INTRODUCTION TO
Accounting

INTRODUCTION TO
Accounting

3rd Edition

Pru Marriott, J.R. Edwards and H.J. Mellett

Los Angeles • London • New Delhi • Singapore • Washington DC

First published 2002
Reprinted twice 2008

SAGE Publications Ltd
1 Oliver's Yard
55 City Road
London EC1Y 1SP

SAGE Publications Inc.
2455 Teller Road
Thousand Oaks, California 91320

SAGE Publications India Pvt Ltd
B 1/I 1 Mohan Cooperative Industrial Area
Mathura Road, New Delhi 110 044

SAGE Publications Asia-Pacific Pte Ltd
33 Pekin Street #02-01
Far East Square
Singapore 048763

British Library Cataloguing in Publication data

A catalogue record for this book is available from
the British Library

ISBN 978-0-7619-7037-8
ISBN 978-0-7619-7038-5(pbk)

Library of Congress Control Number 2001 132896

Typeset by SIVA Math Setters, Chennai, India
Printed in Great Britain by CPI Antony Rowe, Chippenham, Wiltshire

for Hannah and Joe

Contents

Series editor's preface

One of the favourite ploys used by marketing departments is to re-launch the same, unchanged product as '*new and improved*' or '*best ever*'. The publication of an *Introduction to Accounting*, 3rd edition might indicate that something similar could be said about this book. However, in this instance there really are several major changes from the second edition, which are intended to appeal to a new generation of readers.

Most notably, *Introduction to Accounting*, has a new author, Pru Marriott, to complement the talents of John Edwards and Howard Mellett and to provide a fresh perspective on the contribution an introductory textbook can make to current learning and teaching methods. Increasingly, students expect regular feedback from their teachers on their academic progress and modern textbooks must provide a similar response to their readers. It is in this context that the authors have included in each chapter 'activities' that are designed to give students practice in applying the concepts and techniques described in the text. Students are then able to assess their own progress in achieving the learning outcomes against the solutions at the end of the chapter. In addition, the authors have also provided a set of professional examination questions for each topic that can be used as formative assessment in preparation for formal examinations.

The third edition of *Introduction to Accounting* also reflects the recent developments in financial reporting, and in particular the impact of some of the most important accounting standards published since the second edition. Detailed discussion of *FRS3 Reporting financial performance* and *FRS10 Goodwill and intangible fixed assets* have contributed to the increase in the size of the chapter on Company Accounts, making it the largest chapter in the book. Similarly, the importance of understanding financial accounts for the decisions of investors, lenders and creditors has been reflected in a major revision and expansion of the material in the chapter on Interpretation of Accounts.

There is one aspect of the book that has not changed, and that is the authors' highly readable style that has made the previous two editions so popular. The authors have a real knack of explaining the concepts and techniques of accounting in a way that appeals both to students on specialist accountancy courses and to students taking accounting as an option in a business studies or management course. *Introduction to Accounting* has already stood the test of time, and this 'new and improved' third edition will ensure that it remains one of the best, if not the 'best ever' introductory textbooks on accounting.

Michael Sherer
University of Essex

Preface

Recent years have seen an increasing interest in the study of accounting, both as a subject in its own right and as an adjunct to other disciplines, such as engineering, law and medicine. This trend reflects recognition of the fact that the financial aspects of human enterprise cannot be ignored; the activities of almost any undertaking have financial consequences that should be measured and controlled, and this requires the involvement of someone versed in the appropriate techniques. However, it must be remembered that the operation of an accounting system is itself neutral, and the financial information produced has to be interpreted and its relevance weighed, alongside other considerations, before decisions are made. This process requires that the users of accounting information understand what lies behind it and the extent of its uses and limitations.

The authors have produced this book to provide an introduction to accounting that embraces the basic techniques and the underlying theoretical concepts and shows how these are applied in various circumstances. It is designed to meet the needs of both the non-specialist and those intending to specialize in accounting at undergraduate and postgraduate levels. To meet these objectives the text is fully illustrated with worked examples which are reinforced with student activities and end-of-chapter questions. Solutions to all activities are given at the end of each chapter and just over half of the answers to the end-of-chapter questions are provided in the Appendix at the end of the book. The remaining solutions to the end-of-chapter questions are included on the Sage website at: www.sagepub. co.uk/resources/marriott.htm

Questions in the book have been taken from the papers of the following examining bodies: AAT, AEB (now OCR), ACCA and ICSA. We gratefully acknowledge permission granted by these bodies to reproduce the questions contained in this text; the contents of the solutions are entirely our responsibility.

The book has been designed to be read in chapter order, and readers are advised to follow this; however, a number of chapters can be bypassed by the non-specialist. The chapters dealing with the complexities of double entry book-keeping and more technical issues (Chapters 5, 6, 7 and 9) may be less relevant to those studying business studies, engineering, law, etc. The remaining chapters are not dependent on the student having a full understanding of these topics.

The first three chapters introduce the subject, the balance sheet and the calculation of profit as an increase in the value of an enterprise. Chapter 4 examines one of the most basic records, that of cash received and paid, and shows how its contents are converted into a comprehensive set of accounting statements. Chapters 5–7 cover the accounting process based on the double entry system of book-keeping from the initial record of each transaction through to the production of a final report. By this stage the reader should have grasped the underlying techniques, and Chapter 8 discusses the more subjective areas of asset valuation and profit measurement. Chapters 9 and 10 consider the application of accounting theory and techniques to specific forms of enterprise, namely partnerships and limited companies. Chapters 11 and 12 deal with the role of the cash flow statement and ratio analysis in the interpretation of financial information. Chapters 13 and 14 focus on aspects of costing relevant to an introductory text on accounting; specifically, the calculation of total cost, the use of costs as the basis for decision-making and the operation of systems of standard costing and budgetary control.

When the second edition was written it incorporated major changes designed to improve and update the original work. This third edition is a continuation of this evolutionary process. This version naturally includes numerous minor changes to modernize the work. The major revisions compared with the second edition are as follows:

- Chapter 10 incorporates the developments in reporting financial performance and the treatment of goodwill and intangible fixed assets and discusses the issue of research and development activities.
- Chapter 11 on the cash flow statement now deals with the changes introduced by FRS 1 (revised).

The authors are conscious that there are now many modes of study and that some students may be required to work independently without the tutor present. Other students will follow a more traditional route using the text in a classroom environment. In an attempt to meet the needs of both these groups, most worked examples are followed by a student activity. For students studying on their own, these activities can be used to test their knowledge and understanding as they progress through the book. For students whose lecturers adopt the text, the activities can be used in the classroom to reinforce the learning outcomes in an interactive way. Both groups will find the solutions to the activities conveniently placed at the end of the respective chapters.

1 The framework of accounting

The objectives of this chapter are to:

- explain the accounting and decision-making process;
- identify the main entities involved in the supply of accounting information;
- distinguish between financial accounting and management accounting;
- identify the external users of accounting information; and
- outline the nature and content of the principal accounting statements.

THE ACCOUNTING PROCESS

Accounting is a data-processing system that has been vividly described as the 'language of business'. It may be defined as a system for recording and reporting business transactions, in financial terms, to interested parties who use this information as the basis for performance assessment, decision-making and control.

The various stages in the accounting and decision-making process are presented diagrammatically in Figure 1.1. It can be seen that the accounting process contains two basic elements, namely recording business transactions (stages 1–5) and reporting financial information to enable decisions to be taken (stages 6–10). These are interrelated since accounting records form the basis for accounting reports.

The accounting process begins with an economic event, such as the receipt of goods from a supplier. An originating document or voucher is then made out to record the movement of goods, services or cash into, within or out of a business. It is important that the document is made out immediately, since any delay increases the risk of an error that can undermine the entire accounting process. The term 'garbage in, garbage out' has been coined to describe the effect, on the information system, of starting with incorrect data.

Documents and vouchers quite naturally originate in many different departments of a company, but copies of all of them are sent to the accounts department where they are summarized, analysed and then entered in the books of account. Periodically, at least once a year but probably more often, the balances are extracted from the ledger accounts and assembled in a 'trial balance'. This is used as the basis for preparing the final accounts, which consists of a profit and loss account and a balance sheet. These accounting statements are then made available to both management and a variety of 'external' users (see later in this chapter) to help them reach better-informed decisions than would otherwise have been possible. For example, the financial statements prepared for a well-known company,

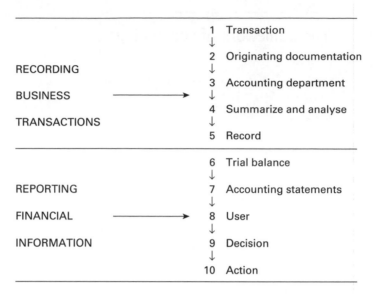

	1	Transaction
	↓	
	2	Originating documentation
RECORDING	↓	
	3	Accounting department
BUSINESS ⟶	↓	
	4	Summarize and analyse
TRANSACTIONS	↓	
	5	Record

	6	Trial balance
	↓	
REPORTING	7	Accounting statements
	↓	
FINANCIAL ⟶	8	User
	↓	
INFORMATION	9	Decision
	↓	
	10	Action

FIGURE 1.1   Accounting and the decision-making process

such as Marks and Spencer plc, may indicate that good (or bad) progress has been made over the last year. On this basis, an individual might decide to purchase some of the company's shares. That individual will use financial statements subsequently published by Marks and Spencer to judge whether the performance has come up to expectations and whether to retain the shareholding, add to it or sell the shares. The profit and loss account and balance sheet of Marks and Spencer plc for 1999 are given in Figure 1.2.

SUPPLIERS OF ACCOUNTING INFORMATION

Suppliers of accounting information include the following business units operating in the private sector of the economy. They are listed in no particular order of priority:

1   *Sole traders.*   These are businesses that have a single owner who also takes all the major managerial decisions. Operations are usually on a small scale, and typical examples are an electrician, the local newsagent and hairdresser. The main reason why accounts are prepared for the sole trader is to help establish the amount of income tax due to the Inland Revenue. He or she makes little use of accounting statements for business decisions. Instead these decisions are based on knowledge obtained as a result of direct contact with all aspects of business activity.

2   *Partnerships.*   These exist where two or more individuals join together to undertake some form of business activity. The partners share between them

ownership of the business and the obligation to manage its operations. Professional people, such as accountants, solicitors and doctors, commonly organize their business activities in the form of partnerships. Accounting statements are required as a basis for allocating profits between the partners and, again, for agreeing tax liabilities with the Inland Revenue.

3   *Clubs and societies.*   There are, in Britain, many thousands of clubs and societies organized for recreational, educational, religious, charitable and other purposes. Members invariably pay an annual subscription and management powers are delegated to a committee elected by the members. The final accounts prepared for (usually large) societies, formed by registering with the Registrar of Friendly Societies, are often controlled by statute. For the local club or society, the form of the accounts is either laid down in the internal rules and regulations or decided at the whim of the treasurer. Conventional accounting procedures are sometimes ignored in a small organization.

Consolidated Profit and Loss Account for the year ended 31 March 1999

	Notes	1999 £m	1998 £m
Turnover continuing operations	2		8,243.3
		8,224.0	
Cost of sales		**(5,450.7)**	(5,322.9)
Gross profit		**2,773.3**	2,904.4
Net operating expenses	3	**(2,261.3)**	(1,816.7)
Operating profit – continuing operations			
Before exceptional operating (charges)/income		**600.5**	1,050.5
Exceptional operating (charges)/income		**(88.5)**	53.2
Total operating profit	2, 3	**512.0**	1,103.7
Profit/(loss) on sale of property and other fixed assets		**6.2**	(2.8)
Net interest income	4	**27.9**	54.1
Profit on ordinary activities before taxation	2	**546.1**	1,155.0
Analysed between:			
Profit on ordinary activities before taxation and exceptional items		**634.6**	1,101.8
Exceptional operating (charges)/income		**(88.5)**	53.2
Taxation on ordinary activities	5	**(176.1)**	(338.7)
Profit on ordinary activities after taxation		**370.0**	816.3
Minority interest (all equity)		**2.1**	(0.4)
Profit attributable to shareholders	6	**372.1**	815.9
Dividends	7	**(413.3)**	(409.1)
Retained (loss)/profit for the year	26	**(41.2)**	406.8

Balance Sheets at 31 March 1999

	Notes	THE GROUP 1999 £m	1998 £m	THE COMPANY 1999 £m	1998 £m
FIXED ASSETS					
Tangible assets:					
Land and buildings		2,954.4	2,755.4	2,629.3	2,530.9
Fit out, fixtures, fittings & equipment		1,317.6	1,086.0	1,094.6	860.1
Assets in the course of construction		115.5	123.4	105.5	54.3
	11	4,387.5	3,964.8	3,829.4	3,445.3
Investments	12	61.2	69.7	406.7	361.6
		4,448.7	4,034.5	4,236.1	3,806.9
CURRENT ASSETS					
Stocks		514.7	500.2	354.0	361.9
Debtors:					
Receivable within one year	13	969.0	948.9	696.7	1,366.1
Receivable after more than one year	13	1,386.7	1,095.2	96.6	175.8
Investments	14	204.0	242.3	–	–
Cash at bank and in hand	15, 16	281.5	614.9	36.1	86.9
		3,355.9	3,401.5	1,183.4	1,990.7
CURRENT LIABILITIES					
Creditors: amounts falling due within one year	17	2,029.8	2,345.0	827.3	1,287.1
NET CURRENT ASSETS		1,326.1	1,056.5	356.1	703.6
TOTAL ASSETS LESS CURRENT LIABILITIES		5,774.8	5,091.0	4,592.2	4,501.5
Creditors: amounts falling due after more than one year	18	772.6	187.2	–	–
Provisions for liabilities and charges	20	54.4	31.0	51.8	27.9
Deferred tax	21	50.6	–	44.5	–
NET ASSETS		4,897.2	4,872.8	4,495.9	4,482.6
CAPITAL AND RESERVES					
Called up share capital	25	717.7	715.6	717.7	715.6
Share premium account		358.5	325.7	358.5	325.7
Revaluation reserve		531.0	506.1	533.2	509.7
Profit and loss account		3,276.7	3,306.3	2,886.5	2,931.6
SHAREHOLDERS FUNDS (all equity)	26	4,883.9	4,853.7	4,495.9	4,482.6
Minority interest (all equity)		13.3	19.1	–	–
TOTAL CAPITAL EMPLOYED		4,897.2	4,872.8	4,495.9	4,482.6

FIGURE 1.2   Profit and loss account and balance sheet of Marks and Spencer plc

Reasons for this are lack of expertise, the meagre quantity of assets belonging to the organization and the fact that the accounts are of interest only to the members.

4 *Limited companies.* A limited company is formed by registering, under the Companies Act, with the Registrar of Companies and complying with certain formalities. The company may be private, indicated by the letters Ltd at the end of its name, or public, in which case the designatory letters are plc. The main significance of the distinction is that only the latter can make an issue of shares to the general public. In the case of public companies there is the further distinction between quoted companies, whose shares are traded on the stock exchange, and unquoted companies. In general, public companies are larger than private companies and quoted companies larger than unquoted.

The directors of all limited companies are under a legal obligation to prepare and publish accounts, at least once in every year, which comply with the requirements of the Companies Act. (It should be noted that there are also in existence a small number of unlimited companies – for example, this method of incorporation is sometimes used by professional firms who are not allowed to have limited liability but want the tax advantages of being a company.)

A limited company may, alternatively, be formed by means of either a private Act of Parliament or a royal charter. These are called statutory and chartered companies, respectively. The form of their accounts may be regulated by the charter or statute. In addition, it is normal practice to comply with the general requirements of the Companies Act.

Reporting units in the *public* sector include local authorities, state colleges and the health service. These are outside the scope of this book, although many of the accounting techniques they employ are exactly the same as those used by organizations in the private sector.

FINANCIAL ACCOUNTING AND MANAGEMENT ACCOUNTING COMPARED

Accounting is conventionally divided into financial accounting and management accounting. The former is concerned with the provision of accounting information for external user groups, while the latter concentrates on the provision of information for management. The principal accounting statements – the balance sheet and the profit and loss account – are of interest to internal and external users but, when presented to the latter, they will normally be in a condensed form. It will be noticed that the final accounts of Marks and Spencer plc (Figure 1.2) summarize on two sheets the financial effect of millions of individual transactions. For example, the balance sheet reports total assets of £7,804.6 million (fixed assets £4,448.7 million + current assets £3,355.9 million) divided into just six categories: tangible assets

£4,387.5 million; investments £61.2 million; stocks £514.7 million; debtors £2,355.7 million; current asset investments £204 million; and cash £281.5 million.

The main factor affecting the amount of detail contained in the accounts is the requirements of the user group. In general, external users wish to assess the overall performance of the entity and an enormous amount of detail is inappropriate both because it is of little interest and because it is likely to obscure the important trends. It is mainly for this reason that information is presented in a highly summarized form in published accounts. A further reason is that the disclosure of too much detail might be used by competitors to analyse the company's strengths and weaknesses.

Financial statements prepared for management contain much more detail. The explanation for this difference may be found in the types of decision to be taken. Shareholders base their decision to sell shares, retain their investment or buy more shares mainly on the level of reported profit and dividends declared. Management, in contrast, is keenly interested in the costs and revenues that make up the profit figure. This is because managers are responsible for taking the following kinds of decisions which influence *individual items* of revenue and expenditure: whether to expand or contract production; whether to substitute one material for another, or one type of worker for another; whether to replace labour-intensive production methods by machinery; whether to acquire property instead of renting it; and which type of power supply to use. In many instances reports must be specially prepared to help reach these decisions, and appraisal techniques have been developed to help the management process. After the decisions have been made, the outcome is monitored to see the extent to which expectations have been fulfilled.

This book introduces accounting techniques that form the basis for both branches of accounting – financial and management – although individual chapters or sections of chapters focus on specialist aspects of each. Chapters 2–8 deal, in detail, with the calculation of profit, the valuation of assets and the preparation of the profit and loss account and balance sheet. As has already been explained, these documents are widely used by both internal and external consumers of accounting information. Chapters 9 and 10 identify the distinctive features of final accounts prepared for partnerships and limited companies. Chapters 11 and 12 explain how the information contained in the accounts may be analysed and interpreted to help both internal and external users decide how to commit resources at their disposal. Chapters 13 and 14 contain an introduction to some of the important accounting techniques used by management for the purposes of planning business activity, allocating resources and monitoring progress made.

EXTERNAL USERS OF ACCOUNTING INFORMATION

In 1975 the accounting profession published a discussion document, called *The Corporate Report*, in an attempt to stimulate interest in the scope and aims of financial reports in the light of modern needs and conditions. The following seven user groups were identified as having a reasonable claim to corporate financial information:

1 The equity investor group made up of existing and potential shareholders.
2 The loan creditor group made up of present and potential holders of debentures and loan stock, and providers of short-term loans and finance.
3 The employee group made up of existing, potential and past employees.
4 The adviser group made up of financial analysts and journalists, economists, statisticians, researchers, trade unions, stockbrokers and credit-rating agencies.
5 The business contact group made up of customers, suppliers, competitors, business rivals, and those interested in mergers, amalgamations and takeovers.
6 The government, particularly the tax authorities, departments and agencies concerned with the supervision of commerce and industry, and local authorities.
7 The public, including taxpayers, ratepayers, consumers and other community and special interest groups such as political parties, consumer and environmental protection societies and regional pressure groups.

Each of these groups has a common interest in company accounts, but they use financial information as the basis for quite different decisions. For instance, shareholders require assistance to help reach share-trading decisions, i.e. whether to retain their present investment, increase it or sell. Employees require financial information to help assess employment prospects and also for the purpose of collective bargaining. Suppliers require accounting information to decide whether to advance credit to a potential customer. Loan creditors, such as the bank, need accounting information to help decide whether to make an initial advance, and to monitor progress and the ability of the customer to repay the amount due at the end of the loan period. A marked deterioration in the company's financial position might well cause the bank to call in the loan before the financial position deteriorates even further.

There are significant variations in the quantity of financial information made available to each of these groups. This results from differential legal requirements, voluntary decisions by management to make financial information available to particular users and the ability of certain individuals to insist on additional disclosures.

PRINCIPAL ACCOUNTING STATEMENTS

The two main accounting statements, the profit and loss account and the balance sheet, are now introduced in a little more detail.

The profit and loss account

Revenues are generated and costs are incurred as the result of undertaking business activity. These revenues and costs are summarized in the profit and loss account, which may be prepared to cover a week, a month, a year or any other chosen interval. Provided total revenue exceeds total expenditure a profit is earned; in the converse situation a loss is suffered.

The published profit and loss account of Marks and Spencer plc (Figure 1.2) covers the 12 months to 31 March 1999. The account starts with turnover and, from this figure, is deducted cost of sales to arrive at the figure for gross profit, and from this figure are deducted operating costs to produce the figure for operating profit. Interest payable (net of interest receivable) to providers of loan finance is then deducted to give the figure for profit before tax. Taxation is then deducted and, next, the amount due to the minority interest (the latter item appears only in accounts prepared for 'groups' of companies – see Chapter 10). Finally, dividends payable to shareholders are deducted to leave the balance of profit retained and reinvested in the business. Full details of each of these items are given in notes 2–8 to the accounts (not reproduced).

The advantages of the profit and loss account are that it sets out the following information: whether a profit has been earned; how much profit has been earned; how the profit figure has been arrived at; and how the profit is appropriated (shared out) between taxation, dividends and the amount retained for reinvestment.

The balance sheet

This sets out the financial position of the business at a chosen point in time. It is the date to which the profit and loss account is made up. The most common accounting dates are the calendar-year end (31 December) and the tax-year end (31 March).

An obvious difference between the profit and loss account and balance sheet is that, whereas the former reports inflows and outflows of resources over a period of time, the latter sets out the assets and liabilities at a particular point in time. It is for this reason that the balance sheet has been likened to a financial photograph of a business. Like all photographs, the position just before or just afterwards may be entirely different. This provides scope for management to undertake cosmetic exercises that present the company's position in the best possible light. For example, it might borrow money just before the year end in order to inflate the cash balance and make repayment on the first day of the next accounting period. Such devices are called 'window dressing', and it is part of the auditor's job to ensure that decision-makers are not misled by the adoption of such procedures.

The balance sheet of Marks and Spencer plc shows fixed assets of £4,448.7 million and current assets of £3,355.9 million. Moving down the balance sheet, a range of liabilities are then deducted, made up of creditors due for payment within one year and creditors and provisions due for payment in more than one year's time. The 'net asset' figure is £4,897.2 million. The remainder of the statement shows how these assets have been financed by shareholders in the form of capital and reserves.

The aim of a business is to make a profit and, if this objective is achieved, the financial position of the business improves and the assets increase. Certainly this is happening at Marks and Spencer, where the shareholders' interest at the end of March 1999 amounts to £4,883.9 million compared with £4,853.7 million a year earlier.

The preparation of the balance sheet is examined in Chapters 2 and 3, and readers are introduced to the profit and loss account in Chapter 4.

2 The balance sheet

The objectives of this chapter are to:

- explain the nature and purpose of the 'entity' concept;
- define the major components of a balance sheet;
- identify and explain the 'accounting equation';
- outline the relationship between 'assets' and 'sources of finance' as disclosed in the balance sheet;
- explain the impact of individual transactions on 'net assets' and 'owner's capital' contained in the balance sheet;
- demonstrate the impact of profit on assets and on the owner's capital;
- show how assets and sources of finance are presented in the balance sheet, distinguishing between 'fixed assets' and 'current assets' on the one hand and 'capital', 'current liabilities' and 'non-current liabilities' on the other;
- outline different possible ways of valuing assets; and
- explain why historical cost is widely used for reporting purposes.

THE ENTITY CONCEPT

In Chapter 1 we saw that there are three main forms of trading organization (clubs and societies do not usually trade) within the private sector of the economy – the sole trader, the partnership and the limited company. There are two important differences between sole traders and partnerships (sometimes referred to as 'firms') on the one hand and limited companies on the other:

1 *The relationship between ownership and management.* In the case of firms, the owner or owners run the business, whereas in the case of the limited company there may well be a significant separation between the ownership and managerial functions. This is particularly likely in the case of the public limited company, where the bulk of the finance is provided by the general public.

2 *The owner's liability for business debts.* Sole traders and partners normally have unlimited liability for the debts of their firm, whereas the shareholders of limited companies are not required to contribute beyond the amount originally paid for shares issued by the company.

The latter distinction is significant when a business runs into financial difficulties. In the case of firms, the creditors claim first against the business assets; if these are insufficient to satisfy the amounts due, the creditors can then claim against the owner's personal wealth. In an extreme situation, the owner of a bankrupt firm could be forced to sell his or her home and all other personal belongings to meet demands from the firm's creditors. (It is to avoid this outcome that a person in business sometimes transfers the ownership of personal assets to his or her partner.) This contrasts with the relative position of investors and creditors of a limited company, where any deficiency of business assets compared with liabilities at the date of liquidation is borne by the creditors.

Company law, therefore, regards a limited company as a separate legal entity. The creditor contracts with the company and can claim only against its assets. No such legal distinction is recognized where the business is carried on by a sole trader or by partners. The position in accountancy, however, is quite different. It is always assumed, for accounting purposes, that the business entity has an existence separate and distinct from its owners, managers or any other individuals with whom it comes into contact during the course of its trading activities. The assumption of a separate existence, usually referred to as the *entity concept*, requires a careful distinction to be drawn between business affairs and personal transactions. One of the reasons for requiring this distinction to be made is that it facilitates performance assessment. A sole trader forms a business in the hope that it will earn him or her a satisfactory profit and, to discover whether this objective has been achieved, profit must be calculated only on the basis of business transactions.

Illustration 2.1

On 1 January 20X1 Mr Old was made redundant and received £30,000 in compensation. He used the cash as follows:

(a)　Purchased a sports car　£19,500.
(b)　Arranged the redecoration of his house　£1,000.
(c)　Paid off his personal overdraft　£3,500.
(d)　Decided to form a business called Old Ventures and, as a first step, opened a business bank account and paid in £6,000.

To comply with the entity concept it is necessary to distinguish between Mr Old's personal transactions and the business transactions of Old Ventures. An examination of the above information shows (a), (b) and (c) to be personal transactions and (d) to be a business transaction.

Joe runs a plumbing business. Indicate which of the following transactions relate to his business and which are personal transactions.

ACTIVITY 2.1

(a)　Joe won £10,000 on the National Lottery and decided to invest it in the business.
(b)　His sister's washing machine broke down and he fixed it for her as a favour.
(c)　She recommended him to a friend who then asked him to plumb in her dishwasher. He charged her £40.
(d)　Joe bought a van for the business costing £8,000.
(e)　He also bought a family car which he will sometimes use in the business.

The solutions to all 'Activities' are at the end of each chapter.

Readers should now attempt Question 2.1 at the end of the chapter. In all cases readers should work through the question and only then compare their answer with the solution provided in the Appendix at the end of the book. (Only the odd-numbered solutions are given in the Appendix – as are solutions 6.2, 6.4 and 6.6; all other even-numbered solutions are to be found in the Solutions Manual located at: www.sagepub.co.uk/resources/marriott.htm.)

CLASSIFICATION OF ASSETS AND SOURCES OF FINANCE

The balance sheet can be described as a 'position' statement that shows the financial position of a business at a particular point in time. It consists of assets, liabilities and capital.

Assets

Business assets may be defined as resources owned by an entity that have the potential for providing it with future economic benefits in the sense that they help to generate future cash inflows or reduce future cash outflows. The fact that a business asset exists, however, does not necessarily mean that it will be reported in the balance sheet. For this to be done, the asset must satisfy the further requirement that the benefit it provides can be measured or quantified, in money terms, with a reasonable degree of precision. This is referred to as the *money measurement* concept. For example, stock-in-trade is reported as a business asset because it is owned by the firm, it has an identifiable monetary value (its cost) and it is expected to produce an at least equivalent cash benefit to the firm when it is sold. Expenditure incurred on training staff, on the other hand, presents a more difficult problem. While it is possible to identify the amount of the expenditure, it is not possible to forecast with a high degree of certainty whether the firm will benefit from the expenditure. Employees may be poorly motivated and fail to improve their competence as the result of attending training courses. In addition, they may leave the firm and take their new expertise elsewhere. Due to this uncertainty concerning the likely extent of any future benefit, such expenditure is not reported as a business asset but is instead written off against profit as an expense as it is incurred.

Assets reported in the balance sheet are divided into two categories:

1   *Current assets.*   These are defined as short-term assets that are held for resale, conversion into cash or are cash itself. There are three main types of current assets: stock-in-trade, trade debtors and cash. A temporary investment of funds in the shares of, say, a quoted company or government securities should also be classified as a current asset. A characteristic of current assets is that the balances are constantly changing as the result of business operations.

    (a)   Stock-in-trade represents the value of items purchased for resale that are still in stock at the year end. They are regarded as a current asset because there is a high chance of the items being converted into cash within the next 12 months.

(b) Debtors represent the amount of money owed to the business and can be sub-divided into trade debtors and others. The former category relates to customers who have bought goods on credit terms and represents the amount of money still outstanding from them at the year end. Other debtors could include dividends receivable from investments in the shares of other companies.

(c) Cash is the amount of funds readily usable by the business and can either be in the form of cash or a balance in the business bank account.

2 *Fixed assets.* These are assets a firm purchases and retains to help carry on the business. It is not intended to sell fixed assets in the ordinary course of business and it is expected that the bulk of their value will be used up as the result of contributing to trading activities. Examples of fixed assets are premises, plant, machinery, furniture and motor vehicles. A characteristic of fixed assets is that they usually remain in the business for long periods of time and will only be sold or scrapped when they are of no further use.

It is important to realize that it is possible to classify an asset as current or fixed only by examining the reason why it was purchased: was it purchased for resale or retention? Assets purchased for resale by one company may be purchased by another for retention. For example, a garage purchases motor vehicles for resale, while a manufacturing concern acquires them as fixed assets to be used by sales representatives.

Assets are reported in the balance sheet in the order of increasing liquidity: the list starts with the items least likely to be turned into cash and ends with the items expected to be converted into cash in the near future. Cash will therefore appear at the bottom of the list as it is the most liquid, and stock will be listed at the top because it is the least liquid.

Sources of finance

The finance of a business can be obtained from three sources: capital, current liabilities and long-term liabilities.

1 *Capital.* This is the amount of money invested in the business by the owner(s). The amount can increase through further investment of funds by the owner(s) or by the business making a profit and can decrease when money is withdrawn from the business for personal use or where a business loss is suffered. Capital is regarded as a permanent source of finance since it is only repayable in full when the business ceases. Until such time the amount is regarded as a liability of the business as the amount is owed to the owner.

2 *Current liabilities.* These liabilities are defined as amounts repayable within 12 months of the balance sheet date. Typical examples include bank overdrafts and creditors. Any loans repayable within the following year are also listed under current liabilities.

Creditors can be divided into trade and other creditors. Trade creditors represent the amount owing to suppliers of stock items that have been purchased on credit terms. Other creditors could include amounts outstanding for miscellaneous services.

3 *Long-term liabilities.* These represent the amounts payable after more than 12 months. They include such items as bank loans and mortgages.

Sources of finance are arranged in order of permanence, with the most permanent sources at the top and amounts repayable (or potentially repayable) in the near future at the bottom of the appropriate section of the balance sheet. Most sources of finance are easily classified into one or other of the three categories, but certain items cause a little more difficulty. For example, the terms of a bank loan may provide for an advance of £100,000 repayable by five equal annual instalments of £20,000. In these circumstances the liability must be divided into two parts, with the next instalment repayable shown as a current liability and the balance reported as a long-term liability. Therefore, at the end of the first year, £20,000 is reported as a current liability and £80,000 as a long-term liability.

Accounting is a device for communicating relevant financial information to interested parties and as such it is important that the information reported should be not only technically accurate but also presented in an orderly fashion so that it can be readily understood by owners, managers and others who wish to assess progress. The balance sheet is drafted so as to help to achieve this objective. It is divided into five sections and, for each of these, an appropriate description is given and subheading provided. (A balance sheet presented in the horizontal format is given in Figure 2.1.)

Users of accounting statements are therefore able to see, at a glance, the amount of finance provided by the owners, the volume of long-term loans and the quantity of short-term finance. The statement also shows how the total finance has been allocated between fixed and current assets. If a firm is to be financially stable, it is normally important for long-term investments in fixed assets to be

Assets	£	£	Sources of finance	£	£
Fixed assets			Capital		179,000
Land and buildings		75,000			
Plant and machinery		49,000	*Non-current*		
Motor vehicles		21,500	*Liabilities*		
		145,500	Loan		50,000
Current assets			*Current liabilities*		
Stock-in-trade	145,700		Bank overdraft	36,700	
Trade debtors	143,700		Trade creditors	170,000	
Investments	2,600		Expense creditor	1,900	
Cash in hand		292,100			208,600
		437,600			437,600

FIGURE 2.1   Balance sheet of Nut and Bolt Engineering at 31 December 20X1

financed substantially by the owners and for current assets to be sufficient to meet current liabilities falling due over the next 12 months. A well-prepared balance sheet enables these and other forms of financial analysis, examined in Chapters 11 and 12, to be efficiently carried out.

THE ACCOUNTING EQUATION

As we have already discussed, the business is regarded as an accounting entity separate from its owner(s). As such all business transactions must be recorded twice: first, to show the effect of the transaction on the assets belonging to the business; and second, to show the effect of the transaction on the owner(s) and other providers of finance of the business. The result is that assets will always be equal to capital plus liabilities:

$$\text{Assets} = \text{Capital} + \text{Liabilities}$$

In other words, what the business owns is equal to what the business owes.

Applying this rule to transaction (d) in Illustration 2.1, we find that its effect is as follows:

Effect on business assets: Assets increase from zero to £6,000 as the result of the injection of cash.

Effect on providers of finance: The business now has capital of £6,000 that is owed to Mr Old.

The financial effect of this transaction may be presented in a balance sheet in the following manner:

Illustration 2.2

Old Ventures

Balance Sheet as at 1 January 20X1

Assets	£	Sources of finance	£
Cash at bank	6,000	Capital: Mr Old	6,000

The left-hand side of the balance sheet shows that the assets belonging to the business consist of cash amounting to £6,000. The right-hand side of the balance sheet shows that Mr Old is owed £6,000. Put another way, the right-hand side shows that Mr Old has made an investment of £6,000 in the business.

We may therefore describe the balance sheet as a financial statement that shows on the one side the assets belonging to the business and on the other the way in which those assets have been financed.

Two obvious differences should be noted between the above balance sheet and that given for Marks and Spencer plc in Figure 1.2:

1   The balance sheet of Marks and Spencer plc contains much more information. This is because it has been in business for many years, and the balance sheet reports the accumulated financial effect of literally millions of transactions undertaken between the date of formation and 31 March 1999. Old Ventures, by way of contrast, has only just been formed and has undertaken only one transaction.
2   The balance sheet of Marks and Spencer plc is presented in vertical format with the assets listed *above* the sources of finance. The balance sheet of Old Ventures is presented in horizontal format with assets on the left and sources of finance on the right. Either presentation is perfectly legal but it is the vertical format that is widely adopted today. (We shall convert to the vertical layout later.)

RAISING FURTHER FINANCE

Before a business commences operations, sufficient finance should be raised to support the planned level of activity. Too many businesses begin their lives with insufficient cash resources and most of them fail before they get off the ground. At best, the early years of a firm's life are marked by a continuous shortage of cash and much of management's time is taken up coping with cash flow problems rather than being directed towards the development of profitable trading activities.

Mr Old has made a personal investment of £6,000 in Old Ventures (see Illustration 2.2), and we will assume that he has estimated that a total initial investment of £10,000 is required to finance the planned level of business operations. He is £4,000 short and is likely to explore a number of avenues in the endeavour to obtain this sum and to place the business on a sound financial footing. One possibility is to borrow from family, friends or the bank; another is to seek government aid; and a third might involve acquiring some of the business assets on hire purchase. We will assume that Mr Old convinces his bank manager that there are good prospects for Old Ventures and on 2 January the bank lends his business £4,000. The effect of the transaction is as follows:

Effect on business assets: Cash increases by £4,000.
Effect on providers of finance: Indebtedness to the bank increases from zero to £4,000.

The equality between assets and sources of finance is retained with the increase in business assets financed by the bank loan. There are now, however, two different types of finance. The amount advanced by Mr Old, his capital, is a permanent investment that will not usually be withdrawn until the business is wound up, whereas the amount advanced by the bank is a liability that must be repaid in due course. The balance sheet below now shows that the business owns assets worth £10,000 and that these assets have been financed by capital (from Mr Old) and a

Illustration 2.3

The revised balance sheet is as follows:

Old Ventures
Balance Sheet as at 2 January 20X1

Assets	£	Sources of finance	£
Cash at bank	10,000	Capital: Mr Old	6,000
		Long-term liabilities:	
		Bank loan	4,000
	10,000		10,000

bank loan. So, in accordance with the accounting equation, assets equal capital plus liabilities:

$$A = C + L$$

Readers should test their understanding of this relationship by working through Question 2.2 at the end of this chapter.

THE INVESTMENT DECISION

It is the job of management to employ profitably the resources that have been placed at its disposal, and to carry out this function many decisions have to be made. These result in a continuous flow of cash and other assets into, through and out of the business. Accounting statements, among which the balance sheet is one of the most important, are prepared at regular intervals to enable management to monitor the results of their decisions and to gauge the extent to which they are achieving the objective of profit maximization. In the case of Old Ventures, Mr Old, when performing his managerial role, must decide how to employ the cash available to the business, i.e. he must make an investment decision. Mr Old decides to go into business as an antiques dealer and purchases on 10 January 20X1 a small warehouse for £7,000 cash. On the same day he acquired various relics, second-hand goods and memorabilia (together called his stock-in-trade) for £2,500 cash. The effect of these transactions is as follows:

Effect on business assets: Premises increase by £7,000.
                              Stock-in-trade increases by £2,500.
                              Cash at bank reduces by £9,500.
Effect on providers of finance: Zero.

Illustration 2.4 sets out the revised financial position of Old Ventures on 10 January. No additional sources of finance have been raised and the right-hand side of the balance sheet remains unchanged. The effect of the investment decision is merely to cause a reallocation of resources between business assets.

Before Old Ventures is ready to commence trading, Mr Old must make sure that his display of antiques is sufficiently extensive to attract customers into his warehouse. Let us assume that a further consignment of furniture, costing £2,000, is

Illustration 2.4

Old Ventures

Balance Sheet as at 10 January 20X1

Assets	£	Sources of finance	£
Fixed assets:		Capital: Mr Old	6,000
Premises	7,000	Long-term liabilities:	
Current assets:		Bank loan	4,000
Stock*	2,500		
Cash at bank	500		
	10,000		10,000

* This is the commonly used abbreviation for stock-in-trade.

required for this purpose. The above balance sheet shows that the company has insufficient cash available for this purpose and an additional source of finance must be obtained. In practice, very few businesses operate entirely on a cash basis. Instead, a proportion – often a high proportion – of purchases and sales are made on credit, i.e. a period of time elapses between the dates on which goods are supplied and paid for. Normally businesses take the maximum period of credit allowed because, during this time, stock is financed by suppliers rather than by the firm itself. The period of credit allowed by suppliers varies a great deal, but 30 days is most common.

Old Ventures takes delivery of furniture costing £2,000 on 11 January 20X1. The supplier allows 30 days' credit. The effect of the transaction is as follows:

Effect on business assets: Stock increases by £2,000.
Effect on providers of finance: Trade creditors increase by £2,000.

The balance sheet below shows that the firm now owns assets totalling £12,000 made up of premises, stock and cash at bank. The finance has been obtained from three sources: ownership, the bank and suppliers who are described as trade creditors for balance sheet purposes. The investment made by the owners is normally permanent, while the loan is likely to be the subject of a formal agreement that covers such matters as the repayment date and the rate of interest payable. Trade creditors expect to be repaid in accordance with the normal practice of the

Illustration 2.5

Old Ventures

Balance Sheet as at 11 January 20X1

Assets	£	Sources of finance	£
Fixed assets:		Capital: Mr Old	6,000
Premises	7,000	Long-term liabilities:	
Current assets:		Bank loan	4,000
Stock	4,500	Current liabilities:	
Cash at bank	500	Trade creditors	2,000
	12,000		12,000

particular trade, in this case 30 days. An important feature of trade credit is that it is a renewable source of finance in the sense that, provided the firm pays money currently owed, it will be able to acquire further supplies on credit, thereby maintaining a constant level of indebtedness.

Readers should now work through Question 2.3 at the end of the chapter.

BUSINESS DEVELOPMENT

Old Ventures is now ready to start trading. Mr Old established the business in the expectation that it would earn profits. Stocks must therefore be sold for sums sufficiently in excess of cost to convince Mr Old that his capital is efficiently employed in the business. This would be the case where the returns from the business are in excess of the returns he could make if the money was invested elsewhere.

On 12 January Old Ventures sells antiques costing £500 to Rustic Relics (a nearby antiques shop) for £1,000 cash. Ignoring operating costs, the profit earned from this sale is £500 (sales price £1,000 minus cost £500). The business operates for the benefit of the owner (Mr Old) and so any profit earned is added to his capital to show that the value of his investment in the business has increased. The effect of the transaction is as follows:

Effect on business assets: Stock decreases by £500.
                                 Cash at bank increases by £1,000.
Effect on providers of finance: Capital increases by £500 profit.

Illustration 2.6

Old Ventures

Balance Sheet as at 12 January 20X1

Assets	£	Sources of finance	£
Fixed assets:		Capital: Mr Old	6,000
Premises	7,000	Add: Profit	500
			6,500
Current assets:		Long-term liabilities:	
Stock	4,000	Bank loan	4,000
Cash at bank	1,500	Current liabilities:	
		Trade creditors	2,000
	12,500		12,500

The total assets of Old Ventures (an alternative description is gross assets) have increased from £12,000 in Illustration 2.5 to £12,500 in Illustration 2.6. This is because one asset (stock) costing £500 has been replaced by an increase in the cash figure of £1,000. A similar increase occurs in the sources of finance as the result of adding the profit earned to Mr Old's initial capital investment. Let us consider his trading activity further and assume that on 15 January he sells some more stock costing £1,500 to Rustic Relics for £2,500, payment to be made by the end of the month. The effect of the transaction is as follows:

Effect on business assets: Stock decreases by £1,500
                                    Trade debtors increase by £2,500.
Effect on providers of finance: Capital increases by £1,000.

Illustration 2.7

Old Ventures

Balance Sheet as at 15 January 20X1

Assets	£	Sources of finance	£
Fixed assets:		Capital: Mr Old	6,000
Premises	7,000	Add: Profit	1,500
			7,500
Current assets:		Long-term liabilities:	
Stock	2,500	Bank loan	4,000
Trade debtors	2,500		
Cash at bank	1,500	Current liabilities:	
		Trade creditors	2,000
	13,500		13,500

It should be noticed that profit is recognized despite the fact that the price paid by
the customer has not yet been received in cash. This brings us to a second assumption made by accountants when preparing accounting statements, namely, the
realization concept (considered further in Chapter 4). This concept assumes that
profit is earned or realized when the sale takes place, and the justification for this
treatment is that Old Ventures now possesses a more valuable asset, since the
£2,500 is a legally enforceable debt.

The trading cycle is completed by Old Ventures collecting £2,500 from Rustic
Relics on 31 January 20X1 and paying £2,000 to its supplier on 8 February 20X1,
30 days after the goods were supplied.

The effects of these transactions are as follows:

Effect on business assets: Trade debtors decrease by £2,500.
                                    Cash increases by £2,500.
                                    Cash decreases by £2,000.
Effect on providers of finance: Trade creditors decrease by £2,000.

Illustration 2.8

Old Ventures

Balance Sheet as at 8 February 20X1

Assets	£	Sources of finance	£
Fixed assets:		Capital: Mr Old	6,000
Premises	7,000	Add: Profit	1,500
			7,500
Current assets:		Long-term liabilities:	
Stock	2,500	Bank loan	4,000
Cash at bank	2,000		
	11,500		11,500

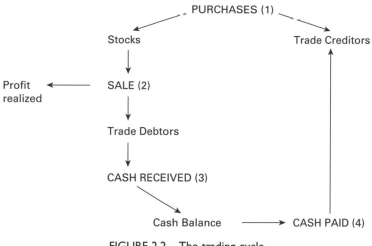

FIGURE 2.2   The trading cycle

Readers should now work through Question 2.4 at the end of this chapter.

THE TRADING CYCLE

The single trading cycle for Old Ventures, examined above, is now complete, and can be expressed in the form of a diagram as in Figure 2.2. The cycle consists of the following four stages:

Stage 1   The purchase of goods on credit that gives rise to balance sheet entries for trade creditors and stock.

Stage 2   The sale of stock on credit results in a profit being realized or a loss incurred. At this stage some of the stock is replaced by trade debtors in the balance sheet.

Stage 3   The collection of trade debts. This produces a change in the composition of the firm's assets, from debtors to cash.

Stage 4   The payment of the amounts due to suppliers. This causes a reduction in cash and the removal of trade creditors from the balance sheet.

A comparison of the position before and after completion of the trading cycle (Illustrations 2.4 and 2.8) shows just two differences: cash has risen by £1,500 and the owner's capital investment has increased by the same amount to reflect profit earned.

The trading cycle examined above is obviously a simplified version of what happens in practice. A business does not complete one cycle before commencing another but is involved in a continuous series of overlapping business transactions. The purchases cycle consists of ordering goods, receiving them into stock as an asset and paying for them by means of a cash outflow, while the sales cycle consists of making a sale, parting with the stocks sold as an asset outflow and collecting the money due from the customer to produce a cash inflow. Therefore even before one creditor is paid another is created and debtors are turned over in a similar manner. It is the responsibility of management to ensure that all these flows are adequately controlled and recorded. Thus no payment should be made without ensuring that the related goods or services have in fact been received, and no goods should be allowed to leave the firm except in exchange for cash or by the creation of a debt. In the latter case there must be adequate follow-up procedures to ensure that the cash is subsequently collected.

A simplified version of the trading cycle occurs when purchases and/or sales are made for cash. There are just two stages: stage 1, the purchase of goods, involves the exchange of cash for stock, stage 2, the sale of goods, involves the exchange of stock for cash of a greater or lesser value, with the amount of the difference recorded as a profit or a loss.

REPORTING CHANGES IN OWNER'S CAPITAL

The capital section of the balance sheet records the indebtedness of the business to its owner. This indebtedness is initially created by the owner(s) advancing money to the business, but the amount changes over time – for example, a profit increases the indebtedness whereas a loss reduces the value of the owner's capital investment. The capital section also reports all other transactions between the business and its owner – for instance, it reports any additional capital investment made by the owner during the life of the business, and also the regular withdrawals of cash and goods made for personal use. The manner in which these matters are reported is shown in Illustration 2.9.

Illustration 2.9

At the end of both February and March Mr Old withdrew £1,500 in cash for personal use. During March he sold the remainder of his stock (which cost £2,500) for £5,000 cash. In April he transferred his car into the business at a value of £2,000.

Old Ventures
Balance Sheet as at 30 April 20X1

Assets	£	Sources of finance	£	£
Fixed assets:		Capital: Mr Old		6,000
Premises	7,000	Add: Additional capital		2,000
Vehicle	2,000			8,000
	9,000			
Current assets:		Add: Profit	4,000	
Cash at bank	4,000	Less: Drawings	(3,000)	
		(1,500 × 2)		1,000
				9,000
		Long term liabilities:		
		Bank loan		4,000
	13,000			13,000

C. Newman started in business on 1 January 20X1 and paid £2,000 into his business bank account. On 30 June he transferred to the business his car valued at £1,400. Each week he withdrew £60 from the business in cash. The accounts prepared for 20X1 showed that his business had earned a profit of £4,100 during the year.

Prepare the Capital section *only* of the balance sheet, taking into account the above transactions.

The owner does not normally wait until profit is calculated before making withdrawals. He or she is often dependent on the business for his or her livelihood and profits are withdrawn, for personal use, as they are earned during the year. Where profits exceed drawings, as is the case in Illustration 2.9, the surplus of £1,000 (profit £4,000 minus drawings £3,000) is retained in the business and increases the owner's capital by an equivalent amount. These extra resources may be used to finance an expansion in the level of business operations. Illustration 2.9 also demonstrates the fact that capital may be introduced in the form of assets other than cash. The motor vehicle, transferred to the business by Mr Old, appears as an asset in the balance sheet and is matched by a corresponding increase in the value of his capital investment. Similarly, drawings may be made in a non-cash form (e.g. the family of a farmer is likely to consume some of the farm produce) though this has not happened in the above illustration.

Readers should now work through Question 2.5 at the end of the chapter.

THE ACCOUNTING EQUATION: A FURTHER ILLUSTRATION

In the case of Old Ventures we saw that the equality between sources of finance and assets was maintained throughout the trading cycle and, because all assets must be financed in some way, we can be confident that this equality will continue throughout the firm's life. In this context there are five basic categories of business transaction:

1   An increase in an asset is matched by a corresponding increase in a source of finance – for example, cash increases as the result of extra capital being invested by the owner.
2   An increase in a source of finance is matched by a decrease in a different source of finance – for example, a loan raised from the bank to enable trade creditors to be paid the amount due to them.
3   A reduction in an asset is matched by a reduction in a source of finance – for example, cash is used to pay trade creditors.
4   An increase in an asset is matched by a reduction in a different asset – for example, a new motor vehicle is purchased for cash.
5   A reduction in a source of finance is matched with a reduction in an asset – for example, the owner of a business withdraws cash from the business bank account.

A complication occurs in the case of a transaction involving the sale of goods, since this gives rise to a profit or a loss that must also be recorded. For example, assume that an item of stock which cost £80 is sold on credit for £100. In the balance sheet stock is replaced by debtors, i.e. a category 4 transaction takes place. In addition a category 1 transaction occurs, because the higher value of debtors, £20, gives rise to a profit that must be added to the owner's capital.

ACTIVITY 2.3   Examine separately the effect of each of the following transactions on the relationship $A = C + L$ and indicate the category of transaction being used.

1   The owner of a business received a legacy of £2,000 and paid it into his business bank account.
2   Machinery costing £3,000 is purchased for cash.
3   Stock is purchased on credit from ABC & Co. for £800.
4   A business computer is purchased for £5,000 financed by a loan from a friend.
5   Trade debts amounting to £750 are collected from customers.
6   Stock costing £1,000 is sold for £1,400 cash.
7   ABC & Co. are paid £220.
8   Stock is purchased for £350 cash.
9   Goods costing £1,000 are sold on credit to XYZ Ltd for £2,500.
10   A filing cabinet is purchased for £60 by increasing an existing bank overdraft.
11   The owner of a business withdrew £100 from the business bank account.

You should present your answer in the following form:

Transaction	Assets =	Capital +	Liabilities	Category of transaction
	+, – or 0	+, – or 0	+, – or 0	
Example 1	+ 2,000	+ 2,000	0	1
Example 2	+ 3,000	0	0	4
	– 3,000			

Readers should now work through Question 2.6 at the end of this chapter.

VALUATION OF ASSETS

The balance sheet contains a list of assets belonging to the company and, for each category, a value is given. For example, a freehold property may be shown in the balance sheet at £50,000. What does this value represent? If a lay person were asked this question, it is quite likely that he or she would say: 'It is what the asset is worth.' This seems reasonable on the face of it, but it leads to further questions, such as: Worth to whom? At what point (i.e. past, current or future) are you valuing the worth? For what purpose (i.e. to retain in the business or to sell in the short term) is the asset being held?

There are four possible methods for valuing assets, although we will see that only one of these normally finds favour with the accountant. The four methods are as follows:

1   *Historical cost.*   The asset is valued at its original purchase price.

2   *Replacement cost.*   The asset is valued at the amount it would cost the business to buy at the balance sheet date.

3   *Realizable value.*   This is the price at which the asset could be sold at the balance sheet date. It differs from replacement cost, as anyone who has ever attempted to sell, say, a second-hand motor vehicle will know.

4   *Present value.*   This is a little more complicated and is the present value of cash expected to be generated, in the future, as a result of owning a particular asset. The estimated cash flows are discounted, at a rate of interest, to take account of the fact that £1 receivable, say, in one year's time is worth rather less than £1 receivable immediately. In other words, the future stream of income is translated into what it is worth today.

The appropriate method of valuation depends on the purpose for which it is required. If the company is contemplating the acquisition of an asset, purchase price is the most relevant. The replacement cost of an asset is likely to be of interest if the existing asset is worn out. Realizable value is relevant if there is an intention to sell the asset in the near future, while the present value calculation should be made if the asset is to continue in use for some time generating a stream of cash flows stretching into the future.

In general, assets are shown in company accounts at their *historical cost* less, in the case of fixed assets, a reduction to reflect wear and tear (depreciation) that has occurred since the acquisition took place.

At first glance this is a little surprising. The analysis in the preceding paragraph shows that although historical cost is of interest at the date of the initial purchase, it is the other valuation methods, particularly market price and present value, that are likely to be more relevant when a balance sheet is prepared at some subsequent date. Why is historical cost so popular? Perhaps the main reason is that this figure is readily available. Most assets are purchased on credit and are entered in the books at their historical cost so as to provide a record of the amount to be paid to the supplier at some future date. Once the figure is in the books it is simply convenient to use it for the purpose of preparing the balance sheet. Many people believe that this is not a sufficient justification for continuing to use historical cost. For example, it seems quite ridiculous to report a building in the balance sheet at £27,000 – the price paid ten years ago – if the building could today be sold for, say, £127,000. But this is what is done. This limitation should be borne in mind when assessing the usefulness of information appearing in accounts. The alternatives to historic cost, however, can be used and we shall look at these later.

ACTIVITY 2.4   Lexington owns a fleet of cars that are rented to customers. One of the cars was purchased a couple of years ago for £7,000. The company has discovered that it could purchase a car in similar condition, today, for £5,000 from the local distributor. Cars no longer needed by Lexington are usually sold to employees. It is estimated that the car costing £7,000 would now sell for £3,800.

The company's intention is to retain the vehicle as part of its fleet for one year. It will be rented to a single customer for an annual rental of £2,000, payable in arrears. The car will then be immediately sold for £3,000. Assume the rental arises at the end of the year and that future cash flows have to be discounted at 10 per cent in order to convert them into an equivalent present value.

Required   Valuations of the car on the following bases:

(a) historical cost;
(b) replacement cost;
(c) realizable value; and
(d) present value.

QUESTIONS   2.1   Indicate which of the following transactions relate to Clive's business as a newsagent and which are his personal transactions:

1   £50 win on Premium Bonds owned by Clive.
2   £100 paid for the following advertisement on a hoarding at the local football ground:'Clive's for all the up-to-date news'.
3   Payment to the newspaper wholesaler, £1,260.
4   Sale of unsold newspapers to a local fish-and-chip shop.
5   Purchase of a new car for family use, although it will be used each morning to collect papers from suppliers.

2.2   John decides to start up in business on 1 April 20X1, and pays £4,000 from his private bank account into a newly opened business bank account. On 2 April 20X1 John's father loans the firm £600 to help with the new venture, and this amount is paid immediately into the business bank account. On 4 April the firm borrows £150 from John's friend, Peter. This amount is kept in the form of 'ready cash' to meet small business expenses.

Required   Balance sheets for John's business after the transactions on:
(a) 1 April; (b) 2 April; (c) 4 April.

2.3   Roger starts up in business on 1 September 20X0 with a capital of £1,200 which he pays into his business bank account on that day. The bank agrees to provide him with a business overdraft facility of £1,500 for the first three months. The following business transactions take place:

2 Sept   A machine is bought, on three months' credit, from Plant Suppliers Ltd for £750. £1,000 is borrowed from the Endridge Local Authority, which is keen to encourage this type of enterprise.

3 Sept   £1,820 is paid for a second-hand machine. Stock is purchased, for £420 cash.

4 Sept   Stock is purchased, on credit, for £215.

Balance sheets for Roger's business following the transactions on: **Required**

(a) 1 September; (b) 2 September; (c) 3 September; (d) 4 September.

2.4   The following balance sheet was prepared for Jeff's business at 1 October 20X0. The firm has an overdraft facility of £700.

Jeff

Balance Sheet as at 1 October, 20X0

	£		£
Fixed assets:			
Machinery	2,200	Capital	5,300
Current assets:		*Current liabilities*	
Stocks	2,870	Trade creditors	690
Trade debtors	800		
Cash at bank	120		
	5,990		5,990

Jeff enters into the following transactions:

2 October   Sells goods that cost £120 for £200 cash. Sells goods that cost £240 for £315 on credit.

3 October   Collects £150 from customers. Purchases stock for £190 on credit.

4 October   Pays trade creditors £75. Purchases a machine for £600 cash.

Balance sheets for Jeff's business following the transactions on: (a) 2 October; (b) 3 October;   **Required**
(c) 4 October.

2.5   (a)   Prepare the balance sheet of Daley from the following list of assets and liabilities at 31 December 20X1:

	£
Cash	1,750
Stock	5,250
Owed by customers	3,340
Owed to suppliers	2,890
Business premises	9,000
Loan from Weakly	3,000

Remember, Assets = Capital + Liabilities.

(b)   Prepare the balance sheet of Daley's business at the end of each of the first seven days of January, taking account of the following transactions:

January 20X2

1   Purchased, on credit, a typewriter for office use, £500.
2   Received £190 from a customer.
3   Paid a supplier £670.
4   Purchased stock, on credit, £260.
5   Sold goods that had cost £350 for £530 cash.
6   Repaid Weakly £1,000 of the balance due to him (ignore interest).
7   Withdrew stock costing £100 for private use.

2.6   Prepare balance sheets to determine the amount missing from each of the following columns of balances at 31 December 20X1:

	A	B	C	D	E	F
	£	£	£	£	£	£
Capital at 1 Jan 20X1	2,500	2,000	3,000	4,000	3,800	?
Profit for 20X1	1,000	3,200	?	5,700	2,300	7,000
Drawings during 20X1	800	3,000	1,000	4,900	?	4,500
Current liabilities	750	?	600	1,300	1,700	2,100
Fixed assets	1,800	1,750	2,800	?	3,700	8,500
Current assets	?	850	1,200	1,900	1,600	3,500

2.7   Review your understanding of the following concepts and terms discussed in this chapter by writing a short explanation of each of them:

1   Accountancy
2   Entity concept
3   Balance sheet
4   Realization concept
5   Trade credit
6   Trading cycle and credit transactions
7   A = C + L
8   Owner's capital
9   Money measurement concept
10   Fixed assets
11   Current assets
12   Current liabilities
13   Gross assets
14   Historic cost

2.8   For a fish-and-chip shop, indicate which of the following items are current liabilities, which are current assets and which are fixed assets:

1   Microwave oven
2   2,000 kilos of King Edward potatoes
3   Cash register
4   Amount owing to the Fat Fishy Company Ltd
5   Capital investment of Mr V. Greasy, owner
6   Mrs Greasy's pearl necklace and gold wrist-watch
7   250 mackerel
8   Loan from V. Greasy's father, repayable in two years' time
9   Last instalment due, in one month's time, on the microwave oven acquired on hire purchase
10 Shop rented from a property company

For items not classified as current liabilities or current assets or fixed assets, describe how they would be reported in the balance sheet, if at all.

2.9   The following list of balances relate to the business of C. Forest at 31 December 20X2:

	£
Plant and machinery	26,500
Stock	14,200
Loan repayable June 20X3	2,500
Capital of C. Forest at 1 January 20X2	52,380
Trade creditors	10,600
Trade debtors	14,100
Cash-in-hand	270
Bank overdraft	3,940
Profit for 20X2	12,600
Owner's drawings during 20X2	10,950
Loan repayable 20X9	9,000
Premises	25,000

The balance sheet of C. Forest's business at 31 December 20X2 presented in good style.   **Required**

**SOLUTIONS
TO
ACTIVITIES**

Business transactions: (a), (c) and (d).   *Solution to*
Personal transactions: (b) and (e).   *Activity 2.1*

		£	£

Solution to
Activity 2.2

Financed by:

Capital (2,000 + 1,400)   3,400

	£	£
Add: Profit	4,100	
Less: Drawings (60 × 52)	(3,120)	
		980
		4,380

Solution to
Activity 2.3

Transaction	Assets	=	Capital	+	Liabilities	Category of transaction
I	+ 2,000		+ 2,000		0	I
2	+ 3,000		0		0	4
	− 3,000					
3	+ 800		0		+ 800	I
4	+ 5,000		0		+ 5,000	I
5	− 750		0		0	4
	+ 750					
6	− 1,000		+ 400		0	4 and I
	+ 1,400					
7	− 220		0		− 220	3
8	+ 350		0		0	4
	− 350					
9	− 1,000		+ 1,500		0	4 and I
	+ 2,500					
10	+ 60		0		+ 60	I
11	− 100		− 100		0	5

Solution to
Activity 2.4

(a)   Historical cost = £7,000, less deduction for wear and tear or depreciation suffered since the date of purchase.

(b)   Replacement cost = £5,000

(c)   Realizable value = £3,800

(d)   Present value =

Rental income at the end of year 1 (2,000 × 1/1.1*)	1,818
Sale proceeds at the end of year 1 (3,000 × 1/1.1)	2,727
	4,545

* The effect of this fraction is to discount the future cash flows to an equivalent present value using an interest rate of 10 per cent. Looked at another way, £4,545 invested at 10 per cent for one year increases to £5,000 (£4,545 × 1.1), which is the cash expected to be received if the asset is retained for use within the business.

3 Profit calculated as the increase in capital

The objectives of this chapter are to:

- explain the importance of profit and outline the way in which it may be appropriated;
- outline the procedure involved in preparing a balance sheet in accordance with the vertical format;
- show how capital is calculated as the difference between assets and liabilities;
- explain the relationship between profits and changes in the owner's capital;
- demonstrate how profit can be calculated as the increase in capital after making allowance for any capital introduced or profit withdrawn during the year.

PROFITABLE ACTIVITY

The maximization of profit has been traditionally regarded as the principal factor motivating the individual to invest in a business venture. However, business organizations, particularly the very large ones, have responsibilities which are wider than the obligation to produce an adequate return for their investors. A list of the responsibilities acknowledged by business people can be obtained by examining the corporate objectives declared by company chairpersons in their annual reports to shareholders. These include such matters as an increase in the market share, the improvement of product quality, a contented workforce, pollution-free production processes, the maximization of exports and survival.

It is difficult to say whether these aims are each of equal importance, but probably they are not. One view is that profit maximization is the main objective, and other stated goals have, as their central purpose, to contribute either directly or indirectly to the long-run achievement of that principal aim. This view may attach rather too much significance to profit, but widespread agreement that profit is an essential product of business activity in the UK can safely be assumed.

There are basically two competing claims on the profits generated by business activity:

1 *Withdrawals.* The owner requires a satisfactory return on his or her investment in the form of drawings or dividends. An inadequate return will cause him or her to close down the business and invest his or her money elsewhere.

2 *Reinvestment.* The second claim on profit arises from the fact that retained profits are a major source of finance for business expansion. For example, the balance sheet of Unilever plc at 31 December 1999 shows share capital as £134 million while retained profits amount to £2,903 million, i.e. over 21

times as much. The retention of profits increases the value of the owner's investment in the business, of course, and should produce higher profits and dividends in the future.

When trading conditions are difficult there may be insufficient profits to finance expansion or even to pay a return on the owner's investment. In these circumstances management must look elsewhere for the finance required for a continuation of business activity. This is not a situation that can persist indefinitely; just as consistent profitability generates the resources necessary for a healthy business, equally a succession of losses gradually deprives a company of the finance needed to support a continuation of business activity. Failure to achieve an adequate level of profitability eventually results in the cessation of business activities. It is part of the accounting function to help management guard against such an outcome by enabling it to monitor progress and ensure that resources are efficiently employed.

PROFIT AND CHANGES IN GROSS ASSETS

In Chapter 2 attention was drawn to the fact that, where management organizes business activity in an efficient manner and a profit is earned, gross assets increase by a similar amount. This relationship was illustrated by means of a series of balance sheets setting out the financial development of a firm called Old Ventures. Readers should now revise their understanding of the link between profit and the level of business assets by doing the following activity.

ACTIVITY 3.1

Larch

Balance Sheet as at 31 December 20X1

	£	£		£
Fixed assets				
Plant and machinery		1,600	Capital	2,000
Current assets			**Current liabilities**	
Stock-in-trade	600		Trade creditors	700
Trade debtors	300			
Cash in hand	200	1,100		
		2,700		2,700

On 1 January 20X2 Larch sold stock (cost price £140) on credit for £220.

Required   The balance sheet of Larch following the transaction on 1 January 20X2.

A comparison of your balance sheet and the one at the end of the chapter shows that the financial effects of the single trading transaction undertaken by Larch are as follows:

1   Gross assets have increased from £2,700 to £2,780 as the result of stock
     costing £140 being replaced by a debt due from a customer of £220.
2   Total sources of finance have increased by the same amount as the result of
     adding the profit realized, of £80, to Larch's opening capital.

BALANCE SHEET PRESENTATION: VERTICAL FORMAT

The balance sheets used, so far, have been presented in what is conventionally
described as the horizontal format, with assets on the left and sources of finance
on the right. Since the early 1960s industry has gradually discarded the horizontal format in favour of the vertical format; see the accounts of Marks and Spencer
plc reproduced in Figure 1.2. The vertical presentation is further illustrated in
Figure 3.1 by rearranging the information taken from Larch's balance sheet in
Activity 3.1.

The main advantage of the vertical presentation is that it is easier to compare
the position of a business at a series of accounting dates. The illustration below
gives the position at just two dates, but a columnar presentation dealing with five
or even ten accounting dates poses no particular difficulty. It is then a relatively
easy matter to glance across the series of figures to discover relative changes and
overall trends. Such an analysis might show that large amounts of money are
being spent each year on fixed assets, suggesting a policy of rapid expansion. By
way of contrast, a continuous decline in the balance of cash, perhaps converting

Larch
Balance Sheet as at

	1 Jan 20X2		31 Dec 20X1	
	£	£	£	£
Fixed assets				
Plant and machinery		1,600		1,600
Current assets				
Stock-in-trade	460		600	
Trade debtors	520		300	
Cash in hand	200		200	
	1,180		1,100	
Less:				
Current liabilities				
Trade creditors	−700		−700	
Working capital		480		400
		2,080		2,000
Financed by:				
Capital				
Opening capital		2,000		2,000
Add: Net profit		80		
		2,080		2,000

FIGURE 3.1   Balance sheet of Larch using the vertical format

into a substantial overdraft, suggests that the company is suffering from increasing cash difficulties.

A second advantage of the vertical presentation is that it contains an item of useful information that does not appear in the horizontal balance sheet, namely *working capital.* This is the balancing figure obtained by deducting current liabilities from current assets. A financially stable business is one that is able to meet its debts as they fall due for payment, and an adequate balance of working capital is an essential requirement if this desirable state of affairs is to exist. It is not possible to specify a figure for working capital that all firms should try to maintain, as much will depend on individual circumstances such as the size of the firm and the speed with which creditors are paid, stocks are sold and cash is collected from customers. Nevertheless managers, shareholders, creditors and other users of accounting statements normally hold firm views concerning what can be regarded as an acceptable balance for a particular business. Working capital is examined further in Chapter 12.

PROFITS, LOSSES AND CHANGES IN NET ASSETS

The vertical balance sheet contains the same basic financial information as does the horizontal balance sheet, since the facts are in no way altered by adopting a different method of presentation. Similarly, the overall financial relationship between sources of finance and assets, expressed in the formula $A = C + L$ (Assets = Capital + Liabilities) remains unchanged. The revised presentation does, however, focus attention on different aspects of the relationship between the three magnitudes, since it emphasizes the fact that capital is equal to gross assets minus liabilities:

$$\text{Assets} - \text{Liabilities} = \text{Capital} \ (A - L = C)$$

In practice, the term 'gross assets minus liabilities' is normally shortened to 'net assets'. We can therefore say that capital equals net assets. Indeed, these are two descriptions of the same financial total; the only difference is the way in which the figure is calculated. Capital is computed by taking the owner's opening investment, adding profit earned and deducting withdrawals for private use to give the closing investment at a particular date. Net assets are computed by adding together the values of the various assets owned at the balance sheet date, and then deducting the amount of finance obtained from suppliers and other creditors. Since assets are, by definition, financed either from capital or from liabilities, the balance that remains must necessarily be equal, in value, to the owner's investment.

Activity 3.1 reminded us that profit produces an equivalent increase in the gross assets of a firm; the profit of £80 resulted in gross assets increasing from £2,700 to £2,780. The presentation of the same data in the form of a vertical balance sheet (see Figure 3.1) draws attention to the fact that profit also results in an equivalent increase in net assets; these are up from £2,000 to £2,080. If the firm were to suffer a loss, net assets, and therefore the owner's capital, would be reduced by the amount of the loss. These circumstances are illustrated in Activity 3.2.

The following balance sheet is prepared in respect of Elm as at 31 December 20X1:   **ACTIVITY 3.2**

Elm

Balance Sheet

as at 31 December 20X1

	£	£		£	£
Fixed assets					
Plant and machinery		4,000	Capital		7,600
Current assets			**Current liabilities**		
Stock-in-trade	1,900		Trade creditors		1,200
Trade debtors	2,200				
Cash in hand	700	4,800			
		8,800			8,800

On 1 January 20X2 Elm sold, on credit for £480, goods that cost £600 some weeks ago.

Calculations of: Required

(a)   Elm's net assets at 31 December 20X1;
(b)   The profit or loss arising on the 1 January sale;
(c)   Elm's capital investment on 1 January 20X2 after the above transaction; and
(d)   Elm's balance sheet at 1 January 20X2, presented in vertical format.

We can conclude from the above examples that

Profit = Increase in net assets (and capital)

Loss = Decrease in net assets (and capital)

An awareness of the relationship between profits, losses and changes in net assets is fundamental to a sound understanding of the financial effects of business activity. The relevant connections between the various financial magnitudes can be expressed diagrammatically as shown in Figure 3.2.

The ownership group invests capital that is used to acquire business assets. These assets form the basis for business activity subsequently undertaken in order to generate profit. Some of the profit is likely to be withdrawn by the owners (sole traders and partnerships) or paid out to them as dividends (limited companies). The remainder is retained and this results in an increased volume of net assets to be used for trading purposes during the following accounting period. The reinvestment takes place in the expectation that the greater volume of net assets will enable a higher profit to be earned.

Readers should now work through Question 3.1 at the end of this chapter.

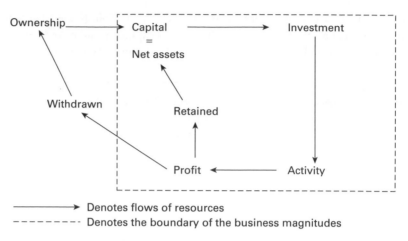

Denotes flows of resources
Denotes the boundary of the business magnitudes

FIGURE 3.2   Connections between financial magnitudes

PROFIT MEASURED BY CAPITAL CHANGES

It sometimes happens that the accountant is faced with the task of measuring profit despite the fact that no record exists of business transactions undertaken during the accounting period under review, for example because the records have been lost or destroyed by fire. In these circumstances it is not possible to calculate profit by comparing the cost of goods sold with their selling price, as in the previous worked examples. Instead the calculation must be based on the fundamental fact, established earlier in this chapter, that profit produces an equivalent increase in net assets or owner's capital, i.e.

Net profit = Closing capital – Opening capital; or
Net profit = Increase in capital

If opening capital exceeds closing capital, the result of the calculation is a negative figure and this means that a loss has been suffered.

The accountant, when faced with the job of calculating profit based on capital changes, must first take steps to establish the proprietor's investment at the beginning and end of the period. This process usually involves a significant element of estimation and judgement, particularly in relation to assets owned at the earlier of the two accounting dates. The existence of fixed assets can usually be established by physical verification, but the valuation of these items may prove more difficult. Evidence of the price paid may well be available in view of the large sums often involved; otherwise it is necessary to use information that can be obtained from suppliers of the relevant items or, alternatively, to arrange for a professional valuation.

Reliable figures for stock are difficult to obtain unless steps were taken to arrange for them to be physically counted and valued at each of the balance sheet dates. If this task has not been undertaken then an estimate of the likely value must be made by the proprietor of the business. Figures for trade debtors and trade creditors can be constructed if the sales and purchase invoices are retained and, where the company deals in products subject to value added tax (see Chapter 10), the likelihood of this information being readily available is much increased. The amount of money due to or from the bank can be established by an examination of the relevant bank statements. The measurement of profit by capital changes can be seen in the following example.

The following information is provided relating to the affairs of James who operates his clothing retail business from rented property: **EXAMPLE 3.1**

Assets and liabilities	31 Dec 20X1	31 Dec 20X2
	£	£
Motor vehicles	1,800	1,350
Fixtures and fittings	450	820
Stocks	1,060	1,610
Trade creditors	730	810
Trade debtors	240	300
Bank overdraft	920	760
Cash in hand	40	50

(a) Calculations of James's capital investment in the business at the end of 20X1 and 20X2.   **Required**

(b) A calculation of the profit earned by James during 20X2.

(c) The balance sheet of James's business at 31 December 20X2, presented in vertical format.

(a) Capital is calculated at each date by deducting liabilities from assets.   **Solution**

Statement of assets, liabilities and capital at 31 December

	20X1		20X2	
	£	£	£	£
Assets				
Motor vehicles		1,800		1,350
Fixtures and fittings		450		820
Stocks		1,060		1,610
Trade debtors		240		300
Cash in hand		40		50
		3,590		4,130
Less: Liabilities				
Bank overdraft	920	−1,650	760	−1,570
Trade creditors	730		810	
Capital		1,940		2,560

(b)   Profit is calculated based on the increase in capital

	£
Closing capital (at 31 Dec 20X2)	2,560
Less: Opening capital (at 31 Dec 20X1)	1,940
Profit	620

(c)   **Balance sheet at 31 December 20X2**

	£	£	£
Fixed assets			
Fixtures and fittings		820	
Motor vehicles		1,350	2,170
Current assets			
Stocks		1,610	
Trade debtors		300	
Cash in hand		50	1,960
Less: Current liabilities			
Bank overdraft	760		
Trade creditors	810		
		− 1,570	
Working capital			390
			2,560
Financed by:			
Opening capital			1,940
Add: Net profit			620
			2,560

ACTIVITY 3.3   The balance sheet of Paul at 30 June 20X3 is as follows:

Balance sheet at 30 June 20X3

	£	£	£
Fixed assets			7,500
Current assets			
Stock		3,280	
Trade debtors		1,750	
		5,030	
Less: Current liabilities			
Bank overdraft	980		
Trade creditors	1,220		
		− 2,200	
Working capital			2,830
			10,330
Financed by:			
Capital			10,330
			10,330

During the year to 30 June 20X4, Paul received a loan of £3,000 from a friend. The loan is interest-free and repayable at the end of 20X6. On 1 December 20X3 Paul purchased fixed assets costing £2,350. At 30 June 20X4, trade creditors amounted to £1,890, stock was valued at £4,270 and debtors amounted to £1,450. In addition, Paul had £570 in the business bank account and cash in hand of £30.

(a) A calculation of Paul's capital investment in the business at 30 June 20X4.   **Required**

(b) A calculation of the profit earned by Paul's business during the year to 30 June 20X4.

(c) The balance sheet of Paul's business at 30 June 20X4, presented in vertical format.

CAPITAL INJECTIONS AND WITHDRAWALS

There are two categories of business transaction which cause capital to increase or decrease during an accounting period:

1 Transactions which produce a profit or a loss.
2 Transactions involving the injection of capital or withdrawals by the owners.

The previous section of this chapter demonstrated the measurement of profit by changes to capital, assuming that there were no capital injections or withdrawals. This assumption is now removed. Where capital injections or withdrawals occur, their financial effects must be isolated if profit is to be measured accurately. This is because, although an investment or withdrawal of funds causes capital, and therefore net assets, to increase or decrease, these changes have not come about as the result of trading activity and therefore give rise to neither a profit nor a loss. The following adjustments must therefore be made:

1 *Drawings.*   These reduce closing capital but because they are not a business expense they must be added back to closing capital before the deduction of opening capital takes place.

2 *Capital injections.*   These increase closing capital but they are not business profits and so their effect must be eliminated by deducting the amount of the additional investment from the closing capital before the deduction of opening capital takes place.

The calculation of profit therefore becomes:

Profit $=$ Increase in capital $+$ Drawings $-$ New capital introduced

EXAMPLE 3.2   Assume the same assets and liabilities as are given in Example 3.1. In addition, you discover that James withdrew cash totalling £1,000 to meet living expenses during 20X2, while on 1 August he paid into his business bank account his 'first prize' winnings of £200 from his golf club's raffle.

Required   (a)   A calculation of the corrected profit earned by James during 20X2.
                  (b)   The capital section of James's balance sheet as at 31 December 20X2.

Solution   (a)   Profit is calculated, based on the increase in capital, as follows:

	£
Closing capital	2,560
Add: Drawings	1,000
Less: New capital introduced	(200)
	3,360
Less: Opening capital	(1,940)
PROFIT	1,420

Note   The assets and liabilities remain the same as in Example 3.1, and so the increase in capital is unchanged at £620 (£2,560 − £1,940). However, account must be taken of the two 'non-trading' transactions that have affected the value of closing capital and cause a net reduction of £800 (cash withdrawals of £1,000, partly compensated by a capital injection of £200). This amount must be added back to the observed increase in capital to produce a 'true' profit figure of £1,420.

(b)   **Balance sheet extract as at 31 December 20X2**

Capital section	£	£
Opening capital		1,940
Add: New capital		200
		2,140
Add: Profit	1,420	
Less: Drawings	(1,000)	
		420
		2,560

Note   The balance sheet now contains a full and accurate statement of transactions affecting the owner's capital during the year. It shows that James made an additional capital investment of £200, that he made personal withdrawals of £1,000 and that a profit figure of £1,420 (not £620) should be used as the basis for assessing the firm's performance and as a starting point for computing tax payable.

An injection of additional capital by the owner is an unusual event and is normally quite easy to identify. Sources of extra capital might include a legacy or gambling winnings or the sale of a non-business asset belonging to the proprietor. Drawings are usually more difficult to calculate as they may well vary from week to week and comprise both cash and stock-in-trade, the latter being particularly likely in the case of a retail business. In the absence of a reliable record of with-drawals, a careful estimate is required from the proprietor.

The various matters discussed in this chapter are incorporated into the follow-ing example.

The following information is provided relating to the affairs of John, who owns a tobacco,   **EXAMPLE 3.3**
confectionery and newspaper kiosk:

Assets and liabilities	I Jan 20XI	31 Dec 20XI
	£	£
Kiosk	2,000	2,000
Stocks of tobacco and confectionery	450	600
Trade creditors	250	320
Bank balance	160	940
Cash-in-hand	20	30

During 20X1 John received a legacy of £800 that was paid into his business bank account. Cash drawings are estimated at £200 per week and, in addition, John took from the business goods worth £150 for his own use during the year.

(a)   A calculation of the profit earned by John during 20X1.   **Required**

(b)   The balance sheet of John's business at 31 December 20X1, presented in vertical format

(a) (i)   Calculation of capital by deducting liabilities from assets: **Solution**

Statements of assets, liabilities and capital at:

	I Jan 20XI	31 Dec 20XI
Assets	£	£
Kiosk	2,000	2,000
Stocks	450	600
Bank balance	160	940
Cash in hand	20	30
	2,630	3,570
Liabilities		
Trade creditors	− 250	− 320
Capital	2,380	3,250

(ii)   Calculation of profit on the basis of the increase in capital:

	£
Closing capital	3,250
Less: Opening capital	(2,380)
Increase in capital	870

Add: Drawings		10,550 W1
Less: New capital introduced		(800)
Net profit		10,620

W1	Drawings:	Cash (£200 × 52)	10,400
		Goods	150
			10,550

(b) **Balance sheet as at 31 December 20X1**

	£	£
Fixed assets		
Kiosk		2,000
Current assets		
Stocks	600	
Bank	940	
Cash in hand	30	
	1,570	
Less: Current liabilities		
Trade creditors	− 320	
Working capital		1,250
		3,250
Capital		
Opening capital		2,380
Add: Capital introduced		800
		3,180
Add: Profit	10,620	
Less: Drawings – cash	(10,400)	
– goods	(150)	
		70
		3,250

The procedure for calculating profit described above is also used by the Inland Revenue where existing business records are unreliable but profit needs to be estimated because the taxpayer is believed to have understated his or her income in his or her tax return. In such cases, the major area of dispute is usually the level of drawings that have been made. The taxpayer will attempt to argue that they have been fairly modest, whereas the Inland Revenue will endeavour to demonstrate that much larger drawings must have been made to support the taxpayer's observed lifestyle. When the amount of the profit understatement has been computed, tax due will be calculated and penalties and interest added. The level of the penalty will depend a great deal on the co-operation received from the taxpayer since the initial discovery of the deception.

Readers should now work through Questions 3.2 and 3.3 at the end of this chapter.

3.1 The following balance sheet relates to the affairs of Columbus who runs a second hand car business. The balance sheet of his business at 31 December 20X1 is as follows:

Balance sheet as at 31 December 20X1

	£	£
Fixed assets		2,000
Current assets		
Stock of cars	2,700	
Trade debtors	1,000	
Bank	1,000	
	4,700	
Less: Current liabilities		
Trade creditors	− 200	
Working capital		4,500
		6,500
Financed by:		
Capital		6,500
		6,500

Transactions undertaken in January 20X2:

1 Columbus collects the £1,000 owing in respect of the second-hand car sold in December 20X1.
2 Columbus wins £500 on the football pools and pays the proceeds into his business bank account.
3 Columbus sells for £1,200 a car that was in stock on 31 December 20X1 at a value of £1,300.
4 Columbus withdraws £50 for private use.
5 Columbus purchases a friend's car for £150, and promises to pay him in February.
6 Columbus purchases a new machine for £700 and pays in cash.

(a) Give the totals for gross assets, net assets and working capital based on the figures in the above balance sheet.

(b) Taking each of the transactions listed above separately, give their effect (increase or decrease) on:

(i)   profit;
(ii)   net assets;
(iii) gross assets;
(iv)   working capital.

3.2 The following information is obtained in connection with the business of G. Haze, a trader:

	31 December	
	20X3	*20X4*
	£	£
Fixed assets at book value	9,000	see below
Stocks	2,650	3,710

Trade debtors	5,200	5,600
Trade creditors	1,710	1,210
Bank balance (overdraft)	(360)	50

During 20X4 motor vehicles were purchased at a cost of £3,144, part of which was met by G. Haze trading in his private motor car at an agreed valuation of £600. Cash drawings made by G. Haze amounted to £150 per week and, in addition, stocks valued at £300 were taken during the year for personal use.

Required

(a) A calculation of the profit earned by G. Haze's business during 20X4.

(b) The balance sheet of the firm at 31 December 20X4 presented in the vertical format.

3.3 The following table shows the cumulative effects of a succession of separate transactions on the assets and liabilities of a business. Each letter identities the assets and liabilities *after each single transaction.*

Transaction		A	B	C	D	E	F	G	H	I	J
Assets:	£000	£000	£000	£000	£000	£000	£000	£000	£000	£000	£000
Buildings, at cost/valuation	200	200	200	200	200	200	200	250	250	250	250
Equipment, at cost	100	100	100	100	125	125	125	125	125	125	125
Stocks, at cost	35	35	46	32	32	22	22	22	22	22	22
Trade debtors	48	43	43	43	43	43	43	43	40	40	40
Prepaid expenses	5	5	5	5	5	5	5	5	5	5	3
Bank	0	0	0	15	15	15	15	15	15	10	10
Cash	3	3	3	3	3	3	1	1	1	1	3
	391	386	397	398	423	413	411	461	458	453	453
Liabilities:											
Capital	235	235	235	241	241	231	230	280	277	278	278
Loan	80	80	80	80	105	105	105	105	105	105	105
Trade creditors	55	55	66	66	66	66	66	66	66	60	60
Accrued expenses	11	11	11	11	11	11	10	10	10	10	10
Bank overdraft	10	5	5	0	0	0	0	0	0	0	0
	391	386	397	398	423	413	411	461	458	453	453

Required

Identify clearly as fully as you can what transaction has taken place in each case. Use the reference letters from the table to identify each transaction. There is no need to copy out the table.

(20 Marks)

(AAT, Basic Accounting, June 1990)

Larch

Balance sheet

as at 31 December 20X2

	£	£		£
Fixed assets				
Plant and machinery		1,600	Capital	2,000
			Add: Net profit	
			(220 – 140)	80
				2,080
Current assets			**Current liabilities**	
Stock-in-trade			Trade creditors	700
(600–140)	460			
Trade debtors				
(300 + 220)	520			
Cash in hand	200	1,180		
		2,780		2,780

		£
(a)	Net assets = Assets	8,800
	Less: Liabilities	(1,200)
		7,600
(b)	Sale proceeds of stock	480
	Less: Cost of stock	(600)
	Loss	(120)
(c)	Capital at 31 December 20X1	7,600
	Less: Loss	(120)
		7,480

(d)

Elm

Balance sheet as at 1 January 20X2

	£	£
Fixed assets		
Plant and machinery		4,000
Current assets		
Stock	1,300	
Trade debtors	2,680	
Cash in hand	700	
	4,680	

Less: Current liabilities		
Trade creditors	− 1,200	
Working capital		3,480
		7,480
Financed by:		
Opening capital		7,600
Less: Net loss		− 120
Closing capital		7,480

Solution to
Activity 3.3

(a) **Statement of assets, liabilities and capital at 30 June 20X4**

Assets		£
Fixed assets		9,850
Stock		4,270
Debtors		1,450
Cash at bank		570
Cash in hand		30
		16,170
Less: Liabilities		
Loan	3,000	
Trade creditors	1,890	
		− 4,890
Capital		11,280

(b) Calculation of profit on the basis of the increase in capital:

	£
Closing capital	11,280
Less: Opening capital	− 10,330
Profit	950

(c) **Balance sheet as at 30 June 20X4**

	£	£
Fixed assets		9,850
Current assets		
Stocks	4,270	
Trade debtors	1,450	
Cash at bank	570	
Cash in hand	30	
	6,320	
Less: Current liabilities		
Trade creditors	− 1,890	
Working capital		4,430
		14,280

Less: Long-term	
liabilities	
Loan	− 3,000
	11,280
Financed by:	
Opening capital	10,330
Add: Net profit	950
Closing capital	11,280

4 The preparation of accounts from cash or incomplete records

The objectives of this chapter are to:

- illustrate the presentation of a summarized statement of receipts and payments;
- explain how profit is measured by matching revenue with expenditure;
- demonstrate the difference between gross profit and net profit;
- explain the significance of the realization concept for the identification of revenue and the benefit principle for the measurement of expenditure;
- demonstrate the preparation of accounts from cash records; and
- outline the special rules relating to the preparation of accounts for clubs and societies.

ACCOUNTING SYSTEMS AND INFORMATION REQUIREMENTS

For the unincorporated enterprise, the complexity of the accounting system for recording and reporting business transactions depends mainly on the size of the organization. (The position is different in the case of a limited company which, irrespective of its size, is legally required to keep formal accounting records.) The large number of transactions undertaken each day, in the case of a substantial business concern, requires a sophisticated accounting system for the dual purposes of *control* and *assessment*. In the small firm the accounting system is usually far more rudimentary, since effective protection of valuable resources is achieved through the owner's close personal contact with all aspects of the firm's business activities. Control is enhanced if the firm's most vulnerable assets, e.g. the cash balance and the bank account, are under the direct control of the owner. Other resources, e.g. stock, which may be in the custody of trusted personnel, nevertheless remains under the close scrutiny of the proprietor.

It is unnecessary, in the small firm, to employ formal reporting procedures as a basis for performance assessment. Trade creditors and customers are likely to be relatively small in number, and any difficulties associated with the supply of, or demand for, the firm's products should come quickly to the attention of a diligent proprietor. Similarly, in the absence of a significant level of capital expenditure, changes in the bank balance are likely to provide a fairly reliable indication of progress. The function of accounting reports, in these circumstances, is simply to provide a basis for agreeing tax liabilities with the Inland Revenue and, where there are a number of proprietors, is a means of allocating profit between the partners. Although an increase in the scale of a firm's activities implies the need for a more formal system of accounting, it does not necessarily follow that transactions will be recorded daily in accordance with the system of double entry described in Chapter 6. It is essential that accounting systems be judged in terms of their usefulness, and a decision to invest the time and money required to operate a complex system must be justified in terms of the benefits it produces.

There is a certain minimum range of financial information that must be made available, however, to enable the accountant to prepare both a trading and profit and loss account (see the Gross Profit and Net Profit section of this chapter) and a balance sheet. The information required consists of

(a) assets at the beginning and at the end of the year;
(b) liabilities at the beginning and at the end of the year; and
(c) cash receipts and payments during the year.

The steps that must be taken to obtain details of assets and liabilities are discussed in Chapter 3. This information is used to compile the closing balance sheet and also the opening balance sheet unless this statement was prepared at the end of the previous year. Details of cash transactions are required as the starting point for preparing the trading and profit and loss account. The business bank statements fulfil an essential role in this context, since they contain a wide range of reliable information concerning cash transactions undertaken during the year. There is, of course, usually a large number of bank statements and the analysis of these documents is a lengthy process, particularly because the statements provide few details. For example, the only information usually given in respect of cheque payments is the amount and the cheque number, and in the case of receipts only a brief description of the source of the receipt is provided. It is, therefore, important for cheque books and paying-in books to be retained so that an accurate description of the various items appearing on the bank statements can be constructed. Details must also be obtained of any cash transactions that have not gone through the bank. This information may be recorded in a 'petty' cash book (see Chapter 5); alternatively, it may be possible to build up the relevant figures from files of cash receipts and payments. In examination questions the analysis work has generally been done, and figures for receipts and payments are given in a summary form similar to that given in Figure 4.1.

The receipts side of the summary shows cash from customers of £23,750 which, when added to the sum available at the start, £510, means that cash totalling £24,260 became available to the business at some stage during 20X1. From this total, cash payments of £21,775 must be deducted, leaving a cash balance at the year end of £2,485.

Provided the rudimentary financial facts referred to in this section can be assembled, it is possible to prepare a full set of final accounts. The process, described as the preparation of accounts from cash records, is examined in this chapter.

Cash transactions, year to 31 December 20X1

Receipts	£	Payments	£
Opening balance of cash	510	Payments to suppliers	17,380
Sale of goods	23,750	Wages	2,560
		Rent and rates	840
		Lighting and heating	620
		General expenses	375
			21,775
		Closing balance of cash	2,485
	24,260		24,260

FIGURE 4.1   Summary of figures for receipts and payments

THE MATCHING CONCEPT

Chapter 3 demonstrated how profit can be measured in the absence of detailed information concerning trading transactions undertaken during a particular accounting period, i.e. it is computed by identifying the change in capital between the beginning and the end of the year. Where an adequate accounting record of transactions undertaken *during the year* exists, profit is computed in accordance with the *matching concept*. That is, the accountant measures profit by comparing or 'matching' the total cost of the many trading transactions undertaken during an accounting period with the total revenues arising from the trading activity:

$$\text{Profit} = \text{Revenue} - \text{Revenue Expenditure}$$

EXAMPLE 4.1   Mex Cars is a motor vehicle distributor that prepares its accounts on the calendar-year basis. Ten cars are purchased during 20X1 for £4,500 each and sold for £6,000 each.

Required   Calculate profit by matching revenues with expenditures.

Solution

	£
Revenue:	
Proceeds from the sale of cars (£6,000 × 10)	60,000
Less: Expenditure:	
Cost of cars sold (£4,500 × 10)	45,000
Profit	15,000

ACTIVITY 4.1   Johanna & Co is a distributor of satellite dishes. The year end is 30 June. For the year ending 20X0 the business sold 100 dishes at £150 each. The cost of each dish was £70.

Required   Calculate the profit earned by Johanna & Co for the year ending 30 June 20X0.

GROSS PROFIT AND NET PROFIT

The balance of profit, which is arrived at by matching sales proceeds with the actual cost of the goods sold, is called *gross profit*. In practice many other costs are also incurred, such as salaries paid to employees, commissions paid to sales people, rent and rates for the showroom and office accommodation, and the numerous incidental expenses such as telephone costs and stationery. Since these outlays are incurred to help generate sales revenue, they must also be deducted to leave a final balance called *net profit*. Revenues and revenue expenditures are matched against one another in the *trading account and the profit and loss account* (usually abbreviated to trading and profit and loss account). The vertical format for this accounting statement is given in Figure 4.2.

The gross profit is calculated in the trading account and the remaining expenses are deducted in the profit and loss account. It might occur to readers that the calculation of profit on the basis of changes in capital is a rather more straight-forward process than by comparing revenue with expenditure. The accumulation of figures for sales revenue and the many items of expenditure incurred during the year is a far more laborious and time-consuming task than the identification of figures for capital at just two dates: the beginning and end of the accounting period. Part of the justification for the extra work is that trading transactions entered into during an accounting period are recorded not only to enable profit to be measured but also to facilitate effective control over inflows and outflows of cash and goods (e.g. to ensure that cash is collected from customers and that employees are paid the amounts due to them).

Mex Cars
Trading and profit and loss account
year ending 31 December 20X1

	£	£
Sales		60,000
Less: Cost of sales		(45,000)
Gross profit		15,000
Less: Expenditure		
Salaries	6,200	
Commissions	600	
Rent and rates	1,400	
Lighting and heating	250	
Telephone	150	
Postage and stationery	220	
Advertising	370	
General expenses	500	
		(9,690)
Net profit		5,310

FIGURE 4.2   Trading and profit and loss account

Detailed accounting records enable management to make a more useful calculation of profit because, although the end result is the same, the preparation of a trading and profit and loss account produces the following advantages:

1   It contains a comprehensive statement of how the net profit balance has been achieved.
2   It is a valuable means for assessing performance, e.g. by comparing this year's gross profit and expenses with results achieved last year.
3   It assists in the decision-making process concerning the future allocation of resources.

THE PROBLEM OF PERIODIC PROFIT CALCULATION

The frequency with which the profit and loss account and balance sheet are prepared varies depending on the circumstances of the particular business. As a minimum, however, accounts must be prepared once a year – limited companies are legally required to prepare annual accounts for publication, while sole traders and partnerships are obliged to prepare annual accounts for tax purposes. To provide the information needed to take day-to-day decisions designed to achieve the most effective use of available resources, management requires more frequent calculations of profit, and the preparation of quarterly or even monthly management accounts is a common feature within commerce and industry today.

The calculation of periodic profit causes difficulties because business activity is continuous. For example, a business may last for ten years but, for accounting purposes, it must be split into at least ten accounting periods, each lasting one year. Many transactions cause no difficulty because they can be easily identified with a particular accounting period. For example, assuming accounts are prepared on the calendar-year basis, an item of stock purchased and paid for in January 20X1 and sold for cash in February 20X1 must clearly be taken into account in computing the profit for 20X1. Problems arise with transactions that *overlap* the end of one accounting period and the beginning of another. Consider the following facts, assuming a 31 December accounting date:

1   Stocks delivered to a customer in December 20X1 but not paid for until January 20X2.
2   Stocks purchased and paid for in November 20X1 but not sold until March 20X2.
3   Rates paid on 1 October 20X1 for the six months to 31 March 20X2.
4   Machinery purchased and paid for in 20Xl, which is expected to last for eight years.

The problem of deciding whether these transactions give rise to revenues and expenditures in 20X1 or 20X2 or another accounting period is solved by the accountant making certain assumptions and applying a range of accounting conventions to the factual information generated by the accounting system. These procedures are examined in the following sections.

THE IDENTIFICATION OF REVENUE:
THE REALIZATION CONCEPT

Revenue is obtained from the sale of goods purchased in the case of a trading organization, from the sale of goods manufactured in the case of an industrial concern, and from the supply of services in the case of a business in the service sector. For accounting purposes, revenue is assumed to arise at the point of sale. In the case of a cash sale, this is when the goods or services are supplied in exchange for cash; in the case of a credit sale, it occurs when the goods or services have been supplied and the sales invoice delivered to the customer. The assumption that revenue, and therefore profit, arises when the sale takes place is called the **realization concept**, and it is a good illustration of how accounting procedures are based on generally agreed conventions rather than indisputable facts.

For example, consider the case of a manufacturer of motor vehicles where demand exceeds supply. A great deal of work goes into building the car and, when completed, little more needs to be done to earn the profit. Demand exceeds supply and so delivery to a motor vehicle distributor is likely to take place fairly soon to satisfy consumer requirements. No profit is recognized during production, however, and the motor vehicle remains in the books at cost until the sale takes place. This procedure demonstrates the rather cautious approach towards profit measurement the accountant generally adopts.

It might be argued that, during the course of the production process, profit is gradually being earned that should be recognized in the accounts, but the accountant prefers to wait until the expected profit is validated by a sale. This view is taken partly because it would be difficult to decide how much extra value to recognize at any interim stage and partly because it is considered imprudent to anticipate sales that may not occur. At the other extreme it might be argued that, in the case of a credit sale, it would be even safer to wait until the cash is actually collected before recognizing a profit. But although the accountant rightly has the reputation of being cautious, he or she is not *that* cautious. The credit sale is recognized as the supply of goods which gives rise to a legally enforceable debt against the customer. The collection of cash will in most cases be a mere formality and no further delay in the recognition of revenue is thought to be justified (the complication of bad debts is examined in Chapter 7).

On 1 January 20X1 Jubilee & Co received an order for an 'indestructible' aluminium pallet.   EXAMPLE 4.2
The pallet was priced in the business's catalogue at £5,000. The pallet was manufactured during the week ended 6 January and production costs totalling £2,000 were incurred. At the close of business, on 6 January, the pallet was transferred to the business's warehouse and held in stock until 15 January when it was dispatched to the customer. Cash, £5,000, was collected from the customer on 12 February 20X1.

Required   Calculate (a) the value recognized in the accounts, and (b) the profit recognized in the accounts at each of the following stages of the transaction:

(i)   receipt of order;

(ii)   production of pallet;

(iii)   transfer of pallet to stock;

(iv)   dispatch of pallet to customer; and

(v)   collection of cash.

Solution

Stage		(a) Value recognized	(b) Profit recognized
		£	£
(i)	Receipt of order	–	–
(ii)	Production of pallet	2,000	–
(iii)	Pallet to stock	2,000	–
(iv)	Dispatch (sale)	5,000	3,000
(v)	Collection of cash	5,000	–

Note   Profit is recognized when the pallet is dispatched to the customer. No additional profit is recognized when cash is collected. The only amendment to the accounts made at this date is that a debtor of £5,000 is replaced by cash of the same amount.

ACTIVITY 4.2   Bart & Co. arranges in 20X0 to sell some goods to a customer. The goods are delivered in 20X1 and the business receives payment for them in 20X2. When would Bart & Co. record the sale in their accounts?

Calculating sales from records of cash receipts

The sales figure is calculated by taking the figure for cash received from customers during the year, deducting opening debtors (i.e. what the debtors owed from last year) and adding closing debtors (i.e. what the debtors still owe for this year). The purpose of the calculation is to convert the figure for cash received into the figure for goods or services supplied.

EXAMPLE 4.3   During 20X1, John received £17,500 from customers in respect of credit sales. On 1 January 20X1 his trade debtors amounted to £3,600 and at 31 December 20X1 they were £4,720.

Required   The calculation of sales for 20X1.

Calculation of sales.   Solution

	£
Cash received in respect of credit sales	17,500
Less: Opening trade debtors	− 3,600
	13,900
Add: Closing trade debtors	4,720
Sales	18,620

Of the £17,500 received during the year, £3,600 was collected from customers to whom goods were sold in 20X0 and that would have been reported as revenue in the trading account for that year. The balance, £13,900, represents cash received in respect of sales actually made *during* 20X1. To this must be added closing debtors for goods sold during 20X1, but not yet paid for, to produce the sales figure of £18,620.
The rule to remember is therefore

Sales = Cash received from customers − Opening debtors + Closing debtors

ACTIVITY 4.3

At the beginning of 20X2 Joe had outstanding debtors amounting to £4,900. During 20X2 he received from debtors £28,000 but at the end of the year he was still owed £7,000. Calculate the amount of sales for 20X2.

Required

MATCHING EXPENDITURE WITH REVENUE: THE BENEFIT PRINCIPLE

The first step in the calculation of profit for the year is to compute revenue; the second step involves identifying the expenditures that must be matched against revenue. The basic test is: 'Which accounting period benefits from the expenditure?' If the answer is the current accounting period then the expenditure is charged against revenue for the current year. If the answer is a future accounting period, then the expenditure must be carried forward as an asset in the balance sheet and charged against the revenue of the future accounting period that benefits. If the answer is both the current period and one or more future periods, an apportionment must be made. This process, which bases the charge on *benefits received* during the year, rather than payments made during the year, is called the **accruals concept**. The application of this concept to specific business facts is examined next.

Accounting for stock

In Example 4.1 and Activity 4.1 we saw that gross profit is calculated as the difference between sales and the cost of the goods sold, and in these two illustrations what the company purchased was sold in its entirety (i.e. 10 cars and 100 satellite dishes were purchased and sold). In many instances, however, a business is not able to, or does not want to, sell all of its purchases. The remaining items in stock are termed *closing stock*. In cases involving stock the cost of sales is not simply the cost of purchases but rather it has to be calculated. To do this the matching principle is applied, which ensures that revenues are charged with the correct amount of expenditure for the period concerned. So, if Mex Cars in Example 4.1 had sold only eight cars then the cost of only eight cars should be included in the profit calculation.

EXAMPLE 4.4   Recalculate the gross profit figure for Mex Cars in Example 4.1, assuming that they sold only 8 cars.

Solution

	£
Revenue:	
Proceeds from the sale of cars (£6,000 × 8)	48,000
Less: Expenditure:	
Cost of cars sold (£4,500 × 8)	(36,000)
Profit	12,000

ACTIVITY 4.4   Recalculate the gross profit figure for Johanna & Co in Activity 4.1, assuming that they sold only 85 dishes.

The calculation of the figure for cost of goods sold, to be matched with sales revenue for the purpose of computing gross profit, involves two steps:

1   *Calculate purchases.* The procedure is the same as that followed when computing sales, and may be summarized using the following formula:

Purchases = Cash paid to suppliers – Opening creditors
+ Closing creditors

2   *Calculate the cost of goods sold.* As already suggested, it is unusual for all the goods purchased during the year to be sold by the end of the year. The items that remain in stock, at the year end, should be deducted from purchases and carried forward, in the balance sheet, to the following accounting period that will benefit from their sale. In a similar manner, stocks brought forward from the previous year and sold during the current accounting period must be added to purchases and matched with the current year's sales proceeds. The calculation that must be memorized in this case is:

Cost of goods sold = Opening stock + Purchases – Closing stock

James made payments by cheque to suppliers of goods on credit amounting to £27,300   EXAMPLE 4.5
during 20X2. In addition, he made cash purchases of £1,600. Trade creditors at 1 January
20X2 and 31 December 20X2 amounted to £4,750 and £6,100, respectively. Opening
stocks were £10,250, while closing stocks amounted to £9,640.

Calculate (a) purchases and (b) the cost of goods sold for 20X2.   Required

(a)   Calculation of purchases: Solution

	£
Cash paid to suppliers:	
Credit purchases	27,300
Cash purchases	1,600
	28,900
Less: Opening creditors	– 4,750
	24,150
Add: Closing creditors	6,100
Purchases	30,250

(b)   Calculation of costs of goods sold:

	£
Opening stock	10,250
Add: Purchases	30,250
	40,500
Less: Closing stock	9,640
Cost of goods sold	30,860

The calculations discussed and illustrated above are central to the measurement
of profit by matching revenue with revenue expenditure. Readers should test their
understanding of these calculations by working through Activity 4.5.

The following information is provided relating to Neil's business for 20X3:   ACTIVITY 4.5

Cash collected from customers in respect of:	£
Credit sales	41,750
Cash sales	12,350
Payments to suppliers	36,590

Balances at	1 January	31 December
Trade debtors	12,650	11,780
Trade creditors	6,540	8,270
Stock	9,150	9,730

(a)   Calculations for 20X3 of: Required
   (i)   receipts from customers;
   (ii) sales;

(iii)   purchases;

(iv)   cost of goods sold.

(b)   The trading, profit and loss account of Neil's business for 20X3.

Accounting for services: accruals and prepayments

When preparing accounts from cash records, it is also necessary to adjust cash payments for services rendered to the company, so that the amount charged in the profit and loss account reflects the cost of benefits actually consumed during the period.

For certain services, payments are made before the associated benefits are received, i.e. the payment is made *in advance*. In the case of rent and rates, advance payments may be made for the right to occupy the property for a fixed future period of time. Where the period of occupation covers the end of one accounting year and the beginning of another, an arithmetical apportionment of the amount paid must be made between the two consecutive accounting periods. For example, if a rental of £600 is paid on 1 April 20X1 for the forthcoming 12 months, and the accounts are prepared on the calendar-year basis (i.e. from January to December), nine months (or three-quarters) of the payment relates to 20X1 and three months (or one-quarter) relates to 20X2. Therefore, $3/4 \times £600 = £450$ is charged against revenue arising during 20X1 and $1/4 \times £600 = £150$ should be charged against the revenue of 20X2. The amount carried forward to the next period is shown in the balance sheet of 20X1 as a current asset called 'prepaid expense'. It is regarded as an asset because until the benefit has been received the amount prepaid is owed to the business.

The majority of expenses are, however, paid *in arrears*, mainly because the amount charged depends on the extent to which the service has been utilized. Examples are electricity charges and telephone charges (except the rental). In these cases the exact amount of the charges may not be known until after the accounting year end, i.e. the bills have not yet been received. Referring back to the matching concept, however, it is important that revenue is matched with the revenue expenditure incurred in generating that income. For this reason, an estimate of the charges should be made and included in the accounts. These charges are termed *accruals* and represent the value of the benefit received but not yet paid for at the end of the accounting period. The amount of the accrual may be estimated on the basis of past experience. Alternatively, where the bill is received by the time the accounts are prepared, an apportionment may be made in the manner described in the previous paragraph. This does not necessarily produce strictly accurate results because the service will not have been utilized at an even rate throughout the period under consideration. However, the error is unlikely to be significant, and the extra work and cost involved in obtaining a more precise apportionment would not be justified. The amount accrued is charged against revenue in the profit and loss account so that a more realistic profit figure is calculated, and it is also included in the balance sheet as a current liability under the heading 'accrued expense'. It is included as a liability since the amount has not been paid, but has been recognized as an expense.

EXAMPLE 4.6

The following information is provided relating to Mark's business for 20X4:

Payments during the year for:

	£
Rates	500
Telephone	375

Balances at	1 January	31 December
	£	£
Rates paid in advance	100	125
Telephone charges outstanding	50	62

Calculations of the amount to be charged against revenue for 20X4 in respect of (a) rates and (b) telephone.

(a) Rates:

	£
Payments during 20X4	500
Add: Amount prepaid at 1 January 20X4*	100
	600
Less: Amount prepaid at 31 December 20X4**	− 125
Charge for the year	475

Note *This amount was paid in 20X3 but relates to the occupation of the premises during 20X4 and must be included in the charge against revenue arising in 20X4.

**This amount is paid in advance for 20X5 and should be excluded from the figure for 20X4.

(b) Telephone:

	£
Payments during 20X4	375
Less: Amount outstanding at 1 January 20X4†	− 50
	325
Add: Amount outstanding at 31 December 20X4††	62
Charge for the year	387

Note † This amount was paid in 20X4 but relates to services received during 20X3; therefore it will have already been charged against revenue in 20X3.

†† This amount should be included for 20X4 as it is a charge for this year even though it will not be paid until 20X5.

ACTIVITY 4.6   The following information is provided relating to Joe's business for 20X1:

Balances at	1 January	31 December
	£	£
Light and heat paid in advance	300	375
Bank interest outstanding	150	162

Payments during the year for:	£
Light and heat	1,500
Bank interest	700

Required   Calculations of the amount to be charged against revenue for 20X1 in respect of (a) light and heat and (b) bank interest.

Accounting for depreciation of fixed assets

Fixed assets are usually paid for at the date of acquisition, or soon afterwards, but they are expected to remain in the firm for many years. For example, a salesman may use a motor vehicle for five years, a machine may produce items to sell for ten years and a building may last for fifty years or more. It would therefore be unreasonable to charge against revenue the entire cost of the asset in the year the asset is acquired on the grounds that the benefits are received over a number of years. At the same time, most fixed assets have a limited useful life, and it would be equally wrong to keep these items indefinitely in the balance sheet at original cost as the older an asset gets the less it is worth.

The term accountants use to describe the fall in the value of a fixed asset between the date it is acquired and the date it is sold or scrapped is *depreciation*. It may be defined as the fall in the value of a fixed asset due to the passage of time, usage or obsolescence. This reduction in value is acknowledged, in the accounts, by making an annual charge designed to spread the loss (fall in value) over the periods that are expected to benefit from using the asset (matching principle). The depreciation charge is included in the expenses deducted from gross profit in the profit and loss account. The annual charge is also deducted from the original cost of the asset in the balance sheet to give the *net book value* (NBV).

There are many different methods of charging depreciation (discussed in Chapter 8), but we will concentrate here on the one that is most common and easy to apply for illustration purposes, namely the straight-line method (sometimes called the equal instalment method). This method assumes that each accounting period receives the same amount of benefit from using the asset and the total decline in its value is therefore spread equally over the period of ownership. The formula used to calculate the depreciation charge for one year is as follows:

$$\text{Straight-line depreciation} = \frac{\text{Original cost} - \text{Estimated disposal value}}{\text{Estimated life}}$$

Paul purchased a machine for £130,000 on 1 January 20X1. It is estimated that the machine will have a useful life of six years and then be sold for £10,000.

EXAMPLE 4.7

(a) Calculate the straight-line depreciation charge for each of the years 20X1–20X6 for inclusion in the profit and loss account.
(b) Calculate the book value of the machine at the end of each of the years 20X1–20X6 to be reported in the balance sheet.

Required

(a) Depreciation charge:

Solution

$$\frac{130,000 - 10,000}{6} = £20,000 \text{ per annum}$$

(b)   Balance sheet extracts, 31 December...

	20X1	20X2	20X3	20X4	20X5	20X6
	£000	£000	£000	£000	£000	£000
Fixed assets	130	130	130	130	130	130
Less: Accumulated depreciation	– 20	– 40	– 60	– 80	– 100	– 120
Net book value (NBV)	110	90	70	50	30	10

The effect of charging depreciation is that the balance sheet value of the machine is gradually reduced to its disposal value. If everything works out as planned, on 31 December 20X6 the written-down value of the machine, £10,000, will be removed from the balance sheet and replaced by cash of an equal value. Events may not progress quite so smoothly, and it may turn out that the estimates on which the calculation was based prove to be wrong, i.e. the machine might not last for six years or sell for £10,000 at the end of its useful life. These complications are considered in Chapters 7 and 8.

Hannah purchased equipment for her hairdressing salon for £14,000 on 1 January 20X0. It is estimated that the equipment will have a useful life of 5 years, after which time it could be sold for £4,000.

ACTIVITY 4.7

(a) Calculate the straight-line depreciation charge for each of the years 20X0–20X4 for inclusion in the profit and loss account.
(b) Calculate the book value of the machine at the end of each of the years 20X0–20X4 to be reported in the balance sheet.

Required

THE PREPARATION OF ACCOUNTS FROM CASH RECORDS: A WORKED EXAMPLE

The preparation of accounts from cash records involves the following four steps:

1 Prepare an opening balance sheet, sometimes called the 'statement of affairs'. This shows the proprietor's opening capital, which is needed when preparing the year-end balance sheet.
2 Calculate revenues and expenditures for inclusion in the trading and profit and loss account.
3 Prepare the trading and profit and loss account.
4 Prepare the closing balance sheet.

EXAMPLE 4.8   William is a trader who commenced business on 1 January 20X1. In his first year a friend of his prepared accounts that were sufficient to enable William to agree his tax liabilities. William's friend has now left the country and is unable to help. William maintains separate files of invoices received from suppliers and issued to customers.

The following summary has been prepared from William's paying-in books, cheque books and bank statements for 20X2:

Bank Summary

	Receipts	Payments	Balance
Opening balance*			− 3,520
Cash sales	39,640		
Proceeds from credit sales	18,750		
Payments to suppliers		− 31,910	
Rates		− 2,800	
Personal drawings		− 6,500	
Wages for part-time staff		− 5,930	
General expenses		− 3,180	
Vehicle		− 4,000	
	58,390	− 54,320	
Closing balance			550

Note   *William is overdrawn in the bank at the start of the year.

The following additional information has been obtained from the files of invoices and other books and records of William:

1 William has paid all sales proceeds into the business bank account except for £200 that was used to pay additional part-time staff over the busy Christmas period.
2 Assets and liabilities at 31 December, based on an analysis of the invoice files and from discussions with William, were as follows:

	20X1	20X2
	£	£
Premises at cost	6,600	6,600
Furniture at net book value (original cost was £3,000)	2,700	2,400
Stock	4,250	5,760
Trade creditors	4,630	4,920
Trade debtors	2,140	2,320
Rates paid in advance	180	200
General expenses accrued	320	290

3 William has charged depreciation at 10% on a straight-line basis. The figures shown are net of depreciation.

4 The vehicle was purchased on 1 July 20X2 and is to be written off over five years assuming a resale value of £1,000 at the end of that period. Ignore depreciation of premises.

The trading and profit and loss account of William's business for the year ended 31 December 20X2 and the balance sheet as at that date.   **Required**

This question is answered by following the four steps outlined at the beginning of this section.   **Solution**

BALANCE SHEET AT 1 JANUARY 20X1   *Step 1*

	£	£	£
Fixed assets			
Premises			6,600
Furniture at cost		3,000	
Less: Accumulated depreciation*		– 300	
			2,700
			9,300
Current assets			
Stock		4,250	
Trade debtors		2,140	
Prepaid rates		180	
		6,570	
Less: Current liabilities			
Bank overdraft	3,520		
Trade creditors	4,630		
Accrued general expenses	320		
		– 8,470	

Working capital[†]	– 1,900
	7,400
Financed by	
Capital	7,400

Notes *Accumulated depreciation means the amount of depreciation charged against profit to date. As this is the first year of trading, only one year's worth of depreciation is included. [†]William has a negative opening working capital. Whilst this is possible, it is not a good position to be in since what he owes exceeds what he is owed.

Step 2

REVENUES AND EXPENDITURE FOR INCLUSION IN THE TRADING, PROFIT AND LOSS ACCOUNT

Workings

			£
W1	Sales:		
	Paid into bank:		
		Cash sales	39,640
		Credit sales	18,750
		Proceeds not paid in but used for	
		part-time Christmas staff	200
	Total cash received		58,590
	Less: Opening debtors		(2,140)
	Add: Closing debtors		2,320
			58,770
W2	Purchases:		
	Payments to suppliers		31,910
	Less: Opening creditors		(4,630)
	Add: Closing creditors		4,920
			32,200
W3	Rates:		
	Paid during year		2,800
	Add: Opening advance payment		180
	Less: Closing advance payment		(200)
			2,780
W4	General expenses:		
	Paid during year		3,180
	Less: Opening accrual		(320)
	Add: Closing accrual		290
			3,150

W5 Wages:

Paid by cheque	5,930
Paid by cash	200
	6,130

W6 Depreciation on furniture:

$$(£3,000 \times 10\%) = £300$$

W7 Depreciation on vehicle:

$$(£4,000 - £1,000) \div 5 \times 1/2* = £300$$

Note *The vehicle has only been owned for six months so half a year's depreciation charge is applicable.

TRADING AND PROFIT AND LOSS ACCOUNT FOR 20X2 *Step 3*

	£		£
Purchases (W2)	32,200	Sales (W1)	58,770
Add: Opening stock	4,250		
Less: Closing stock	− 5,760		
Cost of goods sold	30,690		
Gross profit	28,080		
	58,770		58,770
		Gross profit	28,080
Expenses:			
Rates (W3)	2,780		
General expenses (W4)	3,150		
Wages (W5)	6,130		
Depreciation on furniture (W6)	300		
Depreciation on vehicle (W7)	300		
	12,660		
Net profit	15,420		
	28,080		28,080

BALANCE SHEET AS AT 31 DECEMBER 20X2 *Step 4*

	£	£	£
Fixed assets			
Premises			6,600
Furniture at cost		3,000	
Less: Accumulated depreciation		− 600	
			2,400

Vehicle at cost		4,000	
Less: Accumulated depreciation		− 300	
			3,700
			12,700
Current assets			
Stock		7,760	
Trade debtors		2,320	
Prepaid rates		200	
Bank		550	
		8,830	
Less: Current liabilities			
Trade creditors	4,920		
Accrued general expenses	290		
		− 5,210	
Working capital			3,620
			16,320
Financed by			
Capital			7,400
Add: Net profit			15,420
Less: Drawings			− 6,500
			16,320

Trading and profit and loss account presented in vertical format

Chapter 3 drew attention to the fact that today the balance sheet is usually presented in the vertical format rather than the horizontal format. The same is the case with the trading and profit and loss account as seen in Figure 4.2. The reasons are similar: the layout is thought to be more easily comprehended by the non-accountant, it is possible to present a number of years' results on a single sheet, and comparison of results between years is made much easier. The trading and profit and loss account of William is now reproduced in Figure 4.3. The vertical format is most commonly used nowadays and the one you will most likely be required to produce in an examination. For illustration purposes only, the horizontal format of William's trading, profit and loss account is shown in Figure 4.4.

Readers should now work through Questions 4.1, 4.2, 4.3 and 4.4 at the end of this chapter.

CLUBS AND SOCIETIES

Clubs and societies are a common feature of most local communities. Such organizations are often formed as the result of a group of individuals, possessing a common interest, voluntarily joining together with the objective of providing a

William
Trading, profit and loss account,
period ending 31 December 20X2

	£	£
Sales		58,770
Less:		
Opening stock	4,250	
Add: Purchases	32,200	
Less: Closing stock	– 5,760	
Cost of goods sold		– 30,690
		28,080
Gross profit		
Less expenses:		
Rates	2,780	
General expenses	3,150	
Wages	6,130	
Depreciation of furniture	300	
Depreciation of vehicle	300	
		– 12,660
Net profit		**15,420**

FIGURE 4.3   Trading, profit and loss account of William
for 20X2

William
Trading, profit and loss account,
period ending 31 December 20X2

	£		£
Opening stock	4,250	Closing stock	5,760
Purchases	32,200	Cost of sales	30,690
	36,450		36,450
Cost of sales	30,690	Sales	58,770
Gross profit	28,080		
	58,770		58,770
		Gross profit	28,080
Rates	2,780		
General expenses	3,150		
Wages	6,130		
Depreciation of furniture	300		
Depreciation of vehicle	300		
	12,660		
Net profit	15,420		
	28,080		28,080

FIGURE 4.4   Horizontal version of William's trading, profit and loss account

social facility otherwise not available. For instance, most towns have their own tennis club, parent–teacher association and childrens' play-group. Such clubs and societies are usually described as *non-profit-making organizations* whose objectives are to further recreational, educational or religious activities. This description is a little misleading in that many clubs and societies expect to generate an excess of income over expenditure but, unlike commercial concerns, this is not their principal objective. Furthermore, any profit that does arise is not distributed to members but is instead viewed as a source of finance for facilities required to extend their activities. These facts should be clearly spelled out in the rules governing the activities of the club or society. Provided this is done, the organization is exempted from taxation.

The scale of the activities undertaken by many, though by no means all, clubs and societies is relatively small. The officers of these organizations – the chairperson, secretary, treasurer, etc. – are unpaid volunteers. For these reasons a comprehensive accounting system is unlikely to exist. Indeed, in the majority of clubs and societies, the accounting system is unlikely to consist of more than a record of receipts and payments during the year. At the year end, a decision must be taken concerning the form the final accounts should take. Perhaps because of the absence of necessary expertise, and also perhaps because there is little demand for accounting information from the members, the treasurer may simply prepare a *receipts and payments account* for the year. This is an analysed list of total cash coming into and going out of the club during the year; no attempt is made to take account of debts and liabilities outstanding at the balance sheet date and no balance sheet is prepared. This form of account may be satisfactory for the very small club or society, but is totally inadequate for the larger organization where there exist valuable assets or substantial outstanding liabilities (perhaps because a bank loan has been raised to build a new squash court) of which the members should be made aware. For the larger organizations, the accounts must be prepared in accordance with the accruals concept, and the procedure then followed is almost exactly the same as that described for industrial and commercial concerns earlier in this chapter.

Accounting terms used by clubs and societies

The only distinction of any significance between properly prepared final accounts of clubs and societies, on the one hand, and those of industrial and commercial concerns, on the other, is that different terms are used to describe certain essentially similar financial components. The main differences are as shown in Table 4.1.

Readers should now work through Question 4.5 at the end of this chapter.

Subscriptions and entry fees

The main sources of revenue for clubs and societies are the subscriptions received from members, but it is often considered inappropriate to apply the full force of the accruals concept to these items. At the end of an accounting period, there are usually subscriptions that remain unpaid for that year and subscriptions received in advance for the following year. Strict application of the accruals concept

Table 4.1 Differences in terms used by clubs and societies

Industrial and commercial concerns	Club/society	Comment
Profit and loss account	Income and expenditure	These differences reflect the fact that clubs and societies are not profit-orientated. When computing income and expenditure, however, the accruals concept is usually applied in exactly the same way as when calculating figures for inclusion in the profit and loss account.
Net profit/net loss	Surplus/ deficit	
Capital	Accumulated fund	The term 'capital' denotes a proprietorial interest that does not exist in clubs and societies, e.g. if a member resigns he or she has no right to reclaim his or her joining fee.

requires subscriptions outstanding to be credited to income and treated as a debt due to the club. This treatment is rarely followed in practice, although there may be no doubt that an individual has made use of the club's facilities during the year. The fact that his or her subscription remains unpaid at the year end is a fairly clear indication that it will never be collected. The former member has probably now left the club and the amount outstanding would be insufficient to justify the costs of any legal action needed to achieve its recovery. In accordance with the accruals concept, however, subscriptions received in advance should be shown as a liability in the balance sheet and treated as income of the following accounting period.

At the end of 20X2 subscriptions outstanding amounted to £300 and subscriptions received in advance for 20X3 amounted to £90. During 20X3 subscriptions received amounted to £5,400. This included the £300 outstanding at the end of 20X2 and £120 in advance for 20X4. Subscriptions outstanding at the end of 20X3 amounted to £500.   **EXAMPLE 4.9**

Calculate the amount to be credited to the income and expenditure account for 20X3, assuming that subscriptions are accounted for on (a) a cash basis, (b) the accruals basis and (c) on a prudent basis.   **Required**

	£	**Solution**
(a) Cash basis	5,400	

(b)   Accruals basis:
Cash received in 20X3	5,400
Add: Received in 20X2 for 20X3	90
Oustanding at the end of 20X3	500
	5,990
Less: Outstanding at the end of 20X2	(300)
Received in 20X3 for 20X4	(120)
	5,570

(c)   Prudent basis (subscriptions outstanding ignored):
Cash received in 20X3	5,400
Add: Received in 20X2 for 20X3	90
	5,490
Less: Received in 20X3 for 20X4	(120)
	5,370

Many clubs charge new members an entry fee. These receipts may be credited either to income or direct to the accumulated fund. Either treatment is acceptable, but the method chosen should be applied consistently from year to year, with the amount involved clearly disclosed. Life membership fees may also be accounted for in a variety of ways. There are three main alternatives:

1   Credit to the accumulated fund.
2   Credit in full to the income and expenditure account in the year received.
3   Credit initially to a life membership account, and transfer the fee to the income and expenditure account, in instalments, over an agreed number of years.

The third alternative is theoretically superior, since it attempts to relate income to the periods when the member uses the club's facilities, but it is also the most time-consuming accounting treatment.

Identifying the results of separate activities

It is always important, when deciding what form the annual accounts should take, to consider carefully the information that is likely to be of interest to the recipients of the reports. For this reason the accounts should be designed to reflect the particular nature of the organization's activities. It is quite usual for clubs and societies to have a number of spheres of interest. For instance, a recreation club may provide facilities for lawn tennis, squash, table tennis, bowls, rugby and cricket. It is usually considered useful to identify the contribution of each section, whether positive or negative, to the overall finances of the club. This information is not, however, necessarily required as a basis for deciding to extend or discontinue particular facilities. It must be remembered that it is the aim of clubs to provide recreational facilities, not to make a profit.

However, the extent to which the profitable sections can subsidize the unprofitable is not unlimited and, if a succession of poor results reflects a decline in the demand for a particular sport, the facility may have to be withdrawn in the interests of the club members as a whole. More likely, significant deficits in certain areas will be interpreted as evidence of the need to revise subscriptions upwards. For these reasons a separate income and expenditure account should be prepared for each section, and the balances transferred to a general income and expenditure account where they will be combined with any unallocated items of income and expenditure arising from the club's activities.

Many clubs provide bar facilities at which drinks and perhaps tobacco and refreshments are sold; where this occurs, the relevant items of income and expenditure are collected together in the bar trading account. The balance of this account, whether a profit or a loss, is transferred to the general income and expenditure account.

In the case of industrial and commercial organizations, separate identification of the results of different product lines in order to show whether they are operating at a profit or a loss is a principal basis for management decisions on whether to expand or close down an area of activity.

Readers should now attempt Questions 4.6 and 4.7 at the end of this chapter.

QUESTIONS

The preparation of accounts from incomplete records involves fundamental accounting procedures that must be mastered before readers can expect to make progress in their accounting studies. It is for this reason that questions testing students' understanding of these procedures are extremely common in examinations. Such questions often follow a pattern similar to William (Example 4.8 in this chapter), and solutions should consist of the same four steps recommended for answering that question. Questions 4.1, 4.5, 4.6 and 4.7 are of this type. Some variation is of course possible, and the remaining questions in this section include certain innovations. The opening balance sheet is provided in Question 4.2 so that only steps 2, 3 and 4 need to be processed. Question 4.3 is a revision question that deals with matters covered in Chapter 3 as well as the present chapter. Question 4.4 is a new business and so only steps 2, 3 and 4 apply.

4.1   Stoll, a trader, pays all his business takings into his bank account. All business payments are made by cheque. The following is a summary of his bank account for the year 20X5:

Bank Summary

	Receipts	Payments	Balance
Balance 1 January 20X5			480
Received from debtors	31,560		
Payments to trade creditors		− 24,800	
General expenses		− 2,524	
Rent		− 300	

Drawings		3,600
	31,560	− 31,224
Balance 31 December 20X5		816

The following information is obtained from the available records:

	31 Dec. 20X4	31 Dec. 20X5
Trade debtors	1,900	2,344
Trade creditors	1,630	1,930
Stock	2,040	1,848
Furniture and fittings:		
at cost less accumulated depreciation	400	360

Required

(a) Calculate the balance of Stoll's capital at 31 December 20X4.

(b) Prepare the trading and profit and loss account for the year 20X5 and the balance sheet as at 31 December 20X5. Present these accounting statements in vertical format.

4.2 Bennett commenced business as a retail trader at the beginning of 20X0. He maintains no formal system of ledger accounts for recording business transactions. An accountant has been asked to prepare the accounts for the year ending 20X1 in order to enable tax liabilities to be agreed. The following balance sheet was prepared as at 1 January 20X1:

Bennett

Balance sheet as at 1 January 20X1

	£	£	£
Fixed assets			
Motor vehicle at cost			10,000
Less: accumulated depreciation			− 2,000
			8,000
Current assets			
Stock		3,750	
Trade debtors		1,060	
Prepaid expenses		400	
Bank deposit account		650	
		5,860	
Less: Current liabilities			
Bank overdraft	2,030		
Trade creditors	850		
Accrued expenses	260		
		− 3,140	
Working capital*			2,720
			10,720

Less: Long-term liabilities
   Loan at 15%   − 2,000

                                                        8,720

Financed by
Capital   8,720

The following information is provided regarding 20X1:

1   An analysis of the business bank accounts provided the following information:

Receipts	£	Payments	£
Cash sales	32,100	Paid to suppliers	20,850
Proceeds from credit sales	7,560	General expenses	7,560
Legacy from relative	2,650	Drawings	12,500
Bank interest received	50	Motor vehicle	4,000
	42,360		44,910

2   During the year, a new motor vehicle was purchased for £4,000; Bennett depreciates vehicles at the rate of 20 per cent on cost.

3   Debtors outstanding at the end of 20X1 amounted to £1,840.

4   Amounts due to suppliers at the end of 20X1 totalled £1,140 and stock was valued at £4,600.

5   Accruals and prepayments of general expenses at the end of 20X1 amounted to £310 and £520, respectively.

Required The trading and profit and loss account of Bennett's business for 20X1 and the balance sheet as at 31 December 20X1. (Use the vertical layout for both.)

4.3   The following is the balance sheet of Stondon, a trader, at 31 December 20X3:

Stondon
Balance sheet as at 31 December 20X3

	£	£	£
Fixed assets			
Furniture and fittings			800
Current assets			
Stock		5,384	
Trade debtors		4,162	
Bank		888	
		10,434	
Less: Current liabilities			
Trade creditors		−3,294	
Working capital			7,140
			7,940

Financed by

Capital   7,940

In January 20X3 Stondon sold certain private investments for £4,200; he purchased a motor van for business use for £3,000 and paid the balance of the proceeds into his business bank account.

At 31 December 20X3, trade debtors amounted to £4,124, stock was valued at £6,891 and trade creditors amounted to £3,586. Stondon's business bank account was overdrawn by £782. His drawings during 20X3 were £12,840.

The total of running expenses charged to the profit and loss account for 20X3 amounted to £14,420. This total included £500 for depreciation of the motor van.

Stondon's gross profit is at the rate of 25 per cent of selling price for all goods sold during 20X3.

Required

(a)   Prepare Stondon's balance sheet at 31 December 20X3.
(b)   Calculate Stondon's net profit for 20X3 on the basis of changes in capital.
(c)   Reconstruct the trading and profit and loss account of Stondon's business for the year 20X3.

Note   Ignore depreciation of furniture and fittings.

4.4   Bert Negus inherited £200,000 during February 1995. This provided him with an opportunity to leave his job as an electrical maintenance engineer with a local company and to start up his own business. After giving the matter much consideration he decided to set up as a retailer of electrical appliances from 1 May 1995 and he deposited £150,000 into a business bank account as an initial transaction.

Mr Negus identified leasehold premises which he thought suitable for his purposes. The property included a display room, store room and office. On 2 May 1995 he signed a five year lease at a cost of £80,000. The full lease payment was payable in advance and Mr Negus met this obligation on 4 May 1995. On the same day he also purchased shop fittings for £7,000 which he thought would have a useful life of about five years, and stock for £68,000.

After a slow start, business gradually picked up as the year progressed and on 30 April 1996 Mr Negus wondered whether his business had made a profit during the first year of trading. Mr Negus summarized his bank statements from 1 May 1995 to April 1996.

Receipts	£000	Payments	£000
Initial deposit	150.0	Lease	80.0
Sales	295.7	Shop fittings	7.0
Bank interest	0.5	Stock in trade	244.6
		Wages	9.2
		Motor vehicle	5.7
		Postage and stationery	0.4
		Advertising	4.8
		Heat, light and water	4.1
		Insurance and telephone	1.8
		Drawings	15.0
		Miscellaneous expenses	8.7
		Investment account	30.0
		Balance c/f	34.9
	446.2		446.2

During the year Mr Negus purchased a motor vehicle which he thought was worth £5,100 at 30 April 1996. Mr Negus was allowed discount from suppliers during the financial year. This totalled £600.

At 30 April 1996 unsold stock was valued at £37,500. At the same date Mr Negus owed his suppliers £5,400 and customers owed him £3,800. An electricity bill for £300 in respect of the quarter ending 31 May 1996 was also unpaid.

On 2 January 1996 Mr Negus transferred part of his surplus bank balance into an investment account which carries an interest rate of 5 per cent per annum and where the minimum investment period is two years. Mr Negus banked all of his takings during the year with the exception of £7,900 which he used to pay the wages of casual help in his shop.

(a) Prepare Mr Negus' trading and profit and loss account for the year ended 30 April 1996, and a balance sheet as at that date.   **Required**

(16 marks)

(ICSA, Paper 6, Introduction to Accounting, June 1996) (Adapted)

4.5 The following details are extracted from the books of the Fellowship Club:

Balances at	31 Dec. 20X7	31 Dec. 20X8
	£	£
Bar stock	8,200	11,936
Creditors for bar supplies	4,080	4,568
Creditors for expenses	160	248

Summary of Bank Account for 20X8

Receipts	£	Payments	£
Balance 1 January 20X8	13,280	Bar purchases	80,760

Subscriptions received	12,400	Salaries	16,840
Bar sales	107,600	Rent of club premises	2,800
Interest on investments	4,160	Rates	2,000
		General expenses	5,360
		Cost of new investments	26,000
	137,440		133,760

On 1 January 20X8 the club held temporary investments it had purchased for £49,200, and the furniture in use was valued at £30,400. The club is building up its investments to enable it to purchase its own clubhouse in due course. Depreciation should be charged on the furniture at the rate of 10 per cent per annum on cost.

Required

(a) A bar trading account for 20X8.

(b) A general income and expenditure account for 20X8.

(c) A balance sheet as at 31 December 20X8.

4.6 The Ridlingham Recreation Club consists of a tennis section and a rugby section. The following information has been obtained relating to the position of the club on 1 January 20X1:

	£
Clubhouse at cost	38,000
Creditors for bar purchases	3,720
Creditors for general expenses	500
Tennis courts at cost (£40,000) less depreciation to date	24,000
Furniture and equipment at book value	5,000
Bar stocks	4,400
Bank balance	1,500

The club's bank statements for 20X1 have been analysed and the following summary prepared:

Bank Account 20X1

Receipts	£	Payments	£
Balance 1 January	1,500	New tennis court	16,000
Ten-year membership	12,000	Repairs to tennis court	2,520
Other subscriptions:		Prizes for tennis tournaments	140
Tennis	6,400	Rugby kit	900
Rugby	1,300	Rental of rugby pitch	400
Tennis tournament		Rates on clubhouse	1,100
entry fees	240	Payments for bar supplies	48,400
Bar sales	69,660	Wages of bar steward	7,800
Collections at		General expenses	17,300
rugby matches	180		
Tennis court fees	5,700		
	96,980		94,560

You discover that all cash received is paid into the club bank account and all payments are made by cheque.

During the year a new tennis court was built that was first used on 1 July 20X1. In order to help pay for the new court, ten-year memberships were offered for sale, at the beginning of the first year, at £400 each.

At 31 December 20X1 creditors for bar purchases and general expenses amount to £4,300 and £640, respectively. Bar stocks are valued at £5,280. It is the club's policy to write off the cost of the tennis courts over a ten-year period. Furniture is depreciated at 10 per cent per year. For the purpose of the accounts the rugby kit is considered to possess a nil value.

(a) The bar trading account and a general income and expenditure account for 20X1. The general income and expenditure account should show the net surplus or deficit arising separately from the tennis section and the rugby section.

(b) The balance sheet at 31 December 20X1.

Required

4.7 You have agreed to take over the role of bookkeeper for the AB Sports and Social Club. The summarized balance sheet on 31.12.94 as prepared by the previous bookkeeper, contained the following items.

Assets	£	£
Heating oil for clubhouse		1,000
Bar and café stocks		7,000
New sportswear for sale, at cost		3,000
Used sportswear, for hire, at valuation		750
Equipment for groundsperson: cost	5,000	
depreciation	3,500	
		1,500
Subscriptions due		200
Bank: current account		1,000
deposit account		10,000
Claims		
Accumulated fund		23,150
Creditors: bar and café stocks		1,000
sportswear		300

The bank account summary for the year to 31.12.95 contained the followed items.

Receipts	£
Subscriptions	11,000
Bankings: bar and café	20,000
sales of sportswear	5,000
hire of sportswear	3,000
Interest on deposit account	800
Payments	
Rent and repairs of clubhouse	6,000
Heating oil	4,000
Sportswear	4,500
Groundsperson	10,000

Bar and café purchases	9,000
Transfer to deposit account	6,000

You discover that the subscriptions due figure as at 31.12.94 was arrived at as follows:

	£
Subscriptions unpaid for 1993	10
Subscriptions unpaid for 1994	230
Subscriptions paid for 1995	40

Corresponding figures at 31.12.95 are as follows:

	£
Subscriptions unpaid for 1993	10
Subscriptions unpaid for 1994	20
Subscriptions unpaid for 1995	90
Subscriptions paid for 1996	200

Subscriptions due for more than 12 months should be written off with effect from 1.1.95.

Asset balances at 31.12.95 include the following:

	£
Heating oil for club house	700
Bar and café stocks	5,000
New sportswear, for sale, at cost	4,000
Used sportswear, for hire, at valuation	1,000

Closing creditors at 31.12.95 are as follows:

	£
For bar and café stocks	800
For sportswear	450
For heating oil for clubhouse	200

Two-thirds of the sportswear purchases made in 1995 had been added to stock of new sportswear in the figures given in the list of assets above, and one-third had been added directly to the stock of used sportswear for hire.

Half of the resulting 'new sportswear for sale at cost' at 31.12.95 is actually over two years old. You decide, with effect from 31.12.95, to transfer these older items into the stock of used sportswear, at a valuation of 25% of their original cost.

No cash balances are held at 31.12.94 or 31.12.95. The equipment for the groundsperson is to be depreciated at 10% per annum, on cost.

Required Prepare an income and expenditure account and balance sheet for the AB Sports and Social Club for 1995, in a form suitable for circulation to members. The information given should be as complete and informative as possible within the limits of the information given to you. All workings must be submitted.

(23 marks)

(ACCA, Paper 1, The Accounting Framework, June 1996)

	£	*Solution to*
		Activity 4.1

Revenue:
Proceeds from the sale of satellite dishes
(£150 × 100)   15,000
Less: Expenditure:
    Cost of satellite dishes sold (£70 × 100)   (7,000)
Profit   8,000

Solution to
Activity 4.2

In 20X0 the goods still belong to Bart & Co and no legal title has passed to the customer, so it would be incorrect to record the sale at this point.

It is acceptable to wait for the money to be received in 20X2 before accounting for the sale. This is called cash flow accounting.

The most likely date for the recording of the transaction is 20X1. A contract has been entered into for the supply of goods which have been delivered. The sale is recorded together with the debt outstanding.

Solution to
Activity 4.3

	£
Cash received	28,000
Less: Opening debtors	(4,900)
	23,100
Add: Closing debtors	7,000
	30,100

Solution to
Activity 4.4

Revenue:
Proceeds from the sale of dishes (£150 × 85)   12,750
Less: Expenditure:
    Cost of dishes sold (£70 × 85)   (5,950)
PROFIT   6,800

Solution to
Activity 4.5

(a) (i)   Receipts from customers:

	£
Cash collected in respect of:	
Credit sales	41,750
Cash sales	12,350
Receipts from customers	54,100

(ii)   Sales:

	£
Receipts from customers	54,100
Less: Opening debtors	− 12,650
	41,450
Add: Closing debtors	11,780
Sales	53,230

(iii)   Purchases:

	£
Payments to suppliers	36,590
Less: Opening creditors	− 6,540
	30,050
Add: Closing creditors	8,270
Purchases	38,320

(iv)   Cost of goods sold:

	£
Opening stock	9,150
Add: Purchases	38,320
	47,470
Less: Closing stock	− 9,730
Cost of goods sold	37,740

(b)   Trading account for 20X3

	£	£
Sales		53,230
Opening stock	9,150	
Add: Purchases	38,320	
	47,470	
Less: Closing stock	(9,730)	
Cost of goods sold		(37,740)
Gross profit		15,490

Note   Readers should note that it is conventional practice to show the calculation of cost of goods sold on the face of the trading account, but not the calculations of purchases and sales.

Solution to Activity 4.6

(a)   Light and heat:

	£
Payments made during 20X1	1,500
Add: Payment made in advance in 20X0 for 20X1	300
	1,800
Less: Payment made in advance in 20X1 for 20X2	(375)
	1,425

(b)   Bank Interest.

	£
Payments made during 20X1	700
Add: Payments outstanding for 20X1 to be paid in 20X2	162
	862
Less: Payments outstanding for 20X0 paid in 20X1	(150)
	712

(a)   Straight-line depreciation charge:

$$\frac{\pounds 14,000 - \pounds 4,000}{5} = \pounds 2,000 \text{ p.a.}$$

Solution to Activity 4.7

(b)   Balance sheet extracts 31 December…

	20X0	20X1	20X2	20X3	20X4
	£000	£000	£000	£000	£000
Fixed assets at cost	14	14	14	14	14
Less: Accumulated depreciation	− 2	− 4	− 6	− 8	− 10
Net book value (NBV)	12	10	8	6	4

5 The double entry system 1: the initial recording of transactions

The objectives of this chapter are to:

- show how the record of cash flows is created in the cash book;
- demonstrate the preparation of the bank reconciliation statement and outline its uses;
- explain how to record petty cash transactions;
- explain how cash flows are analysed in the cash book; and
- show how initial records of the flows of goods and services are made using day books.

INTRODUCTION

Accounting reports are based on summarized information, and are accurate only if the initial record of the individual transactions is correct. The operation of a company results in numerous individual transactions taking place; in the case of large companies there is likely to be a massive volume of these. Inflows and outflows of goods, services and cash occur, and it is the responsibility of management to ensure that there is an efficient system of accounting. This system must be designed both to record and to control individual transactions and to enable the production of summarized results in the form of accounting reports. For example, a retail shop that makes a large number of relatively small sales must have controls to ensure that all items that leave the shop are paid for and that all cash received is recorded. Summaries showing the total value of sales, possibly analysed by product, can then be produced for management so that the shop's progress can be monitored. This chapter covers the detailed recording of the separate items in such a way as to provide an adequate foundation for the rest of the accounting process.

CASH FLOWS

Control of cash receipts and payments is obviously of particular importance to the company as resources that are in the form of cash are vulnerable to misappropriation; the cash book, in which all receipts and payments are recorded, is the central element of this control. The objective is to ensure that all cash due to the company is received and retained until its subsequent, properly authorized, disbursement takes place. A simple way to establish this control is to ensure that:

1 all cash receipts are recorded as they are received;
2 all cash receipts are paid with little delay into the company's bank account; and
3 only senior personnel are permitted to authorize the bank to make payments from the bank.

One result of using a bank account is the creation of an additional source of information on cash flows. The bank statement that is provided periodically by the bank should contain the corresponding entries to those entered in the cash book. (The importance of this is discussed later in this chapter.) The initial record of cash receipts is usually in the form of a memorandum list that should be prepared at the point and time of receipt. The necessary documentation is completed as each sale is made when the goods are exchanged directly for cash, as is the case with a retail shop, or at some other point where goods are sold on credit and the cash received some time after the sale. For example, if it is usual for cheques to be received in the post, a reliable employee should be made responsible for opening all letters, removing and listing the cheques enclosed and passing them to the cashier for prompt payment into the bank. The inclusion of a number of different people in this line of control reduces the possibility of undetected theft since the list produced by the person responsible for opening the post is independent of, and can be checked with, the sum accounted for by the cashier. On the payments side, it must be ensured that only a limited number of senior people are authorized to sign documents, such as cheques and standing order mandates, which are accepted by the bank as instructions to pay sums of money out of the account. The official signing the document – for example, the cheque – should require evidence to warrant its completion, such as a valid invoice received from a supplier. In this example, the invoice should be referenced to the cash payment and retained so that the transaction's validity can, if required, be subsequently verified. This involves a system of cross-referencing, with the payment recorded in the cash book cross-referenced to a supplier's account in which the liability has been recorded on the previous receipt of a valid invoice.

The cash account

The cash account is used to record the inflows and outflows of cash and is kept in an accounting record called the cash book. The account consists of two lists of figures, one of which gives details of cash receipts and the other cash payments; in accordance with the rules of double entry book-keeping (explained in detail in Chapter 6), the receipts are known as 'debits' and are placed on the left-hand page of the cash book, while payments are termed 'credits' and are recorded on the right-hand page. (The terms debit and credit are often abbreviated to 'Dr.' and 'Cr.', respectively.) A period of time, such as a week or a month, is covered by the lists and, as well as the cash flows that take place during the period, the opening cash position is included so that the closing balance of cash can be determined. If the company starts the period with cash in hand, the amount is entered at the top of the cash received (debit) column, while an overdraft is entered at the top of the payments (credit) column.

To find the closing balance of cash, the account is 'balanced'. This is done by finding the difference between the total values of debits and credits. The closing balance of one period, known as the 'balance carried down', is the opening balance for the following period, when it is termed the 'balance brought down'; this balance appears in the company's balance sheet.

EXAMPLE 5.1

The following summary of bank receipts and payments was given in Figure 4.1 of the previous chapter.

Receipts	£	Payments	£
Opening balance of cash	510	Payments to suppliers	17,380
Sale of goods	23,750	Wages	2,560
		Rent and rates	840
		Lighting and heating	620
		General expenses	375
	24,260		21,775

Required

Enter the above details in the cash account and balance off the account.

Solution

Cash Account

Cash in = Receipts (Debit)	£	Cash out = Payments (Credit)	£
Balance brought down	510	Payments to suppliers	17,380
Sale of goods	23,750	Wages	2,560
		Rent and rates	840
		Lighting and heating	620
		General expenses	375
			21,775
		Balance carried down	2,485
	24,260		24,260
Balance brought down	2,485		

Notes

1 The balance can either be zero or positive (you can never have negative cash).

2 In this example the receipts exceed the payments by £2,485.

3 Convention dictates that the account is balanced off in the manner shown above, i.e. add up the largest column and enter the total (£24,260); insert the balance required to make the other column add up to this total (£2,485); carry down the balance to its correct side. (£2,485 is a positive balance and so should be brought down to the debit side.)

4 The terms 'balance carried down' and 'balance brought down' are often abbreviated to 'balance c/d' and 'balance b/d', respectively.

Wire & Co balances its cash book each week and at the end of week 8 of 20X7 the business held cash of £782. During week 9 the following receipts and payments took place:

		£
Receipts:	Sales	5,769
	Loan from Newbank Ltd	2,000
Payments:	Purchase of goods for resale	3,150
	Wages	790
	Rent	126
	Advertising	75
	Delivery van	3,500

Prepare the cash account for week 9 of Wire & Co as it would appear in the company's cash book and show the balance brought down to week 10.

Readers should now work through Question 5.1 at the end of this chapter to test their understanding of the preparation of the cash account.

The bank reconciliation

A company's bank account should contain exactly the same receipts and payments as pass through its bank account. A valuable check on the accuracy of the bank account is provided by the routine preparation of the bank reconciliation statement that agrees the bank account's balance with the bank statement. To provide additional control, the reconciliation should ideally be prepared or checked by an official of the company who is otherwise independent of the control and recording of the flows of cash.

The bank reconciliation statement is prepared by comparing items in the bank account with those in the bank statement. Those entries that appear in both the bank account and the bank statement are checked off. In many instances, however, the entries do not correspond exactly. This is the result of some or all of the following:

1 *Payments appear in the bank account but not on the bank statement.* These mainly result from the fact that there is a delay between the issue of a cheque (at which time it is entered in the bank account) and its clearance by the bank (at which time it appears on the bank statement).

2 *Receipts appear in the bank account but not on the bank statement.* A company may enter the cash received each day in the bank account, but pay it into the bank the following day, or even allow it to accumulate for a short period of time. This causes a lapse of time between the bank account record and the bank statement entry. For security reasons, the delay should be kept to a minimum.

3   *Payments appear on the statements but not in the bank account.* Some payments, such as those for bank charges and interest, are generated by the bank. The company may only know that they have been paid when the statement has been received and so would not have entered the amounts in the cash book. Other items that fall into this category are payments made by standing order and direct debit.

4   *Receipts appear on the statement but not in the bank account.*   It is common nowadays for sums to be paid directly into the recipient's bank account, and sometimes they are identifiable only when the statement is received.

5   *Errors in recording amounts.*   *Transposition* errors could occur when entering amounts in the bank account, for example £645 may be entered as £465. Some transactions may not be recorded at all; these are errors of *omission*. In both cases the receipt of the bank statement confirms the amounts involved.

Items 1 and 2 above are merely timing differences and, although appearing in the bank reconciliation, require no further entry in the bank account. However, items 3 and 4 are additional items that, if valid, should be entered in the bank account, and item 5 is an error that should be adjusted.

The procedure for preparing a bank reconciliation statement is to take the entries in the bank account for a certain period of time and mark off in both records those that also appear on the bank statement for the same period. Any items left unmarked must be examined and classified into types 1, 2, 3, 4 or 5. Items of types 3, 4 and 5 are entered in the bank account, from which a new balance is extracted. This balance will still differ from that shown on the bank statement if there are any items of types 1 and 2. If this is the case a reconciliation statement is drawn up that adjusts the balance on the statement for these items after which it should agree with that shown on the bank account.

EXAMPLE 5.2   The following information relates to Check Ltd for the month of March:

Bank Account

Cash in = Receipts			Cash out = Payments		
(Debit)		£	(Credit)		£
March			March		
1	Balance b/d	1,000	4	Cheque no. 11	150
9	Receipts paid into bank	350	9	Cheque no. 12	225
16	Receipts paid into bank	200	15	Cheque no. 13	75
23	Receipt paid into bank	475	22	Cheque no. 14	445
30	Receipt paid into bank	150	30	Cheque no. 15	160
			31	Cheque no. 16	330
				Balance c/d	790
		2,175			2,175
	Balance b/d	790			

Bank statement for the month of March

		Debit £	Credit £	Balance £
March				
1	Balance brought forward			1,000 Cr.
6	Cheque no. 11	150		850
11	Lodgement		530	1,380
	Cheque no. 12	225		1,155
17	Cheque no. 13	75		1,080
18	Lodgement		200	1,280
24	Cheque no. 14	445		835
25	Lodgement		475	1,310
	Standing order	60		1,250
26	Direct credit		50	1,300
31	Bank charges	100		1,200
	Balance carried forward			1,200 Cr.

Note The bank statement is prepared from the point of view of the bank. Money deposited in the bank belongs to the account holder, and so as far as the bank is concerned the amount is a liability because it owes that money to the account holder. Therefore, on the bank statement receipts will be recorded as credit entries. As far as payments are concerned these reduce the amount owing to the account holder and so are recorded as debit entries.

In other words, the terms are the opposite way round compared with the bank account in the books of a business.

(a) Identify and classify by type (1,2,3,4 or 5) the differences between the bank account and the bank statement.

(b) Make the necessary adjustments to the cash account for the month of March and recalculate the balance b/d.

(c) Prepare the bank reconciliation statement at the end of March.

Required

When the entries in the cash account have been checked against those in the bank statement the following differences are found:

Solution

1 Payments in the bank account but not on the bank statement:

Cheque no. 15	£160
Cheque no. 16	£330

2 Receipts in the bank account but not on the bank statement:

Lodgement	£150

3   Payments on the bank statement but not in the bank account:

Standing order   £ 60

Bank charges   £100

4   Receipts on the bank statement but not in the bank account:

Direct credit   £ 50

5   Transposition error:

Receipt recorded in bank account £180 too little

Items 3, 4 and 5 should be entered in the cash account and a revised balance calculated. Items 1 and 2 are timing differences and appear on the bank reconciliation statement only.

(b)   **Bank Account (revised)**

Receipts (Debit)	£	Payments (Credit)	£
March		March	
31 Balance b/d	790	31 Standing order	60
31 Direct credit	50	31 Bank charges	100
31 Receipts paid into bank	180	31 Balance c/d	860
	1,020		1,020
Balance b/d	860		

(c)   Bank reconciliation statement at 31 March

	£	£
Balance as per bank statement		1,200
Less: Outstanding cheques:		
No. 15	160	
No. 16	330	− 490
		710
Add: Outstanding lodgements		150
Balance as per bank account		860

Notes 1 Subsequent bank statements should be checked to ensure that all outstanding items are cleared without undue delay.

2 It is possible for banks to make mistakes. Any unexplained entry on the bank statement (like the difference in the receipt amount of £180) should be investigated and only when it has been confirmed should the bank account be altered.

The cash book of Joe & Co, a trader, for June 20X0 is as follows: **ACTIVITY 5 ?**

Bank Account

Cash in = Receipts		Cash out = Payments	
(Debit)	*£*	*(Credit)*	*£*
June 20X0		June 20X0	
2 Receipts from debtors	2,792	1 Balance b/d	4,300
12 Receipts from cash sales	1,750	3 Payments to creditors	1,500
19 Receipts from debtors	1,700	7 Wages of sales assistant	300
24 Receipts from cash sales	1,400	13 Payments to creditors	950
25 Receipts from debtors	2,600	14 Wages of sales assistant	300
		21 Wages of sales assistant	300
		28 Wages of sales assistant	300
		30 Drawings	1,000
		30 Balance c/d	1,292
	10,242		10,242
Balance b/d	1,292		

Southern Bank plc

Bank Statement for the month of June

Joe & Co – Account Number 13060309

	Debit	Credit	Balance
	£	*£*	*£*
1 Balance brought forward			4,300 Dr
4 Receipts	2,792		1,508 Dr
6 1066759		1,500	3,008 Dr
10 1066760		300	3,308 Dr
15 Receipts	1,750		1,558 Dr
16 1066762		300	1,858 Dr
17 1066761		590	2,448 Dr
21 Receipts	1,700		748 Dr
24 1066763		300	1,048 Dr
27 Receipts	1,400		352 Cr
30 Bank charges		150	202 Cr
Balance carried forward			202 Cr

(a) Identify and classify by type (1,2,3,4 or 5) the differences between the bank account and the bank statement.   **Required**

(b) Make the necessary adjustments to the bank account for the month of June and recalculate the balance b/d.

(c) Prepare the bank reconciliation statement at the end of June.

Readers should now attempt Question 5.2 at the end of this chapter to test their understanding of the preparation of the bank reconciliation statement.

The double column cash book

It was stated above that all cash receipts should be paid into the firm's bank account without delay, and that all disbursements should be made from the bank account. Although this is a very good rule to observe in practice, there are occasions when it is not applied, especially in the case of small businesses. In these circumstances it is particularly important to ensure that all cash flows are recorded so that none are overlooked – for example, a trader may make sales of £100 for cash and out of the proceeds pay wages of £30 and motor expenses of £5 before banking the residual £65. It is incorrect merely to record in the books of the firm the lodgement of £65 in respect of sales, since this ignores the receipt of the additional £35, which was paid out on wages and motor expenses. The effect of the omission would be to understate sales, wages and motor expenses.

Where sums are paid out of cash takings before they are banked, it is necessary to maintain two cash accounts, one to deal with the flows of cash that take place through the bank account, called the 'cash-at-bank account', and one to deal with other cash flows, called the 'cash-in-hand account'. Transfers between the two accounts are made in the usual way, so that, for example, when cash is banked a payment is entered in the cash-in-hand account and a receipt recorded in the cash-at-bank account. Although it is possible to maintain two completely separate accounts, it is usual in these circumstances to modify the traditional cash book format and use what is known as a double column cash book.

EXAMPLE 5.3	Glue & Sticky's business transactions between 1 and 10 June were as follows:	
	Date	*Details*	*£*

Date June	Details	£
1	Cash balance in hand	50
1	Balance at bank	200
3	Received from cash sales	1,275
4	Cash paid into bank	1,000
7	Pay wages in cash	100
8	Make cash purchases	200
9	Draw cash from bank	300
10	Pay for purchases by cheque	150
10	Pay rent in cash	175

Required   Prepare the double column cash book to record the above transactions, carrying down the balances on 10 June.

Double column cash book

Receipts (debits)			Payments (credits)		
Date Details	Cash in hand	Cash at bank	Date Details	Cash in hand	Cash at bank
June	£	£	June	£	£
1 Balance b/d	50	200	4 Cash to bank	1,000	
3 Sales	1,275		7 Wages	100	
4 Cash paid in		1,000	8 Purchases	200	
9 Cash from bank	300		9 Cash withdrawn		300
			10 Purchases		150
			10 Rent	175	
			10 Balance c/d	150	750
	1,625	1,200		1,625	1,200
10 Balance b/d	150	750			

Note that the accounts shown above comply with the usual convention that debits are recorded on the left and credits on the right. It differs from the usual format, though, as there are two columns on each side, one to record the flows of cash and the other to record cash flows that take place through the bank. The opening balances are respectively cash in hand and at the bank on 1 June, and the first transaction increases cash held by £1,275, which is debited in the cash column to represent a cash receipt. Of this cash, £1,000 is paid into the bank on 4 June. Cash in hand is credited with this amount to show that the payment was made out of cash, while the bank is debited to show the corresponding receipt. Conversely, when cash is drawn from the bank to be used for cash payments, cash at bank is credited and the cash in hand column debited.

Jog Ltd undertook the following transactions between 1 and 13 September:

Date	Details	£
1	Cash balance in hand	750
1	Balance at bank	1,500
3	Received from cash sales	3,750
4	Cash paid into bank	1,500
7	Pay wages in cash	700
8	Make cash purchases	900
9	Draw cash from bank	1,900
10	Pay for purchases by cheque	1,150
11	Pay rent in cash	750
13	Paid telephone bill by cheque	400

Required	Prepare the double column cash book to record the above transactions, carrying down the balances on 13 September.

Readers should now work through Question 5.3 at the end of this chapter.

The analysed cash book

To enable accounting reports to be prepared it is necessary to ascertain why particular cash flows have taken place. For example, cash from sales and the receipt of a loan are both recorded as cash inflows, but the former is an element in the calculation of profit while the latter is entered in the balance sheet as a liability. A simple way to break down cash flows into their constituent parts is to maintain an analysed cash book. This has columns not only for cash inflows and outflows but also for different types of flows. When a type of receipt or payment occurs on a regular basis, such as payments for goods or wages, a separate column is devoted to this category of transaction; infrequent transactions are entered in a sundry, or ledger, column. An advantage of the use of an analysed cash book is that the nature of each item must be ascertained at the time it is recorded; errors are more likely to occur if there is delay in this process, due, for example, to lapse of memory.

The fact that the aggregate of the totals in the analysis columns is equal to the total of the 'Total' column provides a useful check of arithmetical accuracy.

EXAMPLE 5.4	The following bank transactions were undertaken by Thorn & Co:

Day	Receipts	£	Payments	£
1	Sales	250	Purchases of stock	125
2	Sales	300	Wages	76
3	Sales	270	Purchases of stock	150
4	Sales	315	Wages	79
4	Loan	150	Rent	50
5	Purchase of fixed asset			200

Required   Prepare the company's analysed cash book to record the above transactions.

Solution   **Bank Account – Receipts (debits)**

Day	Detail	Total £	Sales £	Loan £
1	Sales	250	250	
2	Sales	300	300	

3	Sales	270	270	
4	Sales	315	315	
4	Loan	150		150
		1,285	1,135	150

Bank Account – Payments (credits)

Day	Detail	Cheque No	Total £	Purchases £	Wages £	Rent £	Fixed asset Purchase £
1	Stock purchase	1001	125	125			
2	Wages	1002	76		76		
3	Stock purchase	1003	150	150			
4	Wages	1004	79		79		
4	Rent	1005	50			50	
5	Fixed asset	1006	200				200
			680	275	155	50	200

Another benefit of maintaining an analysed cash book is that the postings to the cash book are less cumbersome and need not be done so frequently. For example, in Example 5.4 instead of entering five receipts and six payments over a period of 5 days, the totals for income and expenditure could be made on day 5. This reduces the number of entries to six (2 for sources of income and 4 for classifications of payments) as follows:

Cash Book

Day	Details	Bank £	Day	Details	Bank £
5	Sales	1,135	5	Purchases	275
5	Loan	150	5	Wages	155
			5	Rent	50
			5	Fixed assets	200

ACTIVITY 5.4

The following represents the bank only transactions of Dolphin Spas for the whole of September:

Date	Details	£
September		
3	Sales	1,275
4	Cash paid into bank	1,000
7	Pay wages	100

8	Purchases	3,200
9	Withdrew pettycash from bank	1,000
10	Pay rent	175
12	Sales	2,000
14	Pay wages	100
15	Received a loan	1,000
20	Purchase a second-hand computer for the office	500
21	Pay wages	100
25	Sales	1,500
28	Pay wages	100
30	Sales	500
30	Purchases	1,000

(Cheque numbers have been omitted)

Required   Prepare the company's analysed cash book to record the above transactions.

Readers should now work through Question 5.4 at the end of this chapter.

The petty cash account

All businesses have to meet small incidental expenses in the course of operating and, as it is often inconvenient to pay these by cheque, it is usual to maintain a petty cash float. The normal procedure is to adopt the 'Imprest' system, which uses a fixed sum as a float from which money is paid in return for a properly authorized petty cash voucher. The size of the float should be sufficient to cover the normal level of disbursements during the length of time between replenishments. At regular intervals the petty cashier exchanges the petty cash vouchers for a cheque equal to their total value, which is then used to restore the fund to its designated amount. An advantage of using this system is that at any time the cash in hand plus that represented by vouchers should total the amount of the initial float. This facilities spot checks by an appropriate official.

Although petty cash expenditure, by definition, covers only relatively small amounts, it is still necessary to ensure that it is properly controlled and accounted for. The use of the Imprest system gives control, and to ensure that a proper record exists it is usual to maintain a petty cash book in which the details of the receipts and payments of petty cash are entered. The petty cash book also acts as the petty cash account. Example 5.5 shows entries in a petty cash account recording the transactions of an Imprest petty cash fund of £50.

Petty cash account   EXAMPLE 5.5

Receipts (debit)			Payments (credit)			
Date		Date Voucher No.	Total	Postage	Travel	Cleaning
	£		£	£	£	£
June		June				
1 Balance b/d	12	4 11	10		10	
3 Bank	38	11 12	7			7
		18 13	5	5		
		24 14	8		8	
		29 15	4	4		
			34	9	18	7
		30 Balance c/d	16	–	–	–
	50		50			
July						
1 Balance b/d	16					
2 Bank	34					

Note   The opening balance of £12 shows that expenditure of £38 has been made in the previous
period and should be represented by vouchers to support the amount of cash drawn from the
bank. The debit entry in the petty cash account of £38 shows the receipt of cash and will correspond with a credit in the cash-at-bank account from which the payment was made. The fund
stands at £50 immediately after the reimbursement. Withdrawals of cash are entered as
payments on the credit side of the book in the cash column and this has the effect of reducing
the petty cash balance. Analysis columns are used to provide a summary of the amount spent
for each purpose. Vouchers 11 to 15 account for £34, and this sum is drawn from the bank to
replenish the fund at the beginning of July.

James Walton is a sole trader who keeps his petty cash on the Imprest system – the Imprest   ACTIVITY 5.5
amount being £50. At the start of business on 1 October 120X2, the petty cash in hand
was £3.75.

Walton's petty cash transactions for the month of October 120X2 were as follows:

1 October	Petty cash restored to Imprest amount
4 October	Wages paid – £11.60
5 October	Stamps purchased – £3.94
8 October	Stationery purchased – £4.09
11 October	Stamps purchased – £2
18 October	Wages paid – £12.93
21 October	Paid to F. Smith, a creditor – £3.42
24 October	Stationery purchased – £4.66
28 October	Stamps purchased – £3.80

Required
Draw up Walton's petty cash book for the month of October 120X2, carry down the balance on 31 October 120X2, and restore the petty cash to the Imprest amount on 1 November 120X2.

Note   Your analysis columns should be Wages, Postage, Stationery and Ledger.

(LCC, Book-Keeping, autumn, adapted)

FLOWS OF GOODS AND SERVICES

Accounts are designed to reflect the economic activity that takes place during a period of time, and this is not accurately shown by simply reporting cash movements. This is because it is usual for sales and purchases to be made on credit and, in these circumstances, the movement of goods is not immediately accompanied by equivalent transfers of cash. Companies must, therefore, keep records of inflows and outflows of goods and services as well as for flows of cash. For example, the fact that goods have been purchased on credit must be reported, even if they have not been paid for.

One reason for making a record of flows of goods and services is that control is needed to ensure that cash is subsequently collected from credit customers and that suppliers are paid on time. This section deals with the initial record of economic events; the control of debtors and creditors is dealt with in Chapter 6.

Day books

In its simplest form a day book is a list of sales or purchases that have taken place on credit, with the name of the customer or supplier entered next to each item. The total of each list gives the value of credit purchases or sales during a period of time.

To make certain that all sales are recorded, steps should be taken to ensure that a sales invoice is made out each time goods are supplied. A number of copies of the sales invoice are normally required, one of which goes to the customer and another to the accounts section as the basis for entering the transaction in the sales day book. A final control, such as pre-numbering, should be used to ensure that copies of all invoices are entered in the day book; any missing numbers should be investigated.

The purchases day book is written up on the basis of invoices received from suppliers. To ensure that payment is made only for goods received, a record should be kept of goods delivered to the company against which the invoice can be checked. The record of goods received (the goods received note) is cancelled after checking the invoice to prevent the possibility of paying twice for one delivery. The invoice should also be matched with its originating order to make sure that goods delivered are actually required by the company. An invoice not supported by both evidence of receipt of the goods and a purchase order should be investigated and not passed for entry in the books until there is sufficient proof that it relates to a valid transaction. Invoices for services, such as cleaning, should be supported by an order or contract and passed for payment only by an authorized official.

To produce final accounts and provide management with relevant information, the inflows and outflows of goods and services must be broken down, and this is achieved by adding analysis columns to the day books, as was done in the case of the cash book. The analysis headings are determined on the basis of which aspects of the organization are to be monitored. Excessive detail impairs comprehension and so too many headings should not be used. On the other hand, significant matters may be masked if the headings are too narrow. Management needs to identify areas of strength and weakness, and this is achieved if, for example, sales and purchases are analysed by type of product, and the department or branch in which they originate.

House & Garden owns a shop that consists of two distinct departments, one selling bricks and the other mortar. All purchases are made on credit and management requires reports that show the individual results of each department.

EXAMPLE 5.6

Prepare from the following details the purchases day book in a manner that provides the information needed by management:

Required

Purchases: 1 March from Builder Ltd – bricks £100; mortar £75
(supplied on one invoice)
2 March from Cement Ltd – mortar £50
3 March from Jerry Ltd – bricks £65

Purchases Day Book

Solution

Date	Supplier	Total £	Bricks £	Mortar £
March				
1	Builder Ltd	175	100	75
2	Cement Ltd	50		50
3	Jerry Ltd	65	65	
		290	165	125

The sales day book would be identical to this, although it is the customers' names that would be entered and the individual columns would represent the categories of products sold. For example, in a printing company the types of products offered could consist of commercial printing, specialized stationery, catalogues and leaflets, and design services.

The use of day books is not restricted to purchases and sales. They can be used for any routine transactions such as the return of goods from customers or to suppliers. In all situations the layout will be identical and in all cases appropriate controls must be established to ensure that only valid entries are made in the records.

ACTIVITY 5.6   During the month of March, the following sales transactions took place for Super Heroes, a business supplying children's toys to both commercial operations and the general public.

March	Customer	Items sold	£
1	Plastic & Co	Fancy dress costumes	4,000
		Face paints	1,000
		Action figures	3,500
5	Kidzone	Fancy dress costumes	1,500
		Action figures	2,000
		Action figure accessories	750
10	Toys Forever	Action figures	2,000
		Fancy dress costumes	1,000
		Action figure accessories	950

Required   Enter the above transactions in the sales day book.

Readers should now work through Question 5.6 at the end of this chapter to test their understanding of the preparation of day books.

QUESTIONS   **5.1**   Mr Wall decided to set up in business as a sole trader on 1 January 20X1. He opened a business bank account into which he pays all the takings and from which he pays all business costs. His transactions for January 20X1 were as follows:

(a)   Pay £5,000 into the bank as capital on 1 January.
(b)   Buy a second-hand delivery van for £4,000 on 2 January paying by cheque.
(c)   Pay one month's rent on premises £100 on 3 January.
(d)   Sell goods for £2,250 cash during the month.
(e)   Collect £450 from debtors and pay £2,500 to creditors during the month.
(f)   Withdraw £110 on 15 January.
(g)   Pay insurance for one year, from 1 January 20X1, of £120 on 30 January.

Required   Write up the bank account for January 20X1 and balance of the account.

5.2   Blue Land plc's financial year ends on 22' May 1998. A number of activities must be undertaken before the final accounts can be prepared.

(a)

DR CASH BOOK OF BLUE LAND PLC CR

Date	£	Date		Cheque number	£
18.05.98 Vitenter Plc.	7,389	18.05.98	Balance b/d		860
20.05.98 Riolettan Inc.	119,432	18.05.98	T Singh	10988	1,716
21.05.98 Solway	9,371	19.05.98	A Inglis	10989	73,429
21.05.98 Trancing Ltd.	10,000	20.05.98	Salaries	10990	32,487
22.05.98 Clavern	4,237	20.05.98	Busses Ltd	10991	1,496
		21.05.98	M Sand & Co.	10992	8,500
		21.05.98	Auster Partners	10993	11,235
		22.05.98	Petty Cash	10994	500
		22.05.98	Balance c/d		20,206
	150,429				150,429

Bank statement of Blue Land plc for week ending 22 May 1998

Date		DR	CR	Balance
18.05.98	Balance b/d			1,100 Cr
18.05.98	Ch.no. 10987	1,960		860 Dr
18.05.98	Interest		38	822 Dr
19.05.98	Credit		7,389	6,567 Cr
19.05.98	Standing order – Lease	16,654		10,087 Dr
20.05.98	Ch.no. 10988	11,716		21,803 Dr
20.05.98	Ch.no. 10990	32,487		54,290 Dr
21.05.98	Bank charges	730		55,020 Dr
21.05.98	Ch.no. 10989	73,429		128,449 Dr
22.05.98	Transfer from Investment Account		100,000	28,449 Dr
22.05.98	Ch.no. 10994	500		28,949 Dr

Update Blue Land plc's cash book and reconcile it with the bank statement. (10 marks)   **Required**

ICSA, Paper 6, Introduction to Accounting, June 1998 (adapted)

5.3 Ray Gunne set up in business on 1 January 20X3. The firm's transactions for the first week of January 20X3 were as follows:

(a) Pay capital of £10,000 into the bank.

(b) Buy premises for £8,000 and equipment for £2,750 – both paid by cheque.

(c) Borrow £5,000 from Gunne's brother. He provided this sum in cash of which £4,000 was used to buy a delivery van and £750 was paid into the bank.

(d) Buy trading stock: £3,000 by cheque and £1,000 for cash.

(e) Make cash sales of £5,500.

(f) Pay wages of £100 in cash.

(g) Take cash drawings of £150.

(h) Pay rates by cheque of £250.

(i) Pay £4,250 of cash into the bank.

Required

Prepare the double column cash book of Gunne's business for the first week of January 20X3 and carry down the balances at the end of the week.

5.4 At the start of a trading week the bank account of Laser Ltd showed that the company was £6,510 overdrawn. During the week the company undertook the following cash transactions:

Day	Receipts	£	Payments	£
1	Sales	1,790	Purchases	2,250
2	Sales	2,190	Wages	380
3	Sales	1,250	Sale of fixed asset	1,000
4	Sales	3,720	Interest on loan	400
5	Sales	1,540	Purchase	3,140
6	Sales	2,710	Wages	450

Required

Prepare the analysed cash book of Laser Ltd to record the above information and carry down the balance at the end of the week.

5.5 A young and inexperienced book-keeper is having great difficulty in producing a bank reconciliation statement at 31 December. He gives you his attempt to produce a summarized cash book, and also the bank statement received for the month of December. These are shown below. You may assume that the bank statement is correct and that the first cheque issued in December was number 7654. You may also assume that the trial balance at 1 January did indeed show a bank overdraft of £7,000.12.

CASH BOOK SUMMARY – DRAFT

	£	Dr £	Cr £	
Jan 1				
Opening overdraft		7,000.12	35,000.34	Jan–Nov payments
Jan–Nov receipts	39,500.54			
Add: discounts	500.02			
		40,000.56		
			12,000.34	Balance Nov 30
		47,000.68	47,000.68	

Dec 1 brought down		12,000.34	Dec payments	Cheque no
Dec receipts	178.19		37.14	7654
	121.27		192.79	7655
	14.92		5,000.00	7656
	16.88		123.45	7657
		329.26	678.90	7658
Dec receipts	3,100.00		1.47	7659
	171.23		19.84	7660
	1,198.17		10.66	7661
		4,469.40	10,734.75	Balance c/d Dec 31
		16,799.00	16.799.00	
Jan 1 balance brought down		10,734.75		

Bank Statement – December 31

	Withdrawals £	Deposits £	Balance £
1 December			800.00
7650	300.00	178.19	
7653	191.91	121.27	
7654	37.14	14.92	
7651	1,111.11	16.88	
7656	5,000.00	3,100.00	
7655	129.79	171.23	
7658	678.90	1,198.17	
Standing order	50.00	117.98	
7659	1.47		
7661	10.66		
Bank charges	80.00		
31 December			3,472.34

Prepare the following. Required

(a) A corrected cash book summary and a reconciliation of the balance on this revised summary with the bank statement balance as at 31 December, as far as you are able.

(20 marks)

(b) A brief note as to the likely cause of any remaining difference. (2 marks)

(22 marks)

(ACCA, Paper 1, The Accounting Framework)

5.6 Office Ltd owns a shop that sells typewriters and also repairs office equipment. The following credit sales took place:

Day 1   Sold a typewriter for £300 and stationery for £75 to Gum Ltd.
         Repaired Clue Ltd's typewriter for £100.
Day 2   Sold stationery to Stick Ltd for £70.
Day 3   Sold a typewriter to Fast Ltd for £450.
         Repaired Stick Ltd's typewriter for £50.

Required

Prepare an analysed sales day book for Office Ltd to record the above transactions. The results of each separate activity are to be ascertained.

5.7   On 2 April 1993 Mostar Motors Ltd received their monthly bank statement which showed that there was a bank overdraft of £2,129. This balance was not in agreement with the balance shown in the bank column of the company's cash book. The chief cashier carried out a reconciliation which revealed the following:

1   Bank charges for the quarter ended 31 March 1993 amounting to £48 had been omitted from the cash book.
2   A page in the cash book of debit entries had been understated by £600 and the incorrect total carried forward to the next page.
3   A dividend cheque received for £340 had been entered twice in the cash book.
4   The company's agent in Southshore had paid into a local bank a sum of £1,550 but this was not shown on the bank statement.
5   A standing order of £110 to a trade association had been duly paid by the bank but there was no entry in the cash book.
6   Cheques totalling £4,920 had been delivered to suppliers on 30 March 1993 but none of these had as yet been presented to the bank.
7   A cheque for £154 had been received from a customer on 25 March 1993 but had been entered in the cash book at £145.
8   A hire–purchase agreement for equipment had been entered into by the company. This required £120 to be paid every month for two years. The first payment was due on 20 January 1993. These amounts were correctly entered by the company but the bank had inadvertently debited another company.
9   The bank statement revealed a credit transfer receivable for £291 but after inquiries it was discovered that this related to another company.
10   The bank statement recorded that a cheque for £185 paid into the bank had been subsequently dishonoured. The company was unaware of this.

After taking appropriate action to update the cash book, the bank reconciliation statement was prepared.

Required

(a)   A corrected cash book and bank reconciliation statement as at 31 March 1993.

(32 marks)

(b)   Explain why it is necessary to prepare bank reconciliation statements.

(12 marks)

(AEB, A-level paper 1, June 1993)

Cash Account				
	£			£
Balance b/d	782	Purchases		3,150
Sales	5,769	Wages		790
Bank loan	2,000	Rent		126
		Advertising		75
		Delivery van		3,500
		Balance c/d		910
	8,551			8,551
Balance b/d	910			

(a)   Entries that do not correspond:

  1   Payments in the cash account but not on the bank statement:
      Creditors   £   950 (but see error below)
      Wages   £   300
      Drawings   £1,000
  2   Receipts in the cash account but not on the bank statement:
      Debtors   £2,600
  3   Payments on bank statement but not in the cash account:
      Bank interest   £ 150
  4   Transposition error:
      Payment to creditor entered in bank account as £950 but should have been entered as £590. A transposition difference has led to a payment of £360 too much being recorded.

(b)   Bank Account (revised)

June 20X0	£	June 20X0	£
2 Receipts from debtors	2,792	1 Balance b/d	4,300
12 Receipts from cash sales	1,750	3 Payments to creditors	1,500
19 Receipts from debtors	1,700	7 Wages of sales assistant	300
24 Receipts from cash sales	1,400	13 Payments to creditors	950
25 Receipts from debtors	2,600	14 Wages of sales assistant	300
30 Correction of error	360	21 Wages of sales assistant	300
		28 Wages of sales assistant	300
		30 Drawing	1,000
		30 Bank charges	150
		30 Balance c/d	1,502
	10,602		10,602
Balance b/d	1,502		

(c) **Bank Reconciliation Statement**

	£	£
Balance as per bank statement		202
Less: Outstanding payments:		
Wages	300	
Drawings	1,000	
		− 1,300
		− 1,098
Add: Outstanding receipts:		
Debtors		2,600
Balance as per accounting records		1,502

Solution to Activity 5.3

Double column cash book

Receipts (debits)			Payments (credits)		
Date Details	Cash in hand £	Cash at bank £	Date Details	Cash in hand £	Cash at bank £
September			September		
1 Balance b/d	750	1,500	4 Bank	1,500	
3 Sales	3,750		7 Wages	700	
4 Cash		1,500	8 Purchases	900	
9 Bank	1,900		9 Cash		1,900
11 Rent	750		10 Purchases		1,150
			13 Telephone		400
13 Balance c/d		450	13 Balance c/d	4,050	
	7,150	3,450		7,150	3,450
Balance b/d	4,050		Balance b/d		450

Note   There is a debit balance on the cash account but a credit balance on the bank account. This situation can be quite common, although with a cash balance of £4,050 the overdraft situation should not last very long.

Solution to Activity 5.4

Bank Account – Receipts (debits)

Date Detail	Total £	Sales £	Loan £	Cash £
September				
3 Sales	1,275	1,275		
4 Cash	1,000			1,000
12 Sales	2,000	2,000		

15 Loan from bank	1,000		1,000		
25 Sales	1,500	1,500			
30 Sales	500	500			
	6,575	5,275	1,000	1,000	

Bank Account – Payments (credits)

Date Detail	Total	Purchases	Cash	Wages	Rent	Computer Purchase
	£	£	£	£	£	£
7 Wages	100			100		
8 Purchases	3,200	3,200				
9 Cash	1,000		1,000			
10 Rent	175				175	
14 Wages	100			100		
20 Computer	500					500
21 Wages	100			100		
28 Wages	100			100		
30 Purchases	1,000	1,000				
	6,275	4,200	1,000	400	175	500

Petty Cash Account

Solution to Activity 5.5

1985			1985		Total	Wages	Postage	Stationery	Purchase Ledger
Oct	Details	£	Oct	Details	£	£	£	£	£
1	Balance b/d	3.75	4	Wages	11.60	11.60			
1	Bank	46.25	5	Postage	3.94		3.94		
			8	Stationery	4.09			4.09	
			11	Postage	2.00		2.00		
			18	Wages	12.93	12.93			
			21	E Smith – creditor	3.42				3.42
			24	Stationery	4.66			4.66	
			28	Postage	3.80		3.80		
					46.44	24.53	9.74	8.75	3.42
			31	Balance c/d	3.56				
		50.00			50.00				

Nov

1 Balance b/d   3.56

Solution to
Activity 5.6

Sales Day Book

Date	Customer	Total	Fancy Dress Costumes	Face Paints	Action Figures	Action Figures Accesssories
		£	£	£	£	£
March						
1	Plastic & Co	8,500	4,000	1,000	3,500	
5	Kidzone	4,250	1,500		2,000	750
10	Toys Forever	3,950	1,000		2,000	950
		16,700	6,500	1,000	7,500	1,700

6 The double entry system II: ledger accounts and the trial balance

The objectives of this chapter are to:

- introduce the concept of double entry book-keeping using ledger accounts;
- show how the double entry system is used to record transactions;
- demonstrate how transactions recorded in the books of prime entry, including the journal, are transferred to the ledger accounts;
- explain the use of control accounts for debtors and creditors;
- show how the trial balance is extracted from the ledger accounts; and
- outline the operation of computerized accounting systems.

INTRODUCTION

The previous chapter explained the manner in which the primary records of flows of goods, services and cash are compiled. This chapter examines how the information on inflows and outflows is recorded by means of the system of double entry book-keeping, thereby enabling control to be exercised and the conversion of prime data into accounting reports to be achieved.

THE INTERLOCKING EFFECT OF TRANSACTIONS

In Chapter 2 the impact on the balance sheet of a number of transactions was examined. Assets remain equal in value to sources of finance after each transaction, and the relationship

$$A(\text{ssets}) = C(\text{apital}) + L(\text{iabilities})$$

remains true in all circumstances. The interlocking effect of transactions is fundamental to the system of double entry book-keeping, and is now given further consideration.

To maintain the relationship $A = C + L$, each transaction must have two equal but opposite effects. The alternatives are shown in Figure 6.1. A single transaction can affect any of the items listed as *Effect 1* and be paired with any item from the *Effect 2* list. The interlocking effect means that the total value of the two impacts must be the same.

Figure 6.1 covers changes in assets, liabilities and capital but can be extended to include revenues and expenses. Items of revenue and expense are recorded

Effect 1 (debit)	Effect 2 (credit)
Increase asset	Decrease asset
or	or
Decrease liability	Increase liability
or	or
Decrease capital	Increase capital

FIGURE 6.1   Alternative effects on relationships A = C + L

separately in the trading, profit and loss account and only the balance (i.e. net profit) is carried forward to the balance sheet and included in capital. The impact of a profit is to increase capital, and a loss will result in a decrease in capital. Considering revenue and expenditure individually, the impact of an expense is to decrease capital, and so it is recorded as an *Effect 1* (i.e. a debit), while revenue increases capital and so is an *Effect 2* (i.e. a credit). Figure 6.2 extends Figure 6.1 to include revenues and expenses. A practical application of the interlocking effect is given in Example 6.1.

Effect 1 (debit)	Effect 2 (credit)
Increase asset	Decrease asset
or	or
Decrease liability	Increase liability
or	or
Decrease capital	Increase capital
or	or
Increase expense	Decrease expense
or	or
Decrease revenue	Increase revenue

FIGURE 6.2   Figure 6.1 extended to include revenues and expenses

EXAMPLE 6.1   The following transactions were undertaken by Bernard Egin, a sole trader, when starting his business:

Transaction number	Description	Value
		£
1	Introduce cash as capital	1,000
2	Raise a loan for cash	500
3	Buy plant for cash	1,000
4	Buy stock for cash	250
5	Buy stock on credit	350
6a	Sell stock on credit	550
6b	Cost of stock sold	350
7	Collect cash from debtors	550

| 8 | Pay cash to creditors | 350 |
| 9 | Pay cash for general expenses | 80 |

The twofold effect of each of these transactions is as follows:

Transaction number	Value £	Effect 1 (debit)	Effect 2 (credit)
1	1,000	+ Asset (cash)	+ Capital
2	500	+ Asset (cash)	+ Loan
3	1,000	+ Asset (plant)	− Asset (cash)
4	250	+ Asset (stock)	− Asset (cash)
5	350	+ Asset (stock)	+ Liability (creditor)
6a*	550	+ Asset (debtor)	+ Revenue
6b*	350	+ Expense	− Asset (stock)
7	550	+ Asset (cash)	− Asset (debtor)
8	350	− Liability	− Asset (cash)
9	80	+ General expenses	− Asset (cash)

Note * Trading transactions 6a and 6b have the combined effect of producing a gross profit of £200 from which general expenses of £80 (item 9) are deducted to leave a net profit of £120. The net profit is added to capital when the balance sheet is prepared.

Both effect 1 and effect 2 have the same value and so their combined impact on the relationship A = C + L is to leave it in balance. For example, transaction 1 adds £1,000 to each side, while transaction 3 both adds and subtracts £1,000 from the same side; the asset cash is exchanged for the asset plant.

The dual effect of each transaction has given rise to the system of *double entry book-keeping,* under which each transaction is recorded twice: its effect 1 is recorded as a debit and its effect 2 is a credit. The equality between debits and credits holds true even if more than two elements are affected by a single deal. For example, a customer buys and takes away goods for £250. The price is settled by an immediate cash payment of £100, and an agreement to pay the remaining £150 in one months time. The facts to be recorded at the time of sale together with their impact are as follows:

	Effect 1 £		Effect 2 £	
Sales			250	(+ Revenue)
Cash received	100	(+ Asset: cash)		
Creation of a debtor	150	(+ Asset: debtor)		
	250		250	

There is a credit of £250 and total debits of £250; equality has been sustained.

Readers should now revise their understanding of the relationship $A - L = C$ by attempting Activity 6.1.

ACTIVITY 6.1   Prepare the balance sheet of Egin as it appears after each individual transaction, given in Example 6.1, has been completed. The layout of your answer should take the following form:

Bernard Egin balance sheet

	1	2	3	4	5	6	7	8	9
Fixed assets									
Plant									
Current assets									
Stock									
Debtors									
Cash	1,000	1,500							
Current liabilities									
Creditors									
Long-term liabilities									
Loan		− 500							
	1,000	1,000							
Financed by									
Capital	1,000	1,000							
Add Revenue									
Less Expenses									
	1,000	1,000							

LEDGER ACCOUNTS

The practical operation of a set of double entry books to record transactions involves the use of a separate record for each type of revenue, expenditure, asset and liability. Each record is named according to the item to which it relates, and is known as an 'account'. For example, each company maintains a bank account, as described in Chapter 5, in which all inflows and outflows of cash are recorded. The guiding principle that must be followed when designing a system of accounts is that it must provide the information needed to prepare the accounting statements, which comprise at least a trading and profit and loss account and a balance sheet. The complete set of accounts kept by a firm is called its *ledger*, and this term is also used to refer to particular groups of the accounts, such as the 'sales ledger', 'purchases ledger' and the 'nominal ledger'.

T accounts

The ledger accounts in which business transactions are recorded are known as 'T' accounts, a name derived from each account's appearance, as is apparent from the following examples. The T account represents an open ledger and has two sides – the left is used to record debits and the right credits. An example, containing no accounting entries, is shown in Figure 6.3.

Account Name

Date	Corresponding Account Name	Amount	Date	Corresponding Account Name	Amount
	DEBIT SIDE			CREDIT SIDE	

FIGURE 6.3   A T account

We can now return to the transactions of Bernard Egin given in Example 6.1. The first was the introduction into his firm of capital in the form of £1,000 cash. The two accounts needed to record this transaction are 'cash' and 'capital': cash, an asset, is increased by an inflow of £1,000 and so is debited with this sum; while capital, the liability to the owner, is increased by £1,000 and the account is credited. The accounts appear as follows when the transaction has been entered:

	Cash Account				Capital Account	
Debit		Credit		Debit		Credit
	£					£
		£		£		
Capital	1,000				Cash	1,000

Note that a system of cross-reference is used whereby, in each account, the location of the corresponding entry is named. Thus, for this transaction, the credit entry corresponding to the debit entry in the cash account can easily be traced to the capital account. This referencing is necessary as the separate accounts would not necessarily be adjacent to each other in the ledger.

The transactions undertaken by Bernard Egin, given in Example 6.1, are reproduced for ease of reference: EXAMPLE 6.2

Transaction number	Description	Value
		£
1	Introduce cash as capital	1,000
2	Raise a loan for cash	500
3	Buy plant for cash	1,000
4	Buy stock for cash	250
5	Buy stock on credit	350
6a	Sell stock on credit	550

6b	Cost of stock sold	350
7	Collect cash from debtors	550
8	Pay cash to creditors	350
9	Pay cash for general expenses	80

Required

Record the transactions of Bernard Egin in a set of T accounts. Insert the transaction number before each item. (The impact of each item was given in Example 6.1 above.)

Solution

Cash Account

	Debit	£		Credit	£
1	Capital	1,000	3	Plant	1,000
2	Loan	500	4	Stock	250
7	Debtor	550	8	Creditor	350
			9	General expenses	80
				Balance c/d	
	Balance b/d				

Capital Account

	Debit	£		Credit	£
	Balance c/d		1	Cash	1,000
				Balance b/d	

Loan Account

	Debit	£		Credit	£
	Balance c/d		2	Cash	500
				Balance b/d	

Plant Account

	Debit	£		Credit	£
3	Cash	1,000		Balance c/d	
	Balance b/d				

Stock Account

	Debit	£		Credit	£
4	Cash	250	6b	Cost of goods sold	350
5	Creditors	350		Balance c/d	
	Balance b/d				

Creditors Account

	Debit	£		Credit	£
8	Cash	350	5	Stock	350

Debtors Account

	Debit	£		Credit	£
6a	Sales	550	7	Cash	550

Sales Account

Debit	£	Credit	£
		6a Debtor	550

Cost of Goods Sold Account*

Debit	£	Credit	£
6b Stock	350		

General Expenses Account

Debit	£	Credit	£
9 Cash	80		

Note   * In this example, the asset 'stock' is converted to the expense 'cost of goods sold' at the time of sale. In practice, the cost of goods sold is found by preparing a trading account in which purchases are adjusted for opening and closing stocks. See Chapter 7 for the explanation of how to achieve this using the double entry technique.

At the end of the accounting period, the accountant prepares the profit and loss account and balance sheet. At this stage it is necessary to balance each of the accounts in the manner described in Chapter 5. The balances, however, on the accounts that relate to items of revenue and expense are not carried down to the next period but are transferred to the trading and profit and loss account where the net result of trading is calculated. These accounts are then left empty for the next accounting period when trading recommences. The balances in the remaining accounts are carried down to the next accounting period where changes in these accounts will continue to be recorded. These balances are also used, together with the net result of trading, to compile the balance sheet.

ACTIVITY 6.2

Required

(a)   Balance off the T accounts for Egin in Example 6.2 above. (Space has been left in the accounts for you to do this.)

(b)   List the balances for the ledger accounts in two columns, one for the debit balances and one for the credit balances. Total each column.

(c)   Prepare Egin's trading and profit and loss account and balance sheet from the balances listed in your answer to part (b).

Alternative formats for ledger accounts

The advent of computer-based systems of accounting has resulted in a move away from the T account format, although all of the rules of double entry are still complied with. There are a number of possible alternatives – for example, there may be separate columns for debits and credits or the transactions in an account may be listed with credits identified by an asterisk. One rule that must be observed is that, irrespective of the method used to distinguish debits from credits, it must be consistently applied. Figure 6.4 lists three ways for recording the same information in a computerized cash account.

| | 1 | | 2 | 3 | | |
	Debit	Credit		Debit	Credit	Balance
	£	£	£	£	£	£
Opening balance	500		500 DR			500 DR
Cash from sales	1,250		1,250 DR	1,250		
Cash for purchases		1,000	1,000 CR		1,000	
Closing balance	750		750 DR			750 DR

FIGURE 6.4   Three ways of recording in a mechanical or computerized cash account

The ledger in practice

Accounts can be classified into the types shown in Figure 6.5. Personal accounts are those that record the relationship between the entity and outsiders, such as debtors, creditors and investors. There should be a separate account for each individual who owes money to or is owed money by the company so that it can be established how much to demand or pay, respectively.

FIGURE 6.5   Classification of accounts

Impersonal accounts are either nominal accounts or real accounts. *Nominal accounts* contain all of the items that are transferred to the trading and profit and loss account and so include such items as sales, purchases, wages and day-to-day running expenses. *Real accounts* are used for the non-personal assets of the company, such as cash, stock and fixed assets.

Personal accounts should be classified first according to general type such as trade debtors, trade creditors, debenture holders and capital. Normally, the totals of these personal accounts are shown in the main ledger with the individual details being held separately for control purposes (see later in this chapter). Some of the real accounts, such as plant and machinery and stock, can also be treated in the same way as personal accounts. In these cases the main ledger contains the total which is backed up by a register of plant and machinery or stock records to show the detail that comprises their total value.

The decision as to which nominal accounts to use should be based on a compromise between providing information that is of little use, because it is too general, and giving detail. The exact selection is based on the type of activity the business undertakes and the items management wishes to monitor and control, but in general the rule applies that accounts should be opened in respect of all items that are likely to be material (see Chapter 8). For example, it would not be deemed important in normal circumstances to identify individually the costs of petrol and motor insurance since they are both consequent upon running a vehicle and are reported under the heading 'motor expenses'. The income derived from sales made in the normal course of trade, however, should be distinguished from the proceeds of the sale of fixed assets. A failure to distinguish between them would mask the sources of revenue and would be seriously misleading if, for example, a large amount had been derived from the sale of a surplus piece of land that had been held as a fixed asset.

BOOKS OF PRIME ENTRY

It is unwieldy to attempt to enter each individual flow of cash, goods or services in the ledger accounts. To overcome this problem each transaction is entered, in the first instance, in a 'book of prime entry'. The initial record of transactions is made in either a day book, the cash book or the journal; each of these is now considered in turn.

Day books

The sales and purchases day books, as described in Chapter 5, contain details of all transactions on credit. It is also advisable to use day books for any type of transaction that occurs frequently, such as the return of goods from customers who decide not to keep them (returns inwards) and the return to suppliers of goods purchased (returns outwards). Day books are used to summarize the flows of goods and services into and out of the company in order to generate entries for the appropriate ledger accounts. The sales day book must produce:

(a) the value of debtors created from sales to be debited to the debtors control account; and
(b) the value of credit sales to be credited in the sales account, possibly analysed according to type of sale.

A transfer of data from the sales day book is highlighted in Figure 6.6.

Sales Day Book

Date	Customer	Total	Computers	Printers	Stationery
April		£	£	£	£
1	Joe Ltd	2,000	2,000		
4	Hannah & Co	700		700	
8	Neil's Supplies	1,250		1,000	250
		3,950	2,000	1,700	250

The totals are posted to their respective accounts in the ledger:

DR.	Debtors Control A/c	3,950
CR.	Sale of Computers	2,000
CR.	Sale of Printers	1,700
CR.	Sale of Stationery	250

The individual amounts are posted to the sales ledger (debtors central account) under their respective customer accounts.

FIGURE 6.6   The transfer of data from the sales day book

Purchases Day Book

Date	Supplier	Total	Fixed Assets	Purchases Computers	Purchases Stationery
May		£	£	£	£
1	Avjay Ltd	4,000	4,000		
4	Raymo & Co	2,700		2,100	600
8	Extra Supplies	2,250		2,000	250
		8,950	4,000	4,100	850

The totals are posted to their respective accounts in the ledger:

DR.	Fixed Assets	4,000	
DR.	Purchase (Computers)	4,100	
DR.	Purchase (Stationery)	850	
CR.	Creditors Control A/c		8,950

The individual amounts are posted to the purchase ledger (creditors central account) under their respective customer accounts.

FIGURE 6.7   The transfer of data from the purchases day book

The purchases day book creates:

(a) the total to be credited to the creditors control account; and
(b) the values to be debited to the various expense and asset accounts.

The transfer of data from the purchases day book is shown in Figure 6.7.

There should be clear cross-referencing between the books of prime entry and the accounts so that the trail can be retraced if necessary. A note should be made in the day book of the account, and its location, to which the figures are posted. The entry in the accounts should refer to the source of the figure, preferably also stating the page in the book of prime entry on which it can be found.

The cash book and discounts

The cash book, unlike the day books, is itself a ledger account; it is therefore necessary only to complete the corresponding double entry for the transactions it contains. At the end of the accounting period the cash book is balanced and the result entered in the balance sheet. Again, only the analysis totals need to be posted and not each separate transaction. For example, the following are the totals from an analysed cash book:

Cash Book

Receipts			Payments			
Total	*Debtors*	*Cash sales*	*Total*	*Wages*	*Creditors*	*Rent*
£	£	£	£	£	£	£
5,000	3,500	1,500	4,000	1,000	2,500	500
			Bal 1,000			
5,000			5,000			
Bal 1,000						

The total of cash received, £5,000, is already debited in the ledger as the result of including it in the total column of the cash book, and so the double entry is completed by making the following credit entries:

	£
Sales (revenue)	1,500 (credit)
Debtors (reduce asset)	3,500 (credit)

The entries to complete the record of the effect of cash payments are:

	£
Wages (expense)	1,000 (debit)
Creditors (reduce liability)	2,500 (debit)
Rent (expense)	500 (debit)

The credits have already been entered in the cash book.

The cash balance of £1,000 (£5,000 debit − £4,000 credit) is entered in the balance sheet as a current asset.

The petty cash book (see Chapter 5) is also part of the double entry accounts, and is operated in the same way as the main cash book. The totals of its analysis columns are posted to the ledger accounts, and its balance is entered in the balance sheet.

Discounts

The full value of each sale made on credit is entered in the debtors account, and in some cases this may be cleared by the receipt of cash together with the grant of a discount for prompt payment. Where a *cash discount* is given the amount of money received from the debtor will not equal the value of the debt and yet the debtor does not owe the balance as a discount has been given. The balance outstanding therefore needs to be removed from the account and so the account is credited with the value of the cash discount. The corresponding debit is to the 'discounts allowed account' into which all such discounts are posted. The balance on this account is transferred to the profit and loss account when the periodic accounting reports are prepared and represents an expense to the business in that it is money that the company will not receive.

Alternatively, the company may take advantage of a cash discount offered by a supplier for early payment of a debt. In this case the creditors account is debited and the 'discounts received account' is credited; the balance on the latter account is income, as it is an amount that the business does not have to pay, and is credited to the profit and loss account.

Where a business receives a discount for purchasing large quantities from a supplier or offers a discount for selling large quantities to a customer, known as a trade discount, the discount received or offered is automatically accounted for on the invoice received or sent and so the amount invoiced is net of trade discounts. There is no need, therefore, to account for *trade* discounts in the ledger system.

The procedure for recording cash discounts for prompt payment is shown in Example 6.3.

EXAMPLE 6.3   Seller sells goods on credit to Buyer for £500. A cash discount of 4 per cent may be taken if the debt is settled within ten days.

Required   On the assumption that the discount is taken, prepare:

(a)   the debtor and discounts allowed accounts in Seller's books; and
(b)   the creditor and discounts received accounts in Buyer's books.

Seller's Books:

Debtor Account

	£			£
Sales	500	Cash		480
		Discount allowed		20
	500			500

Discount Allowed Account

	£		£
Debtor	20	Transfer to Trading	20
		and Profit and Loss a/c	
	20		20

Buyer's Books:

Creditor Account

	£		£
Cash	480	Purchases	500
Discount received	20		
	500		500

Discount Received Account

	£		£
Transfer to Trading and	20	Creditor	20
Profit and Loss a/c			
	20		20
	40		40

Note Cash discounts allowed and received are treated as expenses and revenues respectively in the P&L a/c.

Norm and Co offers credit facilities to its customers with an incentive to pay early of 5% discount. It is also offered a cash discount of 3% by its suppliers.   **ACTIVITY 6.3**

The following transactions occurred during August:

	£
Sold goods on credit to Jean & Co	3,000
Purchase goods on credit from Alex Ltd	2,000
Purchased goods for cash	800
Sold goods for cash	1,500
Sold goods on credit to Edwards Stores	1,500
Purchased goods on credit from Ruth Ltd	1,500

| Required | Record the above transactions in the relevant day books and accounts and balance off the accounts at the end of September. Assume that all discounts are taken and all credit transactions are settled in September. |

It is quite likely that a large number of discounts will be received and allowed during an accounting period. To save time, each transaction is not recorded separately; instead, discounts allowed and received are accumulated in the cash book and transferred to the ledger at the end of the period. Example 6.4 shows how this method is operated. It should be noted that the cash book record of discounts is for information only, i.e. for memorandum purposes.

EXAMPLE 6.4   Disco owes £400 to Dancer and £760 to Tapper. He is owed £540 by Jumper and £880 by Runner. Prepare the cash book for Disco on the assumption that all of the above debts are settled subject to a 5 per cent prompt payment discount.

Solution

Cash Book – Disco

	Discounts Allowed	Receipts Debtors		Discounts Received	Payments Creditors
	£	£		£	£
Jumper	27	513	Dancer	20	380
Runner	44	836	Tapper	38	722
	71	1,349		58	1,102

The cash received of £1,349 is credited to the debtors account and the £1,102 cash paid is debited to the creditors account; this completes the double entry in both cases. Since the columns in which the discounts are recorded are for information only, it is necessary to make both debit and credit entries in respect of their contents. The total of discounts allowed, £71, is debited to the discounts allowed account and credited to the debtors account, while the £58 of discounts received is debited to the creditors account and credited to discounts received. In all cases the value of the discount plus the amount of cash flow is equal to the total amount of indebtedness.

ACTIVITY 6.4   Include discount columns in the cash book and prepare a revised cash book for Activity 6.3.

It is useful to keep the discounts received and discounts allowed in separate accounts, rather than to net them, so that the cost of granting discounts and the benefit of taking them can be easily identified and their impact assessed. If discounts allowed rise in value, the question should be asked whether the terms are too generous, and the benefits of taking discounts must be weighed against the alternative advantages of retaining the cash in the business for a longer period of time.

The three column cash book

Chapter 5 covered the operation of a double or two column cash book in which separate columns are used to record the flows of cash in hand and cash at bank. It is possible to add an extra column to create a three column cash book; the additional column is used to record discounts allowed and received in the manner explained above. The use of a three column cash book is shown in the following example.

Henry York is a sole trader who keeps records of his cash and bank transactions in a three column cash book. His transactions for the month of March 20X1 were as follows:

EXAMPLE 6.5

March

1   Cash in hand £100. Cash at bank £5,672.

4   York received from W. Abbot a cheque for £246 that was paid directly into the bank.

6   Paid wages in cash £39.

8   Sold goods for cash £152.

10   Received cheque from G. Smart for £315, in full settlement of a debt of £344; this was paid directly into the bank.

11   Paid sundry expenses in cash £73.

14   Purchased goods by cheque £406.

18   Paid J. Sanders a cheque of £185 in full settlement of a debt of £201.

23   Withdrew £100 from the bank for office purposes.

24   Paid wages in cash £39.

26   Sold goods for cash £94.

28   Paid salaries by cheque £230.

31   Retained in office cash amounting to £150 and paid the remainder into the bank.

(a)   Enter the above transactions in the three column cash book of Henry York.

Required

(b)   Balance the cash book at 31 March 20X1 and bring down the balances.

(LCCI, Book-keeping, Summer adapted)

Henry York cash book

Solution

	Discount allowed £	Cash-in-hand £	Cash at bank £			Discount received £	Cash-in-hand £	Cash at bank £
		Debit side					*Credit side*	
March					March			
1 Balance b/d		100	5,672		6 Wages		39	
4 W. Abbot			246		11 Sundry			
					expenses		73	
8 Sales		152			14 Purchases			406
10 G. Smart	29		315		18 J. Sanders	16		185
23 Bank		100			23 Cash			100
26 Sales		94			24 Wages		39	
31 Cash			145		28 Salaries			230

				31 Bank		145	
				31 Balance c/d		150	5,457
	29	446	6,378		16	446	6,378
April							
1 Balance b/d		150	5,441				

The journal

There are a few transactions that are not entered in the cash or day books, but are instead initially entered in the 'journal'. The use of a journal ensures that every entry in the ledger first passes through a book of prime entry, which fully explains the nature of the transaction. Each entry in the journal should be authorized to ensure that no unsanctioned changes are made in the ledger. Journal entries are likely to be relatively small in number, and include such items as follows:

1 *Transfers.* These occur when it is necessary to transfer value from one account to another, for example, to correct a mistake made in the original posting that placed the entry in the wrong account.

2 *Adjustments.* The original entry may be made in the correct account in the light of prevailing knowledge, but circumstances may change and require a further entry. For example, a debtor is created when a credit sale is made but if, at a later date, it becomes apparent that the money will not be collected, the debt must be written off by transfer to the bad debts account, since it no longer represents an asset. (Bad debts are considered further in Chapter 7.)

3 *Closing entries.* Adjusting entries must be made at the accounting date to enable the periodic accounts to be drawn up. (These are dealt with in Chapter 7.)

The debit and credit entry for each transaction is entered in the journal together with a brief narrative to explain its purpose. Example 6.6 shows some specimen entries.

EXAMPLE 6.6   A. Jones, a trader, wishes to record the following in his firm's ledger:

(a)   The correction of a wrong posting that entered the purchase of a fixed asset costing £1,000 in the purchase of goods for resale account.

(b)   Capital of £4,000 introduced by A. Jones was incorrectly credited to the loan account.

(c)   The introduction by A. Jones of capital in the form of a fixed asset worth £2,500.

Required   Prepare the journal entries to enter the above facts in the firm's ledger accounts.

A. Jones – Journal   Solution

		Debit (DR) £	Credit (CR) £
(a)	Fixed assets	1,000	
	Purchases		1,000
	Being the transfer to fixed assets of incorrect posting.		
(b)	Loan	4,000	
	Capital		4,000
	Being transfer to capital of incorrect posting.		
(c)	Fixed assets	2,500	
	Capital		2,500
	Being introduction of capital in the form of a fixed asset.		

Although for practical purposes the use of the journal is restricted to those cases where there is no other appropriate book of prime entry, it is theoretically possible to record all entries in journal form. An exercise on these lines provides a useful way for examiners to test students' understanding of double entry accounting without calling for the preparation of a full set of T accounts. For example, the transactions of Bernard Egin given in Example 6.1 could have been recorded in journal form.

Rework Example 6.1 in journal format.   ACTIVITY 6.5

CONTROL ACCOUNTS FOR DEBTORS AND CREDITORS

Businesses require two types of information about debtors and creditors:

1   Their total values must be made available both to provide a record of the total amount due to and from the company and to provide the figures for inclusion in the balance sheet.
2   The amount owed to each individual creditor and by each debtor is needed for day-to-day control; the correct amount must be paid or claimed in each case.

The required information is produced by maintaining two records – in the main double entry ledger 'control' or 'total' accounts are kept, which provide the over-all values of debtors and creditors, while debtors and creditors ledgers (kept for information only), contain a separate account for each individual debtor and creditor. (The debtors ledger is also referred to as the sales ledger and the creditors ledger is also known as the purchase ledger.) The debtors and creditors ledgers are referred to as 'memorandum' as they are subsidiary to, and do not form part of, the main double entry system.

Records of debtors and creditors

The memorandum accounts for debtors and creditors are written up from the day books and cash book using the entries for each separate transaction. The control accounts in the double entry ledger are compiled using totals from the books of prime entry. Example 6.7 shows the operation of this system for sales; the same method is applicable to purchases.

EXAMPLE 6.7   Use the following information to prepare:

(a)   a single-column sales day book;
(b)   the cash book (receipts side only);
(c)   the debtors control account; and
(d)   the sales ledger.

Customer	Balance 1 March £	Sales during March £	Goods Returned £	Cash Received £	Discounts £
Page	100	150	–	98	2
Book	125	130	10	79	1
Volume	150	160	–	150	–
	375	440	10	327	3

Solution

(a)   **Sales Day Book**   £

	£
Page	150
Book	130
Volume	160
	440

The total figure for credit sales is credited to the credit sales account and debited to the sales ledger control account. The individual transactions are debited to the sales ledger.

(b)   **Cash Book (debit side)**

	Discounts £	Cash £
Page	2	98
Book	1	79
Volume		150
	3	327

The total figures for discounts and cash received are credited to the sales ledger control account; the individual amounts are credited to the sales ledger.

(c)   **Sales Ledger Control Account (Debtors)**

	£		£
Balance b/d	375	Cash book	327
Sales day book	440	Discounts allowed	3
		Returns inwards	10
		Balance c/d	475
	815		815
Balance b/d	475		

(d)   **Sales Ledger**
      Page Account

		Balance
	£	£
Balance b/d	100	100
Sales day book	150	250
Cash received	(98)	152
Discounts allowed	(2)	150

Book Account

		Balance
	£	£
Balance b/d	125	125
Sales day book	130	255
Cash received	(79)	176
Discounts allowed	(1)	175
Returns inwards	(10)	165

Volume Account

		Balance
	£	£
Balance b/d	150	150
Sales day book	160	310
Cash received	(150)	160

The same procedures apply to creditors, which you can now attempt in Activity 6.6.

ACTIVITY 6.6

Use the following information to prepare:

(a)   a single-column purchases day book;
(b)   the cash book (payments side only);
(c)   the creditors control account; and
(d)   the purchases ledger.

Supplier	Balance 1 May £	Purchases during May £	Goods Returned £	Cash Paid £	Discounts £
Run	1,100	2,150	500	2,000	200
Walk	2,125	1,130	200	1,500	150
Jog	3,150	1,600	50	2,700	270
	6,375				

Reconciling the control account

The use of control accounts for customers and suppliers reduces the number of entries in the main ledger and enables a cross-check to be performed. The total of the balances on the individual memorandum accounts should agree with the single balance of the control account. Agreement on these lines based on the figures in Example 6.7 is:

Balances from individual accounts:	£
Page	150
Book	165
Volume	160
Balance as per control account	475

The maintenance of the sales and purchase ledgers (i.e. memorandum debtors and creditors ledgers) can be delegated to a responsible person who has no access to the main ledger, which is likely to contain many confidential entries. Where this system is operated, the personnel in charge of the debtors and creditors ledgers should periodically supply a list of balances to the official responsible for the control accounts, who can then check that the totals agree. Any difference must be investigated, but there is the possibility that the totals may agree despite the fact that an error has been made. For example, an invoice may have been posted to the wrong debtor account. However, such an error should be identified when the incorrect amount is demanded from a customer who has been wrongly charged for the goods in question.

EXAMPLE 6.8 A list of the balances on the memorandum individual personal accounts in a company's sales ledger at 31 December 20X1 had a total of £305,640. This did not agree with the balance on the sales ledger control account at that date of £325,000. The following errors were discovered:

1 A sales invoice of £12,900, included in the sales day book, had not been posted to the personal accounts in the sales ledger.
2 Discounts allowed to customers of £1,260 had been credited to the individual accounts in the sales ledger, but no other entries had been made in the books.

3   The returns inwards day book had been wrongly totalled; it was overstated by £3,000.

4   A sales invoice of £9,400 had been entirely omitted from the books.

5   A debit balance of £7,400 on the personal account of a customer had been included in the list of balances as £4,700.

6   The balance on a customer's account in the sales ledger of £5,500 had been omitted from the list of balances.

(a)   Write up the control account to correct it for those errors by which it is affected.   **Required**

(b)   Revise the total value of the list of balances in respect of those errors by which it is affected.

(a)   **Sales Ledger Control Account (Debtors)**   Solution

20X0	£	20X0	£
31 Dec		31 Dec	
Balance b/d	325,000	Discounts allowed (2)	1,260
Returns inwards (3)	3,000		
Sales (4)	9,400	Balance c/d	336,140
	337,400		337,400
Balance b/d	336,140		

(b)

	£
Value of list of balances	305,640
Invoice not in sales ledger (1)	12,900
Invoice omitted (4)	9,400
Balance wrongly extracted (7,400 – 4,700) (5)	2,700
Balance omitted (6)	5,500
	336,140

Note   The same closing balance now appears in the control account and the list of balances; the results obtained from the two separate sources of information have therefore been reconciled.

The control account is likely to include the following entries in addition to those for sales, cash and discounts:

1   *Credit balances on the debtors ledger and debit balances on the creditors ledger.* For example, if a customer overpays, the account in the debtors ledger will be a credit. These balances should be carried down separately in the control account and added to creditors in the balance sheet.

2   *Bad debts.*   Some debtors are unable to pay, and the amounts they owe are known as bad debts. These balances must be removed from debtors, by a journal entry, as they no longer represent an asset.

3 *Settlement by contra.*   A firm may both buy from and sell to another company; this gives rise to a debtor account and creditor account in the same name. The balances on the two accounts may be set off, and the net balance settled for cash.

4 *Interest on overdue debts.*   When a debtor is very slow to pay, a firm may, by agreement, charge interest on the debt; this is added to the amount owed.

5 *Returns.*   Goods may be returned either to or by the company; the related debt must be cancelled. Returns *inwards* relate to goods that are being returned from customers and returns *outwards* relate to goods being returned to suppliers.

EXAMPLE 6.9   Singer & Co maintains memorandum debtors and creditors ledgers in which the individual accounts of customers and suppliers are kept. The following information relates to 20X1:

	£
Debit balances on debtors control account	
1 January 20X1	66,300
Credit balances on creditors control account	
1 January 20X1	50,600
Goods purchased on credit	257,919
Goods sold on credit	323,614
Cash received from debtors	299,149
Cash paid to creditors	210,522
Discounts received	2,663
Discounts allowed	2,930
Cash purchases	3,627
Cash sales	5,922
Interest charged on overdue debtor accounts	277
Returns outwards	2,926
Returns inwards	2,805
Accounts settled by contra between sales and purchase ledgers	1,106

Required   Prepare the sales ledger control account as it would appear in the company's ledger at 31 December 20X1.

Solution

Sales Ledger Control Account (Debtors)

20X1	£	20X1	£
1 Jan		1 Jan	
Balance b/d	66,300	Cash	299,149
Sales	323,614	Discounts allowed	2,930
Interest	277	Returns inwards	2,805
		Contra – creditors	1,106
		31 Dec Balance c/d	84,201
	390,191		390,191
20X2		20X2	
1 Jan Balance b/d	84,201		

Reconciliation with suppliers' statements

Monthly statements should be sent to customers reminding them of the amount due and requesting payment. The customer can then compare this document with the information contained in his or her own ledger. The balances on the statement and in the customer's books are unlikely to be the same – for example, the customer may not have received certain goods appearing on the statement – and so a reconciliation must be prepared. In the same way, the company should receive details of their account from suppliers, and these should be checked with the creditors account in the company's books. This procedure is similar to the preparation of the bank reconciliation (dealt with in Chapter 5) and is shown in Example 6.10.

Included in the creditors ledger of J. Cross – a shopkeeper – is the following account, which disclosed that the amount owing to one of his suppliers at 31 May 20X4 was £472.13.   **EXAMPLE 6.10**

Sales Ledger Control Account (Debtors)

20X4	£	20X4	£
May		May	
18 Purchase returns	36.67	1 Balance b/d	862.07
27 Purchase returns	18.15	16 Purchases	439.85
27 Adjustment		25 Purchases	464.45
(overcharge)	5.80	25 Adjustment	
31 Discount received	24.94	(undercharge)	13.48
31 Bank	1,222.16		
31 Balance c/d	472.13		
	1,779.85		1,779.85
		June 1 Balance b/d	472.13

In the first week of June 20X4, J. Cross received a statement (shown below) from the supplier, which showed an amount owing of £2,424.53.

J. Cross in account with Nala Merchandising Company: Statement of Account

20X4		Debit	Credit	
		£	£	£
May 1	BCE			1,538.70 Dr.
3	DISC		13.40	1,525.30 Dr.
	CHQ		634.11	891.19 Dr.
5	ALLCE		29.12	862.07 Dr.

7	GDS	256.72		1,118.79 Dr.
10	GDS	108.33		1,227.12 Dr.
11	GDS	74.80		1,301.92 Dr.
14	ADJ	13.48		1,315.40 Dr.
18	GDS	162.55		1,477.95 Dr.
23	GDS	301.90		1,779.85 Dr.
25	ALLCE		36.67	1,743.18 Dr.
28	GDS	134.07		1,877.25 Dr.
29	GDS	251.12		2,128.38 Dr.
30	GDS	204.80		2,333.17 Dr.
31	GDS	91.36		2,424.53 Dr.
31	BCE			2,424.53 Dr.

Abbreviations   BCE = Balance; CHQ = Cheque; GDS = Goods; ALLCE = Allowance; DISC = Discount; ADJ = Adjustment.

Required

Prepare a statement reconciling the closing balance on the supplier's account in the creditors ledger with the closing balance shown on the statement of account submitted by the supplier.

(CACA, Level 1 Accounting, December adapted)

Solution

	£	£
Balance per creditors ledger		472.13
Add items on statement not in account:		
May 28 Goods	134.07	
May 29 Goods	251.12	
May 30 Goods	204.80	
May 31 Goods	91.36	
		681.35
		1,153.48
Add items in account not on statement:		
May 31 Paid	1,222.16	
May 31 Discount	24.94	
May 27 Goods returned	18.15	
May 27 Overcharge	5.80	
		1,271.05
Balance per statement		2,424.53

Notes

1 The opening balance on the supplier's account in the creditors ledger and the statement balance on 5 May are the same and so at that point the records are in agreement.

2 Some purchases are combined for entry in the supplier's account: the purchases entered on May 16 of £439.85 consist of the statement entries of May 7 (£256.72), May 10 (£108.33) and May 11 (£74.80); the purchases entry on May 25 of £464.45 consist of the statement entries of May 18 (£162.55) and May 23 (£301.90).

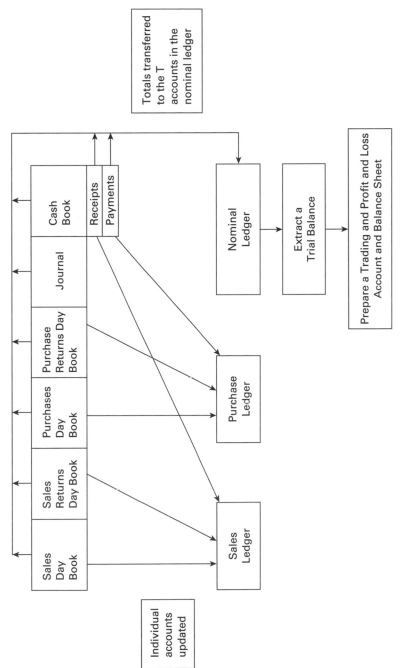

FIGURE 6.8   Summary of the flow of information between the day books and the ledger

A summary of the flow of information between the day books and the ledger is given in Figure 6.8.

THE TRIAL BALANCE

A set of books maintained in accordance with the double entry method provides a comprehensive and appropriately analysed record of all the transactions undertaken by an entity. This record not only enables the day-to-day control of such items as debtors and creditors but also provides the basis from which the final accounting statements, namely the trading, profit and loss account and balance sheet, are prepared.

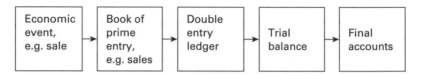

FIGURE 6.9   Process by which an economic event becomes part of the financial accounting statement

The process by which an economic event becomes included in the final accounting statement is as shown in Figure 6.9. It can be seen that the stage prior to the production of the statements from the ledger (covered in Chapter 7) is the preparation of a trial balance. This is a list of all the balances remaining at the end of the accounting period on the many accounts contained in the main ledger; the balances are entered in separate columns according to whether they are debit balances or credit balances. The two columns should possess the same total value since each entry in the books consists of a debit and a credit of equal value and, as described earlier in this chapter, leaves the relationship $A - L = C$. Although it was not described as such, Activity 6.2 (a) involves the trial balance of Bernard Egin.

Readers should now attempt Questions 6.1–6.6 at the end of this chapter.

The fact that the trial balance shows equal totals for both debit and credit balances does not necessarily mean that it is correct, since there are some errors that do not result in an imbalance. These are as follows.

1   *Errors of principle.*   An entry may be made in the wrong account, for example, wages may be debited to purchases.

2   *Duplication.*   Both the debits and credits for a transaction could be entered in the accounts twice.

3   *Omissions.*   A transaction may be omitted altogether.

4 *Compensatory errors.* There may be two or more errors, the effects of which cancel each other out.

5 *Error in the original entry.* An incorrect figure may be used as the basis for the double entry record.

The suspense account

The trial balance, when it is first extracted, does not always balance, and it is then obvious that some error has been made. The first step towards discovering the mistake is to review all the balances to ensure that they have been extracted correctly from the books. The next step is to check that subsidiary memorandum ledgers, for such items as debtors and creditors, have been reconciled with their control accounts. Any discrepancy would indicate a likely area in which the error is to be found. Finally, if the difference is material enough to make its discovery essential, a more thorough check of the records of prime entry to the ledger must be carried out. So as not to delay the preparation of the accounts, a difference on the trial balance may be placed in a suspense account, which is cleared after investigations have been completed. This procedure is shown in Example 6.11.

The trial balance of Wrong at 31 December, as first compiled, contained total debits of £197,500 and total credits of £210,000. The difference of £12,500 was placed to the debit of a suspense account to balance the trial balance. Subsequent investigation revealed the following errors:

1 The balance from the cash book of £3,750 had not been entered in the trial balance.
2 The debtors balance had been wrongly recorded as £71,560 instead of £75,160.
3 A fixed asset purchased for £10,000 had been credited to the fixed asset account instead of being debited.
4 The previous year's profit of £14,850 had not been added to the profit and loss account balance brought forward.

EXAMPLE
6.11

Prepare the suspense account to record the correction of the errors.

Required

Solution

Suspense Account

	£		£
Difference on trial balance	12,500	Cash (1)	3,750
Profit and loss account (4)	14,850	Debtors (2)	3,600
		Fixed assets (3)	20,000
	27,350		27,350

Notes The suspense account now has no value left on it, and the double entry is completed within the trial balance with the following effects:

1 Cash of £3,750 appears as an asset.
2 Debtors are increased by £3,600, to their correct value of £75,160.

3   The incorrect entry in the fixed asset account of £10,000 is cancelled and the correct debit entry of £10,000 is substituted. Note that the total effect of this error was to understate fixed assets by £20,000.

4   The profit and loss account balance is increased by £14,840, being the previous year's profit omitted.

COMPUTERIZED ACCOUNTING SYSTEMS

The overall accounting system of a business consists of a number of sub-systems. For example, there will be a wages system to calculate the amounts due to each employee and allocate the charges to expense headings, such as production, sales and administration, and a purchases system to record creditors and analyse the purchases made between various types of goods and services. Figure 6.10 shows how a firm's accounting system consists of a number of separate, but interlinked, sub-systems.

Computer programs are readily available for each sub-system, indicated by an asterisk in Figure 6.10 and, provided they are from an integrated package of programs, the appropriate links will have been established as part of the program. An entry has to be input only once for all the related aspects to be updated. For example, the fact that a sale has been made, when recorded in the sales system, could also update the stock records and form part of the total sales value automatically posted to the nominal ledger. The sales program may also produce the sales invoice and the stock program may check the resulting stock level to see if more of the item needs to be ordered.

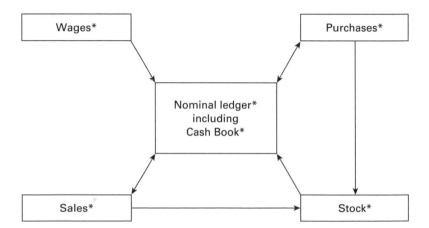

FIGURE 6.10   Some sub-systems in an accounting system (arrows indicate the direction of information flows)

The basic requirements of the sub-systems are fairly standard, and so little adaptation by the user is needed. For example, the principles of calculating wages and the related tax deductions are generally uniform between businesses. However, before a system is acquired, the user must determine the basis on which the analysis is to be carried out, and this, in turn, is largely determined by the content of the reports it is desired to produce. Therefore, before a computerized system is put into operation, careful thought must be given to the accounting system as a whole to ensure that the program is capable of performing the necessary analysis and that the first stages of raw data input will eventually lead to the desired output.

Once the desired analysis has been carried out, a system of coding must be developed to enable the computer to accumulate data in the appropriate accounts in the nominal ledger. Because each business is likely to have its own organization and analysis requirement, and to give flexibility, accounting programs usually leave the setting of codes to the user. The compilation of a list of codes is a straightforward task, and Figure 6.11 shows the steps used to produce some specimen codes in the context of an organization with a number of branches that are subdivided into departments.

Once a code number has been allocated to each branch, department and transaction type in step 1, it is possible, by combining these codes, to develop a code number for each individual transaction, as shown in step 2. Thus, as 441 is the code for a sale in Figure 6.11 then the first code number refers to a sale by department 8 of branch 1 and the second code to a sale by department 9 of the same branch; the third code indicates a sale made by department 8 of branch 2. Transaction type 442 relates to wages, and so the fourth code is the payment to an employee in department 8 of branch 1.

As subsequent analysis and reporting of figures is based on the initial coding of each transaction, a system must be established to ensure that the initial coding is

Step 1: Allocate codes to branches, departments and type of transaction. For example:

Code	Meaning
01	Branch 1
02	Branch 2
08	Department 8
09	Department 9
441	Sales
442	Wages

Step 2: Combine the codes from step 1 to produce detailed codes that can be applied to every transaction the business undertakes:

	Branch	Department	Transaction type
First code	01	08	441
Second code	01	09	441
Third code	02	08	441
Fourth code	01	08	442

FIGURE 6.11   Specimen transaction codes

carried out correctly. In some cases transactions might be coded automatically, for example, the code for each employee may be held by the computer and wage payments allocated accordingly. If this is done, the employee must be recoded when transferred to another department. In other cases, individual transactions must be examined and coded manually, for example, an invoice for repairs to a branch's premises.

It is possible to add extra codes to give additional analysis, which the computer could carry out on an *ad hoc* basis as required by management – for example, data on sales may be analysed by salesperson, location of customer or value of sale. Such exercises emphasize the need to decide and record in advance the necessary basic data; if this is not done, each analysis would involve the laborious procedure of returning to the prime documents to recode them.

The next stage in computerizing the accounts system is to open a nominal ledger account for each valid code. Such an account would be opened for each code produced under step 2 in Figure 6.11 but, although it could be derived, one would not be needed, for example, for sales by the accounts department that only provides a service for the rest of the organization. The computer can then post every transaction with the appropriate code to an account, and copies of each account can be printed out to show the individual transactions that have been combined to give the closing balance. The usual cross-referencing is done automatically so that each entry can be traced to its source.

The computer is also able to construct and print out the books of prime entry (that is, the day books, cash book and journal) in the form of a list of all the transactions that have been entered in a particular batch. Security is achieved by numbering all such lists consecutively and producing them as an automatic part of the operation; they can then be filed and checked for completeness. Additional security is given if access to parts of the system, such as the cash book and journal, is granted with the use of passwords known only to authorized personnel.

Finally, the trial balance is periodically prepared, usually monthly, and converted into a trading and profit and loss account and balance sheet. This process can be handled by the computer and the reports can be prepared on a number of bases, such as monthly, cumulatively, or in comparison with budgets or the same period of the previous year. The production of reports highlights the speed and flexibility of a computerized accounting system as a single set of input data can be manipulated and presented in a number of different ways with great ease.

ADVANTAGES OF DOUBLE ENTRY

The double entry system is very flexible. In this chapter reference has been made to books of account and pages within these books. The records could, in practice, be kept on separate cards or be produced as computer print-outs. Whichever method of operation is employed, however, the benefits derived from the use of double entry are as follows:

1 It enables all types of transactions undertaken by the business, which can be expressed in monetary terms, to be recorded. Provided an economic event has a measurable financial impact, it can be entered into the double entry framework.

2 It enables large numbers of transactions to be recorded in an orderly manner, with similar transactions being grouped together.

3 Economic events are recorded both from the personal point of view (that is, their impact on the relationship between the entity and outsiders) and also from their impersonal aspect (that is, their effect on the business itself in terms of assets owned, revenue and expenses).

4 The debits entered to record a particular transaction must be of equal value to the credits. This equality enables a trial balance to be prepared that gives an initial check on the arithmetical accuracy of the records, although there are errors that are not revealed.

5 The trial balance, an end product of the double entry system, is the basis for the preparation of the trading, profit and loss account and balance sheet. The former gives an indication of the return made by the entity on the resources invested in it, while the latter presents a picture of the extent to which management has carried out its custodial duties in the form of a statement of the financial position.

Readers should now attempt Questions 6.7–6.14 at the end of this chapter.

Questions 6.1–6.6 trace the transactions of a business from the opening balances of the accounting period through to the closing trial balance. The remaining questions test other aspects covered in this chapter.

QUESTIONS

6.1 The following are the balances on the accounts of Radio on 1 January:

Credit balances	£	£
Capital		8,500
Trade creditors:		
Tele	2,300	
Trany	1,000	
Valve	1,300	
		4,600
		13,100
Debit balances		
Plant and machinery at written-down value		4,500
Stock		2,700
Debtors: Vision	2,500	
Sister	1,500	
Batty	1,200	
		5,200
Cash		700
		13,100

Required   Prepare the journal entries to record the opening balances in Radio's books on 1 January.

6.2   During January, Radio undertook the following transactions:

Credit transactions with customers during January

Customer	Sales	Returns Inwards	Cash Received	Prompt Payment Discount
	£	£	£	£
Vision	7,000	300	6,350	50
Sister	4,000	–	3,500	40
Batty	2,700	200	2,600	25
Flat	200	–	–	–
Broke	300	–	–	–

Credit transactions with suppliers during January

Supplier	Detail	Purchases	Returns Outwards	Cash Paid	Prompt Payment Discount
		£	£	£	£
Tele	Goods for resale	3,000	–	2,950	55
Tranny	Goods for resale	2,000	100	1,950	35
Valve	Goods for resale	2,400	150	2,200	20
Garage	Motor expenses	100	–	–	–
Paper	Office supplies	50	–	–	–

Other cash transactions during January

Payee	Detail	£
Plantmax	Purchase of plant	1,000
Cash	Wages	1,500
Accom	Rent for 6 months to 30 June	600
Supplies	Office expenses	250
Garage	Motor expenses	300

£100 was received from Scrap for machinery that was disposed of.

Required   Enter this information in the books of prime entry, i.e. the day books and cash book.

6.3   Use the information in Questions 6.1 and 6.2 to prepare the ledger accounts, other than cash, in Radio's main ledger.

6.4   Use the information in Questions 6.1 and 6.2 to prepare the memorandum debtors and creditors ledger.

6.5   Use the information in Questions 6.3 and 6.4 to prepare reconciliations of the purchases and sales ledger accounts with their memorandum ledgers.

6.6   Prepare Radio's trial balance from the accounts produced in Questions 6.2 and 6.3.

6.7 (a) Define and distinguish, with examples, the following three classifications of ledger accounts:

    (i) real accounts;

    (ii) personal accounts;

    (iii) nominal accounts.

    (b) Give the appropriate classification for each of the following account balances:

       (i) fixed assets at cost, £10,000;

       (ii) wages paid, £700;

       (iii) discounts received, £1,400;

       (iv) balance due from Double Ltd, £1,500.

6.8 Explain how the accountant makes use of the trial balance.

6.9 The following particulars have been extracted from the books of a trading concern for the year ended 30 September 20X1:

		£	
1	Sales ledger debit balances at 1 October 20X0	102,300	
2	Sales ledger credit balances at 1 October 20X0	340	
3	Credit sales	630,800	
4	Cash sales	140,100	
5	Cash received from debtors	498,660	
6	Returns outwards	8,300	
7	Returns inwards	2,700	
8	Discounts received	15,200	
9	Discounts allowed	11,790	
10	Accounts settled by contra to purchase ledger	5,200	
11	Bad debts written off		3,950
12	Sales ledger credit balances 30 September 20X1	510	

Prepare the sales ledger control account for the year to 30 September 20X1.   *Required*

6.10 Ian Error has produced a trial balance for his business for the year to 30 September 20X2 that does not balance, and the error has been placed in a suspense account. An examination of the company's books reveals the following errors:

(a) An invoice from Zed amounting to £1,000, for goods purchased, has been omitted from the purchases day book and posted direct to the purchases account in the nominal ledger and to Zed's account in the memorandum purchase ledger. It has not been included in the creditors control account in the trial balance.

(b)   The sales day book has been understated by £2,400.

(c)   Discounts allowed for the month of June amounting to £4,890 have not been debited to the ledger.

(d)   Goods received from Wye on 30 June 20X2, which cost £24,100, have been included in the stock but the invoice has not yet been received and entered in the books.

(e)   A cheque for £1,920 received from Exe, a debtor, has been debited to cash and credited to the sales account in the nominal ledger.

Required

(i)   Prepare the journal entries to correct these errors.

(ii)   Prepare a statement that shows the effect of the corrections on the company's profit for the year.

(iii) Calculate the difference between the sides of the trial balance that was placed to suspense account.

6.11   (a)   Aries Ltd maintains a creditors ledger control account in its general ledger as part of its double entry system. Individual accounts for suppliers are maintained on a memorandum basis in a separate creditors ledger.

The following totals are available for the financial year ended 30 November 1990:

	£
Discounts received	3,608
Cash and cheques paid to suppliers (per cash book)	231,570
Set-offs to sales ledger control account	818
Credit purchases	249,560
Returns outwards	4,564

The audited total for creditors as at 1 December 1989 was £45,870.

Required   Reconstruct the creditors ledger control account for the year ended 30 November 1990.

(8 marks)

(b)   The total of the balances on the individual creditors accounts as at 30 November 1990 was £51,120. When the records were checked the following errors were discovered:

1   An invoice for £1,125 which was correctly entered into the purchases book has not been posted to the individual supplier's account.

2   Another invoice for £1,850 has been omitted from the purchases book.

3   A credit note from a supplier for £870 has been completely omitted from the records.

4   During the year ended 30 November 1990 petty cash payments to suppliers totalled £625. These have been correctly recorded in the petty cash book and posted to the individual suppliers accounts but no other entry has been made.

5   The total of the individual creditors balances as at 30 November 1990 has been understated by £2,000.

Prepare a clear calculation of

(i)   The corrected balance on the creditors ledger control account; and

(6 marks)

(ii) The corrected total of the balances on the individual creditors accounts as at 30 November 1990.

(6 marks)

(Total 20 marks)

(AAT Preliminary, December 1990)

6.12 The following information for the financial year ended 31 May 1991 has been extracted from the accounting system of George Peace Ltd:

	£
Discounts allowed to credit customers	4,170
Cash and cheques received from credit customers	144,700
Discounts received from suppliers	3,910
Cash and cheques paid to suppliers	156,770
Bad debts written off	1,730
Set-offs from customers to suppliers accounts	3,600
Credit sales	167,800
Credit purchases	175,510
Returns in	4,220
Returns out	6,330
Trade debtors as at 1 June 1990	27,490
Trade creditors as at 1 June 1990	21,810

All sales and purchases during the year were made on credit.

(a)   Use the above information to prepare a sales ledger control account and a purchases ledger control account for the year ended 31 May 1991.

(14 marks)

(b)   Indicate the source of each of the above totals in the accounting system of George Peace Ltd.

(6 marks)

(Total 20 marks)

(AAT Preliminary, June 1991)

6.13 The following is a list of typical business transactions:

(a)   The purchase of goods on credit.

(b)   Allowances to credit customers upon the return of faulty goods.

(c)   Refund from petty cash to an employee of an amount spent on entertaining a client.

(d)   Credit card sales.

(e)   The recovery of a debt previously written off as bad.

For each transaction identify clearly:

(i)   the original documents for the data;

(ii) the book of original entry for the transaction; and

(iii)   the way in which the data will be incorporated into the double entry system.

(4 marks each)

(Total 20 marks)

(AAT Preliminary, June 1991)

6.14   After completing a training course at a technical college, Michael Faraday set up in business as a self-employed electrician on 1 January 19X5. He was very competent at his job but had no idea how to maintain proper accounting records. Sometime during 19X5 one of his friends asked Michael how well his business was doing. He replied, 'All right ... I think ... but I'm not quite sure'. In the ensuing conversation his friend asked whether he had prepared accounts yet, covering his first quarter's trading, to which Michael replied that he had not. Hs friend then stressed that, for various reasons, it was vital for accounts of businesses to be prepared properly.

Shortly afterwards Michael came to see you to ask for your help in preparing accounts for his first quarter's trading. He brought with him, in a cardboard box, the only records he had, mainly scribbled on scraps of paper.

He explained that he started his business with a car worth £700, and £2,250 in cash of which £250 was his savings and £2,000 had been borrowed from a relative at an interest rate of 10 per cent per annum. It was his practice to pay his suppliers and expenses in cash, to require his customers to settle their accounts in cash and to bank any surplus in a business bank account. He maintained lists of cash receipts and cash payments, of supplies obtained on credit and of work carried out for customers and of appliances sold, on credit.

The list of credit suppliers comprised the following:

Date Supplied 19X5	Supplier	Amount Owed £	Date Paid 19X5	Amount Paid £	Remarks
Jan	Dee & Co	337.74	March	330.00	Received discount £7.74
	AB Supplies	528.20	March	528.20	
Feb	Simpson	141.34	March	138.00	Received discount £3.34
	Cotton Ltd	427.40	March	130.00	Payment on account
			April	297.40	Remainder
	Dee & Co	146.82	March	140.00	Received discount £6.82
Mar	AB Supplies	643.43	April	643.43	
	Simpson	95.60			Not yet paid

The purchase in January from Dee & Co. was of tools and equipment to enable him to carry out electrical repair work. All the remaining purchases were of repair materials, except for the purchase in February from Cotton Ltd that consisted entirely of electrical appliances for resale.

In addition to the above credit transactions, he had bought repair materials for cash, as follows:

19X5	£
January	195.29
February	161.03
March	22.06

Other cash payments comprised:

19X5	£
January	
Rent of premises for January to June 19X5	400.00
Rates of premises for January to March 19X5	150.00
Stationery	32.70
Car running expenses	92.26
February	
Sundries	51.54
Car running expenses	81.42
March	
Sundries	24.61
Car running expenses	104.52
Transfer to bank	500.00

He had also withdrawn £160.00 in cash at the end of each month for living expenses.

The list of credit customers comprised:

Date of sale 19X5	Customer	Amount owed £	Date received 19X5	Amount received £	Remarks
Jan	D. Hopkins	362.80	Feb	357.00	Allowed discount £5.80
	P. Bolton	417.10	March	417.10	
Feb	G. Leivers	55.00	March	55.00	
	M. Whitehead	151.72	April	151.72	
	N. John Ltd	49.14	April	49.14	
	A. Linneker	12.53	March	12.53	
Mar	E. Horton	462.21	April	462.21	
	S. Ward	431.08	March	426.00	Allowed discount £5.08
	W. Scothem	319.12			Not yet received
	N. Annable	85.41			Not yet received

The above amounts relate to charges for repair work he had carried out, except that the amounts shown in February for G. Leivers, N. John Ltd and A. Linneker are for sales of electrical appliances.

In addition to the above credit transactions, he had cash takings, as follows:

19X5		£
January	Repair work	69.44
February	Repair work	256.86
March	Repair work	182.90
	Appliances	112.81

He estimated that, at the end of March 19X5, his stock of electrical repair materials was £691.02 and of electrical appliances for resale was £320.58, his tools and equipment were worth £300.00 and his car £600.00.

Apart from loan interest, the only accrual was for heating and lighting, £265.00.

Required

1   Prepare:

    (a)   purchases day book with analysis columns for type of purchase; and

    (b)   sales day book with analysis columns for class of business undertaken.

2   Open, post to 31 March 19X5 only, and balance a columnar cash book suitably analysed to facilitate ledger postings.

3   Open, post to 31 March 19X5 only, and balance a creditors ledger control account and a debtors ledger control account. Use the closing balances in your answer to (7) below. (*N.B.* Individual accounts for creditors and debtors are not required.)

4   Open, post and balance sales and cost of sales accounts, each with separate columns for 'Repairs' and 'Appliances'.

5   Prepare M. Faraday's trading account for the quarter ended 31 March 19X5, distinguishing between gross profit on repairs and on appliance sales.

6   Prepare M. Faraday's general profit and loss account for the quarter ended 31 March 19X5.

7   Prepare M. Faraday's balance sheet as at 31 March 19X5.

(CACA, Preliminary, June)

SOLUTIONS TO ACTIVITIES

Solution to Activity 6.1

Bernard Egin balance sheet

	1	2	3	4	5	6	7	8	9
Fixed assets									
Plant			1,000	1,000	1,000	1,000	1,000	1,000	1,000
Current assets									
Stock				250	600	250	250	250	250

Debtors						550			
Cash	1,000	1,500	500	250	250	250	800	450	370
Current liabilities									
Creditors						− 350	− 350	− 350	
Long-term liabilities									
Loan		− 500	− 500	− 500	− 500	− 500	− 500	− 500	− 500
	1,000	1,000	1,000	1,000	1,000	1,200	1,200	1,200	1,120
Financed by									
Capital	1,000	1,000	1,000	1,000	1,000	1,000	1,000	1,000	1,000
Add: Revenue						200	200	200	200
Less: Expenses									− 80
	1,000	1,000	1,000	1,000	1,000	1,200	1,200	1,200	1,120

(a)

Solution to Activity 6.2

Cash Account

		£			£
1	Capital	1,000	3	Plant	1,000
2	Loan	500	4	Stock	250
7	Debtor	550	8	Creditor	350
			9	General expenses	80
				Balance c/d	370
		2,050			2,050
	Balance b/d	370			

Capital Account

		£			£
	Balance c/d	1,000	1	Cash	1,000
		1,000			1,000
				Balance b/d	1,000

Loan Account

		£			£
	Balance c/d	500	2	Cash	500
		500			500
				Balance b/d	500

Plant Account

		£			£
3	Cash	1,000		Balance c/d	1,000
		1,000			1,000
	Balance b/d	1,000			

Stock Account

		£			£
4	Cash	250	6b	Cost of goods sold	350
5	Creditors	350		Balance c/d	250
		600			600
	Balance b/d	250			

Creditors Account

		£			£
8	Cash	350	5	Stock	350

Debtors Account

		£			£
6a	Sales	550	7	Cash	550

Sales Account

	£			£
Transfer to trading & profit and loss a/c	550	6a	Debtor	550
	550			550

Cost of Goods Sold Account

		£		£
6b	Stock	350	Transfer to trading & profit and loss a/c	350
		350		350

General Expenses Account

		£		£
9	Cash	80	Transfer to trading and profit and loss a/c	80
		80		80

(b)

	Debit	Credit
	£	£
Cash	370	
Capital		1,000
Loan		500
Plant	1,000	
Stock	250	
Sales		550
Cost of goods sold	350	
General expenses	80	
	2,050	2,050

Notes
1. There are no debtors or creditors as, in this instance, their respective inflows and outflows are exactly equal in value and so cancel each other out.
2. The debit balances are equal in value to the credit balances; this provides a check of accuracy.

(c) Bernard Egin – Trading and profit and loss account

	£
Sales	550
Less: Cost of goods sold	– 350
Gross profit	200
Less: General expenses	– 80
Net profit	120

Bernard Egin – Balance sheet

	£	£
Fixed assets		
Plant		1,000
Current Assets		
Stock	250	
Cash	370	
		620
Long-term liabilities		
Loan		– 500
		1,120
Capital		
At start of period		
Introduced		1,000
Profit for period		120
		1,120

The balance carried forward in the sales, cost of goods sold and general expenses accounts are zero. The transactions that were entered in them relate to a period of time; at the end of the period the accounts are cleared to the trading and profit and loss account and appear as above.

Once the balances on all the accounts cleared to the trading and profit and loss account have reverted to zero, these accounts are ready to record information for the next period.

The assets and liabilities shown in the balance sheet are carried forward to the next accounting period in their individual accounts where they will continue to be adjusted for changes that subsequently occur.

Sales Day Book

Date	Customer	Amount
August	Jean & Co	3,000
	Edwards Stores	1,500
		4,500

Purchases Day Book

Date	Supplier	Amount
August	Alex Ltd	2,000
	Ruth Ltd	1,500
		3,500

Solution to Activity 6.3

Sales Account

	£			£
September Transfer to trading and profit and loss account	6,000	August	Debtors	4,500
			Cash	1,500
	6,000			6,000

Debtors Account

	£		£
August Sales	4,500	Sept Cash	4,275
		Sept Discount allowed	225
	4,500		4,500

Discount Allowed Account

	£		£
Sept Debtor	225	September Transfer to trading and profit and loss a/c	225
	225		225

Cash Account

	£		£
August Sales	1,500	August Purchases	800
September Debtors	4,275	September Creditors	3,395
		Balance c/d	1,580
	5,775		5,775
Balance b/d	1,580		

Purchases Account

	£		£
August Creditors	3,500	Transfer to trading and profit and loss a/c	4,300
Cash	800		
	4,300		4,300

Creditors Account

	£		£
Sept Cash	3,395	August Purchases	3,500
Sept Discounts received	105		
	3,500		3,500

Discount Received Account

	£		£
Transfer to trading and profit and loss A/c	105	Sept Creditors	105
	105		105

Cash Book – Norm Ltd

Solution to
Activity 6.4

	Discounts Allowed £	Debtors £	Cash Sales £	Total		Discounts Received £	Total	Creditors	Cash Purchases
Aug			1,500	1,500	Aug		800		800
Sales					Purchases				
Sept					Sept				
Jean	150	2,850		2,850	Alex	60	1,940	1,940	
Edwards	75	1,425		1,425	Ruth	45	1,455	1,455	
	225	4,275	1,500			105	4,195	3,395	800
					Balance c/d		1,580		
				5,775			5,775		
Balance b/d				1,580					

Bernard Egin – Journal

Solution to
Activity 6.5

Transaction number		Debit £	Credit £
1	Cash	1,000	
	Capital		1,000
	Receipt of capital in the form of cash		
2	Cash	500	
	Loan		500
	Loan raised		
3	Plant	1,000	
	Cash		1,000
	Purchase of plant for cash		
4	Stock	250	
	Cash		250
	Purchase of stock for cash		
5	Stock	350	
	Creditor		350
	Purchase of stock on credit		
6(a)	Debtor	550	
	Sales		550

6(b)	Cost of goods sold	350	
	Stock		350
	Sale of goods on credit		

7	Cash	550	
	Debtors		550
	Collection of cash from debtors		

8	Creditors	350	
	Cash		350
	Payment of cash to creditors		

9	General expenses	80	
	Cash		80
	Payment of general expenses in cash		

These entries can be checked against the T accounts in Example 6.1.

Solution to
Activity 6.6

(a) **Purchases Day Book**

	£
Run	2,150
Walk	1,130
Jog	1,600
	4,880

The total figure for credit purchases sales is debited to the purchases account and credited to the purchase ledger control account. The individual transactions are credited to the purchase ledger.

(b) **Cash Book (credit side)**

	Discounts	*Cash*
	£	£
Run	200	2,000
Walk	150	1,500
Jog	270	2,700
	620	6,200

The total figures for discounts and cash paid are debited to the purchase ledger control account; the individual amounts are debited to the purchase ledger.

(c)   Purchase ledger contol account (creditors)

	£		£
		Balance b/d	6,375
Cash payments	6,200	Purchases	4,880
Discounts	620		
Returns outwards	750		
Balance c/d	3,685		
	11,255		11,255
		Balance b/d	3,685

(d)   **Purchase ledger**
Run account

	£	Balance £
Balance b/d	1,100	1,100
Purchases day book	2,150	3,250
Returns outwards	(500)	2,750
Cash paid	(2,000)	750
Discounts received	(200)	550

Walk account

	£	Balance £
Balance b/d	2,125	2,125
Purchases day book	1,130	3,255
Returns outwards	(200)	3,055
Cash paid	(1,500)	1,555
Discounts received	(150)	1,405

Jog account

	£	Balance £
Balance b/d	3,150	3,150
Purchases day book	1,600	4,750
Returns outwards	(50)	4,700
Cash paid	(2,700)	2,000
Discounts received	(270)	1,730

Purchase ledger control account (creditors)

20X1 Jan	£	20X1 Jan	£
Cash	210,522	Balance b/d	50,600
Discounts received	2,663	Purchases	257,919

Solution to
Activity 6.7

Returns outwards	2,926		
Contra – debtors	1,106		
31 Dec Balance c/d	91,302		
	308,519		308,519
_20X2_		_20X2_	
		1 Jan	
		Balance b/d	91,302

Note The cash sales and cash purchases do not appear in the control accounts. They do not affect the recorded value of debtors and creditors.

7 The double entry system III: periodic accounting reports

The objectives of this chapter are to:

- recap on the purpose of the trading, profit and loss account and balance sheet.
- explain how a set of accounts is prepared from the trial balance;
- show how the value of closing stock is included in a set of accounts;
- demonstrate how depreciation is included in a set of accounts;
- describe how to account for the disposal of fixed assets;
- explain the terms 'prepayments' and 'accruals' and their impact on final accounts;
- show how to account for bad and doubtful debts; and
- illustrate the use of the extended trial balance.

PERIODIC ACCOUNTS

The preparation of accounting statements should be a routine procedure as they are regularly needed by managers, owners and other interested parties, such as banks, to monitor the progress and position of the business. The principal accounting statements used for these purposes are the trading and profit and loss account and the balance sheet. It is normal to prepare these statements at least once a year to comply with legal and taxation requirements, but they can be produced more frequently if required. Their usefulness depends, first, on the ability of the recipients to base decisions on them and, second, on the time lags between the occurrence of events, their financial effects being reported and decisions taken. If decisions are delayed because of a lack of financial information, then opportunities may be missed, possibly with disastrous consequences. For this reason management, and sometimes other interested parties, will require statements more frequently than once a year, usually monthly, but possibly even more often. For example, when losses are being made it is important to realize this fact at an early stage; this is helped by the frequent and prompt production of a profit and loss account. The first evidence that losses are being incurred may otherwise be the collapse of the business, an eventuality that might have been avoided if the losses had been identified earlier and remedial action taken.

The procedures described in Chapters 5 and 6 provide the foundations of the accounting process as they are used to record the flows of cash, goods and services and provide a summary of these flows in the form of the trial balance. This chapter deals with the adjustments necessary to the information contained in the trial balance to enable the production of the trading and profit and loss account and balance sheet.

Profit and loss account and balance sheet

The trading, profit and loss account is a statement spanning two time periods, normally the beginning and end of the accounting year. It is sometimes referred to as a 'period' statement. Included in this statement is the income from trading activity, together with the expenditure incurred in generating that income (i.e. the day to day running expenses of the business). The difference between income and expenditure is referred to as profit which is transferred to the balance sheet and added to the owner's capital. A summary trading, profit and loss account, showing the transactions covered in the previous sections of the book, is given in Illustration 7.1.

Illustration 7.1
Trading, profit and loss account period ending 31 December 20X1

	£	£
Sales		XXX
Less: Returns inwards (sales returns)		(XXX)
		XXX
Purchases	XXX	
Less: Returns outwards (purchase returns)	(XXX)	
Cost of goods sold		(XXX)
Gross profit		XXX
Additional income		
Discounts received		XXX
		XXX
Expenditure		
Salaries	XXX	
Commissions	XXX	
Rent and rates	XXX	
Lighting and heating	XXX	
Telephone	XXX	
Postage and stationery	XXX	
Advertising	XXX	
General expenses	XXX	
Discounts allowed	XXX	
		(XXX)
Net profit		XXX

The balance sheet is a statement showing the financial position of a business at a particular point in time, normally at the accounting year end. It is referred to as a 'position' statement. The balance sheet shows what the business owns (i.e. its fixed and current assets) and how it has been financed (i.e. its capital, long-term liabilities and short-term liabilities). A summary balance sheet is given in Illustration 7.2.

Illustration 7.2

Balance sheet as at 31 December 20X1

	£	£	£
Fixed Assets			
Land and buildings			XXX
Plant and machinery			XXX
Fixtures and fittings			XXX
Vehicles			XXX
			XXX
Current Assets		XXX	
Debtors		XXX	
Bank		XXX	
Cash		XXX	
Less: Current Liabilities			
Bank overdraft	XXX		
Creditors	XXX		
		(XXX)	
Working capital			XXX
Less: Long-term Liabilities			
Mortgage		XXX	
Bank Loan		XXX	
			(XXX)
Net assets			**XXX**
Financed by			
Capital			XXX
Add: Additional capital			XXX
Add: Profit		XXX	
Less: Drawings		(XXX)	
			XXX
			XXX

The information contained in the profit and loss account and balance sheet comes from the trial balance which would have been prepared from the balances contained in the ledger accounts. However, before this transfer of information takes place, adjustments to the trial balance may be required because the transactions in the ledger accounts do not reflect precisely the economic events that have occurred during the period covered by the accounting statements. The following adjustments may need to be taken into account:

ADJUSTMENTS TO THE TRIAL BALANCE

1 *Timing differences.* These occur when an item recorded in the books during an accounting period has significance for the business not only in that accounting period but also in previous or subsequent ones. In these circumstances an adjustment must be made to distribute the item accordingly. For example, the purchase of a fixed asset is initially recorded at cost in the year of purchase, but it is necessary to apportion this cost over the years that derive benefit from the expenditure. Timing differences also operate in the opposite direction. For example, there may be an interval between the receipt of goods and the arrival of the related invoice. (For a fuller explanation, see later in this chapter.)

2 *Incomplete information.* The entries in the books may not reflect all the economic changes that must be reported, since some events are not supported by a documented flow of value on which a day book entry can be made. For example, a debtor may be unable to pay the sum due to the company, or a machine may be scrapped (see later in this chapter). The routine documentation procedures for a sale or purchase do not apply in these cases, and care must be taken to ensure that allowance has been made for them when the accounts are prepared. The accountant must be satisfied that all the items that relate to the period under review have been included and also that all items that are not relevant have been excluded.

The adjustments made to the trial balance must comply with the rules of double entry – each must comprise a debit and a credit of equal value. The implementation of the adjustments that routinely arise when periodic accounts are prepared are examined in this chapter; the principles of valuation on which the adjustments are based are dealt with in Chapter 8.

STOCK (INVENTORIES)

Gross profit is measured by comparing the value of sales for a period of time with their related costs, and so it is necessary to determine the value of goods consumed, or used up, in the manner described in Chapter 4. Companies may hold many different types of stock such as raw materials, work in progress and finished goods, and the general equation to find the cost of items consumed is

$$\text{Cost of goods consumed} = \text{Opening stock} + \text{Inflow of goods} - \text{Closing stock}$$

Care must be taken to ensure that all inflows of goods are included. Any items received prior to the accounting date and included in stock, but which have not been entered as purchases as they have not yet been invoiced, must be identified. An adjustment in the form of an accrual is then made, which increases the value of purchases (debit) and is shown as a liability in the balance sheet (credit); for a fuller explanation, see the section on prepayments and accruals in this chapter.

In a system of double entry accounting, unless continuous stock control as described in Chapter 8 is used, it is usual to enter the opening stock in one account and to accumulate in another account, called purchases, the cost of all acquisitions made during the accounting period. The effect of this procedure is that the trial balance contains separate balances for opening stock and purchases; these provide two of the three elements in the formula given above. The missing element is the figure for closing stock, and this is usually determined by means of a physical stocktake to find the quantities of each type of stock, which are then valued.

To find the cost of goods sold in the trading account the values of opening stock and purchases contained in the trial balance are transferred to the debit of this account. The accounting entry to record closing stock in the final accounts must then be made:

> *Debit*   *Credit*   *With*
> Stock account   Trading account   Value of closing stock

The closing balance on the stock account appears as an asset in the balance sheet and is subsequently included as opening stock in the trading account for the following accounting period.

From the following information, calculate the cost of sales figure to be included in the trading and profit and loss account.   **EXAMPLE 7.1**

	£
Stock as at 31 December 20X0	20,000
Stock as at 31 December 20X1	30,000
Purchases during the year	150,000

Opening Stock	20,000	Solution
Add: Purchases	150,000	
	170,000	
Less: Closing Stock	(30,000)	
Cost of Sales	140,000	

From the following information calculate the cost of sales figure to be included in the trading and profit and loss account.   **ACTIVITY 7.1**

	£
Stock as at 31 March 20X5	620,000
Stock as at 31March 20X6	530,000
Purchases during the year	3,150,000

Example 7.2 involves the preparation of final accounts from the trial balance where an adjustment has to be made for closing stock.

The trial balance of Button, a sole trader, at 31 December 20X4 was: **EXAMPLE 7.2**

	Debit	*Credit*
	£	£
Capital		10,000
Drawings	8,000	

Sales		75,500
Purchases	45,250	
Stock: 1 January 20X4	6,750	
Debtors	4,300	
Creditors		3,200
Cash	3,125	
Delivery costs	875	
Wages	11,225	
Sundry expenses	3,000	
Freehold premises	6,175	
	88,700	88,700

The stock at 31 December 20X4 was £7,150.

Required

Prepare the trading and profit and loss account of Button for the year to 31 December 20X4 and a balance sheet at that date. The accounts should be presented in vertical format.

Solution

Button Trading and profit and loss account, year ending 31 December 20X4

	£	£
Sales		75,500
Opening stock	6,750	
Purchases	45,250	
	52,000	
Less: Closing stock	−7,150	
Cost of goods sold		44,850
Gross profit		30,650
Wages	11,225	
Delivery costs	875	
Sundry expenses	3,000	
		15,100
Net profit		15,550

Button Balance sheet as at 31 December 20X4

	£	£
Fixed assets		
Freehold premises		6,175
Current assets		
Stock	7,150	
Debtors	4,300	
Cash	3,125	
	14,575	
Current liabilities		
Creditors	−3,200	
		11,375
		17,550

Capital

At I January 20X4	10,000
Profit for 20X4	15,550
	25,550
Drawings	−8,000
	17,550

The trial balance of Finis, a sole trader, at 31 December 20X4 was: ACTIVITY 7.2

	Debit	Credit
	£	£
Capital		57,600
Drawings	15,000	
Sales		155,000
Returns inwards	700	
Purchases	90,000	
Returns outwards		800
Stock: I January 20X4	18,000	
Debtors	17,000	
Creditors		8,000
Cash at bank	5,000	
Wages	19,000	
Discount received		1,000
Rent	6,000	
Freehold premises	38,000	
Delivery costs	3,000	
Sundry expenses	3,700	
Heat and light	5,000	
Advertising	2,000	
	222,400	222,400

The stock at 31 December 20X4 was £20,000.

Prepare the trading and profit and loss account for Finis for the year to 31 December 20X4   Required
and a balance sheet at that date. The accounts should be presented in vertical format.

DEPRECIATION

Fixed assets and their related depreciation are recorded in the double entry ledger
by using three types of account:

	Account name	Value	Destination of balance
1	Specific fixed asset	Original value	Balance sheet

| 2 | Specific fixed asset accumulated depreciation | Total depreciation to date | Balance sheet |
| 3 | Depreciation charge | One year's charge | Profit and loss account |

The number of accounts to be opened depends on the nature of the business, but usually separate accounts for land and buildings, plant and machinery, motor vehicles and furniture and fittings suffice along with their individual accumulated depreciation accounts. Further accounts can be used if appropriate, for example, computer equipment may have a value significant enough to warrant separate identification. The totals of these accounts should be backed up by detailed analysis in a fixed asset register so that the individual assets can be identified.

When the trial balance is extracted it contains for each type of fixed asset (as a debit) the cost and (as a credit) the accumulated balance of depreciation brought forward at the start of the accounting period. The value of the depreciation charge for the period for each class of asset has then to be calculated, and the amounts are debited to the profit and loss account and credited to the accounts containing the opening balances of accumulated depreciation. (The calculation of the depreciation charge is dealt with in Chapter 8.) The balances destined for the balance sheet, as described above, would appear in the statement as follows:

Balance sheet (extract)

Fixed assets

Land and buildings (at cost)	100,000	
Less: Accumulated depreciation	(20,000)	
Net book value		80,000
Plant and machinery	70,000	
Less: Accumulated depreciation	(35,000)	
Net book value		35,000
		115,000

The debit balance on each of the fixed asset accounts is entered in the balance sheet, and from it the credit balance on the related accumulated depreciation account is deducted to give the net book value (or written-down value). That is, the portion of the original cost that has not yet been written off and is therefore carried forward to the next accounting period. It is helpful to the users of the accounts if both the total cost and the total related depreciation are shown in the balance sheet, rather than just the net figure. This procedure indicates how much of the value has been used up and, therefore, how long it is likely to be before replacement becomes necessary. In the case of a limited company, such disclosure is a legal requirement that is shown in a note to the accounts as opposed to on the face of the balance sheet.

The following information relates to the machinery owned by Clip & Co: EXAMPLE 7.3

	£
At cost 1 January 20X1	65,000
Accumulated depreciation at 1 January 20X1	25,000
Acquired during 20X1	10,000
Depreciation charge for 20X1	8,000

(a) Prepare the ledger accounts for 20X1 to record the above information.   Required
(b) Show the balance sheet extract for machinery at 31 December 20X1.

(a)   Solution

Machinery Account

	£		£
1 Jan 20X1			
Balance b/d	65,000		
Acquisitions	10,000	31 Dec 20X1	
		Balance c/d	75,000
			75,000
	75,000		
1 Jan 20X2	75,000		
Balance b/d			

Accumulated Depreciation Account Machinery

	£		£
		1 Jan 20X1	
		Balance b/d	25,000
31 Dec 20X1		Depreciation 20X1	8,000
Balance c/d	33,000		33,000
	33,000	1 Jan 20X2	
		Balance b/d	33,000

Depreciation Charge Account Machinery

	£		£
31 Dec 20X1			
Accum Dep'n	8,000	Transfer to P&L account	8,000
	8,000		8,000

(b) Balance sheet (extract), 31 December 20X1

	£
Machinery at cost	75,000
Less: Accumulated depreciation	(33,000)
	42,000

ACTIVITY 7.3   The following information relates to the plant and machinery owned by Heavy Duty:

	£
At cost 1 January 20X0	650,000
On 1 Jan 20X3 acquired more plant	100,000
Depreciation is charged on the basis of 10% of cost	

Required   It is now the end of 20X3.

(a)   Draw up the ledger accounts recording all transactions from 20X0 to 20X3.
(b)   Show the balance sheet extract for plant and machinery as at 31 December 20X3.

Readers should now attempt Questions 7.1 to 7.3 at the end of this chapter.

DISPOSAL OF FIXED ASSETS

When a fixed asset is disposed of, its cost and related depreciation must be eliminated from the books and any profit or loss on disposal calculated. Any proceeds from disposal must not be included in the company's sales figure as they do not relate to routine trading activity. Instead, the proceeds are credited to a disposal of fixed assets account, the balance on which appears as a credit entry in the trial balance which is then transferred to the profit and loss account and treated as additional income.

The calculation of the profit or loss arising on disposal is made in the disposal of fixed assets account using the following entries:

Account debited	*Account credited*	*With*
Disposal of fixed assets	Fixed assets at cost	Historical cost of the asset
Accumulated depreciation	Disposal of fixed asset	Accumulated depreciation on the asset

---

EXAMPLE 7.4   The fixed assets of Case at the beginning of 20X3 included machinery that cost £100,000. The accumulated depreciation on this machinery was £55,000. At the end of 20X3 a piece of machinery is sold, for £6,500 cash, having cost the company £25,000. At the time of sale, the accumulated depreciation on the asset was £20,000.

Required   Enter the above information in the relevant ledger accounts. (Ignore annual depreciation for 20X3.)

Solution

Machinery Account

	£		£
1 Jan 20X3		31 Dec 20X3 Disposal	25,000
Balance b/d	100,000	31 Dec 20X3	
		Balance c/d	75,000
	100,000		100,000
1 Jan 20X3			
Balance b/d	75,000		

Accumulated Depreciation Account – Machinery

	£		£
31 Dec 20X3 Disposal	20,000	1 Jan 20X3	
		Balance b/d	55,000
31 Dec 20X3			
Balance c/d	35,000		
	55,000		55,000
		1 Jan 20X4	
		Balance b/d	35,000

Disposal of Machinery Account

	£		£
31 Dec 20X3		31 Dec 20X3	
Machinery	25,000	Accum dep'n	20,000
31 Dec 20X3		31 Dec 20X3	
Profit on sale*	1,500	Cash	6,500
	26,500		26,500

Note *Balancing figure credited to the profit and loss account.

Enter the following transactions in the appropriate ledger accounts and balance off each account.   **ACTIVITY 7.4**

	£
Fixed assets (at cost)	2,000,000
Accumulated depreciation to 20X0	500,000
Proceeds from sale of fixed asset in 20X1	500,000
Acquisition of fixed assets in 20X1	750,000

Notes   1 The sale of the fixed asset took place at the beginning of 20X1. The cost of the fixed asset disposed of was £800,000 and the accumulated depreciation at the date of sale was £200,000.

2 Annual depreciation is calculated on the basis of 8% on cost.

Prepare the ledger accounts to record the above transactions.   **Required**

Sometimes a disposal of fixed assets account is not maintained during the year and instead any proceeds are credited to the fixed assets at cost account. This happens especially where a 'trading-in' allowance is received, for example when changing motor vehicles, as a reduction in the amount paid for the new asset. In these circumstances, the proceeds or trading-in allowance must be transferred to the disposal account by the following entry:

Account debited	Account credited	With
Fixed assets at cost	Disposal of fixed assets	Proceeds of disposal or trading-in allowance.

Instead of making the appropriate entries in a disposal of fixed assets account, the profit or loss on the disposal of an individual asset may alternatively be calculated by using the following formula:

$$\begin{matrix} \text{Proceeds on} \\ \text{disposal} \end{matrix} - \left(\begin{matrix} \text{Historical} \\ \text{cost} \end{matrix} - \begin{matrix} \text{Accumulated} \\ \text{depreciation} \end{matrix} \right) = \begin{matrix} \text{Profit/loss on} \\ \text{disposal} \end{matrix}$$

Questions can be framed so that any one element from this equation is unknown and has to be found as the balancing figure after the others have been determined and entered.

EXAMPLE 7.5 Shed bought a fixed asset for £10,000 in 20X1, which was sold for £6,250 in 20X5 to give a profit on disposal of £1,250.

Required

(a) Calculate the accumulated depreciation that had been charged on the asset up to the time it was sold.

(b) Explain why, when the amount of profit on disposal is known, it is necessary to calculate the depreciation figure.

Solution

(a) £6,250 (Proceeds) − (£10,000 (Cost) − Accumulated depreciation)

= £1,250 (profit)

∴ £ 6,250 − £10,000 + Accumulated depreciation

= £1,250

∴ Accumulated depreciation = £10,000 − £6,250 + £1,250

= £5,000.

(b) It is necessary to know the value of accumulated depreciation as, when an asset is disposed of, all the related entries in the books must be removed. This is done by using the double entry procedures to complete a disposal of fixed assets account:

Disposal of Fixed Assets Account

	£		£
Fixed asset at cost	10,000	Accumulated depreciation	5,000
Profit on disposal	1,250	Proceeds of sale	6,250
	11,250		11,250

Readers should now attempt Question 7.4 at the end of this chapter, which tests all the aspects of asset disposal described in this section.

PREPAYMENTS AND ACCRUALS

A business makes a number of payments that give it the right to enjoy certain benefits over a period of time. Some of these payments, such as rates on the occupation of property, are paid in advance of the receipt of the benefit and are known as *prepayments*, while others, such as for the consumption of gas or electricity, are made in arrears and are known as *accruals*. The accruals concept, as explained in Chapter 4, is applied, and so, unless the period of time covered by these payments coincides exactly with the accounting period, an adjustment is needed. The adjustment will either be an asset, to account for payments made in advance, or a liability, where payments are made in arrears. The value of accruals and prepayments for items that relate to a period of time is normally found by apportioning the cost on a time basis.

Illustration 7.1

Accounting period 1	Accounting period 2
Jan	July Dec	Jan June

Jan	July Dec	Jan June
	Pay 12 months car insurance in July	
	←————————→	←————————→
	6 months falls in the current accounting period and so is charged against profit this year.	6 months falls in the following accounting period and so will be charged against profit next year.

Illustration 7.2

Accounting period 1

Jan	Sept	Dec
Electricity bills have been received for quarters 1,2 and 3.	Final quarter bill is still outstanding.	

A charge to the profit and loss account is required for electricity that covers the full 12 months. (This will include the actual amounts paid plus an estimate of the final quarter s charge.)

Prepayments

The entries in the accounts to record a prepayment are:

Account debited	Account credited	With
Prepayment	Expense	Value of prepayment

The credit of the prepayment in the expense account reduces the expense, and the prepayment is shown in the balance sheet as a current asset. In practice, the prepayment may be carried down in the expense account to which it relates. This is illustrated in Example 7.6.

EXAMPLE 7.6   Gelco makes up its accounts to 31 December, and made the following cash payments in respect of rent:

Year	Month	Payment
		£
20X0	October	900
20X1	April	1,000
20X1	October	1,000

The payments for rent relate to the six-month period starting with the month in which they are paid.

Required   Prepare the rent account for 20X1.

Solution

Rent Account

20X1	£	20X1	£
1 Jan. Balance b/d	450	31 Dec. Transfer to	
April Cash	1,000	P&L account	1,950
October Cash	1,000	31 Dec. Balance c/d	500
	2,450		2,450
20X2			
1 Jan. Balance b/d	500		

The balance brought down at the start of the year is half of the payment of £900 made in October 20X0 and covers January, February and March 20X1. The balance of £500 carried down at the end of 20X1 is an asset since it pays in advance for the first three months of 20X2 and will appear as a current asset in the balance sheet at 31 December 20X1. The transfer to the profit and loss account is found as a balancing figure once all the other entries have been made. The balance brought down on 1 January 20X2 will be charged against profit as an expense in 20X2, even though the payment was made in 20X1.

At the beginning of 20X1 Joe had a prepayment for advertising in his balance sheet amounting to £500. During the year an additional £1,600 was spent. A final payment in December amounting to £1,500 included a prepayment of £350 for advertising booked for 20X2.

Prepare the advertising account to reflect the information given above and calculate the figure that will be transferred to the profit and loss account.

ACTIVITY 7.6

Required

Accruals

The entries in the accounts to record an accrual are:

Account debited	*Account credited*	*With*
Expense	Accrual	Value of accrual

The accrual increases the expense figure charged in the profit and loss account (debit) and is included as a current liability in the balance sheet (credit). In practice, the accrual may be carried down in the expense account to which it relates. This is shown in Example 7.7.

Gelco makes up its accounts to 31 December, and made the following cash payments in respect of electricity:

Year	Month	Payment
		£
20X0	October	400
20X1	January	600
20X1	April	630
20X1	July	400
20X1	October	500
20X2	January	750

The payments are for electricity consumed during the three months immediately prior to the months in which they are made.

Record the above transactions in the company's electricity account for 20X1 and 20X2.

EXAMPLE 7.7

Required

Solution

Electricity Account

20X1		£	20X1		£
			1 Jan. Balance b/d		600
Jan. Cash		600	31 Dec. P&L account		2,280
April Cash		630			
July Cash		400			
Oct. Cash		500			
31 Dec Balance c/d		750			
		2,880			2,880
20X2			20X2		
Jan. Cash		750	1 Jan. Balance b/d		750

The credit balance of £600 brought down would have appeared in the balance sheet at
31 December 20X0 as a liability and relates to the electricity consumed in the last three months
of 20X0. It can be seen that it is cancelled by the actual cash payment made in January
20X1 since at that point the balance on the account is zero. The same reasoning relates to
the £750 carried down at the end of 20X1.

ACTIVITY 7.7   At the year end, Hannah & Co have not yet received an electricity bill for the final quarter of
the year. The amount of money they paid for the first three quarters is £1,550 and the estimate for the last quarter, based on last year's bill, is £400. The accrual at the beginning of
the year amounted to £350.

Required   Enter the above details in the electricity account and balance off the account.

Readers should now attempt Question 7.5 at the end of this chapter.

BAD DEBTS

When a company makes sales on credit there is a possibility that some customers
will not be able to pay their debts, with the result that bad debts are suffered.
Although known bad debts may be written off during the year, it is usual to review
carefully the list of debtors outstanding when the annual accounts are prepared
and write off any additional bad debts at the year end. The fact that a debt is likely
to prove bad becomes apparent when a great deal of time has elapsed since the
goods were supplied and no cash has been received despite repeated efforts to
collect the amount outstanding. This emphasizes the importance of monitoring
debtors on a routine basis so that, when the terms for payment are exceeded,
further supplies can be stopped; such action encourages the customer to pay the
amount owed and also minimizes the loss if the debt should prove to be bad.
When it becomes apparent that the full amount of the debt will not be received
from the debtor, it is necessary to remove the value of the irrecoverable debt from
the total debtors account and record the loss. The double entry to achieve this is:

Account debited	Account credited	With
Bad debts	Debtors control	Value of bad debt

The amount is also credited to the individual personal account of the debtor in the sales ledger. The balance on the bad debts account appears as a debit balance in the trial balance, and is written off to the profit and loss account when the annual accounts are prepared since it represents the loss of an asset and, therefore, is an expense.

In addition, a company may know, from experience, that a consistent proportion of the debts outstanding at the balance sheet date will prove to be bad, although it is not possible to tell in advance which specific debts will remain unpaid. The most prudent course of action to take in these circumstances, is to make an allowance for the likely bad debts contained in the value of debtors outstanding at the year end by the introduction of a provision for doubtful debts. When the amount of the provision has been determined, the provision is created by a debit to the doubtful debts account with the corresponding credit to a provision for doubtful debts account; this credit balance is offset against the value of debtors in the balance sheet to show the net amount that is expected to be collected. The fact that this provision is general, or not related to any particular debtor, means that no consequential adjustments are made in the debtor's individual sales ledger personal accounts.

Once a provision has been created, it appears as a credit balance in the trial balance prepared at the end of the period. In subsequent periods it is necessary only to account for the increase or decrease in the provision. The provision required is likely to change from year to year as the amount of debtors at the end of each accounting period is not a consistent balance. The balance in the provision accounts is therefore based on the amount of debt outstanding at the end of any particular year. The double entry to record adjustments for doubtful debts is:

Account debited	Account credited	With
Doubtful debts in the P&L account	Doubtful debt provision in the balance sheet	Increase in the provision
or		
Doubtful debt provision in the balance sheet	Doubtful debts in the P&L account	Decrease in the provision

---

The following balances appeared in the books of Fifth at the end of 20X1:   EXAMPLE 7.8

	Debit	Credit
	£	£
Bad debts written off during 20X1	950	
Provision for doubtful debts brought forward		900
Debtors control account	125,000	

It is decided, after a review of the debtors balances at the end of the year, to write off a further £1,000 of bad debts and create a provision of 1 per cent of the value of the remainder for doubtful debts.

Required

Write up the T accounts to deal with these matters and show the appropriate extracts from the profit and loss account and balance sheet.

Solution

Bad Debts Account

		£		£
20X1	Debtors	950	31 Dec.20X1 Profit and loss	1,950
31 Dec. 20X1	Debtors	1,000		
		1,950		1,950

Debtors Control Account

		£		£
31 Dec. 20X1	Balance	125,000	31 Dec. 20X1 Bad debts	1,000
			31 Dec. 20X1 Balance c/d	124,000
		125,000		125,000

Provision for Doubtful Debts Account

	£		£
31 Dec. 20X1 Balance c/d	1,240*	31 Dec. 20X1 Balance b/d	900
		31 Dec. 20X1 Doubtful debts	340
	1,240		1,240

Note *1 % of £124,000 = £1,240.

Doubtful Debts Account

		£		£
31 Dec. 20X1	Provision for doubtful debts	340	31 Dec. 20X1 Profit and loss	340

Profit and loss account (extract)

	£		£
Bad debts	1,950		
Doubtful debts	340		
			2,290

Balance sheet (extract)

	£	£
Debtors	124,000	
Less: Provision for		
doubtful debts	1,240	
		122,760

Notes 1 The bad debts of £950 have already been written off the value of debtors and so no further adjustment to the debtors control account is required in respect of this loss.

2 All bad debts arising during 20X1 have been written off against profit. It is therefore necessary only to increase the provision to the revised value, that is, by £340 to £1,240. In some cases the review of debtor balances results in a reduction of the provision and hence a credit to the profit and loss account.

ACTIVITY 7.8

At the beginning of the 20X1 PM has balances of £28,000 on its debtors control account and £1,400 on its provision for bad debts account. During 20X1 the company makes credit sales of £40,000, receives cash of £25,000 and receives confirmation of the liquidation of a customer who owes them £5,000. The latter amount will have to be written off. As a result of the bad debt, the company decides to increase its provision for bad debts to 7% of the closing debtor figure.

Required

Write up the T accounts to deal with the above information and show the appropriate extracts from the profit and loss account and balance sheet.

Readers should now work through Question 7.6 at the end of the chapter, which tests the book entries related to bad debts, and Question 7.7, which revises the preparation of final accounts from the trial balance with some additional adjustments.

THE ADJUSTED TRIAL BALANCE

The adjustments made to the trial balance when the trading and profit and loss account is prepared must be carried out in a systematic manner that complies with double entry procedures. Example 7.9 shows how this can be done.

EXAMPLE 7.9

The following trial balance was extracted from the books of T. Jones on 31 December 20X5:

	£	£
Sales		100,000
Purchases	50,000	
Stock – 1 January	10,000	

Rent	5,000
Wages	12,000
Electricity	1,500
Debtors	9,000
Trade creditors	8,000
Cash	1,000
Fixed assets at cost	34,000
Accumulated depreciaion – I January	13,000
Other expenses	6,000
Capital – I January	17,000
Drawings	9,500
	138,000 138,000

The following additional information is provided:

1 Goods that cost £1,000 were received during 20X5 and were included in closing stock. No invoice was included in purchases for them in 20X5.
2 Rent of £500 is prepaid.
3 Electricity of £350 is accrued.
4 The depreciation charge for the year is £6,000.
5 Jones took stock for his own use that cost £450. No entry was made in the books in respect of this.
6 The closing stock is £12,000.
7 Bad debts of £150 are to be written off.
8 A provision for doubtful debts of £100 is to be created.

Required

(a) Prepare the adjusted trial balance of T. Jones as at 31 December 20X5.
(b) Prepare the trading and profit and loss account of T. Jones for the year to 31 December 20X5 and the balance sheet as at that date.

Solution

(a) **Adjusted trial balance**

	Original trial balance at 31 Dec. 20X5		Adjustments		Trading and profit and loss account		Balance sheet	
	£ Dr.	£ Cr.	£ Dr.	£ Cr.	£ Dr.	£ Cr.	£ Dr.	£ Cr.
Sales		100,000				100,000		
Purchases	50,000		1,000 (1)	450 (5)	50,550			
Stock	10,000		12,000 (6)	12,000 (6)	10,000	12,000	12,000	
Rent	5,000			500 (2)	4,500			
Wages	12,000				12,000			
Electricity	1,500		350 (3)		1,850			
Debtors	9,000			150 (7)			8,850	
Creditors		8,000		1,000 (1)				9,000

	Original trial balance at 31 Dec. 20X5		Adjustments		Trading and profit and loss account		Balance sheet	
	£ Dr.	£ Cr.	£ Dr.	£ Cr.	£ Dr.	£ Cr.	£ Dr.	£ Cr.
Cash	1,000						1,000	
Fixed assets								
at cost	34,000						34,000	
Accumulated								
depreciation								
1 January		13,000		6,000 (4)				19,000
Other								
expenses	6,000				6,000			
Capital								
1 January		17,000						17,000
Drawings	9,500		450 (5)				9,950	
Accruals				350 (3)				350
Prepayments			500 (2)				500	
Depreciation								
charge			6,000 (4)		6,000			
Bad and								
doubtful debts			100 (8) 150 (7)			250		
Provision for								
doubtful								
debts				100 (8)				100
	138,000	138,000	20,550	20,550	91,150	112,000		45,450
						−91,150		20,850
							20,850 66,300	66,300

Notes 1 The adjustment columns show the debit and credit entries needed to give effect to the additional information. The number in brackets by such figures refers to the note in the question on which it is based.

2 The opening balance of each line is taken, adjusted and then entered in the final trial balance.

3 The fact that the two adjustment columns have the same total shows that the double entry rules have been complied with.

4 The final trial balance is separated into the trading and profit and loss account and the balance sheet. This is to aid the preparation of the final accounts. The proof of the trial balance in this format is that each section has an equal, but opposite, difference. This is the profit figure.

5 The accrual of £1,000 for the goods received but not invoiced at the year end represents a trade creditor and so is added to the existing balance of £8,000.

(b) **Trading and profit and loss account, year to 31 December 20X5**

	£	£
Sales		100,000
Opening stock	10,000	
Purchases	50,550	
Closing stock	(12,000)	
Cost of goods sold		48,550
Gross profit		51,450
Rent	4,500	
Wages	12,000	
Electricity	1,850	
Other expenses	6,000	
Depreciation	6,000	
Bad and doubtful debts	250	
		30,600
Net profit		20,850

Balance sheet at 31 December 20X5

	£	£	£
Fixed assets			
Fixed assets at cost			34,000
Less: Accumulated depreciation			19,000
			15,000
Current assets			
Stock		12,000	
Debtors	8,850		
Less: Provision for doubtful debts	100		
		8,750	
Prepayment		500	
Cash		1,000	
		22,250	
Current liabilities			
Creditors	9,000		
Accruals	350		
		9,350	
Working capital			12,900
			27,900
Capital			
Balance at 1 January			17,000
Profit for year			20,850
			37,850
Less: Drawings			9,950
			27,900

An adjusted trial balance, as used in Example 7.9, should be completed for inclusion in a set of permanent working papers when final accounts are prepared in practice. In examinations it is often too time-consuming to prepare this but, with practice, this process can be avoided. The important requirement is that students should adopt a systematic approach so as to ensure that all necessary adjustments are properly made. One useful technique is to note the double entry effects of all the adjustments to the trial balance on the question paper. The adjusted balances are then used to prepare the final accounts. This approach is now shown in Example 7.10, which uses the data given in Example 7.9 for T. Jones. The notes on the trial balance, which would in practice be made by hand, are shown in italics, and the final accounts include notes on how the figures have been calculated.

The following trial balance was extracted from the books of T. Jones on 31 December 20X5   **EXAMPLE 7.10**
and shows, in italics, the adjustments needed to prepare the final accounts:

	£			£	
Sales				100,000	
Purchases	50,000	*+ 1,000*	*– 450*		
Stock – 1 January	10,000				
Rent	5,000	*– 500*			
Wages	12,000				
Electricity	1,500	*+ 350*			
Debtors	9,000	*– 150*			
Trade creditors				8,000	*+ 1,000*
Cash	1,000				
Fixed assets at cost	34,000				
Accumulated depreciation –					
1 January				13,000	*+ 6,000*
Other expenses	6,000				
Capital – 1 January				17,000	
Drawings	9,500	*+ 450*			
	138,000			138,000	
Prepayments	*500*				
Accruals				*350*	
Depreciation	*6,000*				
Bad debts	*150*				
Doubtful debt provision	*100*			*100*	

The additional information on which the adjustments (in italics) are based is given in Example 7.9.

Care must be taken to include workings with the answer submitted to ensure that the examiner understands how the figures were derived. In this example, the workings are given in brackets on the face of the accounts:

Trading and profit and loss account, year to 31 December 20X5

	£	£
Sales		100,000
Opening stock	10,000	
Purchases (50,000 + 1,000 − 450)	50,550	
Closing stock	(12,000)	
Cost of goods sold		48,550
Gross profit		51,450
Rent (5,000 − 500)	4,500	
Wages	12,000	
Electricity (1,500 + 350)	1,850	
Other expenses	6,000	
Depreciation	6,000	
Bad and doubtful debts (100 + 150)	250	
		30,600
Net profit		20,850

Balance sheet at 31 December 20X5

	£	£	£
Fixed assets			
Fixed assets at cost			34,000
Less: Accumulated depreciation			
(13,000 + 6,000)			19,000
			15,000
Current assets			
Stock		12,000	
Debtors (9,000 − 150)	8,850		
Less: Provision for doubtful debts	100		
		8,750	
Prepayment		500	
Cash		1,000	
		22,250	
Current liabilities			
Creditors (8,000 + 1,000)	9,000		
Accruals	350		
		9,350	
Working capital			12,900
			27,900
Capital			
Balance at 1 January			17,000
Profit for year			20,850
			37,850
Less: Drawings (9,500 + 450)			9,950
			27,900

The following trial balance was extracted from the books of Trotters & Co, a retail business, as at 31 December 20X1:

ACTIVITY 7.9

	£	£
Freehold land and buildings (at cost)	220,000	
Accumulated depreciation on buildings (at 1 Jan 20X1)		26,400
Motor vehicles (at cost)	70,000	
Accumulated depreciation on vehicles (at 1 Jan 20X1)		37,500
Debtors and creditors	62,000	48,000
Sales		500,000
Purchases	350,000	
Stock (at 1 Jan 20X1)	40,000	
Advertising	16,000	
General expenses	10,000	
Wages	40,000	
Bad debts written off	13,000	
Provision for doubtful debts (at 1 Jan 20X1)		1,500
Drawings	36,000	
Bank	50,000	
Capital		293,600
	907,000	907,000

You are given the following additional information:

1 Wages outstanding at 30 December 20X1 amount to £1,000.
2 The provision for doubtful debts should be adjusted to represent 6% of debtors.
3 Stock at 31 December 20X1 amounted to £50,000.
4 Advertising includes a prepayment of £2,000.
5 A debtor returned goods to the value of £20,000. This has not been accounted for in the above figures.
6 During the year a vehicle, which had cost £20,000 and had a written down value of £12,000, was sold for £15,000. No entries have been made for this transaction.
7 Depreciation should be charged as follows: Buildings £4,400; Vehicles £10,000.

A trading, profit and loss account for the period ending 31 December 20X1 and a balance sheet as at that date.

Required

Errors may come to light during the examination of the books that takes place when the periodic accounts are prepared. The correction of these errors must be made in accordance with the double entry techniques described in this chapter. This aspect of preparing final accounts is tested in Questions 7.8 and 7.9 at the end of this chapter, which readers should now attempt.

QUESTIONS   **7.1**   The following is the trial balance of Push, a sole trader, at 30 June 20X7:

	£	£
Capital		30,350
Sales		108,920
Purchases	72,190	
Drawings	12,350	
Debtors	7,350	
Creditors		6,220
Cash	1,710	
Stock	9,470	
Plant and machinery at cost	35,000	
Accumulated depreciation at 1 July 19X6		12,500
Rent	1,000	
Wages	14,330	
Other costs	4,590	
	157,990	157,990

Notes   1 The value of stock at 30 June 20X7 was £9,960.
2 The depreciation charge for the year to 30 June 20X7 was £3,000.

Required   Prepare the trading and profit and loss account of Push for the year to 30 June 20X7 and the balance sheet at that date.

7.2   Tip was established and started trading on 1 January 20X1 and draws up its accounts to 31 December each year. Its purchases and disposals of fixed assets over the subsequent three years were as follows:

Asset	Date of purchase	Cost	Date of disposal	Proceeds on disposal
		£		£
A	1 January 20X1	5,000	–	–
B	1 January 20X1	2,000	1 January 20X3	900
C	1 January 20X3	7,000	–	–

Required   Use this data to:

(a)   prepare the fixed assets at cost, accumulated depreciation and disposal of fixed assets accounts based on straight-line depreciation of 20 per cent per year for 20X1, 20X2 and 20X3; and

(b)   show the fixed asset extracts from the balance sheets at the end of each year.

7.3 Prepac Ltd prepared its accounts to 31 December. The following facts relate to 20X8:

	£
Balance on insurance account 1 January	450 (Dr.)
Balance on electricity account 1 January	300 (Cr.)
Balance on rates account 1 January	290 (Dr.)
Balance on gas account 1 January	600 (Cr.)
February – pay for electricity consumed during quarter to 31 January	900
March – pay for gas consumed during quarter to 28 February	850
– pay rates for the half year to 30 September	780
May – pay for electricity consumed during quarter to 30 April	820
June – pay for gas consumed during quarter to 31 May	840
– pay insurance for the year to 30 June 20X9	1,020
August – pay for electricity consumed during quarter to 31 July	690
September – pay for gas consumed during quarter to 31 August	610
– pay rates for 6 months to 31 March 20X9	780
November – pay for electricity consumed during quarter to 31 October	550
December – pay for gas consumed during quarter to 30 November	960
Electricity consumed in November and December 20X8	390
Gas consumed in December 20X8	680

Prepare the insurance account, electricity account, rates account and gas account for 20X8 as they appear in the books of Prepac Ltd and show clearly in each case the transfer to profit and loss account.

Required

7.4 At 31 December 20X3 the trial balance of Damp Ltd contained the following balances in repect of motor vehicles:

	Debit	Credit
	£	£
Motor vehicles at cost	127,000	
Accumulated depreciation at 1 January 20X3		76,000
Disposal of motor vehicles		1,600

You ascertain that during 20X3 the following occurred:

1 A delivery van, which was fully depreciated and had cost £2,000, was scrapped. No proceeds were received.

2 A car that cost £5,000, on which accumulated depreciation was £3,000, had been traded in for a new model with a full cost of £8,000. A trade-in allowance of £1,500 was received, and only the net cost of the new car, £6,500, has been entered in the books.

3 A car that cost £4,000 and had a written-down value of £1,250 was sold for £1,600 (credited to the disposals account).

4 A delivery van was sold for £2,500. This vehicle had cost £10,000 and a loss of £750 was made on its sale. The proceeds have been credited to the fixed asset account.

5 The depreciation charge for the year is £25,000.

Required

(a) Prepare the motor vehicles at cost account, motor vehicles accumulated depreciation account and disposal of motor vehicles account for 20X3 to show the effect of the above information and the transfer to the profit and loss account.

(b) Show the extract for motor vehicles that would appear in the company's balance sheet at 31 December 20X3.

7.5 At 31 December 20X0 the following balances were shown in the books of E. Rider Ltd:

	£
Sales control account	156,937 (Dr.)
Provision for doubtful debts	2,600 (Cr.)
Bad debts	750 (Dr.)

The list of debtors contained balances that were considered to be bad or doubtful as indicated in the 'remarks' column of the schedule below:

Schedule of bad and doubtful debts, 31 December 20X0

Customer	Account number	Account balance	Remarks
B. Clyde	C6	£560	Irrecoverable
S. Wars	W2	£680	In liquidation. At least 50p in the £ is anticipated, but full recovery is a possibility
M. Poppins	P4	£227	Irrecoverable
M. Express	E9	£390	This debt is doubtful to the extent of 20%
M. Ash	A1	£240	A provision of £80 is to be made against this debt

The general provision for doubtful debts in respect of debts other than those dealt with individually above is to be raised to £3,750.

Required

(a) Prepare the sales ledger control account, bad debts account, doubtful debts account and provision for doubtful debts account as they appear after recording the above transactions.

(b) Show the balance sheet extract for debtors at 31 December 20X0.

7.6 At 31 December 19X7 the totals of the ledger balances of Theta Limited, were as follows:

		£
Sales	debit	384,600
	credit	2,900
Purchases	debit	1,860
	credit	222,230

After reviewing these balances in preparing the financial statements for the year ended 31 December 19X7, a number of adjustments are necessary:

(i) A contra settlement had been agreed during the year offsetting an amount due from Zeta Limited in the sales ledger of £1,080 against the balance due to that company in the purchase ledger. No entry had been made for this contra.

(ii) The following amounts due from sales ledger customers are to be written off:

Customer	£
P	840
Q	120
R	360
S	2,090
T	180

(iii) The provision for doubtful debts, which stood at £3,060 after the debts in (ii) above had been written off, is to be increased to £5,200.

(iv) During the year £200 cash received from Tau Limited had mistakenly been entered into the account of Vau Limited in the sales ledger.

Further information:

The purchase ledger balances included £56,000 relating to a purchase in September 19X7 on extended credit terms.

The £56,000 balance is due to be cleared by payments in four equal instalments at six-monthly intervals as follows:

	£
31 March 1998	14,000
30 September 1998	14,000
31 March 1999	14,000
30 September 1999	14,000

No ledger control accounts are kept by Theta Limited.

(a) Prepare journal entries to give effect to adjustments (i)–(iv). (4 marks)

(b) Calculate the amounts which should appear under the various headings in the company's published balance sheet as at 31 December 19X7 for debtors and creditors, assuming that there are no other items for inclusion apart from those stated above. (6 marks)

(ACCA, Paper 1, The Accounting Framework, June 1998) (modified)

7.7 During the preparation of the accounts from the books of S. Top, a sole trader, for the year to 30 June 20X7, the following items were found:

1 Included in the repairs to machinery account was £2,750, which was paid on 29 June 20X7 and was for the purchase of a new lathe.

2 Manufacturing wages account included £350 paid to an employee for time spent repairing a machine.

3 A debt of £1,290 due from J. Jones was included in debtors, but in fact was irrecoverable.

4 The rates on S. Top's private house of £200 had been paid by the business and charged to the rates account.

5 Goods worth £1,500 had been received into stock on 30 June and included in the value of stock for accounts purposes. No entry had been made in the books to record this purchase.

6 An old machine that had cost £1,000 and was fully depreciated had been scrapped during the year. This fact had not been recorded in the books.

7 S. Top had taken stock to the value of £150 for his own use during the year. No entry appeared in the books in respect of this usage.

8 A payment of £125 for delivery of goods to customers had been entered in the purchases account.

Required

(a) Prepare the journal entries to record the adjustments.

(b) Prepare a statement to show the effect of these adjustments on the profit for the year to 30 June 20X7.

SOLUTIONS
TO
ACTIVITIES

Solution to
Activity 7.1

	£
Opening stock	620,000
Add: Purchases	3,150,000
	3,770,000
Less: Closing stock	(530,000)
Cost of sales	3,240,000

Finis

Trading and profit and loss account,

year ending 31 December 20X4

Solution to
Activity 7.2

	£	£	£
Sales			155,000
Less: Returns inwards			(700)
			154,300
Opening stock		18,000	
Purchases	90,000		
Less: Returns outwards	(800)		
		89,200	
		107,200	
Less: Closing stock		(20,000)	
Cost of goods sold			87,200
Gross profit			67,100
Discount received			1,000
			68,100
Wages		19,000	
Rent		6,000	
Delivery costs		3,000	
Heat and light		5,000	
Sundry expenses		3,700	
Advertising		2,000	
			(38,700)
Net profit			29,400

Finis

Balance sheet

as at 31 December 20X4

	£	£
Fixed assets		
Freehold premises		38,000
Current assets		
Stock	20,000	
Debtors	17,000	
Cash	5,000	
	42,000	
Current liabilities		
Creditors	(8,000)	34,000
		72,000

Capital

At 1 January 20X4	57,600
Profit for 20X4	29,400
	87,000
Drawings	(15,000)
	72,000

Solution to
Activity 7.3

(a)   **Plant and Machinery Account**

	£		£
1 Jan 20X0			
Balance b/d	650,000	31 Dec 20X6	
20X6 Acquisitions	100,000	Balance c/d	750,000
	750,000		750,000
1 Jan 20X7			
Balance b/d	750,000		

Accumulated Depreciation Account – Plant and Machinery

	£		£
31 Dec 20X0		31 Dec 20X0	
Balance c/d	65,000	Depreciation	65,000
	65,000		65,000
		1 Jan 20X1	
		2 Balance b/d	65,000
31 Dec 20X1		31 Dec 20X1	
Balance c/d	130,000	Depreciation	65,000
	130,000		130,000
		1 Jan 20X2	130,000
		Balance b/d	
31 Dec 20X2		31 Dec 20X2	
Balance c/d	195,000	Depreciation	65,000
	195,000		195,000
		1 Jan 20X3	
		2 Balance b/d	195,000
31 Dec 20X3		31 Dec 20X3	
Balance c/d	270,000	Depreciation	75,000
	270,000		270,000
		1 Jan 20X4	
		Balance b/d	270,000

Depreciation Charge Account – Machinery

	£			£
31 Dec 20X0		Transfer to		
Accum dep'n	65,000	P&L account		65,000
	65,000			65,000
31 Dec 20X1		Transfer to		
Accum dep'n	65,000	P&L Account		65,000
	65,000			65,000
31 Dec 20X2		Transfer to		
Accum dep'n	65,000	P&L account		65,000
	65,000			65,000
31 Dec 20X3		Transfer to		
Accum dep'n	75,000	P&L account		75,000
	75,000			75,000

(b) **Balance sheet (extract), 31 December 20X1**

	£
Plant and machinery at cost	750,000
Less: Accumulated depreciation	(270,000)
	480,000

Fixed Assets Account

Solution to Activity 7.4

	£		£
1 Jan 20X0 Balance b/d	2,000,000	31 Dec 20X1 Disposal	800,000
31 Dec 20X1 Acquisition	750,000	31 Dec 20X1 Balance c/d	1,950,000
	2,750,000		2,750,000
1 Jan 20X7 Balance b/d	1,950,000		

Accumulated Depreciation Account – Fixed Assets

	£		£
31 Dec 20X0 Disposal	200,000	1 Jan 20X0 Balance b/d	500,000
31 Dec 20X0 Balance c/d	456,000	31 Dec 20X0 Depreciation*	156,000
	656,000		656,000
		1 Jan 20X1 Balance b/d	456,000

Note $*2,000,000 - 800,000 + 750,000 \times 8\% = 156,000$

Depreciation Charge Account

	£		£
31 Dec 20X1		31 Dec 20X1	
Accum dep'n	156,000	Transfer to P&L a/c	156,000
	156,000		156,000

Disposal of Fixed Assets Account

	£		£
31 Dec 20X1		31 Dec 20X1	
Fixed asset	800,000	Accum dep'n	200,000
		31 Dec 20X1 Bank	500,000
		31 Dec 20X1	
		Loss on sale*	100,000
	800,000		800,000

Note   *A loss on sale has been suffered on this occasion.

Solution to Activity 7.5

8,000 (proceeds) − (Cost − 40,000 (Accumulated depreciation))

$$= (£2,000) \quad \text{(loss)}$$
$$\text{Cost} = 40,000 + 8,000 + 2,000$$
$$= £50,000$$

Check: 8,000 − (50,000 − 40,000) = (£2,000)

Solution to Activity 7.6

Advertising Account

	£		£
1 Jan 20X1		31 Dec 20X1 Transfer to	
Balance b/d	500	P&L account	3,250
30 June 20X1 Bank	1,600		
31 Dec 20X1 Bank	1,500	31 Dec 20X1 Balance c/d	350
	3,600		3,600
1 Jan 20X2 Balance b/d	350		

Solution to Activity 7.7

Electricity Account

	£		£
Bank	1,550	Balance b/d	350
Balance c/d	400	Transfer to P&L account	1,600
	1,950		1,950
		Balance b/d	400

Debtors Control Account

Solution to
Activiity 7.8

	£		£
Balance b/d	28,000	Bank	25,000
Sales	40,000	Bad debt	5,000
		Balance c/d	38,000
	68,000		68,000
Balance b/d	38,000		

Bad Debts Account

	£		£
Debtors control account	5,000	Transfer to P&L account	5,000
	5,000		5,000

Provision for Doubtful Debts Account

	£		£
		Balance b/d	1,400
Balance c/d	2,660	Doubtful debts	1,260
	2,660		2,660
		Balance b/d	2,660

Doubtful Debts Account

	£		£
Provision for doubtful debts	1,260	Transfer to P&L account	1,260
	1,260		1,260

Profit and Loss Account (extract)

	£	£
Bad debts	5,000	
Provision for bad debts	1,260	
		6,260

Balance Sheet (extract)

	£	£
Debtors	38,000	
Less: Provision for doubtful debts	(1,260)	36,740

Solution to
Activity 7.9

Trotters & Co
Trading, profit and loss account
period ending 31 December 20X1

	£	£
Sales		500,000
Less: Returns inwards (sales returns)		(20,000)
		480,000
Opening stock	40,000	
Purchases	350,000	
	390,000	
Less: Closing stock	(50,000)	
Cost of goods sold		(340,000)
Gross profit		140,000
Additional income		
Profit on sale of vehicle (W1)		3,000
		143,000
Expenditure		
Advertising(16,000 – 2,000)	14,000	
General expenses	10,000	
Wages (40,000 + 1,000)	41,000	
Bad debts written off	13,000	
Depreciation of buildings	4,400	
Depreciation of vehicles	10,000	
Increase in doubtful debt provision (W2)	1,020	
		(93,420)
Net profit		49,580

Trotters & Co
Balance Sheet
as at 31 December 20X1

	£	£	£
Fixed Assets			
Freehold land and buildings (at cost)		220,000	
Less: Accumulated depreciation (W3)		(30,800)	
			189,200
Vehicles (at cost) (W4)		50,000	
Less: Accumulated depreciation (W5)		(39,500)	
			10,500
			199,700

Current Assets

Stock		50,000	
Debtors	42,000		
Less: Provision for doubtful debts (W2)	(2,520)		
		39,480	
Prepayment		2,000	
Bank (50,000 + 15,000)		65,000	
		156,480	
Less: Current Liabilities			
Creditors	48,000		
Accruals	1,000		
		(49,000)	
Working capital			107,480
Net assets			307,180
Financed by			
Capital			293,600
Add: Profit		49,580	
Less: Drawings		(36,000)	
			13,580
			307,180

Workings

W1	Sale proceeds	15,000	
	Net book value	(12,000)	
	Profit	3,000	
W2	Debtors	62,000	
	Goods returned	(20,000)	
		42,000	
	Provision for doubtful debts	6%	
	New provision	2,520	
	Current provision	(1,500)	
	Increase in provision	1,020	
W3	Accumulated depreciation b/f	26,400	
	Add: Charge for year	4,400	
		30,800	

W4	Vehicles at cost	70,000
	Less: Disposal	(20,000)
		50,000
W5	Accumulated depreciation b/f	37,500
	Less: Depreciation on disposal	
	(20,000 – 12,000)	(8,000)
		29,500
	Add: Charge for year	10,000
		39,500

8 Asset valuation, profit measurement and the underlying accounting concepts

The objectives of this chapter are to:

- explain the effect of different methods of asset valuation on the level of reported profit;
- distinguish between capital expenditure and revenue expenditure;
- identify and distinguish between different methods of depreciation;
- distinguish between tangible and intangible assets;
- explain the difference between purchased and non-purchased goodwill;
- distinguish between different methods of accounting for purchased goodwill;
- provide an understanding of the methods available for valuing non-purchased goodwill;
- provide an appreciation of the nature of research and development expenditure and its treatment in company accounts;
- explain the effect of the 'lower of cost and net realizable value' rule on the valuation of stock;
- show how to value stock on the marginal cost basis and total cost basis;
- distinguish between FIFO, LIFO and AVCO as methods of matching purchases with production or sales;
- outline the operation of a system of perpetual inventory; and
- introduce the main accounting concepts and indicate the effect of their application on accounting reports.

ASSET VALUATION AND PROFIT MEASUREMENT

The level of profit reported in the accounts depends on the amounts at which assets, listed in the balance sheet, are valued. Any error made when valuing assets has a corresponding effect on the level of reported profit and, therefore, reduces its usefulness as a basis for assessing performance. For example, if closing stock is overvalued by £1,000, the figure for cost of goods sold is understated and reported profit is overstated by this amount. Great care should therefore be taken when calculating asset values for inclusion in the accounts. The procedures that are followed, in practice, are examined below.

TANGIBLE FIXED ASSETS

Fixed assets are reported in the balance sheet at cost less accumulated depreciation. The identification of cost and the calculation of the depreciation charge are considered below.

Distinguishing capital expenditure from revenue expenditure

The expenditure incurred by a business must be accounted for as either capital expenditure or revenue expenditure. The basic test applied to distinguish between the two types of expenditure is the effect that the outlay has on the company's long-term ability to earn profits. If it is enhanced, the expenditure is capital; if the expenditure merely enables the business to continue to operate at its existing level, it is revenue. The distinction is of crucial importance because it affects how the expenditure is reported in the profit and loss account and balance sheet. Capital expenditure on fixed assets is recorded in the balance sheet at cost, and is subsequently charged against revenue over the period of years that benefit from the use of the asset. Revenue expenditure, on the other hand, is normally charged in the profit and loss account against revenue arising during the period when the cost is incurred. A proper classification is important, otherwise the reported balances for profit and net assets will be incorrectly stated and wrong conclusions may be reached regarding the performance and position of the firm. The effects of incorrect allocations are shown in Figure 8.1.

	Effect on	
	Profit	*Net Assets*
Capital expenditure wrongly allocated to revenue	Understated	Understated
Revenue expenditure wrongly allocated to capital	Overstated	Overstated

FIGURE 8.1   Effect of wrongly allocating expenditure to capital or revenue

Most items of expenditure are easily classified as capital or revenue, but there are some 'grey areas' where judgement is needed to help make a proper allocation in the light of all the available facts. The cost of fixed assets acquired or built by the firm itself, to form the basis for business activity, is clearly capital expenditure. Difficulties arise in connection with expenditure incidental to the acquisition of the fixed asset and expenditure on fixed assets currently in use. The following rules should be followed to achieve a proper allocation:

1   Expenditure incurred in getting a new fixed asset ready for business use is a capital expense. This includes, for example, any transportation costs, import duties and solicitors' fees. In addition, costs incurred in modifying existing premises to accommodate a new fixed asset should also be capitalized (i.e. put on the balance sheet).
2   Expenditure on an existing fixed asset that enhances its value to the business, e.g. by increasing its capacity, effectiveness or useful life, should be capitalized.
3   Expenditure on an existing fixed asset intended to make good wear and tear and keep it in satisfactory working order is a revenue expense. Where the expenditure contains an element of improvement, as well as repair, an apportionment between capital expenditure and revenue expenditure must be made.

Indicate for each of the following items whether the expenditure is of a capital or revenue   EXAMPLE 8.1
nature:

1   Legal expenses incurred when acquiring a new building.
2   Giving the factory a fresh coat of paint.
3   Replacing 200 tiles on a roof damaged by a gale.
4   Expenditure incurred demolishing part of a wall to make room for a recently purchased
    machine.
5   Replacing wooden office windows by double-glazed metal windows.
6   Installing a system of ventilation in the factory.

1   *Capital.* This is part of the cost of acquiring the new asset.   Solution
2   *Revenue.* This makes good wear and tear.
3   *Revenue.* This merely restores the roof to its pre-gale condition.
4   *Capital.* This is part of the cost of bringing the fixed asset into use.
5   *Part capital, part revenue.* The new windows should be more effective in eliminating
    draughts and making the office sound-proof
6   *Capital.* Working conditions and employee performance should improve.

Indicate for each of the following items whether it is capital or revenue expenditure: ACTIVITY 8.1

1   Repairs and maintenance of factory machinery.
2   Replacement parts for machinery.
3   Lubrication oil for machinery.
4   Import duties on the purchase of a new machine.
5   Delivery costs associated with the purchase.

Readers should now attempt Questions 8.1 and 8.2 at the end of this chapter.

Depreciation methods

Depreciation is charged in the accounts to reflect the fact that the business has
benefited from using fixed assets that, as a result, have declined in value. The pattern of benefit that arises differs from one type of fixed asset to another. For
example, some fixed assets produce a greater benefit in the early years of ownership, when the asset is more efficient, whereas others make a fairly steady contribution over their entire useful life. There are a number of different methods of
charging depreciation and management should choose the one that most closely
reflects the forecast pattern of benefits receivable.

Straight-line (equal instalment) method   Under this method the difference between original cost and ultimate disposal value is spread equally over the asset's estimated useful life. This method is described and illustrated in Chapter 4, and has been used in all the previous examples and questions requiring a charge to be calculated. The method assumes that each accounting period benefits to an equal extent from using the fixed asset, and the annual charge is calculated on the basis of the following formula:

$$\frac{\text{Original cost} - \text{Estimated disposal value}}{\text{Estimated useful life}}$$

The estimated useful life of the asset represents the length of time the business intends to use the asset and not the overall life of the asset. For example, a machine might have a total life of 10 years but if the company intends to use the machine for only 6 years, then it is depreciated over 6 years and not 10. An attraction of this method is that it is easy to apply once the initial estimates have been made and, for this reason, it is widely used in the UK.

EXAMPLE 8.2   On 1 January 20X1 a manufacturing company acquired a new lathe for £23,000. It is estimated to have a useful life of four years during which time it will produce 100,000 units of output: 50,000 units in 20X1; 10,000 units in 20X2; 10,000 units in 20X3; and 30,000 units in 20X4. The lathe is expected to be sold for £3,000 at the end of four years.

The annual straight-line charge is calculated as follows:

$$\text{Depreciation charge} = \frac{£23,000 - £3,000}{4}$$

$$= £5,000$$

ACTIVITY 8.2   A printing company purchased a new printing press at the beginning of 20X0. The cost of the asset was £45,000 and the manufacturer guarantees that it will last for 15 years. The company has estimated that it will keep the press for 10 years after which time it should have a scrap value of £4,000.

Required   Calculate the annual depreciation charge for the printing press.

Reducing (declining) balance method   This is the second most popular method. A depreciation rate is decided upon and then applied to the net book value (original cost less accumulated depreciation) of the asset brought forward at the beginning of each accounting period. The charge is highest in year 1 and then falls each year because the depreciation rate is applied to a reducing (or declining) balance. The rate is usually given in examinations but, where it is not provided, it may be calculated using the following formula.

$$\text{Depreciation rate} = \left(1 - \sqrt[n]{\frac{s}{c}}\right) \times 100\%$$

where n is the expected useful life, s is the expected scrap value and c is the original cost.

Apply this formula to the facts provided in Example 8.2.   **EXAMPLE 8.3**

$$\text{Depreciation rate} = \left(1 - \sqrt[4]{\frac{3,000}{23,000}}\right) \times 100\%$$ Solution

$$= 39.9\%$$

Depreciation charges for 20X1–20X4

	£
Original cost	23,000
20X1 depreciation charge (£23,000 × 39.9%)	(9,177)
Net book value at 31 December 20XI	13,823
20X2 depreciation charge (£13,823 × 39.9%)	(5,515)*
Net book value at 31 December 20X2	8,308
20X3 depreciation charge (£8,308 × 39.9%)	(3,315)*
Net book value at 31 December 20X3	4,993
20X4 depreciation charge (£4,993 × 39.9%)	(1,993)*
Net book value at 31 December 20X4	3,000

*As a rule, when rounding, round up all numbers greater than 0.5 and round down all numbers less than 0.5. Make any final rounding adjustment in the last year.

It should be noticed that the charge for 20X1 (£9,177) is over four times as high as the charge for 20X4 (£1,993). Clearly, the method is appropriate only when the bulk of the benefit arises early on. An argument sometimes put forward for this method (and the sum of the digits method, see below) is that repair and maintenance costs normally increase as a fixed asset becomes older and the reducing balance basis therefore helps to ensure that the total annual charge (depreciation plus maintenance) remains steady over the asset's useful life.

Taking the information given in Activity 8.2, calculate the depreciation charge and the net   **ACTIVITY 8.3**
book values for each of the 10 years using the reducing balance method.

Sum of the digits method   This method also produces larger charges in the early years, but the differences that occur are less dramatic than with the reducing balance method. Each year of the asset's life is represented by a digit which represents the number of years' life remaining at the beginning of the year. The earliest year, therefore, would be allocated the highest number and each subsequent year would be allocated a number which is one less than the previous number. For example, if you were considering an asset with a four-year life, year 1 would be allocated the digit 4, year 2 would be 3, year 3 would be 2 and year 4 would be 1. The depreciation for each year is calculated by applying the following formula:

$$\frac{\text{Original cost} - \text{Estimated disposal value}}{\text{Sum of the year's digits}} \times \begin{array}{l}\text{Number of years' life}\\ \text{remaining at the}\\ \text{beginning of the year}\end{array}$$

The sum of the digits is the total of all the numbers allocated to all the years. For example, for a six-year-old asset this would be:

$$6 + 5 + 4 + 3 + 2 + 1 = 21$$

A quick method of summing the digits is to use the following formula:

$$\frac{1}{2} n (n + 1)$$

where n is the number of years of the asset's life. Taking our example of 6 years:

$$\frac{6(6 + 1)}{2} = 21$$

EXAMPLE 8.4   Apply the formula to the facts provided in Example 8.2 and calculate the depreciation charge per year using the sum of the digits method.

Solution $$\text{Sum of the digits} = \frac{4(4+1)}{2} = 10$$

Depreciation charge:

20X1 $£20,000 \times \dfrac{4}{10} = £8,000$

20X2 $£20,000 \times \dfrac{3}{10} = £6,000$

20X3 $£20,000 \times \dfrac{2}{10} = £4,000$

20X4 $£20,000 \times \dfrac{1}{10} = £2,000$

Using the information provided in Activity 8.2, calculate the annual depreciation charges for the asset using the sum of the digits method.

ACTIVITY 8.4

The units of service method This method relates the charge to the extent the asset is used during an accounting period. For this purpose usage may be measured on the basis either of the number of units produced or the number of hours in service. The formula used to calculate the annual charge is as follows:

$$\frac{\text{Original cost} - \text{Estimated disposal value}}{\text{Total estimated number of units (hours)}} \times \begin{array}{c} \text{Number of units (hours)} \\ \text{in use} \end{array}$$

Applying the units of service method to the facts provided in Example 8.2, calculate the depreciation charge per year.

EXAMPLE 8.5

Depreciation charge:

Solution

20X1 $\dfrac{£20,000}{100,000} \times 50,000 = £10,000$

20X2 $\dfrac{£20,000}{100,000} \times 10,000 = £2,000$

20X3 $\dfrac{£20,000}{100,000} \times 10,000 = £2,000$

20X4 $\dfrac{£20,000}{100,000} \times 30,000 = £6,000$

This depreciation method is considered to be the most rational because it produces a variable charge that depends on the level of activity. The lathe is capable of producing 100,000 units, of which 50,000 are produced in 20X1. Half of the total benefit provided by the asset arises in 20X1 and half of its net cost to the business (£20,000 × $\frac{1}{2}$) should therefore be charged against revenue arising during that year. Only the units of service method produces this result. In the following year, 20X2, when 10,000 units are produced, one-tenth of the asset's net cost, i.e. £2,000, is charged against revenue. The disadvantage of this method is the difficulty of estimating the units of service that a fixed asset will provide, and it is not widely used.

ACTIVITY 8.5   At the beginning of year 1 a manufacturing company acquired a new moulding machine for £80,000. It is estimated to have a useful life of six years during which time its output will be:

Year		
	1	200,000 units
	2	150,000 units
	3	175,000 units
	4	200,000 units
	5	180,000 units
	6	190,000 units

The machine is expected to have a scrap value of £10,000.

Required   Calculate the annual depreciation for each of the six years using the units of service method.

Comparing the methods   The charges made under each of the four methods in Examples 8.2–8.5 are as follows:

	20X1	20X2	20X3	20X4	Total
	£	£	£	£	£
Straight-line	5,000	5,000	5,000	5,000	20,000
Reducing balance	9,177	5,515	3,315	1,993	20,000
Sum of the digits	8,000	6,000	4,000	2,000	20,000
Units of service	10,000	2,000	2,000	6,000	20,000

It can be seen that the pattern of charges differs a great deal depending on the method used. For example, the highest charge arises in 20X1 from using the units of service method, in 20X2 from using the sum of the digits method, in 20X3 from using the straight-line method and in 20X4 again from using the units of service method. Within particular years the difference is also marked. For example, in 20X1 the units of service method produces a charge that is twice as high as under the straight-line method. Looked at another way, reported profit for 20X1 is £5,000 more if the straight-line basis is used. This shows that great care should be taken when choosing the depreciation method as this can have a substantial effect on the level of reported profit. The choice is rarely easy, however, as the depreciation policy must be decided upon when the asset is acquired and management does not know, at that stage, the precise benefit that will arise in each future accounting period. The decision is, therefore, to some extent arbitrary and, if an error is made, profit will be either under- or overstated.

Readers should now attempt Question 8.3 at the end of this chapter.

Estimation errors

In addition to the difficulty of selecting the most appropriate method, there is the problem of making accurate estimates of the useful life of the fixed asset, measured in terms of years or output, and its disposal value at the end of that period. Care should be exercised when making these estimates as errors produce an incorrect charge for depreciation and a consequent under- or overstatement of profit.

A machine is purchased for £60,000 on 1 January 20X1. It is estimated that the machine will last for five years and then have a zero disposal value. Management believes that each accounting period will benefit equally from the use of the machine and the straight-line method of depreciation is therefore considered appropriate.

EXAMPLE 8.6

(a)   Calculate the depreciation charge to be made each year, 20X1–20X5.   **Required**

(b)   Assuming it turns out that all management's estimates are correct, except that it totally misjudges the second-hand demand for the machine, which eventually sells for £20,000, calculate the depreciation charge that *would* have been made each year if the disposal value had been accurately estimated.

(a)   Depreciation charge $= \dfrac{£60,000}{5} = £12,000$ **Solution**

(b)   Depreciation charge $= \dfrac{£60,000 - £20,000}{5} = £8,000$

Because the disposal value was wrongly estimated, the annual charge is overstated and profit is understated by £4,000 during each of the five years of ownership. This is balanced by crediting £20,000 to the profit and loss account when the fixed asset, by this time completely written off, is sold for that figure. Where the profit on sale of a fixed asset is abnormally large, as in this case, the amount should be separately disclosed in the accounts so that users do not assume that the highly favourable results are derived from normal business operations.

A machine is purchased for £180,000 in year 1. It is estimated to have a residual value of £20,000 at the end of its estimated useful life of 8 years. The depreciation policy of the company is to depreciate such machinery on a straight-line basis over its estimated useful life.

ACTIVITY 8.6

(a)   Calculate the depreciation charge and net book value each year on the basis of the information given above.   **Required**

(b)   Recalculate the depreciation charge and net book value each year on the assumption that the asset's life is only 5 years and the residual value is only £14,000.

INTANGIBLE FIXED ASSETS

Business assets may be classified as either tangible or intangible. Both categories of asset are valuable because they help the business to earn a profit. The most common examples of tangible assets are stock and fixed assets. The main types of intangible assets are goodwill and research and development (R&D) expenditure.

Goodwill

Goodwill arises as the result of business connections built up over a period of time. It was described as follows by Lord MacNaughton in *CIR v. Muller* (1901), AC 217:

> It is the benefit and advantage of the good name, reputation and connection of a business. It is the attractive force which brings in custom. It is the one thing which distinguishes an old established business from a new business at its first start.

Goodwill may be classified as 'purchased goodwill', which arises on the acquisition of an existing business, and 'non-purchased goodwill', which has been internally created but has no value because no transaction has taken place.

Purchased goodwill   This is calculated as the difference between the price paid for the business as a whole and the aggregate of the 'fair' (current) values of its various identifiable assets – both tangible and intangible.

EXAMPLE 8.7   Ted Anthony who had been in business for many years decided to retire and sold his business assets, other than cash and debtors, to William Jones for £30,000. The tangible assets transferred consisted of premises worth £20,000, machinery worth £3,500 and stocks valued at £2,500.

Required   Calculate the value of goodwill arising on the sale of Ted Anthony's business to William Jones.

Note   William Jones took over none of the creditors or other liabilities of Ted Anthony.

	£	£	Solution
Purchase price		30,000	
Less: Tangible assets acquired: Premises	20,000		
Machinery	3,500		
Stock	2,500		
		26,000	
Goodwill		4,000	

The total value of the tangible assets is £26,000 and we can therefore conclude that William Jones was willing to pay an extra £4,000 to cover the goodwill built up by Ted Anthony over the years.

In the above example, goodwill is the 'balancing' figure which results from comparing the agreed purchase price with the total value of the tangible assets acquired.

T Jones
Balance sheet
as at 31 December 20X5

ACTIVITY 8.7

	£	£	£
Fixed assets			
Fixed asset at cost			34,000
Less: Accumulated depreciation			− 19,000
			15,000
Current assets			
Stock		12,000	
Debtors	8,850		
Less: Provision for doubtful debts	− 100		
		8,750	
Prepayment		500	
Cash		1,000	
		22,250	
Current liabilities			
Creditors	9,000		
Accruals	350		
		− 9,350	
Working capital			12,900
			27,900
Capital			17,000
Add: Profit			20,850
			37,850
Less: Drawings			− 9,950
			27,900

T. Jones has decided to sell his business as at 31 December 20X5 to S. Bassey for £40,000. S. Bassey will take over all the business liabilities.

Required   Calculate the value of goodwill.

The price paid for goodwill is initially recorded in the books of the acquiring company at cost. The subsequent treatment of it depends on the accounting policy of the business. Two options are available:

1   Write it off annually against profit over its estimated useful life.
2   Retain it in the balance sheet indefinitely (this option requires an annual impairment review of the value of goodwill, any decrease in its value being charged against profit).

EXAMPLE 8.8   Shrapnel & Co purchased the assets, including the goodwill, of Mr Bullet on 1 January 20X1 for £196,000. The balance sheet of Mr Bullet consisted of tangible fixed assets of £120,000 and net current assets of £26,000.

Required

(a)   Calculate the value of goodwill.
(b)   Prepare the balance sheet of Shrapnel & Co at 1 January assuming that goodwill is retained in the balance sheet.
(c)   Prepare the balance sheet of Shrapnel & Co at 31 December assuming that goodwill is to be written off over 5 years and that the business made a cash profit of £20,000.

Solution

(a)   Goodwill = £196,000 − (£120,000 + £26,000)
              = £50,000

(b)

Shrapnel & Co
Balance sheet as at 1 January 20X1

Fixed assets	£
Intangible assets: Goodwill	50,000
Tangible fixed assets	120,000
	170,000
Net current assets	26,000
	196,000
Capital	196,000
	196,000

(c)

Shrapnel & Co
Balance sheet as at 31 December 20X1

Fixed assets	£
Intangible assets: Goodwill (W1)	40,000
Tangible fixed assets	120,000
	160,000

Net current assets (26,000 + 20,000)	46,000
	206,000

Capital	196,000
Profit for 20X1 (20,000 – 10,000)	10,000
	206,000

W1   Goodwill write-off = 50,000 / 5 = 10,000 p.a.

Referring back to Activity 8.7, prepare the balance sheet of S. Bassey   **ACTIVITY 8.8**

(a)   as at 1 January 20X6;

(b)   as at 31 December 20X6, assuming goodwill is written off over 5 years and the cash profit made during 20X6 was £30,000.

Non-purchased goodwill   Goodwill is built up gradually over the years and, when a business person 'sells up', he or she expects the buyer to pay a price which covers the value of this asset. In these circumstances it is useful to prepare a valuation as a basis for negotiations. We consider two methods which may be used:

Goodwill may be valued as a multiple of past profits. For this purpose a number of years' profits may be averaged and 'weights' attached to the profits arising each year, giving rise to the weighted average profits method.

The profits of a partnership for the last three years are as follows: 20X1, £20,000; 20X2,   **EXAMPLE 8.9**
£26,000; 20X3, £31,000.

Calculate goodwill on the basis of 1.5 times the weighted average profits of the last three   **Required**
years, using weights of 3 for the most recent year, 2 for the previous year and 1 for the earliest year.

Weighted average profits are calculated as follows: **Solution**

Year	Weight	Profits	Total
		£	£
19X1	1	20,000	20,000
19X2	2	26,000	52,000
19X3	3	31,000	93,000
Total	6		165,000

$$\text{Weighted average} = \frac{£165,000}{6} = £27,500$$

Goodwill = £27,500 × 1.5 = £41,250

ACTIVITY 8.9   A sole trader wants to put his business up for sale and is aware that the business is worth
                    more than the value of the net assets. He has built up a good reputation and has a very
                    sound customer base. The profits for the last three years were as follows:

                    20X0   £70,000
                    20X1   £70,000
                    20X2   £90,000

Required   Calculate the value of goodwill on the basis of 2 times the weighted average profits of the
                    last three years, giving more weight to the most recent profits.

We can also calculate goodwill on a 'super' profit basis. This method seeks to identify the extra profit earned by a firm because of the existence of good connections. It then values goodwill as the capitalized value of this surplus, i.e. at the amount that would have to be invested, assuming a given rate of return, to produce the extra profit for an indefinite time period. The rate of return considered appropriate naturally differs from one type of business to another.

EXAMPLE   Leake has earned profits averaging £20,000 per annum in recent years. It is estimated that
8.10   £17,000 represents a reasonable return on the existing tangible assets.
Required   Calculate goodwill on the 'super' profit basis.

Solution   £

                        Actual profit   20,000
                        Normal profit   17,000
                        Super profit   3,000

The amount a buyer is willing to pay for the 'super profit' depends on what is considered a reasonable rate of return on intangible assets in this line of business. If a return of 20 per cent is considered reasonable, goodwill is worth:

$$\text{Goodwill} = £3,000 \times \frac{100}{20} = £15,000$$

i.e. at a 20 per cent rate of interest, £15,000 must be invested to give an annual return of £3,000.

ACTIVITY   Using the information in Activity 8.9, calculate goodwill on a 'super profit' basis, assuming
8.10   that a reasonable return on assets is £65,000 and that a buyer considers a return of 20%
                   on intangible assets acceptable.

Both of the above approaches enable goodwill to be valued, but it does not necessarily follow that a buyer will be willing to pay either of these amounts, or that the seller will accept them. The price actually paid for goodwill depends on negotiation between these two parties, and the main use of the above calculations is that they produce measures of value which can be referred to during discussions.

FRS 10, *Goodwill and Intangible Fixed Assets* (see Chapter 10 for discussion of FRSs and SSAPs), categorically states that only purchased goodwill should be recognized in the accounts. The main reason for excluding non-purchased goodwill is that its value is subject to wide fluctuation due to both internal and external circumstances, making any assessment of its worth highly subjective and problematic. It is probably the right conclusion.

Readers should now attempt Question 8.4 at the end of this chapter.

Research and development expenditure

Research is undertaken to discover new products and processes and to improve those products and processes already in existence. The development stage involves the conversion of these ideas into marketable products or services. In large organizations separate departments are established to undertake these kinds of activities. The record-keeping system normally provides for the accumulation of research and development costs in a separate ledger account. The appropriate accounting treatment of such expenditure, at the end of an accounting period, has been the subject of debate for many years.

Because R&D is undertaken to help a company generate higher revenues in the future, it is reasonable to argue that it represents an asset that should be capitalized and written off against related revenues when they arise. Indeed, the proper application of the accruals concept would seem to require this procedure to be followed. In practice, however, companies are legally required to write off research expenditure immediately it is incurred, and also development expenditure unless a number of stringent conditions are met. These include requirements that development work should be reasonably well advanced, that the development costs can be accurately identified and that sufficient resources exist to cover them, and there exists a strong demand for the product.

The reason for the cautious accounting treatment of R&D expenditure is the difficulty of establishing whether a future benefit is likely to occur, and in one particularly well-known case R&D was heavily overvalued and investors and creditors totally misled. The case involved Rolls-Royce, which collapsed in 1971 despite the fact that it had reported satisfactory profits and paid healthy dividends for many years. The company's problems were concealed by the capitalization of large amounts of R&D expenditure that were valueless and should have been written off. A more prudent, and realistic, treatment of this expenditure would have brought the company's difficulties to the attention of the investing public at a much earlier stage.

STOCK VALUATION METHODS

The categories of stock owned by business organizations differ depending on the way in which their affairs are organized. For example:

1 *Trading organizations (i.e. businesses which purchase and sell goods but do not produce them).* Stock consists of goods purchased, in their completed state, and remaining unsold at the end of the accounting period.

2 *Manufacturing concerns.*   Here the term 'stock' covers raw materials, work in progress and finished goods awaiting sale.

3 *Service organizations (e.g. accountants and bankers).*   These hold very little, if any, stock in the conventional sense of the term, though accountants will have a significant balance of work in progress (representing services provided but not yet billed), while banks possess large investments which present their own valuation problems.

For many businesses stock is a large proportion of gross assets. For example, the accounts of Somerfield plc, the food retailer, for the period ending 29 April 2000 included stock amounting to £372.6 million, and this represented 21.6 per cent of its total assets.

The calculation of the figure for stock involves two steps: first, the physical quantities of stocks must be established; and second, these physical quantities must be valued.

The quantity of stock on hand is usually established by a physical count after close of business at the end of the accounting period. Because of the importance of the 'stock count', stocktaking procedures should be worked out well in advance and the exercise undertaken in a systematic manner by reliable employees who are fully aware of their responsibilities. In these circumstances the likelihood of error, as the result of items being incorrectly described, counted twice or completely omitted, is reduced to a minimum. It is also necessary for management to take steps to ensure that all goods sold and invoiced to customers on the last day of the accounting period have been dispatched from the premises by the time the count takes place. Failure to ensure this happens may mean that profit will be substantially overstated as the result of including certain items both in sales for the year and in the year-end stock figure. For similar reasons management operates controls designed to ensure that all goods on the premises, and included in stock, are recorded in the books as purchases made during the year.

We will now examine the way in which quantities of stock, once identified, are valued.

The basic rule

The fundamental rule is that stock should be valued at the *lower* of cost and net realizable value. Readers will be broadly familiar with what is meant by cost (examined further in this chapter in the section on calculating cost), but the term 'net realizable value' (NRV) is met here for the first time. Basically, NRV is the market selling price of stock less any further costs to be incurred in its sale or disposal by the firm.

The following information is provided relating to a vehicle held in stock by Thornhill Carsales:

EXAMPLE 8.11

	£
Cost	3,700
Market selling price	5,000

Sales people are paid a commission of 2 per cent on market selling price, and it is the company's policy to allow the customer a full tank of petrol at an estimated cost of £20.

Calculate the net realizable value of the vehicle.

Required

Net realizable value:	£	£
Market selling price		5,000
Less: Further costs – commission	100	
petrol	20	
		120
		4,880

Solution

You have decided to sell your car, which you bought at a car auction at a cost of £7,000 two months ago. You receive a phone call from a prospective purchaser, who saw the advert you placed in the local newspaper, who offers you £7,900 for the vehicle. The cost of the advert was £500 for three months.

ACTIVITY 8.11

(a) Calculate the net realizable value of the vehicle.
(b) If you were a business and were keeping the vehicle as a current asset, what value would you place on it, given the above information?

Required

NRV normally exceeds cost in a profitable concern, as is the case in Example 8.11 above – NRV (£4,880) exceeds cost (£3,700) by £1,180. Sometimes NRV is below cost. For example, where an existing model of car is to be replaced, the firm will be anxious to clear its 'old' stock before it becomes unsaleable, and is likely to accept a lower price.

EXAMPLE
8.12

The following information is provided for three vehicles held in stock by
Reliable Cars:

Vehicle	Cost	NRV
	£	£
A	5,400	6,200
B	5,200	8,500
C	7,100	6,200

Required

Calculate the value of Reliable Cars stock for the purpose of its accounts.

Solution

Vehicle	Cost	NRV	Value for the accounts (lower of cost and NRV)
	£	£	£
A	5,400	6,200	5,400 (cost)
B	5,200	8,500	5,200 (cost)
C	7,100	6,200	6,200 (NRV)
	17,700	20,900	16,800

The total cost of the three vehicles is £17,700 compared with a total NRV of £20,900, i.e.
total NRV exceeds total cost. For accounting purposes, however, the total value is calculated
on an item-by-item basis. Using this method it can be seen that the fall in value of vehicle
C is taken into account.

ACTIVITY
8.12

The following information relates to the stock of Busy Bees:

Stock item	Cost	Selling price	Distribution cost
	£	£	£
A	1,500	3,500	500
B	2,000	2,500	600
C	4,000	3,500	200
D	2,100	4,000	900

Required

Calculate the value of stock for Busy Bees for inclusion in the accounts.

Where the comparison between the cost and NRV of stock on an individual
items basis would be excessively time-consuming, for example, because of
the large number of items involved, groups of similar items of stock may be
compared.

Most of a company's stock is usually valued at cost, with a small number of
items reduced to NRV either because they are damaged or because they are no
longer popular with customers.

Readers should now attempt Question 8.5 at the end of this chapter.

Calculating cost

The calculation of the cost of stock is a straightforward matter in the case of a trading organization, and normally consists of the price paid to the supplier plus delivery charges (sometimes described as 'carriage inwards') where these are not included in the purchase price. The calculation is more difficult for a manufacturing organization because, in these businesses, cost consists of the price paid for raw materials *plus* the processing costs incurred to convert these materials into finished goods. This raises the question of which processing costs should be included. Clearly, the wages paid to employees working with the materials should be included as part of the cost of the finished item, but what about the wages paid to supervisors and other essential manufacturing costs such as lighting and heating, rent and rates of the factory and depreciation of the machinery? In practice, one of the following two procedures is followed:

1 *The marginal cost basis.*   Only those costs which can be traced directly to the item manufactured are included in the valuation, e.g. materials costs and the wages paid to those employees directly involved in processing the materials.

2 *The total cost basis.*   All manufacturing costs are included, i.e. the marginal costs plus a fair proportion of incidental manufacturing expenses, called 'manufacturing overheads'.

The total cost figure for stock therefore exceeds the marginal cost figure by the amount of the fixed manufacturing overhead costs.

The following data are provided relating to the manufacture of Nexo for the month of January 20X1:

EXAMPLE 8.13

	£
Raw materials (£5 per unit)	6,000
Wages paid to staff directly involved in manufacture	8,400
Salary paid to supervisor	850
Rent	420
Light and heat	670
Depreciation of machinery	460

During January 1,200 items were manufactured, of which 1,000 were sold. There was no opening stock at the beginning of the month and no work in progress at the beginning or end of the month. Closing stock consists of 200 completed items.

(a) Valuations of closing stock on the

Required

   (i)   marginal cost basis;
   (ii) total cost basis.

(b) Comment on your results.

Solution   (a)   (i)   Marginal cost basis

	£
Raw materials	6,000
Labour	8,400
	14,400

Marginal cost per unit manufactured = 14,400 / 1,200 = £12
Marginal cost of unsold stock = £12 × 200 = £2,400

(ii) Total cost basis

	£	£
Direct costs		14,400
Manufacturing overheads:		
Salary	850	
Rent	420	
Light and heat	670	
Depreciation	460	2,400
		16,800

Total cost per unit manufactured = 16,800/1,200 = £14
Total cost of unsold stock = £14 × 200 = £2,800

(b)   The total cost basis produces a cost per unit that is £2 more (£14 − £12). This results from the inclusion of a proportion of manufacturing overheads that amount, in total, to £2,400, or £2,400 / 1,200 = £2 per unit manufactured.

A company must be able to cover all its costs if it is to survive and flourish in the long run and, for this reason, companies are required to use the total cost basis when valuing stock for inclusion in the accounts published for external use. For internal reporting purposes, however, either total costs or marginal costs can be used and management may well regard the latter as the more relevant basis for short-run business decisions. For example, a business operating below its full productive capacity may find it worthwhile to accept orders at prices below total costs, provided marginal costs are covered, since overhead costs will be incurred anyway.

ACTIVITY   The following data are provided relating to the manufacture of Alpho for the month of
8.13   June 20X2:

    Direct materials (4,000 units @ £10 per unit)
    Direct labour (12 employees earning £2,000 per month)
    Indirect labour (2 supervisors earning £2,500 per month each)

Rent	£1,600
Light and heat	£3,000
Depreciation of machinery	£4,000

    Sales (3,500 units @ £20)

Required   Valuations of closing stock on the marginal cost and total cost basis.

Readers should now attempt Question 8.6 at the end of this chapter.

First in first out (FIFO) and last in first out (LIFO)

We saw in Chapter 4 that profit is calculated by matching costs with revenues arising during an accounting period. The difficulty, in the case of stock, is to decide which costs to match with sales revenue in view of the large number of items acquired. It is theoretically possible to identify the actual items sold and, where a firm deals in a relatively small number of high-value items that can be easily identified – for example, cars – this procedure is followed in practice. Where there are a large number of transactions, however, the heavy additional cost involved in keeping such detailed records rules out this option. Instead the matching process is facilitated by making one of a number of arbitrary assumptions concerning the flow of goods into and out of the business. Two possibilities are as follows:

1 *First in first out (FIFO).* This assumes that the first items purchased are the first items sold. The items assumed to be in stock are therefore the most recent acquisitions.

2 *Last in first out (LIFO).* This assumes that the last items purchased are the first sold. The items assumed to be in stock are therefore likely to have been purchased months or even years ago. (It should be noted that the use of LIFO complies with legal requirements but it is not favoured by Standard Accounting Practice (see Chapter 10).)

The following information is provided for Frame for 20X2:   **EXAMPLE 8.14**

	£
Opening stock, 200 units at £5 each	1,000
Purchases during 20X2, 1,000 units at £6 each	6,000
Sales during 20X2, 900 units at £10 each	9,000
Closing stock, 300 units	

Calculate the value of Frame's closing stock using: **Required**

(a) FIFO;
(b) LIFO.

(a) 300 units at £6 = £1,800   **Solution**

Note The 900 units sold are assumed to be made up of the opening stock of 200 units, plus 700 units purchased during the year. Closing stock, therefore, consists of the remaining 300 units purchased during the year which are valued at £6 each.

(b)   200 units at £5   £1,000
       100 units at £6   £ 600
                           £1,600

Note   The 900 items sold are assumed to have been made entirely from purchases during the year.
        Closing stock is, therefore, assumed to consist of the opening stock of 200 units, plus the 100
        units purchased during the year that were not sold.

ACTIVITY 8.14

The following information is provided for Frame for 20X3:

	£
Opening stock, 300 units at £6 each	1,800
Purchases during 20X3, 4,000 units at £8 each	32,000
Sales during 20X3, 3,900 units at £15 each	58,500
Closing stock, 400 units	

Required

Calculate the value of Frame's closing stock using:

(a) FIFO;
(b) LIFO.

Perpetual inventory

In the previous section the total number of items sold was deducted from the total number of items that became available for sale (i.e. opening stock plus purchases), during the accounting period and the balance that remained was valued at the latest purchase prices (under FIFO) or earliest purchase prices (under LIFO). This is called the 'periodic basis' for matching stock sold with those available for sale.

Many large companies operate a system of perpetual inventory. In such circumstances the stock records contain details of quantities, and sometimes also values, of the various types of stock on hand throughout the year. This enables the transaction basis to be used for matching stock sold with those available for sale, i.e. each batch of goods dispatched is matched with stock on hand at that point in time, using FIFO or LIFO as appropriate. Other advantages that result from the maintenance of detailed records are as follows:

1   They provide an element of control by showing the quantity of goods that *should* be in stock at a particular point in time. Any discrepancies compared with *actual* holdings can then be investigated.

2   Steps can be taken, in good time, to replenish stocks when they fall to a predetermined minimum level.
3   Stock values are readily available for the purpose of management accounts, which are perhaps prepared monthly, and the annual accounts published for external use. At least once a year, however, and perhaps more often, it is necessary to have a physical stocktake to check the accuracy of the stock records.

The following purchases and sales were made by Trader during the first two weeks of January 20X1. There are no opening stocks.

EXAMPLE 8.15

		Purchases		Sales	
		Units	Price per £	Units	Price per £
January	1	100	7	10	9
	2			20	9
	5			50	9
	7	75	8		
	10			20	9
	12			50	10
		175		150	

The physical stocktake confirmed that there were 25 units in stock at the month end.

Write up the stock records of Trader using the transaction basis on the following alternative assumptions:

Required

(a)   Issues are made from stock on the FIFO basis.
(b)   Issues are made from stock on the LIFO basis.

(a)   FIFO basis: stock card

Solution

Date	Receipts			Issues			Balance		
	Units	Price	£	Units	Price	£	Units	Price	£
1 Jan	100	7	700	10	7	70	90	7	630
2				20	7	140	70	7	490
5				50	7	350	20	7	140
7	75	8	600				20	7	140
							75	8	600
10				20	7	140	75	8	600
12				50	8	400	25	8	200
	175		1,300	150		1,100			200

(b)   LIFO basis: stock card

Date	Receipts			Issues			Balance		
	Units	Price	£	Units	Price	£	Units	Price	£
1 Jan	100	7	700	10	7	70	90	7	630
2				20	7	140	70	7	490
5				50	7	350	20	7	140
7	75	8	600				20	7	140
							75	8	600
10				20	7	140	20	7	140
							55	8	440
12				50	8	400	20	7	140
							5	8	40
	175		1,300	150		1,120			180

Stock valuation methods and changing prices

The FIFO and LIFO assumptions have the following different effects on the figure for cost of goods sold and the valuation of stock during a period of rising prices:

1   Cost of goods sold.   This is higher under LIFO due to the fact that most recent purchases are matched with sales.

2   Stock.   This is valued at a higher figure under FIFO due to the fact that the most recent purchases are assumed to remain in stock.

The effect on the gross profit of Trader of using the two different methods (Example 8.15) is shown in the following summarized trading accounts:

Summary trading accounts, transaction basis

	FIFO £	LIFO £
Sales (100 × £9) + (50 × £10)	1,400	1,400
Cost of goods sold	(1,100)	(1,120)
Gross profit	300	280

The above example shows that, when prices are rising, reported profit is higher using the FIFO cost-flow assumption. The opposite is the case when prices are falling. It is important that readers should recognize that actual events are unaffected by the choice of valuation method, but the selection usually alters the level of reported profit.

The following purchases and sales were made by Striker & Co. during the first four months of 20X0. There are no opening stocks.

| | Purchases | | Sales | |
	Units	Price per unit	Units	Price per unit
		£		£
Jan	1,000	10		
	900	10	1,200	20
Feb	1,200	14	1,000	24
Mar	2,000	16	500	24
Apr	500	17		
	200	18	1,700	26
	5,800		4,400	

The physical stocktake confirmed that there were 1,400 units in stock at the end of April.

(a) Write up the stock records of Striker & Co. using the transaction basis on the following alternative assumptions:

(i)   Issues are made from stock on the FIFO basis.
(ii) Issues are made from stock on the LIFO basis.

(b) Calculate the gross profit figure under the two alternatives.

Weighted average cost (AVCO)

A further option is for firms to value cost of goods sold and closing stock at its weighted average cost (AVCO). This is fairly popular with companies and produces results that fall between those achieved by using FIFO or LIFO. The procedure is shown in Example 8.16.

Using the information given in Example 8.15:

EXAMPLE
8.16

(a) Calculate the AVCO value of Trader's stock using (i) the periodic basis and (ii) the transaction basis.

(b) Prepare a summary trading account for Trader using AVCO and the transaction basis.

(a) (i)   Periodic basis:

		Units	Price	£
Purchases	1 Jan	100	7.00	700
	7 Jan	75	8.00	600
		175		1,300

Stock is valued at:

$$1,300 / 175 = £7.43$$

Closing stock = £7.43 × 25 units = £186

Note This method uses the average purchase value of the period.

(ii) Transaction basis: cost card

Date	Receipts			Issues			Balance		
	Units	Price	£	Units	Price	£	Units	Price	£
1 Jan	100	7	700	10	7.00	70	90	7.00	630
2				20	7.00	140	70	7.00	490
5				50	7.00	350	20	7.00	140
7	75	8	600				95	*7.79	740
10				20	7.79	156	75	7.79	584
12				50	7.79	389	25	7.79	195
	175		1,300	150		1,105			195

Note This method uses the weighted average value of items remaining in stock.

*(20 × £7) + (75 × £8) = £740 / 95 units

(b) **Summary trading account - AVCO (transaction basis)**

	£
Sales	1,400
Less: Cost of goods sold	(1,105)
Gross profit	295

ACTIVITY 8.16

Using the information given in Activity 8.15:

(a) Calculate the AVCO value of Striker & Co.'s stock using (i) the periodic basis and (ii) the transaction basis.

(b) Prepare a summary trading account for Striker & Co. using AVCO and the transaction basis.

Readers should now work through Questions 8.7–8.10 at the end of this chapter.

ACCOUNTING CONCEPTS

Accounting records and statements are based on a number of assumptions, called accounting concepts. The ten considered most important are examined below. The treatment is brief in those cases where the concept has already been discussed in an earlier chapter.

Entity concept

This fixes the boundary for the financial affairs contained in an accounting statement and was examined in Chapter 2. The boundary is often the business, but it may be a smaller or even a larger unit. For instance, a business may be split into a number of departments, each of which is treated as a separate entity for the purpose of preparing accounting statements for management (see Chapter 11). At the other extreme, a number of companies may be regarded as a single entity for accounting purposes. This occurs where a company owns the shares of one or more other companies. The connected companies together form a 'group', and their separate accounts are 'consolidated' for the purpose of reporting to shareholders (see Chapter 10).

Money measurement concept

A business asset is reported in the balance sheet only if its value can be measured in money terms with a reasonable degree of precision. This concept was discussed in Chapter 2. A good example of the application of this concept concerns the accounting treatment of goodwill. We saw earlier in this chapter that goodwill consists of the reputation and business connections built up over a period of time. Most firms enjoy an element of goodwill, but its value continuously fluctuates and is therefore difficult to quantify with any degree of precision. For this reason the existence of goodwill is usually acknowledged by an entry in the accounts only when its value is proved by a market transaction involving its purchase and sale.

Matching (accruals) concept

The accountant measures profit for a period of time, such as a year, by comparing or 'matching' revenue and expenditure identified with that period. The first step is to identify revenues and the second step is to deduct the expenditures incurred in producing the revenues. This concept was examined in Chapter 4. It should be noted that many of the concepts are closely interrelated. For example, the matching concept is put into effect by applying the realization concept and the accruals concept. These are considered next.

Realization concept

Revenue is assumed to be earned when a sale takes place and a legally enforceable claim arises against the customer. The effect of this rule is that stock usually remains in the books at cost until the sale takes place at which stage a profit arises or a loss is incurred. This concept was discussed in Chapter 4.

The accruals concept

Costs are matched against revenues when the benefit of the expenditure is received rather than when the cash payment is made. Where the benefit is received before the payment is made, the amount owed is treated as a liability in the balance sheet. Where the benefit is received after the payment is made, the amount paid is treated as an asset in the balance sheet, and charged against revenues arising during whichever future accounting period benefits from the payments. This concept was examined in Chapter 4.

Readers should now attempt Question 8.11 at the end of this chapter.

Historical cost concept

Assets are initially recorded at the price paid to the supplier. In certain circumstances further costs may be added. For example, in the case of a manufacturing concern, a proportion of the production costs should be added to the cost of raw materials to arrive at the cost of finished goods (see earlier in this chapter). In the case of fixed assets, their recorded cost includes not only the price paid to the supplier but also all incidental costs incurred to make the item ready for use (see earlier in this chapter). A major advantage of this concept is that the accounting records are based on objective facts. A disadvantage of using historical cost is that, during a period of rising prices, the reported figures may significantly understate the asset's true value to the business. It is for this reason that some companies periodically revalue their fixed assets and/or publish supplementary accounts designed to take account of the effects of inflation (see further discussion in Chapter 10).

Going concern concept

This assumes that the business is a permanent venture and will not be wound up in the foreseeable future. Many fixed assets, which cost a great deal, have low resale value because they have been specially designed for a particular business. The going concern concept allows accountants to ignore this low resale value and instead spread the cost of an asset over the accounting periods that benefit from its use. The assumption that the business will continue indefinitely as a going concern is, however, in certain circumstances false and must be dropped. For example, if a company is about to be liquidated, forecasts of the amounts likely to be received by various providers of finance should be based on estimates of what the business assets are expected to realize in the market rather than their historical book value.

Consistency concept

The same valuation methods should be used each year when preparing accounting statements. We have seen that there exist a number of methods for valuing fixed assets and stocks. There are arguments for and against most of them and, to some extent, an arbitrary choice must be made. The effect on reported profit is unlikely to be significant provided similar procedures are adopted each year. For example, the total cost method of valuing stock produces a higher figure for stock than the marginal cost method, but the overall effect of this increased value will be zero since the closing stock of one year becomes the opening stock of the following year. The consistent use of total cost produces a higher figure for stock at both dates and so the beneficial effect on profit of a high closing stock figure in year 1 will be cancelled out against the detrimental effect on profit of a high opening stock figure in year 2.

The higher opening and closing valuations, on the total cost basis, cancel out, and gross profit is unaffected by the valuation method adopted. It should be noted, however, that the balance sheet figure for stock, and therefore gross assets and net assets, will be higher if total cost is used. It should also be noted that reported profit does vary when there are changes in the level of stock because, in these circumstances, the opening and closing balances no longer cancel out. However, the difference is unlikely to be large unless the change in the level of stock is substantial, such as occurs when new business operations commence.

The following information is provided for one of the products manufactured by Mill during 20X8:

EXAMPLE 8.17

Opening stock – 100 units valued as follows:

	£
Marginal cost basis, £5 per unit × 100	500
Total cost basis, £8 per unit × 100	800
Production cost of 500 units:	
Marginal costs, £5 per unit	2,500
Fixed costs	1,500
Sales, 500 units at £12	6,000

(a) Valuations of closing stock using

    (i) the marginal cost basis; and

    (ii) the total cost basis.

(b) Profit statements for 20X8 using each of the above bases.

Required

Solution

(a) Opening stock is 100 units and, as the same number of items are produced as are sold, closing stock is also 100 units.

		£	£
(i)	Marginal cost basis:		
	Marginal costs, £5 × 100		500
(ii)	Total cost basis:		
	Marginal costs	500	
	Fixed costs	300 W1	800

W1 £1,500 (total fixed costs) ÷ 500 (number of items produced) × 100 (number of items in stock at year end)

(b) **Profit statement, 20X8**

	(i) Marginal cost basis		(ii) Total cost basis	
	£	£	£	£
Sales		6,000		6,000
Less: Opening stock	500		800	
Production costs	4,000		4,000	
Closing stock	(500)		(800)	
Cost of goods sold		4,000		4,000
Gross profit		2,000		2,000

The level of reported profit can be significantly inflated or deflated if a company changes from one method to another.

EXAMPLE
8.18

Assume the same facts as for Example 8.17, except that the marginal cost is used at the beginning of the year and total cost at the end.

Required

The revised profit statement for 20X8.

Solution

Profit statement 20X8

	£	£
Sales		6,000
Less: Opening stock (marginal cost)	500	
Production cost	4,000	
	4,500	
Closing stock (total cost)	(800)	
Cost of goods sold		(3,700)
Gross profit		2,300

Gross profit is £2,300 in Example 8.18 as compared with £2,000 in Example 8.17. Profit is therefore inflated by £300 as the result of switching from one valuation method to another and using the total cost closing stock figure, £800, instead of the marginal cost closing stock figure, £500. As a result of the change, reported profits are greater than actual profits and wrong conclusions may be reached concerning the performance of Mill. It is therefore important for valuation procedures to be consistently applied so that reported results fairly reflect performance during the year, and valid comparisons can be made with results achieved in a previous accounting period.

While consistency is a fundamental accounting concept (see Chapter 10), it does not mean that methods, once adopted, should never be changed, but sound and convincing arguments must be put forward to justify departures from existing practice. The essential test is whether management can show that the new procedures result in a fairer view of the financial performance and position of the concern. If it is decided that a change should be made to a previously accepted method of valuation, the impact on comparability between two sets of figures must be noted and, wherever possible, also quantified, so that it can be taken into account when measuring performance. For example, when a firm switches from marginal cost to total cost to comply with regulatory requirements, relevant balances for the previous year, which are also reported, must be recomputed, using total cost, so that a proper assessment of comparative performance can be made.

It must be emphasized that inconsistent accounting methods can have a marked effect on the information contained in accounting statements. The changes are not always explained as clearly as they should be, and the user must scrutinize the accounts vigilantly to ensure that distorted financial information does not cause him or her to make a wrong investment decision.

Readers should now attempt Question 8.12 at the end of the chapter.

Prudence concept

The prudence concept (sometimes called the concept of conservatism) requires the accountant to make full provision for all expected losses and not to anticipate revenues until they are realized. A good example of how this concept affects accounting practice is the basic rule that stock should be valued at the lower of cost and NRV. Where NRV is above cost, the profit likely to arise in the near future is ignored and stock remains in the accounts at the lower figure until the sale occurs, i.e. revenue is not anticipated. On the other hand, where NRV is below cost, stock must be immediately restated at the lower figure so that full provision is made for the foreseeable future loss.

Approval of a prudent approach to profit measurement is based on the potential dangers of an over-optimistic calculation that may be used as the basis for an excessive distribution of funds, to ownership, that deprives the business of much needed resources. Another possible pitfall is that an attractive presentation of the current position, not justified by the underlying facts, may cause management to expand the level of operations wrongly and incur heavy losses. New projects often involve a substantial commitment of resources, the bulk of which is tied up in fixed assets. The only way the firm is likely to recoup its money is by using the assets to produce and sell goods at a profit. Caution is, therefore, highly desirable when management is considering whether to make an investment, and any accounting statement used to help reach this decision should be prepared on a prudent basis. This may mean that, occasionally, good opportunities are missed, but this will not happen often, and the likely loss from an ill-conceived investment will be many times greater than the profit possibly forgone.

It is important, however, not to take the prudence concept too far. Where there are a number of likely outcomes it is usually wise to choose the lower figure, but profit should not be deliberately understated. Accounting statements are used as the basis for decision-making, and they should contain realistic, not excessively pessimistic, financial information. Understatement can be just as misleading as overstatement and, although the potential loss from the misallocation of resources that may result is less, losses can be minimized by preparers of accounting reports exercising no more than a reasonable level of caution.

Materiality

Accounting statements should contain only those financial facts that are material, or relevant, to the decision being taken by the recipient of the report. It is, therefore, important for the accountant to be familiar with the user's requirement so that he or she can decide which information should be included and excluded. For example, if an accounting statement is prepared to help management assess which departments are most successful, it is clearly essential for the report to show the profits earned by each of them. This means identifying the revenues and expenditures that relate to each department, but unnecessary detail is omitted – for example, a manager is interested in knowing the individual amounts expended on materials, wages, power, depreciation, etc., but not on Christmas gratuities, the ingredients for morning coffee and paper towels. Trivial items are, therefore, grouped together under the heading 'sundry expenses'. For similar reasons balance sheets contain values for the main categories of assets and liabilities but do not give figures for each item of plant, stock, etc.

Accounting statements prepared for shareholders of limited companies contain even less detail. This is partly because such information is of little interest to them. It is management's job to decide how to allocate resources between various investment opportunities, while the shareholder is primarily interested in assessing whether the overall performance is satisfactory. It is, therefore, considered desirable to keep to a minimum detailed facts that may be difficult to assimilate, and instead concentrate on the broad overall pattern of developments. It must be admitted that the sophisticated institutional investor would welcome far more detail than is sometimes provided in the published accounts, but there is a natural reluctance to publish sensitive material that could be of use to competitors.

There is another aspect of materiality, and this concerns the amount of detail the accountant goes into when measuring profit. A good example is the use of FIFO, AVCO and LIFO instead of attempting to match individual purchases with sales. Another example is the decision not to distinguish between capital and revenue expenditure where the amount spent on a fixed asset is small. For example, minor items of office equipment such as staplers and punches last for a number of years, but it is not usually considered worthwhile to capitalize and depreciate them systematically over their expected useful life. Instead they are written off immediately against revenue. A detailed treatment is justified only if the extra costs involved produce a significant improvement in the quality of the information contained in accounting statements. When applying this test, it must be remembered that, because of the need for estimates to be made and judgement to be exercised, the reported profit figure is at best an approximation and is unlikely to be improved by making precise adjustments for trivial items.

Readers should now attempt Questions 8.13 and 8.14 at the end of this chapter.

8.1 (a) How would you distinguish between capital and revenue expenditure, and why is it important to make a correct allocation?   **QUESTIONS**

(b) State, with reasons, in which of the two categories you would place the following items:

  (i) Replacement of the blade on a cutting machine damaged as the result of using poor-quality raw material inputs.

  (ii) A feeding device costing £1,000 that is fixed to a machine so as to enable a 20 per cent increase in throughput each hour.

  (iii) The cost of transporting to the factory a new machine supplied by a Japanese company.

  (iv) Second-hand plant purchased at a cost of £1,500.

  (v) Repairs to the plant mentioned in (iv), costing £800, before it is ready for use.

8.2 Simon is a surveyor who purchases old properties in poor condition. He incurs expenditure on improving these properties, which he then resells. His balance sheet at 31 December 20X2 was as follows:

	£
Properties on hand (including expenses on purchase):	
1	30,250
2	29,350
Bank balance	19,400
	79,000
Capital	79,000

During 20X3 he bought three more properties:

	Cost	Legal expenses borne by Simon	Cost of improvements
	£	£	£
3	36,250	1,000	260
4	24,000	750	1,000
5	25,000	800	520

He also sold the following three properties:

	Sale price	Legal expenses incurred by Simon
	£	£
1	34,000	400
3	42,500	500
4	31,250	350

General expenses incurred and paid during 20X3 amounted to £2,500.

Required

(a) Simon's bank account for 20X3.

(b) A profit and loss account for the year 20X3 covering Simon's property deals and a balance sheet at 31 December 20X3.

Notes 1 Cash due from the sale of property 4 was not received until 5 January 19X4.

2 There were no other transactions during the year and all receipts and payments were by cheque.

8.3 On 1 January 199X a business purchased a Minilab to process and print films. The Minilab costs £28,000 and has an estimated economic life of 4 years, after which it will have no residual value. The financial year of the business ends on 31 December. It is estimated that the output from the Minilab will be:

	Films processed
Year 1	40,000
Year 2	50,000
Year 3	55,000
Year 4	55,000
	200,000

(a) Calculate the annual depreciation charges on the Minilab for each of the four years on
each of the following bases:

    (i)   The straight-line basis.

    (ii)   The diminishing balance method at 55 per cent per annum.

    (iii) The units of output method.

Required

Note Your workings should be to the nearest £.

(10 marks)

(b) Suppose that the business sold the Minilab half way through the third year for £10,000
and that depreciation had been provided for using the straight-line method applied on
a month-for-month basis.

Reconstruct the following accounts *for the third year only:*

    (i)   The Minilab account.

    (ii)   The provision for depreciation – Minilab account.

    (iii) The assets disposals account.

(10 marks)

(Total 20 marks)

(AAT, Basic Accounting, December 1990)

8.4 Buy paid Mr Sale £120,000 cash to acquire his business, Sale & Co., as a going
concern on 1 January 20X1. The assets taken over were considered to be worth the
following amounts:

	£
Fixed assets	71,500
Stock	20,000
Debtors	10,000

In addition, Buy assumed responsibility for paying Sale & Co.'s outstanding creditors, which
amounted to £5,000. The policy of Buy is to write off goodwill over a five-year period.

(a) Calculate the goodwill arising on the acquisition of Sale & Co.

(b) Show how goodwill will appear in the balance sheet of Buy Ltd as at 31 December 20X1.

Required

8.5 Give the basic rule for valuing stock. Apply this rule to the facts provided below and
calculate the total value of stock to be included in the accounts.

Product	Cost	Net realizable value
	£	£
A	2,400	2,760
B	1,290	740
C	3,680	750
D	2,950	4,760
E	6,280	9,730

8.6   Brothers manufacture one type of high-quality ornament for the export market. The firm plans its activities three months in advance and its estimates for January, February and March 1994 are as follows:

		Units
Stock of ornaments at 1 January		Nil
Ornaments produced during:	January	450
	February	480
	March	500
Expected sales for:	January	400
	February	450
	March	520
Unit selling price		£21
Unit variable manufacturing cost		£12
Manufacturing overheads per month		£1,800
Fixed administrative expenses per month		£600

Required

(a)   Prepare profit statements for each of the months January, February and March 1994, adopting

  (i)   a marginal costing approach; and

  (ii)   an absorption costing approach.

(14 marks)

(b)   Using examples from your answer to part (a), explain why the resultant profit figures differ for each approach.

(4 marks)

(Total: 18 marks)

(ICSA, Introduction to Accounting, December 1993)

8.7   What do you understand by the terms 'perpetual inventory' and 'periodic stocktake'? In the case of a trader, how is the figure for cost of goods sold obtained under each of these systems?

8.8   D. Hart, a trader dealing in one product only, has the following transactions over a six-month period:

	Date	Quantity (in units)	Unit cost (£)
Purchases	1 June 1992	1,500	90
	1 August 1992	2,000	92
	1 October 1992	3,000	93
Sales	June 1992	340	140
	July 1992	700	140
	August 1992	800	144
	September 1992	450	144
	October 1992	900	144
	November 1992	630	145

The trader held no stock at 31 May 1992.

(a) Applying the following principles of stock valuation, calculate D. Hart's gross profit or loss for the six months ended 30 November 1992:

Required

   (i)   first in first out; and

   (ii) last in first out.

(Ignore other expenses which may have been incurred for the period.)

(14 marks)

(b) If a trader uses last in first out as the basis of stock valuation, does this mean that he is left with the 'oldest' intake of stock at the end of the period? Briefly explain your answer.

(4 marks)

(ICSA, Introduction to Accounting, December 1992)

8.9 Airwaves Ltd are retailers who sell mobile telephones. During January to March 1993 they decided to concentrate their selling activities on the 'Meteor' model, which experienced several cost price fluctuations during the period. The company found that because of this it had to adjust its own selling price.

During the period the following transactions took place:

1   1 Jan.: an opening stock of 50 telephones was obtained at a total cost of £8,250.

2   10 Jan.: initial sales were good so extra telephones had to be obtained from abroad; 200 telephones were purchased at a cost of £135 each, but in addition there was a freight charge of £3 each, as well as a customs import duty of £5 each.

3   31 Jan.: during the month 180 telephones were sold at a price of £175 each.

4   1 Feb.: a new batch of 120 telephones was purchased at a cost of £170 each.

5   28 Feb.: the sales for February were 120, at a selling price of £215 each.

6   2 Mar.: a further 220 telephones were purchased at a cost of £240 each and these were subject to a trade discount of 12.5 per cent each.

7   31 Mar.: 250 telephones were sold during March at a price of £230 each.

All purchases were received on the dates stated.

   The accountant of Airwaves Ltd decided he would apply the first in first out (FIFO) and weighted average (AVCO) methods of stock valuation in order that the results could be compared.

(a) Calculate the stock value at 31 March 1993 using each of the methods indicated (if necessary, calculate to one decimal place). *(16 marks)*

Required

(b) Prepare the trading accounts using each of the above methods for the period January–March 1993. *(8 marks)*

(c) What considerations should an accountant bear in mind in deciding on a basis of stock valuation? Reference should be made to relevant accounting concepts. *(20 marks)*

(AEB, Accounting, November 1993)

8.10   Stoval Ltd started to trade on 1 January 20X1. Its purchases of trading stock, at cost, during the first three years of business were

	£
20X1	240,000
20X2	252,000
20X3	324,000

The values of stock at 31 December, under different valuation methods, were

31 December	LIFO cost	FIFO cost	Lower of FIFO cost and net realizable value
20X1	£96,480	£96,000	£88,800
20X2	£87,360	£86,400	£81,600
20X3	£100,320	£105,600	£105,600

Required

(a)   Assuming that in any one year prices moved either up or down, but not both:

   (i)   Did prices go up or down in 20X1?

   (ii)   Did prices go up or down in 20X3?

(b)   Which stock valuation method would show the highest profit for 20X1?

(c)   Which stock valuation method applied to opening and closing stock would show the highest profit for 20X3?

(d)   Which stock valuation method would show the lowest profit for all three years combined?

8.11   Where accounts are prepared in accordance with the *accruals concept*, cash receipts and payments may precede, coincide with or follow the period in which revenues and expenses are recognized. Give two examples of each of the following:

(a)   A cash receipt that precedes the period in which revenue is recognized.

(b)   A cash receipt that coincides with the period in which revenue is recognized.

(c)   A cash receipt that follows the period in which revenue is recognized.

(d)   A cash payment that precedes the period in which expense is recognized.

(e)   A cash payment that coincides with the period in which expense is recognized.

(f)   A cash payment that follows the period in which expense is recognized.

8.12   The summarized trading account of Change Ltd for 20X1 contained the following information:

Trading Account for 20X1

	£	£
Sales		100,000
Less: Opening stock	7,000	
Purchases	80,000	
Closing stock	(11,000)	
Cost of goods sold		76,000
Gross profit		24,000

Opening stock is valued at marginal cost, but the directors have now decided that total cost is more suitable, and this basis was used for the purpose of valuing closing stock. The value of opening stock, on the total cost basis, is found to be £10,000.

(a) Prepare a revised trading account for Change Ltd complying with the consistency concept.

(b) Indicate the effect of the revision on the *net* profit figure reported by Change Ltd for 20X1.

Required

8.13

   (i)   Dual aspect;

  (ii)   consistency;

 (iii)   prudence;

 (iv)   matching/accruals; and

  (v)   going concern.

(a) Briefly explain each of the concepts mentioned above.   *(10 marks)*

(b) Explain how each of the concepts will affect the preparation of the final accounts of a company.   *(10 marks)*

                                        (Total: 20 marks)

            (ICSA, Introduction to Accounting, December 1993)

Required

8.14   (a)   SSAP 9, *Stocks and Long-Term Contracts*, requires stocks of raw materials and finished goods to be valued in financial statements at the lower of cost and net realizable value.

        (i)   Appendix 1 to SSAP 9 states that in arriving at the cost of stock, methods such as last in first out (LIFO) are not usually appropriate. Explain how LIFO is applied.

                                           (2 marks)

        (ii)   Describe three methods of arriving at cost of stock which are acceptable under SSAP 9 and explain why they are regarded as acceptable, and LIFO is not.

                                           (5 marks)

       (iii)   Explain how the cost of a stock of finished goods held by the manufacturer would normally be arrived at when obtaining the figure for the financial statements.

                                           (3 marks)

Required

    (b)   Sampi is a manufacturer of garden furniture. The company has consistently used FIFO (first in, first out) in valuing stock, but it is interested to know the effect on its stock valuation of using LIFO (last in, first out) and weighted average cost instead of FIFO.

        At 28 February 19X8 the company had a stock of 4,000 standard plastic tables and has computed its value on each of the three bases as:

Basis	Unit cost	Total value
	£	£
FIFO	16	64,000
LIFO	12	48,000
Weighted average	13	52,000

During March 19X8 the movements on the stock of tables were as follows:
Received from factory:

Date	Number of units	Production cost per unit £
8 March	3,800	15
22 March	6,000	18

Sales:

Date	Number of units
12 March	5,000
18 March	2,000
24 March	3,000
28 March	2,000

On a FIFO basis the stock at 31 March 19X8 was £32,400.

Required

Compute what the value of the stock at 31 March 19X8 would be using:

(i) LIFO;   (5 marks)

(ii) weighted average cost.   (5 marks)

In arriving at the total stock values you should make calculations of two decimal places (where necessary) and deal with each stock movement in date order.

(20 marks)

ACCA, Paper 1, The Accounting Framework, June 1998 (adapted)

SOLUTIONS
TO
ACTIVITIES

Solution to
Activity 8.1

1 Revenue expenditure.

2 Depends: if the replacement parts increase production capacity or estimated useful life then it is capital expenditure; if not, it is revenue expenditure.

3 Revenue expenditure.

4 Capital expenditure.

5 Capital expenditure.

Solution to
Activity 8.2

$$\frac{\text{Cost} - \text{Residual value}}{\text{Estimated useful life}} - \frac{45,000 - 4,000}{10} = £4,100 \text{ p.a.}$$

Solution to
Activity 8.3

$$\text{Depreciation rate} = \left(1 - \sqrt[10]{\frac{4,000}{45,000}}\right) \times 100\%$$

$$= 21.5\%$$

Depreciation charge and NBV for 20X0–20X9

	£
Original cost	45,000
20X0 depreciation charge (£45,000 × 21.5%)	(9,675)
Net book value at 31 December 20X0	35,325
20X1 depreciation charge (£35,325 × 21.5%)	(7,595)
Net book value at 31 December 20X1	27,730
20X2 depreciation charge (£27,730 × 21.5%)	(5,962)
Net book value at 31 December 20X2	21,768
20X3 depreciation charge (£21,768 × 21.5%)	(4,680)
Net book value at 31 December 20X3	17,088
20X4 depreciation charge (£17,088 × 21.5%)	(3,674)
Net book value at 31 December 20X4	13,414
20X5 depreciation charge (£13,414 × 21.5%)	(2,884)
Net book value at 31 December 20X5	10,530
20X6 depreciation charge (£10,530 × 21.5%)	(2,264)
Net book value at 31 December 20X6	8,266
20X7 depreciation charge (£8,266 × 21.5%)	(1,777)
Net book value at 31 December 20X7	6,489
20X8 depreciation charge (£6,489 × 21.5%)	(1,395)
Net book value at 31 December 20X8	5,094
20X9 depreciation charge (£5,094 × 21.5%)	1094*
Net book value at 31 December 20X9	4000

*Rounding adjustment made in final charge.

Solution to
Activity 8.4

Depreciable amount = £45,000 − £4,000 = £41,000

$$\text{Sum of the digits} = \frac{10 (10 + 1)}{2} = 55$$

Depreciation charge:

$$20X0 = £41,000 \times \frac{10}{55} = £7,455$$

$$20X1 = £41,000 \times \frac{9}{55} = £6,709$$

$$20X2 = £41,000 \times \frac{8}{55} = £5,964$$

$$20X3 = £41,000 \times \frac{7}{55} = £5,218$$

$$20X4 = £41,000 \times \frac{6}{55} = £4,473$$

$$20X5 = £41,000 \times \frac{5}{55} = £3,727$$

$$20X6 = £41,000 \times \frac{4}{55} = £2,982$$

$$20X7 = £41,000 \times \frac{3}{55} = £2,236$$

$$20X8 = £41,000 \times \frac{2}{55} = £1,491$$

$$20X9 = £41,000 \times \frac{1}{55} = £745$$

Total charge £41,000

Solution to Activity 8.5

Total number of units
$= (200,000+150,000+175,000+200,000+180,000+190,000)$
$= 1,095,000$

Depreciation charge:

$$\text{Year } 1 = \frac{70,000}{1,095,000} \times 200,000 = £12,785$$

$$\text{Year } 2 = \frac{70,000}{1,095,000} \times 150,000 = £\ 9,589$$

$$\text{Year } 3 = \frac{70,000}{1,095,000} \times 175,000 = £11,187$$

$$\text{Year } 4 = \frac{70,000}{1,095,000} \times 200,000 = £12,785$$

$$\text{Year } 5 = \frac{70,000}{1,095,000} \times 180,000 = £11,507$$

$$\text{Year } 6 = \frac{70,000}{1,095,000} \times 190,000 = £12,146$$

Solution to Activity 8.6

(a)
$$\text{Depreciation charge} = \frac{180,000 - 20,000}{8} = 20,000 \text{ p.a.}$$

	Year 1	Year 2	Year 3	Year 4	Year 5	Year 6	Year 7	Year 8
	£000	£000	£000	£000	£000	£000	£000	£000
Cost	180	180	180	180	180	180	180	180
Accum Dep'n	20	40	60	80	100	120	140	160
NBV	160	140	120	100	80	60	40	20

(b)

$$\text{Depreciation charge} = \frac{180,000 - 14,000}{5} = 33,200 \text{ p.a.}$$

	Year 1 £000	Year 2 £000	Year 3 £000	Year 4 £000	Year 5 £000
Cost	180.0	180.0	180.0	180.0	180.0
Accum Dep'n	33.2	66.4	99.6	132.8	166.0
NBV	146.8	113.6	80.4	47.2	14.0

Solution to
Activity 8.7

	£
Purchase price	40,000
Less: Net assets	(27,900)
Goodwill	12,100

(a)

Solution to
Activity 8.8

S. Bassey
Balance sheet
as at 1 January 20X6

	£	£	£
Fixed assets			
Intangible fixed assets – goodwill			12,100
Tangible fixed assets at cost		34,000	
Less: Accumulated depreciation		−19,000	
			15,000
			27,100
Current assets			
Stock		12,000	
Debtors	8,850		
Less: Provision for doubtful debts	−100		
		8,750	
Prepayment		500	
Cash		1,000	
		22,250	
Current liabilities			
Creditors	9,000		
Accruals	350		
		−9,350	
Working capital			12,900
			40,000
Capital			40,000

(b)

S. Bassey
Balance sheet
as at 31 December 20X6

	£	£	£
Fixed assets			
Intangible fixed assets – goodwill			9,680
Tangible fixed assets at cost		34,000	
Less: Accumulated depreciation		– 19,000	
			15,000
			24,680
Current assets			
Stock		12,000	
Debtors	8,850		
Less: Provision for doubtful debts	– 100		
		8,750	
Prepayment		500	
Cash (1,000 + 30,000)		31,000	
		52,250	
Current liabilities			
Creditors	9,000		
Accruals	350		
		– 9,350	
Working capital			42,900
			67,580
Capital			40,000
Add: Profit (30,000 – 2,420)			27,580
			67,580

Solution to
Activity 8.9

Year	Weight	Profits	Total
20X0	1	70,000	70,000
20X1	2	70,000	140,000
20X2	3	90,000	270,000
	6		480,000

Weighted Average $= \dfrac{480,000}{6} = 80,000$

Goodwill $= £80,000 \times 2 = £160,000$

Solution to
Activity 8.10

Average profits	76,667
Reasonable profit	65,000
	11,667

Goodwill $= 11,667 \times \dfrac{100}{20} = £58,335$

		£
(a)	Selling price	7,900
	Advertising cost	(500)
	NRV	7,400

		£
(b)	Cost	7,000
	NRV	7,400

Value at the lower of cost and net realizable value = 7,000

Stock Item	Cost	NRV*	Lower of cost and NRV
	£	£	£
A	1,500	3,000	1,500
B	2,000	1,900	1,900
C	4,000	3,300	3,300
D	2,100	3,100	2,100
	9,600	11,300	8,800

* NRV = selling price – distribution costs

Stock should be valued at £8,800

(i) Marginal cost basis:

	£
Direct materials (4,000 × £10)	40,000
Direct labour (12 × £2,000)	24,400
	64,400

Marginal cost per unit manufactured = 64,400/4,000 = £16.10

Unsold stock = 4,000 – 3,500 = 500

Marginal cost of unsold stock = £16.10 × 500 = £8,050

(ii) Total cost basis:

	£	£
Direct costs		64,400
Manufacturing overheads:		
Indirect wages (2 × £2,500)	5,000	
Rent	1,600	
Light and heat	3,000	
Depreciation	4,000	
		13,600
		78,000

Total cost per unit manufactured = 78,000 / 4,000 = £19.50

Total cost of unsold stock = £19.50 × 500 = £9,750

(a)   FIFO = 400 units at £8   £3,200

(b)   LIFO = 300 units at £6   £1,800

100 units at £8   £800

£2,600

(a)   (i)   FIFO basis: stock card

Date	Receipts			Issues			Balance		
	Units	*Price*	*£*	*Units*	*Price*	*£*	*Units*	*Price*	*£*
Jan	1,000	10	10,000						
	900	10	9,000	1,200	10	12,000	700	10	7,000
Feb	1,200	14	16,800	700	10	7,000			
				300	14	4,200	900	14	12,600
Mar	2,000	16	32,000	500	14	7,000	400	14	5,600
							2,000	16	32,000
Apr	500	17	8,500	400	14	5,600	700	16	11,200
	200	18	3,600	1,300	16	20,800	500	17	8,500
							200	18	3,600
	5,800		79,900	4,400		56,600			23,300

(ii)   LIFO basis: stock card

Date	Receipts			Issues			Balance		
	Units	*Price*	*£*	*Units*	*Price*	*£*	*Units*	*Price*	*£*
Jan	1,000	10	10,000				1,000	10	10,000
	900	10	9,000	1,200	10	12,000	700	10	7,000
Feb	1,200	14	16,800	1,000	14	14,000	700	10	7,000
							200	14	2,800
Mar	2,000	16	32,000	500	16	8,000	700	10	7,000
							200	14	2,800
							1,500	16	24,000
Apr	500	17	8,500	200	18	3,600	700	10	7,000
	200	18	3,600	500	17	8,500	200	14	2,800
				1,000	16	16,000	500	16	8,000
	5,800		79,900	4,400		62,100			17,800

(b)   **Trading account (extract)**

		FIFO basis		LIFO basis
		£		£
Sales		104,200		104,200
Purchases	79,900		79,900	
Less: Closing stock	(23,300)		(17,800)	
		(56,600)		(62,100)
Gross profit		47,600		42,100

(a) (i) Periodic basis:

Purchases:	Units	Price	£
Jan	1,000	10	10,000
	900	10	9,000
Feb	1,200	14	16,800
Mar	2,000	16	32,000
Apr	500	17	8,500
	200	18	3,600
	5,800		79,900

Stock is valued at:

79,900 / 5,800   =   £13.78

Closing stock   =   £13.78 × 1,400 units = £19,292

(ii) Transaction basis: cost card

Date	Receipts			Issues			Balance		
	Units	Price	£	Units	Price	£	Units	Price	£
Jan	1,000	10	10,000				1,000	10.00	10,000
	900	10	9,000				900	10.00	9,000
							1,900	10.00[1]	19,000
				1,200	10.00	12,000	700	10.00	7,000
Feb	1,200	14	16,800				700	10.00	7,000
							1,200	14.00	16,800
							1,900	12.53[2]	23,800
				1,000	12.53	12,530	900	12.53	11,277
Mar	2,000	16	32,000				900	12.53	11,277
							2,000	16.00	32,000
							2,900	14.92[3]	43,277
				500	14.92	7,460	2,400	14.92	35,808
Apr	500	17	8,500				2,400	14.92	35,808
	200	18	3,600				500	17.00	8,500
							200	18.00	3,600
							3,100	15.45[4]	47,908
				1,700	15.45	26,265	1,400	15.45	21,630

Note 1 £19,000 / 1,900 units

2 £23,800 / 1,900 units

3 £43,277 / 2,900 units

4 £47,908 / 3,100 units

(b) **Summary trading account - AVCO (transaction basis)**

	£	£
Sales		104,200
Purchases	79,900	
Less: Closing stock	(21,630)	
		(58,270)
Gross profit		45,930

9 Partnerships

The objectives of this chapter are to:

- explain what a partnership is;
- outline the legal rules governing their operations;
- explain and illustrate how profit is divided;
- describe how the interest of each partner in the firm is recorded;
- show how changes in membership or the profit-sharing ratio are recorded; and
- demonstrate the accounting aspects of dissolving a partnership.

INTRODUCTION

Partnerships use the same basic accounting techniques as those described so far in this book in the context of the sole trader, although some modifications are required in their application to suit the different constitution of the partnership. There is no legal requirement for partnerships to prepare annual accounts, but the need to share profits between the partners and for partners to submit tax returns makes their routine production essential if the conduct of the partnership is to proceed smoothly. As with sole traders, there is no requirement for the contents of partnership accounts to be made public, even though they may relate to significant economic entities: this contrasts with the disclosure requirements imposed on limited companies described in Chapter 10.

The legal background is provided by the Partnership Act 1890, which defines a partnership as 'the relation which subsists between persons carrying on a business in common with a view of profit'. There is no formal legal procedure necessary to create a partnership; it can be deemed to exist because people are trading in a way that brings them within the definition. It is very important to determine whether a person is a partner as the liability of each partner for all of the firm's debts is unlimited; if the firm cannot pay, then each partner becomes personally liable to the extent of the entire debt. (The Limited Partnership Act 1907 makes special provision for a partnership to have limited partners whose liability is restricted to the value of their capital investment, provided there is at least one general partner who accepts full liability for all of the firm's debts. This provision is not widely used.)

The most common reasons for forming a partnership are to raise the necessary finance to fund planned operations, and to pool together complementary skills, for example, an engineer who is very good at developing new products may need the services of a sales person to market them.

The number of partners allowed to combine in a partnership is limited to 20, although some specific exemptions are granted: for example, firms of chartered accountants can have any number of partners. If a firm limited to 20 partners wishes to seek funds from a larger group, then incorporation as a limited company is first necessary (see Chapter 10).

THE PARTNERSHIP AGREEMENT

The owners of a partnership, the partners, also manage it, and each partner can enter into contracts on behalf of the firm that are binding on the partnership as a whole. In these circumstances, the partners must have a great deal of mutual trust, and it is best for the manner in which the partnership is to be conducted to be set out formally in a legally binding partnership agreement signed by all of the partners. Examples of the matters to be covered by such an agreement are as follows:

1   The purpose for which the partnership is formed.
2   The amount of capital each partner is to contribute.
3   Regulations to be observed when the partnership is created.
4   How profits and losses are to be divided among the partners.
5   Whether separate capital and current accounts are to be maintained.
6   The extent to which partners can make drawings.
7   The frequency with which accounts are to be prepared and whether they are to be subjected to an independent audit.
8   Regulations to be observed when a partner retires or a new partner is admitted, the profit-sharing ratio changes or the partnership is dissolved.

Where no formal agreement exists, the terms of the partnership may be concluded from past behaviour: for example, if profits have always been divided between two partners in the ratio 2 : 1, without dissent from either partner, then this is presumed to be the agreed ratio. The Limited Partnership Act 1890 provides a 'safety net' of regulations that apply when there is no agreement, either formal or informal, to the contrary. Among the major of these provisions are the following:

1   All profits and losses are to be shared equally among the partners.
2   No interest on capital or remuneration for conducting the partnership business is payable to any partner.
3   A partner is entitled to 5 per cent per annum interest on any loans to the partnership in excess of his or her agreed capital contribution.
4   Every partner is authorized to take part in the firm's management.
5   All existing partners must agree to the admission of a new partner.

THE CREATION OF A PARTNERSHIP

When a partnership is formed, the contribution of each partner is recorded in its books at its current, agreed value. The capital may consist simply of cash or, where the partner already operates as a sole trader, comprise a collection of assets and possibly liabilities. As was the case with the sole trader, the value of the capital of each partner is equal to, and can be calculated as, the value of the assets contributed less any liabilities. The entries made in the books to record the assets, liabilities (if any) and capital introduced by a partner, on the formation of a partnership, are:

Debit	*Credit*	*With*
Various asset accounts		Assets contributed
	Various liability accounts	Liabilities taken over
	Capital account	Value of assets less liabilities

The merging of two sole traders to create a partnership is shown in Example 9.1.

Beaver and Burroughes are two sole traders who decide to enter into partnership as from 1 March 1986. Their respective balance sheets as at the close of business on 28 February 1986 were as follows:

EXAMPLE 9.1

Beaver

	£		£
Capital account	2,990	Office furniture	500
Creditors	850	Delivery van	660
Bank overdraft	320	Stock	1,440
		Debtors	1,530
		Cash-in-hand	30
	4,160		4,160

Burroughes

	£		£
Capital account	5,200	Office furniture	550
Creditors	920	Delivery van	750
		Stock	1,970
		Debtors	1,730
		Bank	1,120
	6,120		6,120

The partnership acquired *all* the assets and took over *all* the liabilities at the figures shown in the above balance sheets except that:

		Beaver	*Burroughes*
		£	£
1	Office furniture is to be revalued	400	480
2	Stock is to be revalued	1,300	1,900
3	Goodwill is valued at	–	400
4	Bad debts are to be written off	120	80
5	The bank accounts are to be closed and a new partnership bank account opened		

Required

(i)   Calculate the opening capital of each of the two partners. (Calculations *must* be shown.)

(ii) Draw up the *opening* balance sheet of the partnership.

(LCC, Elementary Book-Keeping, Winter 1986)

Solution

(i)

	Beaver	*Burroughes*	*Total*
	£	£	£
Office furniture	400	480	880
Delivery vans	660	750	1,410
Stock	1,300	1,900	3,200
Debtors	1,410	1,650	3,060
Goodwill	–	400	400
Cash	30	–	30
Bank	(320)	1,120	800
Creditors	(850)	(920)	(1,770)
	2,630	5,380	8,010

(ii) **Partnership Balance Sheet, 1 March 1986**

	£	£
Goodwill		400
Office furniture		880
Delivery vans		1,410
		2,690
Stock	3,200	
Debtors	3,060	
Bank	800	
Cash	30	
	7,090	
Creditors	(1,770)	

	5,320
	8,010
Financed by:	
Beaver – capital account	2,630
Burroughes – capital account	5,380
	8,010

THE DIVISION OF PROFIT

The net profit of a partnership is calculated in the usual way, and is then transferred to the appropriation account where it is divided among the partners in the agreed manner. The agreement may provide for a straightforward allocation in accordance with a specific ratio, such as 3 : 2; alternatively, precise adjustments may be made to take account of the following factors:

1 The partners may provide different amounts of capital; this involves sacrificing different amounts of interest that could have been earned by, for example, putting the money in a bank deposit account. Compensation for this can be achieved by allowing a deduction to be made in the appropriation account for interest on partners' capital. The rate of interest may be fixed in the agreement or, because rates of interest fluctuate, it could be tied to some external indicator, such as the rate paid on long-term deposit accounts by banks. In whichever way the rate is determined, the greater the amount of capital a partner has invested in the firm, the greater is the interest received.

2 By deciding to join a partnership, each partner forgoes potential earnings as an employee of another firm. The sacrifice of alternative income may not be the same for each partner, for example, one may contribute more valuable skills. This can be recognized by giving each partner a salary related to potential 'outside earnings'. Such salaries are also deducted from profit in the appropriation account.

3 Partners make drawings from the firm that reduce the amount of their investment, and it may be decided to recognize this by charging partners interest on their drawings. This interest is then added to the profit to be shared among the partners.

4 After any interest and salaries have been deducted, there must be agreement on how to divide the residual profit or loss. The ratio in which it is shared may be designed to reflect the partners' relative seniority, or some other basis, such as equality, may be adopted.

The steps necessary to carry out the division of partnership profit are as follows:

1 Determine the manner in which profit is to be divided.

2 Determine the value of profit or loss to be shared. The value found takes no account of any payments to the partners, for example, in the form of salaries, and is transferred to the appropriation account.

3   Add to profit any interest charged on drawings made by the partners.
4   Deduct from profit any interest allowed on capital account balances and any salaries payable to partners.
5   Split the residual profit or loss in the agreed ratio.

Steps 3–5 are recorded in the firm's books with the following entries:

Debit	Credit	With
Capital account*	Profit and loss appropriation account	Interest charged on drawings
Profit and loss appropriation account	Capital account	Interest allowed on capital, salaries and share of profit
Capital account*	Profit and loss appropriation	Share of losses account

Note   *These entries are instead made in the current accounts of partners where such accounts are maintained (see the section on capital and current accounts that follows).

The division of profit in the appropriation account is demonstrated in Example 9.2.

EXAMPLE 9.2   Oak and Tree are in partnership and prepare their accounts on a calendar-year basis. They have agreed that profits are to be shared as follows:

1   Oak is to receive an annual salary of £5,000 and Tree one of £10,000.
2   Interest at 10 per cent per annum is to be paid on each partner's capital account balance as on 1 January.
3   Residual profits and losses are to be shared equally.

On 1 January 20X6 the balance on Oak's capital account was £64,000 and on Tree's it was £30,000.

Required   Prepare the partnership's appropriation account on the alternative asssumptions that the profit for 20X6 was

(a)   £30,000,
(b)   £20,000.

(a) **Appropriation Account**   Solution

		£			£
Salary:	Oak	5,000	Profit		30,000
	Tree	10,000			
Interest:	Oak	6,400			
	Tree	3,000			
Residue:	Oak	2,800			
	Tree	2,800			
		30,000			30,000

(b) **Appropriation Account**

		£			£
Salary:	Oak	5,000	Profit		20,000
	Tree	10,000	Share of loss: Oak		2,200
Interest:	Oak	6,400		Tree	2,200
	Tree	3,000			
		24,400			24,400

Note   If there is no agreement to the contrary, the profits in the above example would have been divided between the partners in accordance with the terms of the Partnership Act 1890. Each would have received an equal share, namely, £15,000 in (a) and £10,000 in (b).

Readers should now attempt Activity 9.1, which extends the above example to three partners and includes interest charged on drawings, and Activity 9.2.

Jack, Jill and Jane trade together in partnership, and they have agreed to share profits and   **ACTIVITY 9.1** losses on the following basis:

1 Annual salaries of £10,000, £7,500 and £5,000 are to be paid to Jack, Jill and Jane, respectively.
2 Interest of 12 per cent is to be allowed on the average balance of each partner's capital account for the year.
3 Interest of 12 per cent is to be charged on drawings.
4 Residual profits and losses are to be shared: Jack and Jill 40 per cent and Jane 20 per cent.

You are given the following additional information:

1   On 1 January 20X2, the balances on the partner's capital accounts were:

	£
Jack	30,000
Jill	20,000
Jane	40,000

On 30 June 20X2, Jill introduced further capital of £5,000.

2   The charges for interest on drawings for 20X2 are:

	£
Jack	600
Jill	450
Jane	400

3   The firm made a profit of £42,000 in 20X2.

Required   Prepare the partnership appropriation account for 20X2.

ACTIVITY 9.2   (a)   Prepare the partnership appropriation account of the Jack, Jill and Jane partnership using
Required   the information given in Activity 9.1 above assuming that no partnership agreement exists.
           (b)   Explain the basis on which you have divided the profit in part (a).

CAPITAL AND CURRENT ACCOUNTS

The capital each partner invests in the business can be divided into two elements:

1   The part permanently required to finance the ability of the firm to trade. It is invested in fixed assets and working capital and cannot be withdrawn without reducing the capacity of the business.
2   The part that can be withdrawn by the partners as drawings.

The permanent capital of each partner is entered in a 'capital account'. The partnership agreement usually stipulates the amount of permanent capital invested by each partner, and the balances remain constant until the partners agree to a change. Routine transactions among partners and the firm are entered in a 'current account'. The current account balance fluctuates as it is credited with each partner's share of profits, in the form of interest, salary and share of residue, and is debited with drawings and interest on drawings. To prevent partners withdrawing more than their entitlement, the partnership agreement should state that no current account is allowed to have a debit balance without the consent of the other partners.

Disk and Drive trade in partnership. The following information relates to 20X7.

EXAMPLE 9.3

	Disk	Drive
	£	£
Current account balance 1 January 20X7	9,130	8,790
Interest allowed on capital	1,000	1,500
Interest charged on drawings	150	390
Salary	5,000	3,000
Share of residual profit	6,250	6,250
Cash drawings	7,160	8,240
Stock drawings	120	80

Prepare the current accounts of Disk and Drive for 20X7. For each entry indicate clearly the location of its corresponding double entry.

Current accounts

	Disk	Drive		Disk	Drive
	£	£		£	£
Appropriation			Balance b/d	9,130	8,790
Account:			Appropriation		
Interest on drawings	150	390	Account:		
Drawings:			Interest	1,000	1,500
Cash account	7,160	8,240	Salary	5,000	3,000
Purchases a/c	120	80	Residue	6,250	6,250
Balance c/d	13,950	10,830			
	21,380	19,540		21,380	19,540

It is possible for substantial balances to accumulate in the current accounts where partners consistently withdraw less than their share of the profits. The funds represented by these balances may have been invested in trading assets, and so have taken on the aspect of permanent capital, that is, they are not available for quick withdrawal. This position is shown in Figure 9.1. It is clear that the current account balances could not be withdrawn without reducing the size of the business, since a large proportion of these balances has been invested in fixed assets that would have to be sold to release cash. This is unlikely to happen, and so to bring the balance sheet into line with economic reality, the partners may agree that each of them should transfer, say, £25,000 from current to capital account. The transfer is entered in the books by a debit in each current account and a corresponding credit in each capital account. This increase in capital account balances does not provide the firm with any additional funds, but simply recognizes that the partners have invested funds previously available as drawings in the permanent structure of the undertaking. When additional capital funds are required by a partnership, they must be introduced by the partners and credited to their capital accounts.

		£000
Fixed assets		75
Working capital		25
		100

	Paper	Clip	Total
	£000	£000	£000
Capital accounts	20	20	40
Current accounts	30	30	60
	50	50	100

FIGURE 9.1   Summarized balance sheet of Paper and Clip at 31 December 20X9

ACTIVITY 9.3

Ice and Cube are in partnership, sharing profits and losses equally. The balances on their capital and current accounts at 1 January 20X4 are:

	Capital	Current
	£	£
Ice	50,000	30,000
Cube	60,000	20,000

The trading profit for 20X4 was £45,000, and during the year the cash drawings of Ice were £12,500 and of Cube £14,000. In addition, Ice took over one of the firm's cars at its book value of £1,500 to give to his daughter as an eighteenth-birthday present.

The partners review the accounts for 20X4 and decide that, as some of their current account balances have been invested in the expansion of the firm, Ice should transfer £20,000 and Cube £10,000 from current to capital account.

Required

Prepare the partners' current and capital accounts for 20X4.

CHANGES IN MEMBERSHIP

The partnership business, unlike a limited company, is not recognized in law as a separate legal entity, and so a change in the ownership creates a new business. For accounting purposes, the firm is treated as a continuing entity and the same set of books usually remains in use when a new partner joins or an existing one retires, but entries must be made in the books to give effect to any financial adjustments needed.

Each partner is entitled to their share of the profits, or losses, that have accrued during the period of time for which they have been a partner. Adjustment must be made, when a partner retires or joins, for any increase in value not yet recognized in the accounts, otherwise the retiring partner is not credited with the full amount due and the incoming partner is credited with a share of the assets at below their current value. This is demonstrated in Example 9.4.

The following is the summarized balance sheet of Lamp and Bulb, who share profits in the ratio 3 : 2, at 31 December 20X5:

EXAMPLE 9.4

	£
Net assets	2,000
Financed by:	
Lamp – capital account	1,000
Bulb – capital account	1,000
	2,000

The following is agreed:

1 Bulb is to retire on 1 January 20X6.
2 The net assets have a current value of £3,000.
3 Bulb is to be paid the sum due to him in cash immediately.
4 Socket is to be admitted as a partner on 1 January 20X6.
5 Socket and Lamp agree to share future profits and losses equally.
6 Socket agrees to introduce cash equal to the value of Lamp's capital after the assets have been adjusted to current values.
7 Current accounts shall not be maintained.

(a) Calculate the amount due to Bulb on his retirement. **Required**
(b) Calculate the amount of capital to be introduced by Socket.
(c) Prepare the opening balance sheet of the Lamp and Socket partnership.
(d) Comment on the consequences of not adjusting the assets to current values.

(a) **Solution**

	£	£
Current value of net assets		3,000
Historical cost of net assets		2,000
Increase in value		1,000
Share of increase: Lamp	600	
Bulb	400	
		1,000

Amount due to Bulb:

Capital	1,000
Revaluation surplus	400
Total due	1,400

(b)   Lamp and Socket have agreed to share profits equally and the amount Socket should therefore introduce as capital is the same as the balance on Lamp's capital account:

1,000 (balance) + 600 (revaluation surplus) = 1,600

(c)   **Balance sheet of Lamp and Socket**

	£
Net assets	3,200*
Financed by:	
Lamp – capital account	1,600
Socket – capital account	1,600
	3,200

Note   *2, 000 (Original value) + 1, 000 (Revaluation) − 1,400 (Paid to Bulb) + 1,600 (Cash from Socket) = £3,200.

(d)   Without the revaluation, Bulb would withdraw only the balance on his capital account, i.e. £1,000. He therefore leaves £400 in the business that has accrued under his ownership. Socket would introduce only £1,000, the same as the balance on Lamp's capital account, but would be buying a half share in assets with a current value of £3,000.

ACTIVITY 9.4   Amber and Beryl are in partnership sharing profits in the ratio 60 : 40 after charging annual salaries of £20,000 each. They regularly make up their accounts to 31 December each year.

On 1 July 1996 they admitted Coral as a partner and agreed profit shares from that date of 40% Amber, 40% Beryl and 20% Coral. The salaries credited to Amber and Beryl ceased from 1 July 1996.

The partnership trial balance at 31 December was as follows:

	£	£
Capital accounts as at 1.1.96		
Amber		280,000
Beryl		210,000
Capital account Coral (see note (d) below)		140,000

Current accounts as at 1.1.96		
Amber		7,000
Beryl		6,000
Drawings accounts		
Amber	28,000	
Beryl	24,000	
Coral	15,000	
Loan account Amber		50,000
Sales		2,000,000
Purchases	1,400,000	
Stock 1.1.96	180,000	
Wages and salaries of staff	228,000	
Sundry expenses	120,000	
Provision for doubtful debts at 1.1.96		20,000
Freehold land at cost (see note (e) below)	200,000	
Buildings: cost	250,000	
aggregate depreciation 1.1.96		30,000
Plant, equipment and vehicles: cost	240,000	
aggregate depreciation 1.1.96		50,000
Trade debtors and creditors	420,000	350,000
Cash at bank	38,000	
	3,143,000	3,143,000

In preparing the partnership accounts the following further information is to be taken into account.

(a) Closing stock at 31 December 1996 was £200,000.

(b) Debts totalling £16,000 are to be written off and the provision for doubtful debts increased by £10,000.

(c) Provision is to be made for staff bonuses totalling £12,000.

(d) The balance of £140,000 on Coral's capital account consists of £100,000 introduced as capital and a further sum of £40,000 paid for a 20% share of the goodwill of the partnership. The appropriate adjustments to deal with the goodwill payment are to be made in the capital accounts of the partners concerned and no goodwill account is to remain in the records.

(e) It was agreed that the freehold land should be revalued upwards on 30 June, prior to the admission of Coral, from £200,000 to £280,000. The revised value is to appear in the balance sheet at 31 December 1996.

(f) Amber's loan carried interest at 10% per annum and was advanced to the partnership some years ago.

(g) Provide depreciation on the straight-line basis on cost as follows:
Buildings 2%
Plant, equipment and vehicles 10%

(h) Profits accrued evenly during the year.

Required

(a) Prepare a trading account, profit and loss account and appropriation account for the year ended 31 December 1996 and a balance sheet as at that date.   (17 marks)

(b) Prepare the partner's capital accounts and current accounts for the year in columnar form.   (7 marks)

(24 marks)

(ACCA, Paper 1, The Accounting Framework, June 1997)

We will now examine how these matters are recorded in the books of the partnership. To record the revaluation of assets a revaluation account is used in which the following entries are made:

Debit	Credit	With
Revaluation account	Asset account	Reduction in asset value
Asset account	Revaluation account	Increase in asset value

The revaluation account contains all the increases and decreases in value, and its balance – the net surplus or deficit – is shared among the partners in the agreed ratio. Each partner's share of the net adjustment is entered in his or her capital account as it is permanent in nature. The revaluation account and capital accounts of Lamp, Bulb and Socket, from Example 9.4, would contain the following information:

Revaluation Account

	£		£
Surplus shared:		Increase in value	
Lamp – capital	600	of net assets	1,000
Bulb – capital	400		
	1,000		1,000

Capital Accounts

	Lamp £	Bulb £	Socket £		Lamp £	Bulb £	Socket £
				Balance b/d	1,000	1,000	
Cash		1,400		Revaluation	600	400	
Balance c/d	1,600		1,600	Cash			1,600
	1,600	1,400	1,600		1,600	1,400	1,600
				Balance b/d	1,600		1,600

As well as adjusting the values of tangible assets included in the balance sheet, it is usually necessary to create a balance for goodwill, since the partners are also entitled to share in the value of this intangible asset. The appropriate share of goodwill created during his or her period of ownership is due to a retiring partner, and an incoming partner must expect to pay for a share of existing goodwill.

The partners in the new firm may decide to record the assets taken over at their revalued figures; alternatively they may choose to restate some, or all, of the assets at their pre-revaluation amounts. If the latter course is adopted, the adjustment must be shared among the partners in the new firm in accordance with their agreed profit-sharing ratio. Usually, the revised figures for tangible assets are accepted and goodwill is written off.

Bill, Ben and Flo are in partnership together and share profits and losses in the ratio of 2 : 2 : 1 respectively. The balance sheet of the partnership at 31 December 20X0 was as follows:

EXAMPLE 9.5

	£000	£000
Fixed assets		
Land and buildings		50
Plant and equipment		175
		225
Current assets		
Stock	80	
Debtors	90	
Cash	5	
	175	
Less: Trade creditors	110	
		65
		290
Financed by:		
Capital accounts		
Bill	90	
Ben	80	
Flo	70	
		240
Current accounts		
Bill	10	
Ben	25	
Flo	15	
		50
		290

The following information is relevant:

1   Bill decides to retire on 31 December 20X0, while Ben and Flo intend to continue trading, sharing profits and losses equally.

2   To determine the amount due to Bill, the partners agree that the assets should be revalued as follows:

	£000
Land and buildings	165
Plant and equipment	180
Stock	75
Debtors	85
Goodwill	100

3   After the retirement of Bill, the assets are to be left in the books at their revalued amounts, with the exception of goodwill, which is to be written off. All adjustments are to be made through the partners' capital accounts.

4   All sums due to Bill are to be transferred to a loan account.

Required

Prepare the partnership balance sheet for Ben and Flo after all the above adjustments have been put into effect. Show clearly your calculation of the balances on Ben's and Flo's capital accounts and the amount due to Bill.

Solution

Ben and Flo balance sheet

	£000	£000
Fixed assets		
Land and buildings		165
Plant and equipment		180
		345
Current assets		
Stock	75	
Debtors	85	
Cash	5	
	165	
Less: Trade creditors	110	
		55
		400
Less: Loan from Bill		184
		216
Financed by:		
Capital accounts		
Ben	114	
Flo	62	
		176

Current accounts

Ben	25	
Flo	15	
		40
		216

Revaluation Account

	£000			£000
Stock		5	Goodwill	100
Debtors		5	Land and buildings	115
Surplus			Plant and equipment	5
Bill (loan a/c)	84			
Ben: Capital account	84			
Flo: Capital account	42			
		210		
		220		220

Capital Accounts

	Ben £000	Flo £000		Ben £000	Flo £000
Goodwill	50	50	Balance b/d	80	70
Balance c/d	114	62	Surplus	84	42
	164	112		164	112

Amount due to Bill

	£000
Balance: Capital account	90
Current account	10
Surplus	84
	184

Note All sums due to the retired partner are shown as a loan rather than as capital as he is no longer a partner.

Bush and Shrub are in partnership and share profits and losses in the ratio 1 : 2 respectively. The firm's balance sheet at 31 December 20X4 was:

	£			£
Fixed assets	15,000	Capital: Bush		10,000
Working capital	15,000	Shrub		20,000
	30,000			30,000

The following is agreed:

1 Flower is to join the firm as a partner on 1 January 20X5.
2 After 1 January 20X5 the partners are to share profits and losses equally.
3 Flower is to introduce cash of £14,000 as capital.
4 The assets are to be revalued:

	£
Fixed assets	20,000
Working capital	13,000
Goodwill	9,000

5 The original asset values are to be reinstated after the adjustments resulting from Flower's joining have been made, and goodwill is to be written off.

Required

(a) Prepare the revaluation account of the partnership.
(b) Prepare the partners' capital accounts.
(c) Prepare the partnership balance sheet on 1 January 20X5 after Flower has been admitted and all the consequent adjustments made.

CHANGE IN PROFIT-SHARING RATIO

It is necessary to revalue the assets when there is an alteration in the ratio in which profits are split, so that changes in value up to that time are shared in the ratio that prevailed while they accrued; subsequent changes are shared in the new ratio. Failure to adopt this approach means that all value changes would be shared in the new ratio, even though this did not apply while some of the changes took place. Some assets may have increased in value while others may have lost value, and a value should be assigned to goodwill. The necessary adjustments to values are again made through a revaluation account, the balance on which is shared among the partners in the old profit-sharing ratio. If the original values of any assets are to be reinstated, the adjustments are also made through the revaluation account, the balance on which is transferred to the partners' capital accounts in accordance with the new ratio.

Cut and Hack are in partnership sharing profits and losses equally. The firm's summarized balance sheet at 30 June 20X7 was   **EXAMPLE 9.6**

	£
Fixed assets	7,000
Working capital	3,000
	10,000
Financed by:	
Capital accounts	
Cut	5,000
Hack	5,000
	10,000

Hack decides to reduce the amount of time he spends working for the business, and it is agreed that from 1 July 20X7 profits should be shared between Cut and Hack in the ratio 2 : 1.

The partners consider that fair current values for the assets on 30 June 20X7 are:

	£
Fixed assets	10,000
Working capital	3,500
Goodwill	5,500

The assets are to be recorded in the books at their original values, after the necessary adjustments consequent upon the change in the profit-sharing ratio have been effected.

(a)   Prepare the revaluation account of the partnership to record all the adjustments made to asset values.   **Required**

(b)   Prepare the partners' capital accounts showing clearly the balances after all adjustments have been made.

(c)   Prepare the revised balance sheet of Cut and Hack.

(a)   **Revaluation Account**   **Solution**

	£		£
Surplus: Cut	4,500	Fixed assets	3,000
Hack	4,500	Working capital	500
		Goodwill	5,500
	9,000		9,000
		Written off:	
Fixed assets	3,000	Cut	6,000
Working capital	500	Hack	3,000
Goodwill	5,500		
	9,000		9,000

(b) **Capital Accounts**

	Cut	Hack		Cut	Hack
	£	£		£	£
Revaluation account	6,000	3,000	Opening balance	5,000	5,000
Balance c/d	3,500	6,500	Revaluation account	4,500	4,500
	9,500	9,500		9,500	9,500

(c) **Revised Balance Sheet**

	£
Fixed assets	7,000
Working capital	3,000
	10,000
Financed by:	£
Capital accounts	
Cut	3,500
Hack	6,500
	10,000

ACTIVITY 9.6 (a) A and B are in partnership sharing profits equally. The summarized balance sheet of AB & Co. at the close of business on 30 June 1995 is as follows.

	£000		£000
Land	30	Capital A	50
Buildings	100	Capital B	70
Other assets	70	Creditors	80
	200		200

The partners have agreed between themselves as follows.

(i)   With effect from 1 July 1995 profits are to be shared in the ratio A three-fifths, B two-fifths.
(ii) As at 30 June 1995 the land is valued at £55,000. The new valuation is not to be recorded in the asset account.
(iii) As at 30 June 1995 the buildings are valued at £65,000. This new valuation is to be recorded in the asset account.
(iv) As at 30 June 1995 the business, i.e. the net assets, is valued at £170,000 (the 'other assets' and 'creditors' figures are valued as shown in the above balance sheet). The assets side of the balance sheet at commencement of business on 1 July 1995 is not to be altered from the figures at close of business on 30 June 1995 except for the figure for buildings which is to be reduced to the newly agreed value.

Required   Prepare a summarized balance sheet at the commencement of business on 1 July 1995, taking account of the above agreement between the partners. Show workings clearly.

(8 marks)

(b) Partner A, on receipt of the balance sheet you have prepared in part (a), is not pleased. He is particularly concerned because the balance on his capital account, as compared with B's, has changed in both absolute and relative terms.

Draft a memorandum to A clarifying the whole situation. Your memorandum is required to contain five sections. The first four, referenced (i), (ii), (iii) and (iv), should explain the implications of the corresponding point in the four-part agreement between the partners given in the question. The final section, referenced (v), should summarize the reasons for the change in the balance on A's capital account and should include a comparison with the change in the balance on B's capital account.   (12 marks)

Required

(c) It is often said that the function of a balance sheet is to show the financial position of a business at a point in time.

To what extent do you believe that the balance sheets for AB & Co., one given in the question and one prepared in your answer to part (a), satisfy that function?
Explain your answer briefly.   (5 marks)

Required

(25 marks)

(ACCA, Paper 1, The Accounting Framework, December 1995) (adapted)

DISSOLUTION OF PARTNERSHIPS

When a partnership comes to the end of its life, perhaps because the partners decide to sell up and retire, the firm is dissolved. In these circumstances, the assets are sold, the liabilities settled and the partnership ceases to exist. The Partnership Act 1890 requires that the money raised from the sale of assets must be applied in the following order:

1   To settle all the firm's debts, other than those to the partners.
2   To repay any loans owed to partners.
3   To settle amounts due to partners on their capital and current accounts.

A realization account is used to record the dissolution of the partnership. The following entries are made in it:

Debit	Credit	With
Realization account	Sundry asset accounts	Book values of assets
Cash account	Realization account	Receipts from sale of assets
Realization account	Cash account	Expenses of realization
Capital accounts	Realization account	Assets taken over by partners at valuation

Capital accounts	Realization account	Share of loss on realization
Realization account	Capital accounts	Share of profit on realization
Creditor accounts	Realization account	Any gains (e.g. discounts) on settlement

EXAMPLE 9.7   Tape and Ribbon trade in partnership and share profits and losses equally. The firm's summarized balance sheet at 31 December 20X8 is as follows:

	£		£
Fixed assets	20,000	Capital: Tape	15,000
Current assets	12,500	Ribbon	12,500
			27,500
		Overdraft	1,000
		Sundry creditors	4,000
	32,500		32,500

The partners agree to dissolve the firm. Tape is to take over some of the fixed assets at a valuation of £14,000. The remaining fixed assets are sold for £20,000 and the current assets realize £15,000.

    The expenses of realization are £1,000 and a prompt payment discount of £200 is received from the creditors.

Required

(a)   The firm's realization account.

(b)   The partners' capital accounts.

(c)   The firm's cash account.

Solution

(a)   **Realization account**

	£		£
Fixed assets	20,000	Tape (fixed assets)	14,000
Current assets	12,500	Cash (fixed assets)	20,000
Cash (expenses)	1,000	Cash (current assets)	15,000
Tape	7,850	Discount received	200
Ribbon	7,850		
	49,200		49,200

(b)   **Capital accounts**

	Tape	Ribbon		Tape	Ribbon
	£	£		£	£
Realization a/c	14,000	–	Balance b/d	15,000	12,500
Cash	8,850	20,350	Realization a/c	7,850	7,850
	22,850	20,350		22,850	20,350

(c)   **Cash account**

	£		£
Realization account:		Balance b/d	1,000
Fixed assets	20,000	Realization expenses	1,000
Current assets	15,000	Sundry creditors	3,800
		Tape	8,850
		Ribbon	20,350
	35,000		35,000

Green, Brown and Gray are in partnership, sharing profits and losses in the ratio 2 : 1 : 1.   **ACTIVITY 9.7**
The balance sheet of the firm as at 31 May 19X9 was as follows.

Balance Sheet of Green, Brown and Gray

	£	£		£	£	£
				Cost	Depn	Net
Capital accounts			Fixed assets			
Green	40,000		Premises	60,000	–	60,000
Brown	20,000					
Gray	20,000		Plant and			
		80,000	equipment	10,000	3,440	6,560
				70,000	3,440	66,560
Current liabilities			Current assets			
Bank overdraft	1,300		Stock	16,000		
Trade creditors	5,500		Debtors	4,240		
		6,800				20,240
		86,800				86,800

On 31 May 19X9 it was agreed to dissolve the partnership and as Brown is continuing in business on his own account he agrees to take over the stock, plant and debtors at valuations of £18,000, £5,500 and £4,100, respectively. He also agrees to acquire the premises at a cost of £105,000 and obtains a mortgage loan of £80,000 which is paid to the partnership. The balance owing by Brown is charged against Green's capital account as the two parties have agreed that Brown will repay the loan to Green over a period of three years. Realization expenses amounting to £1,000 are paid in cash and the creditors of the firm are paid in full.

You are required to record the above transactions in the ledger accounts of the partnership.   **Required**

(20 marks)

(ACCA, Paper 1, The Accounting Framework)

If, after all the assets have been sold, debts have been settled and loans have been repaid, any partner has a net debit balance on his or her combined capital and current accounts, he or she must introduce cash to cover the deficiency so that the other partners can receive the amounts due to them. For example, Red, Green and Blue, after trading in partnership for a number of years, decide to dissolve the business. The balance sheet after all of the assets had been sold and the firm's liabilities settled was as shown in Figure 9.2. In these circumstances, Blue must pay £5,000 into the firm's bank account: this raises its balance to £25,000 and eliminates the debit balance on Blue's capital account. Red and Green can then withdraw cash of £15,000 and £10,000 respectively to complete the dissolution.

	Balance Sheet
	£
Cash	20,000
Capital accounts:	
Red	15,000
Green	10,000
Blue	(5,000)
	20,000

FIGURE 9.2   Effect of debit balance of one partner at dissolution of a partnership

The rule in *Garner v. Murray*

If a partner is personally bankrupt and so cannot introduce cash to make good a debit balance on his or her capital account when a partnership is dissolved, then the rule laid down in the case of *Garner v. Murray* must be applied. This requires the deficiency from the realization account to be shared between the remaining partners in the agreed profit-sharing ratio; the irrecoverable debit balance on a partner's capital account is then borne by the solvent partners in the ratio of their capital account balances before the start of the dissolution. The application of this rule is examined in Example 9.8.

Readers should now attempt Questions 9.1–9.5

EXAMPLE 9.8   The following is the balance sheet of Pink, Blink and Wink, who share trading profits and losses equally, after all the firm's assets have been sold:

	£
Cash	20,000
Deficiency from realization account	3,000
	23,000
Capital accounts:	
Pink	15,000
Blink	10,000
Wink	(2,000)
	23,000

Wink is personally bankrupt and cannot contribute anything towards the debit balance on his capital account.

Prepare the capital accounts of the partners showing the distribution of the available cash, and explain the basis on which Wink's deficiency has been shared between Pink and Blink.

Required

Capital accounts

Solution

	Pink	Blink	Wink		Pink	Blink	Wink
	£	£	£		£	£	£
Balance b/d	–	–	2,000	Balance b/d	15,000	10,000	–
Share of loss on realization	1,000	1,000	1,000				
Wink	1,800	1,200		Pink			1,800
Cash	12,200	7,800		Blink			1,200
	15,000	10,000	3,000		15,000	10,000	3,000

The £3,000 debit balance on Wink's account after debiting the loss on realization, is split between Pink and Blink in accordance with the ruling in *Garner v. Murray*, that is, it is shared in the ratio of the capital account balances of the remaining partners prior to the dissolution. Hence, Pink bears 15,000/25,000 × 3,000 = £1,800, and Blink bears 10,000/25,000 × 3,000 = £1,200. The cash balance of £20,000, which remains, is used to pay off the balances on capital accounts of Pink and Blink.

9.1 Jupiter, Mars and Saturn are in partnership sharing profits and losses in the ratio 2 : 1 : 1. The balance sheet of the partnership as at 30 June 1984 disclosed the following financial position:

QUESTIONS

	£	£		£	£	£
				Cost	Dep.	Net
Capital accounts			*Fixed assets*			
Jupiter	55,000		Freehold land			
Mars	32,000		and premises	80,000	–	80,000
Saturn	25,000		Equipment	15,000	6,000	9,000
		112,000	Motor car	5,000	2,000	3,000
Current liabilities				100,000	8,000	92,000
Creditors	4,100					
Bank overdraft	6,400		*Current assets*			
		10,500	Stock	24,000		
			Debtors	6,500		
						30,500
		122,500				122,500

On 30 June 1984 it was agreed that the partnership should be dissolved as from that date. Mars will continue in business on his own account; he agrees to take over the equipment, stock and debtors at valuations of £11,000, £26,000 and £6,100 respectively. He also agrees to purchase the freehold land and premises at an agreed valuation of £120,000, and obtains a bank loan over ten years of £90,000, to help finance the purchase. The proceeds are paid into the partnership. It is agreed that any balance owing by Mars at the finalization of the dissolution transactions will be charged to the capital account of Jupiter as the two parties have agreed that the balance owing by Mars and settled by Jupiter will represent a personal loan to be repaid by Mars, over a four-year period. Saturn agrees to purchase the motor car for £2,900.

Realization expenses amount to £1,500 and, together with amounts owing to creditors, are paid out of the partnership resources. All transactions were completed on 1 July 1984.

Required

(a) The partnership realization account. *(6 marks)*

(b) The partnership bank account. *(4 marks)*

(c) The capital accounts of the partners. *(7 marks)*

(d) The balance sheet of Mars as at 1 July 1984, indicating what the balance on the capital account of Mars represents. *(5 marks)*

(Total: 22 marks)

(ICSA, Financial Accounting I, December, 1984)

9.2 Second and Minute started trading as retail grocers in partnership on 1 January 20X4, but did not keep a set of double-entry books. The firm's bank account, for 20X4, prepared from the record of cheques issued and cash paid into the bank, was

	£		£
Capital introduced:		Purchases	160,000
Second	20,000	Wages	17,000
Minute	20,000	Rent and rates	3,500
Sales receipts banked	200,000	Light and Heat	1,260
		Delivery van	19,000
		Drawings: Second	18,000
		Minute	16,000
		Balance c/d	5,240
	240,000		240,000

Notes 1 The following payments were made directly from cash sales receipts:

	£
Petrol for van	2,000
Maintenance	1,000

Advertising	900
Purchases	2,500
	6,400

2   The van, purchased on 1 January 20X4, is expected to have a life of five years, at the end of which its scrap value will be £3,000.

3   The partners agree that separate capital and current accounts are to be kept and all profits and losses are to be shared equally.

4   At 31 December 20X4:

	£
Debtors	5,460
Trade creditors	3,800
Prepaid rent	100
Light and heat accrued	140
Stock	9,200

5   During 20X4 both Second and Minute took groceries for personal use at cost price as follows:

	£
Second	1,000
Minute	1,260
	2,260

Prepare the trading and profit and loss account for the year to 31 December 20X4 and the balance sheet at that date.   **Required**

9.3   The following is the trial balance of Bean and Stalk, who trade in partnership, at 31 March 20X3:

	£	£
Capital account balances at 1 April 20X2:		
Bean		30,000
Stalk		10,000
Current account balances at 1 April 20X2:		
Bean		3,000
Stalk		5,000
Sales		150,000
Stock at 1 April 20X2	30,000	
Wages	14,500	
Rent	5,000	
Expenses	3,000	
Heat and light	1,200	
Debtors/creditors	14,000	11,500
Delivery costs	5,300	

Drawings:		
Bean	7,000	
Stalk	9,000	
Cash	4,500	
Fixed assets	6,000	
Purchases	110,000	
	209,500	209,500

Notes

1 Stock at 31 March 20X3 was valued at £40,000.

2 Depreciation of £1,500 is to be written off the fixed assets for the year to 31 March 20X3.

3 At 31 March 20X3 wages accrued amounted to £500 and rent of £1,000 was prepaid.

4 On 1 February 20X3 the firm ordered and paid for goods costing £700. These were recorded as purchases but were never received as they were lost by the carrier responsible for their delivery. The carrier accepted liability for the loss during March 20X3 and paid full compensation of £700 in April 20X3. No entries had been made in the books in respect of the loss or claim.

5 Bean took goods that had cost the firm £340 for his own use during the year. No entry had been made in the books to record this.

6 The partnership agreement provided that profits and losses should be shared equally between the partners after:

(a) allowing annual salaries of £2,000 to Bean and £4,000 to Stalk;

(b) allowing interest of 5 per cent per annum on the balance of each partner's capital account; and

(c) charging Bean £200 and Stalk £300 interest in drawings.

7 The balances on the capital accounts shall remain unchanged, all adjustments being recorded in the current accounts.

Required Prepare the trading, profit and loss and appropriation accounts for the Bean and Stalk partnership for the year to 31 March 20X3 and the balance sheet at that date.

9.4 Amir and Barry are in partnership with contributed capitals of £70,000 and £50,000, respectively. They have agreed the following appropriation scheme:

(a) Interest is to be allowed on contributed capital at 12 per cent per annum.

(b) Interest is to be charged on drawings.

(c) Amir and Barry are to receive salaries of £10,000 and £13,000 per annum, respectively.

(d) Amir and Barry are to share profits and losses in the ratio 3 : 2 respectively.

During the financial year ended 30 November 1990 Amir and Barry made drawings from the business totalling £37,000 and £40,400, respectively. Amir and Barry are to be charged interest on their drawings amounting to £1,900 and £3,500, respectively.

The balances on the partners' current accounts were Amir £250 and Barry £1,240 as at 1 December 1989. Both were credit balances.

The draft net profit for the partnership for the year ended 30 November 1990 was £95,000 but this is before allowing for the following:

1   It has been discovered that the receipt of a cheque for £3,000 has been correctly recorded in the cash book but has been posted in error to the sales account.

2   The provision for bad debts has still to be adjusted so that it is 2 per cent of trade debtors as at 30 November 1990. The balance on the provision for bad debts account is £3,400 which represents the provision made as at 30 November 1989. Trade debtors totalled £153,000 as at 30 November 1990.

(a) Prepare journal entries to record the correction of the posting error and the adjustment to the provision for bad debts. Dates and narratives are not required.   **Required**

(4 marks)

(b) Calculate net profit for the year after taking the above into account.

(2 marks)

(c) Prepare the partnership appropriation account for the year ended 30 November 1990.

(8 marks)

(d) Calculate the balances on the partners' current accounts as at 30 November 1990.

(6 marks)

(Total 20 marks)

(AAT Preliminary Examination, December 1990)

9.5   Alpha, Beta and Gamma were in partnership for many years, sharing profits and losses in the ratio 5 : 3 : 2 and making up their accounts to 31 December each year. Alpha died on 31 December 19X7, and the partnership was dissolved as from that date. The partnership balance sheet at 31 December 19X7 was as follows:

Alpha, Beta and Gamma
Balance sheet as at 31 December 19X7

	Cost	*Aggregate depreciation*	*Net book value*
	£	£	£
Fixed assets			
Freehold land and buildings	350,000	50,000	300,000
Plant and machinery	220,000	104,100	115,900
Motor vehicles	98,500	39,900	58,600
	668,500	194,000	474,500
Current assets			
Stock		110,600	
Trade and sundry debtors		89,400	
Cash at bank		12,600	
		212,600	
Less:			
Current liabilities – trade and sundry creditors		118,400	
			94,200
			568,700

Less:

Long-term liability – loan Delta

(carrying interest at 10 per cent per year)   40,000

       528,700

	£	£
Capital accounts		
Alpha	233,600	
Beta	188,900	
Gamma	106,200	
		528,700
		528,700

In the period January to March 19X8 the following transactions took place and were dealt with in the partnership records.

(i)   Fixed assets   £

     Freehold land and buildings – sold for   380,000

     Plant and machinery – sold for   88,000

     Motor vehicles: Beta and Gamma took over the cars they had been

       using at the following agreed values:

       Beta   9,000

       Gamma   14,000

       The remaining vehicles were sold for   38,000

(ii)   Current assets

     Stock – taken over by Gamma at agreed value   120,000

     Trade and sundry debtors:

     Cash received   68,400

     Remainder taken over by Gamma at agreed value   20,000

(iii)   Current liabilities

     The trade and sundry creditors were

     all settled for a total of   115,000

(iv)   Long-term liabilities

     Delta's loan was repaid on 31 March 19X8 with

     interest accrued since 31 December 19X7

(v)   Expenses of dissolution £2,400 were paid

(vi)   Capital accounts

     The final amounts due to or from the estate of Alpha,

     Beta and Gamma were paid/received on 31 March 19X8

Prepare the following accounts as at 31 March 19X8 showing the dissolution of the partnership:

Required

(a) realization account;

(b) partners' capital accounts;

(c) cash book (cash account).

Ignore taxation and assume that all partners have substantial resources outside the partnership.

(20 marks)

(ACCA, Paper 1, The Accounting Framework, June 1998)

SOLUTIONS
TO
ACTIVITIES

Solution to
Activity 9.1

Appropriation Account

	£	£
Profit		42,000
Add: Interest on drawings		
Jack	600	
Jill	450	
Jane	400	1,450
		43,450
Less: Salaries		
Jack	10,000	
Jill	7,500	
Jane	5,000	− 22,500
		20,950
Less: Interest on capital		
Jack	3,600	
Jill (W1)	2,700	
Jane	4,800	− 11,100
		9,850
Share of profit:		
Jack	3,940	
Jill	3,940	
Jane	1,970	
		9,850

W1 12% × 20,000 (opening capital) + 12% × 5,000 × ½ (capital introduced half way through the year) = 2,700.

Solution to Activity 9.2

(a) **Appropriation Account**

Profit		42,000
Share of profit:		
Jack	14,000	
Jill	14,000	
Jane	14,000	
		42,000

Solution to Activity 9.3

Current Accounts

	Ice £	Cube £		Ice £	Cube £
Drawings:			Balance b/d	30,000	20,000
Cash	12,500	14,000	Share of profit	22,500	22,500
Car disposal a/c	1,500				
Transfer to capital a/c	20,000	10,000			
Balance c/d	18,500	18,500			
	52,500	42,500		52,500	42,500
			Balance b/d	18,500	18,500

Capital Accounts

	Ice £	Cube £		Ice £	Cube £
			Balance b/d	50,000	60,000
			Transfer from		
			current a/c	20,000	10,000
Balance c/d	70,000	70,000			
	70,000	70,000		70,000	70,000
			Balance b/d	70,000	70,000

Solution to Activity 9.4

(a)
Amber, Beryl and Coral
Trading, Profit and Loss Account and Appropriation Account
period ending 31 December 1996

	£000	£000
Sales		2,000
Opening stock	180	
Purchases	1,400	
	1,580	
Less: Closing stock	− 200	
Cost of goods sold		1,380
Gross profit		620

Less Expenses:

Wages and salaries (228 + 12)	240	
Sundry expenses	120	
Bad debts written off	16	
Increase in provision for doubtful debts	10	
Depreciation of buildings (2% × 250)	5	
Depreciation of plant (10% × 240)	24	
Interest on loan (10% × 50)	5	
		− 420
Net profit		200

Appropriation Account:

Jan–June 1996

Salaries:	A	10
	B	10
Share of profit:	A ((½ × 200) − 20) × 60%)	48
	B ((½ × 200) − 20) × 40%)	32

July–Dec 1996

Share of profit:	A (½ × 200 × 40%)	40	
	B (½ × 200 × 40%)	40	
	C (½ × 200 × 20%)	20	
			200

Amber, Beryl and Coral
Balance sheet as at
31 December 1996

	£000	*£000*	*£000*
Fixed assets	Cost	Accum	NBV
		Dep'n	
Land	280	Nil	280
Buildings	250	− 35	215
Plant	240	− 74	166
			661
Current assets			
Stocks		200	
Trade debtors (420 − 16)	404		
Less: Provision for doubtful debts	− 30	374	
Bank		38	
		612	
Current liabilities			
Trade creditors	350		
Accruals	12	− 362	
Working capital			250
			911

Long-term liabilities

Loan		− 50
		861

Financed By

Capital Accounts:	Amber	368	
	Beryl	242	
	Coral	100	
			710

Current Accounts:	Amber	82	
	Beryl	64	
	Coral	5	
			151
			861

(b)   **Partners' Capital Accounts (vertical presentation)**

	Amber	Beryl	Coral
	£000	£000	£000
Balance b/d	280	210	−
Cash			140
Goodwill (W1)	120	80	
Goodwill written off (W2)	− 80	− 80	− 40
Revaluation	48	32	
	368	242	100

W1   Total goodwill = 40/0.2 = 200 of which 60% is credited to Amber and 40% to Beryl
W2   Goodwill is written off in accordance with the new profit-sharing ratio (40 : 40 : 20)

Partners' Current Accounts (vertical presentation)

	Amber	Beryl	Coral
	£000	£000	£000
Balance b/d	7	6	−
Salaries	10	10	−
Share of profit	88	72	20
Interest on loan	5	−	−
Drawings	− 28	− 24	− 15
	82	64	5

Solution to Activity 9.5

Revaluation account

	£		£
Working capital	2,000	Fixed assets	5,000
Bush	4,000	Goodwill	9,000

Shrub	8,000			
	14,000		14,000	
Fixed assets	5,000	Working capital	2,000	
Goodwill	9,000	Bush	4,000	
		Shrub	4,000	
		Flower	4,000	
	14,000		14,000	

AB & Co.
Balance Sheet as at 1 July 1995

Solution to
Activity 9.6

	£000	£000
Fixed assets		
Land (W1)		30
Buildings (W2)		65
		95
Other current assets	70	
Current liabilities	− 80	
		− 10
		85
Financed by		
Capital accounts (W3): A	24	
B	61	
		85

W1   Land Account

	£000		£000
Balance b/d	30.0		
Revaluation of 25:		Removed from accounts:	
Capital − A	12.5	Capital − A	15.0
B	12.5	B	10.0
		Balance c/d	30.0
	55.0		55.0
Balance b/d	30.0		

W2   Buildings Account

	£000		£000
Balance b/d	100.0	Devaluation of 35	
		Capital − A	17.5
		B	17.5

		Balance c/d		65.0
	100.0			100.0
Balance b/d	65.0			

W3   Capital Accounts

	A	B		A	B
	£000	£000		£000	£000
Land	15.0	10.0	Balance b/d	50.0	70.0
Buildings	17.5	17.5	Land	12.5	12.5
Goodwill	36.0	24.0	Goodwill (W4)	30.0	30.0
Balance c/d	24.0	61.0			
	92.5	112.5		92.5	112.5
			Balance b/d	24.0	61.0

W4

Goodwill =   Value of business as a whole minus fair value of net assets.

Value of business as a whole	170,000
FV of net assets (55 + 65 + 70 − 80)	(110,000)
	60,000

Solution to
Activity 9.7

Realization Account

	£		£
Premises	60,000	Assets taken over by Brown:	
Plant and equipment	6,560	Stock	18,000
Stocks	16,000		
Debtors	4,240	Plant and equipment	5,500
Realisation expenses	1,000	Debtors	4,100
Gain on realization:		Premises	105,000
Green	22,400		
Brown	11,200		
Gray	11,200		
	132,600		132,600

Bank Account

	£		£
Brown	80,000	Balance b/d	1,300
		Creditors	5,500
		Realization expenses	1,000

		Green capital	41,000
		Gray capital	31,200
	80,000		80,000

Green's Capital Account

	£		£
Loan to Brown	21,400	Balance b/d	40,000
Cash	41,000	Gain on realization	22,400
	62,400		62,400

Brown's Capital Account

	£		£
Assets taken over	132,600	Balance b/d	20,000
		Gain on realization	11,200
		Cash	80,000
		Loan from Green (bal)	21,400
	132,600		132,600

Gray's Capital Account

	£		£
Cash	31,200	Balance b/d	20,000
		Gain on realization	11,200
	31,200		31,200

Company accounts

The objectives of this chapter are to:

- explain the procedures followed in the creation of a registered company;
- distinguish between the different types of company;
- introduce the concept of limited liability;
- distinguish between ownership and control of a company;
- familiarize readers with the main content of the annual report;
- explain the nature and purpose of regulations which set out standard accounting practice;
- indicate the nature of accounting policies with reference to Financial Reporting Standard (FRS) 18.
- identify sources of information available to external users additional to that contained in the annual accounts;
- distinguish between and show how to account for the issue and forfeiture of shares;
- identify the distinctive features of loan capital and debentures;
- demonstrate how to account for taxation and dividends in the appropriation account;
- introduce the treatment of taxation in company accounts;
- define and distinguish between provisions and reserves, and discuss the restrictions on provisions imposed by FRS 12, *Provisions, Contingent Liabilities and Contingent Assets*;
- explain and identify the impact of fixed asset revaluations on published accounts;
- outline the procedures involved in the redemption of debentures;
- explain the nature of a bonus issue and show how it affects a company's accounts;
- explain and illustrate the changes, introduced by FRS 3, *Reporting Financial Performance*, to the layout of the profit and loss account;
- introduce the concept of group companies and discuss the treatment of goodwill in accordance with FRS 10, *Goodwill and Intangible Fixed Assets*;
- describe research and development and show how it is dealt with in the accounts of companies as per SSAP 13, *Accounting for Research and Development*; and
- outline the main limitations of company accounts.

FORMATION OF REGISTERED COMPANIES

A limited company is formed by registering under the Companies Act 1985 (as amended in 1989) – hence the term 'registered' company. Registration is a fairly simple process, but certain formalities must be complied with. It is possible for the individuals wishing to form a limited company to do the work themselves; alternatively they may choose to employ a specialist company registration agent who charges a fee for the work carried out. The following information must be filed with the Registrar of Companies at, or soon after, the registration date:

1 The names and addresses of the first directors.
2 A statement showing the amount of the company's authorized share capital.
3 The address of the company's registered office.
4 The company's memorandum of association and articles of association.

The memorandum gives the company's name and the nature of its proposed operations, which are contained in the 'objects' clause(s).

The articles of association set out the internal rules and regulations of the company, which must be observed by both shareholders and management; they deal with such matters as the voting rights of shareholders, the appointment and powers of directors and the borrowing powers of the company. The Companies Act contains a model set of articles that apply to any limited company not filing articles of its own. The specimen articles also apply to the extent that they are not specifically modified or excluded by any articles the company files. The model articles are rarely entirely suitable and articles 'tailor-made' to the company's individual requirements are usually prepared.

Types of company

There are a number of different types of registered company (see Figure 10.1) and the option chosen will depend on the nature and scale of expected business operations. It is first necessary to decide whether the company is to be registered with limited liability or unlimited liability. Usually the main reason for forming a company is to obtain the protection of limited liability for business activities that, by their very nature, are likely to involve a significant element of risk. For this reason unlimited companies are few and far between, and we do not, therefore, need to consider them further.

There are two basic categories of limited company: the public company and the private company. The public company must include the designatory letters plc after its name, and must have a minimum issued share capital of £50,000, of which at least one-quarter must be collected at the outset. Private companies must use the designatory letters Ltd and are not allowed to make an issue of shares or debentures (see the section on loan capital and debentures in this chapter) to the general public. For a plc there must be a minimum of two shareholders; there is no maximum for either public or private limited companies. Public companies are able to increase the marketability of their shares and debentures by making arrangements for these securities to be listed on the Stock Exchange, but this is a feasible exercise only for very large concerns.

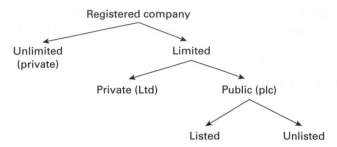

FIGURE 10.1   Types of registered company

Small and medium-sized companies

Small and medium-sized companies are allowed certain 'filing exemptions': the accounts they lodge with the Registrar of Companies, and which are available for public inspection, need not contain all the information which must be published by large companies. This concession, however, does not relieve them of the obligation to publish full statutory accounts for approval by the shareholders. The conditions to be satisfied for a company to be classified as small or medium-sized are outlined in Figure 10.2. It must be noted that public companies, regardless of their size, can never be entitled to the filing exemption.

A company qualifies as small or medium in a particular financial year if, for that year, two or more of the following conditions are satisfied:

	Turnover	Balance sheet total	Average number of employees
Small	≤ £2.8 million	≤ £1.4 million	≤ 50
Medium	≤ £ 11.2 million	≤ £5.6 million	≤ 250
Large	Any other company		

FIGURE 10.2   Definition of small and medium-sized companies

Limited liability

Both sole traders and partnerships are financed by capital contributed by the owners. Should the businesses run short of funds, or become insolvent, the owners are responsible for making good any shortfalls and could face losing their personal possessions to finance business debts, i.e. they have unlimited personal liability for the debts of the business.

Assuming a company is limited, the liability of its shareholders is limited to the amount of money invested in share capital. This means that no further call can be made on the private possessions of the shareholders and that the maximum amount they can lose is the amount of their investment in share capital.

Ownership and control

The powers delegated to the board of directors, in the articles of association, are considerable but they are nevertheless restricted to those needed to manage a business organization on a day-to-day basis. The shareholder theoretically retains overall control in the following respects:

1 Only shareholders are able to authorize a change in the nature of the company's operations, as set out in the memorandum of association.
2 Shareholders control the extent of the company's operations. The level of share capital and borrowing are both stated in the company's constitution and these levels can be raised only with the approval of the shareholders.
3 Shareholders can remove all or any of the directors by passing an appropriate resolution at a general meeting of the company.

These powers are more apparent than real. In a large company there is likely to be a wide dispersal of shares (for example, the shareholding in GlaxoWellcome plc set out in Figure 10.3) and most shareholders regard themselves as passive recipients of dividends rather than active participants in policy-making.

	Number of accounts	Number of accounts (%)	Ordinary shares	Ordinary shares (%)
Holding of ordinary shares				
Up to 1,000	108,442	66.38	44,128,304	1.22
1,001 to 5,000	39,745	24.33	86,421,134	2.38
5,001 to 100,000	13,594	8.32	230,852,033	6.37
100,000 to 1,000,000	1,200	0.73	369,523,005	10.19
Over 1,000,000	383	0.24	2,894,773,422	79.84
Totals	**163,364**	**100.00**	**3,625,697,898**	**100.00**
Held by				
Nominee companies	37,665	23.06	2,944,396,238	81.21
Investment and trust companies	686	0.42	28,229,398	0.78
Insurance companies	138	0.08	77,276,506	2.13
Individuals and other corporate bodies	124,873	76.44	318,675,838	8.79
BNY (Nominees) Ltd	2	0.00	257,119,918	7.09
Totals	**163,364**	**100.00**	**3,625,697,898**	**100.00**

FIGURE 10.3 Analysis of shareholdings in GlaxoWellcome plc

The directors are usually able to exert effective control through their ownership of a significant block of votes, and the fact that many shareholders are absent from the annual general meeting (AGM) empowers the directors to cast their 'proxy' votes in the manner the directors think fit.

An unusually important issue is required to arouse a sufficient body of shareholders to act, in concert, to outvote the directors. The increased involvement of the institutional investor has made shareholder power a greater reality in recent years. Even then, however, activity is likely to occur behind the scenes, resulting in the resignation of a director and the appointment of a capable replacement. In the case of the individual shareholder, dissatisfaction with performance or perhaps policies, for example, lack of attention to environmental issues, simply results in shares being sold.

THE ANNUAL REPORT

The form and content of accounts published for outsiders is set out in Schedule 4 of the Companies Act 1985, as amended by the First Schedule to the Companies Act 1989. In addition to the statutory requirements there are guidelines issued by the ASB in the form of FRS 3, *Reporting Financial Performance.* The standard requires companies to publish the following information in addition to the profit and loss account and balance sheet:

- Statement of total recognized gains and losses;
- Note on historical cost profits and losses;
- Reconciliation of movements in shareholders funds.

Balance Sheet

	£	£
Fixed assets		
Intangible assets: Goodwill	XXX	
Research and development	XXX	XXX
Tangible assets: Land and buildings	XXX	
Plant and machinery	XXX	
Fixtures and fittings	XXX	XXX
Investments		XXX
		XXX
Current assets		
Stock	XXX	
Trade debtors	XXX	
Prepayments	XXX	
Temporary investments	XXX	
Cash at bank	XXX	
	XXX	
Less: Creditors amounts falling due within one year		
Debenture loans repayable within one year	XXX	
Unsecured loans repayable within one year	XXX	
Bank loans and overdrafts	XXX	
Trade creditors	XXX	
Taxation	XXX	
Dividends payable	XXX	
Accruals	XXX	
	XXX	
Net current assets (working capital)		XXX
Total assets less current liabilities		XXX

Less: Creditors amounts falling due after more than one year

Debentures	XXX
Unsecured loans	XXX
	XXX
	XXX

Financed by:

Share capital: Authorized	XXX
Issued	XXX
Share premium account	XXX
Revaluation account	XXX
General reserve	XXX
Retained profit	XXX
	XXX

Trading, Profit and Loss and Appropriation Account

	£	£
Turnover		XXX
Less: Cost of sales		XXX
Gross profit		XXX
Less: Distribution costs	XXX	
Administrative expenses	XXX	
		XXX
Net profit before tax		XXX
Less: Corporation tax		XXX
Net profit after tax		XXX
Less: Dividends	XXX	
Transfer for reserves	XXX	
		XXX
Retained profit for the year		XXX
Retained profit at the beginning of the year		XXX
Retained profit at the end of the year		XXX

In the case of fixed assets, figures for original cost (or revalued amount) and accumulated depreciation should be provided. The above accounting statements broadly comply with the legal requirements concerning the form of company accounts contained in the Companies Act 1985, Schedule 4, format 1.

FIGURE 10.4 Specimen accounts for a limited company

(small entities are exempt this additional disclosure requirement). Students are not usually required to prepare accounts in accordance with the detailed legal and professional requirements at an introductory level. However, answers should be presented in a good form and, for this purpose, specimen layouts are given in Figure 10.4, which complies broadly with legal requirements.

Copies of the profit and loss account and balance sheet must be sent to every shareholder and debenture holder at least 21 days before the AGM. A copy of the accounts approved by the AGM must be filed with the Registrar of Companies, at Companies House, where it is available for inspection by any other interested party. In the case of small and medium-sized companies, as defined by the Act, the accounts filed with the Registrar may be abridged versions of the shareholders' accounts. The reason for this concession is to allow what are, in many cases, small, family businesses a measure of confidentiality. A drawback of the information available at Companies House is that accounts need not be filed until seven months (ten months for a private company) after the end of the accounting period to which they relate, and many companies even fail to keep to this generous timetable; hence the material is often hopelessly out of date.

The profit and loss account and balance sheet are normally published in a document called the 'annual report'. For a large company, it is an extensive document; to take an example, the 1999 annual report of Marks and Spencer plc covers 45 pages. A typical annual report, prepared for a large public company, contains the following range of financial and general information in *addition* to the balance sheet and profit and loss account:

1   *The chairperson's review.*   This is one area of the annual report not subject to any requirements regarding its content. The chairperson is therefore free to say exactly what he or she wishes, but his or her comments will generally cover the following broad areas:

   (a)   An assessment of the year's results.
   (b)   An examination of factors influencing those results, for example, the economic and political climate or the effect of strikes.
   (c)   A reference to major developments, for example, takeovers or new products.
   (d)   Capital expenditure plans.
   (e)   An assessment of future prospects.

   The chairperson's message usually conveys a fair amount of optimism even if the financial facts published later in the report make depressing reading. A strong point in favour of the chairperson's review is that it is readable and easily understood by the lay person. A major drawback is that, with regard to future prospects, it must be based on opinion rather than fact, but it is useful background material when attempting to assess progress by an interpretation of the financial information contained in the accounts.

2   *The directors' report.*   The content of the directors' report is closely regulated by the Companies Act. It must contain a wide range of information, including the following: details of the principal activities and the changes in those activities during the year; recommended dividends and transfers to reserves, if any; significant changes in fixed assets during the year; substantial differences between the book value and market value of land and buildings; details of political and charitable contributions where they exceed specified levels; certain details regarding the company's employment policies; names of the directors and details of their interests in shares and debentures of the company; and details of any acquisitions, by the company, of its own shares.

3   *The auditors' report.*   We have seen that the directors are legally obliged to prepare accounts that are relied upon by external users to reach a wide range

of decisions. The directors usually wish to portray a company's results in the best possible light in order, for example, to persuade the public to buy its shares. It is for this reason that an independent auditor is appointed, by the shareholders, to examine and report on the information contained in the profit and loss account, balance sheet and directors' report. The auditor is not required to report on the chairperson's review, but he or she should not sign an unqualified report if the review contained an erroneous factual statement, for example, where the entire loss for the year was blamed on a strike by the workforce, whereas it was actually caused by falling demand. The auditors' report on the accounts of Marks and Spencer plc for 1999 is shown in Figure 10.5.

The first section sets out the respective responsibilities of the directors and the auditors, while the second section informs shareholders of the scope of the audit, i.e. that work done complies with the instructions issued by the professional accounting bodies for the guidance of auditors. The third section sets out the auditors' findings – their 'opinion'. You will notice that it does not certify the accuracy of the accounts, but instead expresses the opinion that the accounts show a true and fair view. The auditor of a limited company must be professionally qualified, however, and would be expected to exercise appropriate skill and judgement in reaching his or her conclusions. If the auditors have any reservations regarding the truth and fairness of the accounts, for example, perhaps they believe that the provision for bad debts is inadequate, they must refer to this fact in their report. Details of the qualification, in these circumstances, normally appear at the beginning of the section.

There is now an audit exemption available for private limited companies whose turnover currently falls below the £1,000,000 threshold.

4   *The cash flow statement.*   The purpose of this statement is to provide a full record of the cash implications of transactions undertaken during an accounting period. It is, therefore, more broadly based than the profit and loss account, which gives details only of revenues and expenditures during an accounting period. The statement also contains information about capital raised during the year and expenditure on fixed assets. Its function is to provide an insight into the overall financial policy pursued by management and the effect of that policy on the financial structure and stability of the concern. The statement is considered in detail in Chapter 11.

Again, for small entities, there is an exemption available which removes the requirement for a cash flow statement.

Standard accounting practice

Accounting practices were the subject of a great deal of criticism in the late 1960s. The main reason for this criticism was increased public awareness of the fact that, by adopting alternative valuation procedures, it was possible to report vastly different profit figures. In 1965, Professor Chambers drew attention to the fact that conventionally acceptable procedures provided scope for 'a million sets of mutually exclusive rules' (*Abacus*, September 1965, p. 15) for profit measurement. The event that brought matters to a head, however, was the GEC bid for AEI in October 1967.

ANNUAL REPORT AND FINANCIAL STATEMENTS 1999

REPORT OF THE AUDITORS

AUDITORS REPORT TO THE MEMBERS OF MARKS AND SPENCER P.L.C.

We have audited the financed statements on pages 20 to 43.

RESPECTIVE RESPONSIBILITIES OF DIRECTORS AND AUDITORS

The directors are responsible for preparing the Annual Report including, as described on page 6, the financial statements. Our responsibilities, as independent auditors, are established by statute, the Auditing Practices Board, the Listing Rules of the London Stock Exchange and our profession s ethical guidance.

We report to you our opinion as to whether the financial statements give a true and fair view and are properly prepared in accordance with the Companies Act. We also report to you if, in our opinion, the directors report is not consistent with the financial statements, if the Company has not kept proper accounting records, if we have not received all the information and explanations we require for our audit or if information specified by law or the Listing Rules regarding directors remuneration and transactions is not disclosed.

We read the other information contained in the Annual Report and consider the implications for our report if we become aware of any apparent misstatements or material inconsistencies with the financial statements.

We review whether the statement on pages 6 and 7 reflects the Company s compliance with those provisions of the Combined Code specified for our review by the London Stock Exchange, and we report if it does not.

We are not required to form an opinion on the effectiveness of the Group s corporate governance procedures or its internal controls.

BASIS OF AUDIT OPINION

We conducted our audit in accordance with Auditing Standards issued by the Auditing Practices Board. An audit includes examination, on a test basis, of evidence relevant to the amounts and disclosures in the financial statements. It also includes an assessment of the significant estimates and judgements made by the directors on the preparation of the financial statements, and of whether the accounting polices are appropriate to the Company s circumstances, consistently applied and adequately disclosed.

We planned and performed our audit so as to obtain all the information and explanations which we considered necessary in order to provide us with sufficient evidence to give reasonable assurance that the financial statements are free from material misstatement, whether caused by fraud or other irregularity or error. In forming our opinion we also evaluated the overall accuracy of the presentation of information in the financial statements.

OPINION

In our opnion the financial statements give a true and fair view of the state of affairs of the Company and the Group at 31 March 1999 and of the profit and cash flows of the Group for the year then ended and have been properly prepared in accordance with the Companies Act 1985.

PricewaterhouseCoopers

Chartered Accountants and Registered Auditors
London
17 May 1999

FIGURE 10.5   Auditors' report on the accounts of Marks and Spencer plc for 1999

In an attempt to resist the takeover bid, the directors of AEI issued a profit forecast of £10 million for 1967. The takeover nevertheless went ahead and, when AEI reported in April 1968, the investing public was amazed to discover that its accounts showed a loss of £4.5 million. Subsequent investigations proved that a major cause of the £14.5 million discrepancy between forecast and actual results was simply the adoption of more conservative valuation procedures by the new management.

The result was a public outcry, and a great deal of dissatisfaction was expressed with the degree of latitude allowed to those responsible for preparing financial reports. In the endeavour to restore public confidence, the accounting profession established the Accounting Standards Committee (ASC). The job identified for this committee was to prepare Statements of Standard Accounting Practice (SSAPs) designed to achieve the following objectives:

1 To encourage the adoption of best accounting practices.
2 To ensure, as far as possible, that companies adopt similar procedures.
3 To disclose the procedures that have actually been adopted.

The ASC did much to raise the standard of financial reporting, but it was the subject of increasing criticism during the late 1980s. This criticism was a result of the ASC's failure to devise a satisfactory system of inflation accounting and because of a growing tendency to issue standards which were sufficiently flexible to gain acceptability by the business community rather than insisting on what it considered to be best practice.

As the result of criticism a review committee was established, in November 1987, under the chairmanship of Sir Ronald Dearing. It reported in 1988 and its recommendations for the revision of the standard-setting process found favour with the government which, on 26 February 1990, announced the establishment of the Financial Reporting Council under Dearing's chairmanship. The Financial Reporting Council has two 'subsidiaries': the Financial Reporting Review Panel (FRRP) and the Accounting Standards Board (ASB) (see Figure 10.6). The job of

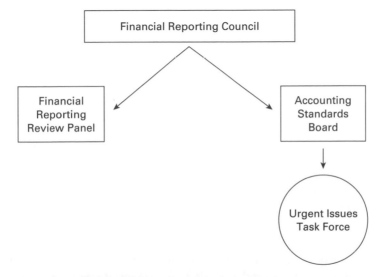

FIGURE 10.6 The standard-setting regime

the review panel is to examine published accounts where there is evidence that the requirements of the Companies Act have been breached, particularly where it appears that they failed to show a true and fair view. The review panel may apply to the Court to issue revised accounts where those previously issued have been shown to be defective. This was done in the case of Groupe Chez Gérard, the restaurant chain, which was ordered to change its depreciation policy and to restate its 2000 accounts.

The function of the ASB is to issue new accounting standards and withdraw any which are considered out of date. It is thus the successor of the ASC. The ASB is assisted by the Urgent Issues Task Force to deal with conflicts between accounting standards and statutory provisions, which possibly lead to different interpretations. Although the ASB may be seen as the successor of the ASC, it is different in a number of important respects. The ASB owes its existence to statutory edict and may issue accounting standards in its own name, whereas the ASC merely prepared standards to be issued by the professional accounting bodies. The independence of the ASB is underlined by the fact that it is financed not only by the accounting profession (as was the ASC) but also by the financial community and the government. The fact that there is now a requirement for companies to disclose and explain material departures from accounting standards further increases its authority.

The ASB adopted the 22 SSAPs issued by the ASC and still extant at the date of the latter's demise. The new body issues Financial Reporting Standards, five of which are considered in this book: FRS 3, *Reporting Financial Performance*, FRS 10, *Goodwill and Intangible Fixed Assets*, FRS 12, *Provisions, Contingent Liabilities and Contingent Assets*, and FRS 18, Accounting Policies are discussed later in this chapter and FRS 1, *Cash Flow Statements* (which has subsequently been revised since its initial introduction), is considered in Chapter 12. FRSs will gradually replace SSAPs; for example, FRS 1 replaces SSAP 10 *Source and Application of Funds*; FRS 10 replaces SSAP 22 on goodwill.

Accounting Policies   FRS 18, entitled *Accounting Policies* (issued December 2000), deals primarily with the selection, application and disclosure of accounting policies. Its objective is to ensure that for all material items:

1   An entity adopts the accounting policies most appropriate to its particular circumstances for the purpose of giving a true and fair view.
2   The accounting policies adopted are reviewed regularly to ensure that they remain appropriate and are changed when a new policy becomes more appropriate to the entity's particular circumstances.
3   Sufficient information is disclosed in the financial statements to enable users to understand the accounting policies adopted and how they have been implemented.

The document requires accounting policies to be consistent with accounting standards and companies legislation. Where a choice of treatment is allowed, a company should select the most appropriate policy to its particular circumstances for the purpose of giving a true and fair view.

The appropriateness of a company's accounting policies is judged against the objectives of relevance, reliability, comparability and understandability and should be reviewed regularly to ensure that they remain the most appropriate for the particular circumstances.

The purpose of the standard is to ensure that accounting policies adopted are appropriate, are amended when necessary, and are adequately disclosed for uses purposes. Three definitions are given, as follows:

Accounting policies Those principles, bases, conventions, rules and practices applied by an entity that specify how the effects of transactions and other events are to be reflected in its financial statements through:

- recognizing;
- selecting measurement bases for; and
- presenting

assets liabilities, gains, losses and changes to shareholders' funds. Accounting policies do not include estimation techniques.

Accounting policies define the process whereby transactions and other events are reflected in financial statements. For example, an accounting policy for a particular type of expenditure may specify whether an asset or a loss is to be recognized; the basis on which it is to be measured; and where in the profit and loss account or balance sheet it is to be presented.

Estimation techniques The methods adopted by an entity to arrive at estimated monetary amounts, corresponding to the measurement bases selected, for assets, liabilities, gains, losses and changes to shareholders' funds.

Estimation techniques implement the measurement aspects of accounting policies. An accounting policy will specify the basis on which an item is to be measured; where there is uncertainty over the monetary amount corresponding to that basis, the amount will be arrived at by using an estimation technique. Estimation techniques include, for example:

(a) methods of depreciation, such as straight-line and reducing balance, applied in the context of a particular measurement basis, used to estimate the proportion of the economic benefits of a tangible fixed asset consumed in a period;

(b) different methods used to estimate the proportion of trade debts that will not be recovered, particularly where such methods consider a population as a whole rather than individual balances.

Measurement bases Those monetary attributes of the elements of financial statements – assets, liabilities, gains, losses and changes to shareholders' funds – that are reflected in financial statements.

Monetary attributes fall into two broad categories – those that reflect current values and those that reflect historical values. Some monetary attributes will be suitable for use in financial statements only in conjunction with others. A monetary attribute, or combination of attributes, that may be reflected in financial statements is called a measurement basis.

FRSs and SSAPs often deal with the valuation and presentation of individual items in the accounts. For example, SSAP 9, *Stocks and Long-Term Contracts*, favours the total cost rather than the marginal cost basis for valuing stocks, and FIFO rather than LIFO. It also requires, where applicable, the classification of stocks into each of its main categories, such as work in progress, raw materials and finished goods. FRS 1, by way of contrast, requires companies (although there are a few exemptions such as small entities as defined by the Companies Act) to publish an additional accounting statement, i.e. the cash flow statement.

OTHER SOURCES OF INFORMATION

Accounts published by limited companies are an important source, but by no means the only source, of information available for shareholders and other interested parties.

There is a whole range of additional information provided by the company itself:

1   A public limited company offering shares to the general public must issue a 'prospectus' containing an accountant's report, which includes the most recent balance sheet and certain specified profit and loss account data for each of the last five years. In addition, the company must provide a forecast of its current year's profits and the planned dividend payment.

2   Companies whose shares are quoted on the London Stock Exchange are required to comply with a range of obligations contained in the Listing Agreement. These include the publication, every year, of an interim statement, which is not audited, setting out key profit and loss account and balance sheet data in respect of the first six months of the company's financial year.

3   It is a growing practice for companies to produce house magazines or newsletters for employees. These summarize the company's results in a manner that is easy to assimilate, making use of pictorial presentations such as bar charts, pie charts and graphs. Although produced principally for employees, it is not unusual for the information to be circulated to shareholders. It is also quite common for such data to be reproduced in the financial press.

4   Shareholders and debenture holders are entitled to attend the AGM where they have the opportunity to ask questions about past performance and the directors' future plans. It is not usual for these meetings to be heavily attended unless the company's affairs are the subject of some controversy, for example, where there is a contested takeover bid. Usually the directors are willing to

answer reasonable questions, although they will tend to become evasive if asked for information considered to be particularly sensitive and unsuitable for public disclosure.

5   Shareholders, particularly institutional shareholders, may be able to obtain information about a company's affairs as the result of informal discussions with one or more of a company's directors, perhaps over lunch.

Information about a company's affairs may also be obtained from external sources:

1   A limited company is under a legal obligation to file a copy of its accounts with the Registrar of Companies. This information is available for inspection at Companies House in London and in Cardiff. On payment of a small charge, an applicant is issued with a microfiche that can be taken away. This contains a copy of the company's accounts, a copy of the company's constitution, details of the company's share capital and debentures, details of each mortgage and charge on the assets of the company, a list of the directors and secretary and the address of the registered office. An extra charge is made for the list of shareholders.

2   There are now a number of websites that give accounting information on quoted companies ranging from the financial reports themselves to an analysis of the results over a number of years. Two useful addresses are:

www.carol.co.uk
www.hemscott.net

The remainder of this chapter examines a number of important aspects in which a limited company's accounts differs from those prepared for sole traders and partnerships.

SHARE CAPITAL

The memorandum of association contains details of the share capital with which the company is to be initially registered and the division of that share capital into shares of a fixed monetary value. The figure for the company's registered share capital is described as the authorized share capital, and the face value of each share is called the 'nominal' or 'par' value. A company may be registered, for example, with an authorized share capital of £500,000 divided into 500,000 shares of £1 each. There is no fixed rule regarding the nominal value of each share, though £1 is often used.

There are a number of different categories of share capital – the two most common are *preference* shares and *ordinary* (or equity) shares. As the name implies, preference shares are given priority over ordinary shares as regards both payment of the annual dividend and repayment of capital on liquidation. Unlike ordinary shares, though, preference shares do not carry any voting rights at the company's AGM.

1   *Dividends.*   The annual dividend payable on preference shares is fixed at, say, 8 per cent per annum, and the dividend is usually paid if profits are sufficient; if profits are insufficient the dividend is lost. If, however, the shares are cumulative preference shares the amount of unpaid dividends is accumulated and, when trading results improve, paid. The payment of preference dividends must be made before any dividend is paid to ordinary shareholders. The dividend payable on ordinary shares is entirely at the discretion of the directors; if profits are low and/or the directors wish to retain all profits earned within the company, they may decide to pay no dividend whatsoever.

2   *Capital repayment.*   On the liquidation of a company, the assets of the business are used, firstly, to settle outstanding liabilities, and secondly, to repay the preference shareholders the nominal value of their investment. Any balance remaining is paid out to the ordinary shareholders as they possess the equity interest in the concern. If a company is wound up because of financial difficulties there is often nothing left over for shareholders after repaying creditors the amounts due.

The directors do not necessarily issue the company's entire authorized share capital at the outset. The figure initially registered represents the company's estimated financial requirements over, say, the next ten years. To begin with, however, the scale of activity may be relatively modest and the volume of shares issued should be restricted accordingly. The way in which the shares are issued may differ depending on whether the company is private or public. It is likely that the issued share capital of private companies will be acquired entirely by members of the first board of directors, and perhaps also their families and friends. In the case of a public company, an invitation may be made to the general public to acquire some, if not all, of the share capital the directors plan to issue. In the latter case the shares are advertised in the prospectus, the content of which is regulated by company law and, in the case of listed companies, also by the Stock Exchange rules.

EXAMPLE 10.1	Griffin Ltd, a newly established private company, is registered with a share capital of £1,000,000 divided into 1,000,000 ordinary shares with a nominal value of £1 each and £450,000 6% preference shares with a nominal value of £1.50. On 1 January 20X1, 400,000 ordinary shares and all of the preference shares are issued at par (nominal value) to members of the board of directors and paid for immediately in cash.
Required	Prepare the T accounts to record the above transactions.

Solution

Ordinary Share Capital Account

	£		£
		1 Jan Bank	400,000

6% Preference Share Capital Account

	£		£
		I Jan Bank	450,000

Bank Account

	£		£
I Jan Ordinary shares	400,000		
Preference shares	450,000		

ACTIVITY 10.1

Milliott Ltd is an established company with an authorized share capital of £4,000,000 divided into 8,000,000 shares of 50p each. At the beginning of 20X1 the company issues a further 2,000,000 shares in addition to the 5,000,000 already in issue at that date. The shares are paid for in full.

Prepare the T accounts to record the above transactions.   **Required**

EXAMPLE 10.2

Using the information from Example 10.1, prepare the capital section of Griffin Ltd's balance sheet as at 1 January 20X1.

Solution

Griffin Ltd
Balance sheet (extract) as at
1 January 20X1

	£
Share capital:	
Authorized: 1,000,000 ordinary shares of £1 each	1,000,000
300,000 preference shares of £1.50 each	450,000
Issued: 400,000 ordinary shares of £1 fully paid	400,000
300,000 preference shares of £1.50 fully paid	450,000

The location of these items in a full balance sheet can be seen by referring back to Figure 10.4.

ACTIVITY 10.2

Using the information from Activity 10.1, prepare a balance sheet extract for Milliott Ltd as at the beginning of 20X1.

Shareholders are not necessarily required to pay immediately the full price of the shares. For example, in the case of a £1 share issued at par, 15p may be payable when the shares are applied for, a further 25p when the shares are issued (called the allotment) and two further instalments, designated calls, of 30p each at some future date. Where shares are offered to the general public, it is extremely unusual for applications to match exactly the number of shares available for issue. If the issue is 50 per cent oversubscribed, one way of dealing with the problem is to issue each subscriber with two-thirds of the shares applied for. If the issue is under-subscribed it is likely to fail unless the company has taken the precaution of arranging for the issue to be underwritten. The function of the underwriter, often a finance house or an insurance company, is to guarantee the success of an issue by undertaking to subscribe for a new issue of shares to the extent it is not taken up by the general public. The transaction is in the nature of a speculation: if the issue is popular the underwriter receives a commission and does nothing; if the issue fails to attract the required number of subscriptions the underwriter is obliged to acquire shares for which there is little demand and whose price, initially, is likely to fall.

EXAMPLE 10.3

A plc has just issued a prospectus offering 500,000 shares for sale at a nominal value of £2.00. The shares are to be paid for as follows: 20% on application; 50% on allotment; and 15% on calls 1 and 2. Exactly 500,000 applications were received and approved.

Required

Enter the above information in the ledger accounts of the company and prepare an extract of the balance sheet.

Solution

Applications and Allotment Account

		£			£
2	Capital	200,000	1	Bank	200,000
4	Capital	500,000	3	Bank	500,000
		700,000			700,000

First Call Account

		£			£
5	Capital	150,000	6	Bank	150,000

Second Call Account

		£			£
7	Capital	150,000	8	Bank	150,000

Capital Account

	£			£
		2	Applic and allotment	200,000
		4	Applic and allotment	500,000
		5	First Call	150,000
Balance c/d	1,000,000	7	Second Call	150,000
	1,000,000			1,000,000
			Balance b/d	1,000,000

Bank Account

		£			£
1	Applic and allotment	200,000			
3	Applic and allotment	500,000			
6	First call	150,000			
8	Second call	150,000	Balance c/d		1,000,000
		1,000,000			1,000,000
	Balance b/d	1,000,000			

Repeat Activity 10.1 supposing that, instead of the cash being received all at once the following pattern of receipts occurred: 30% on application; 50% on allotment; and 20% on first and final call.

ACTIVITY
10.3

SHARE PREMIUM ACCOUNT

The initial issue of shares is normally made at par value and if, a few days later, one of the shareholders decides to sell his or her investment, he or she is likely to obtain a price not materially different from the issue price. This is because the prospects of the company are unlikely to have altered, materially, during the short time since the company was formed. As time goes by the position changes and, assuming the company is successful, the demand for its shares is likely to rise. Where this happens, the original shareholders are able to sell their shares at a profit to new investors. It must be recognized, however, that any rise or fall in the market price of the company's shares has no effect on the finances of the company itself and that the shares continue to be reported in the balance sheet at their issue price (which was £1 in the case of Griffin Ltd).

The directors may decide, at some later stage, to make a further issue of shares to help finance an expansion of the company's scale of operations. This additional issue will be made not at nominal value but at the best price then obtainable. If the market value of the shares has risen to £1.50, the issue price will be fixed at approximately that figure. An accounting problem arises here because of a legal requirement that all share issues, not only the initial issue, must be recorded in the share capital account at nominal value. This problem is solved, however, by recording the excess of the issue price over nominal value in an account called the share premium account.

Assume the same facts as in Example 10.1. Also, on 31 December 20X5 Griffin Ltd issues, for cash, a further 200,000 ordinary shares at a price of £1.50 each. All cash was received immediately.

EXAMPLE
10.4

Required   (a)   Prepare the nominal accounts for Griffin Ltd to record the above transactions.

(b)   Prepare an extract of Griffin Ltd's balance sheet as at 31 December 20X5.

Solution   (a)

Ordinary Share Capital Account

20X5		£	20X5		£
			1 Jan	Balance b/d	400,000
31 Dec	Balance c/d	600,000	31 Dec	Applic and allot	200,000
		600,000			600,000
20X6			20X6		
			1 Jan	Balance b/d	600,000

6% Preference Share Capital Account

	£			£
		1 Jan	Balance b/d	450,000

Applications and Allotment Account

20X5		£	20X5		£
31 Dec	Capital	200,000	31 Dec	Bank	300,000
31 Dec	Share premium	100,000			300,000
		300,000			

Share Premium Account

20X5		£	20X5		£
			31 Dec	Applic and allot	100,000

Bank Account

20X5		£	20X5		£
1 Jan	Balance b/d	850,000			
31 Dec	Applic and allot	300,000	31 Dec	Balance c/d	1,150,000
		1,150,000			1,150,000
20X6			20X6		
1 Jan	Balance b/d	1,150,000			

(b)

Griffin Ltd
Balance sheet (extract) as at
31 December 20X5

Share Capital:	£
Authorized: 1,000,000 ordinary shares of £1 each	1,000,000
300,000 preference shares of £1.50 each	450,000

Issued: 600,000 ordinary shares of £1 fully paid	400,000
300,000 preference shares of £1.50 fully paid	450,000
Share premium account	100,000

ACTIVITY 10.4

Following on from Activities 10.1 and 10.3, at the end of 20X2 Milliott Ltd issues, for cash, a further 1,000,000 ordinary shares at a price of £1.00 each. All cash was received immediately.

(a) Prepare the nominal accounts for Milliott Ltd to record the above transactions.
(b) Prepare an extract of Milliott Ltd's balance sheet as at end of 20X2.

Required

SHARE FORFEITURE

A subscriber to a new issue of shares sometimes pays his or her application money but defaults either when required to pay the amount due on allotment or on one of the later calls. This may happen because he or she is short of money or because he or she feels that the shares are no longer a good buy. Since he or she has contracted to acquire the shares, it is possible for the company to sue for the balance due; however, even where the defaulting shareholder is perfectly solvent, this course of action is unlikely to be considered worthwhile. The directors are more likely to exercise their right, under the company's articles, to consider the shares forfeited. The directors then endeavour to find an investor who is willing to acquire the shares at a price at least equal to the balance outstanding. Any excess received is credited to the share premium account.

EXAMPLE 10.5

Thatchers Ltd is registered with a share capital of £500,000 divided into 1,000,000 ordinary shares with a nominal value of £0.50 each. On 1 January 20X2, 600,000 shares are issued with the agreement that £0.30 is paid immediately and the balance outstanding on 31 March 20X2. The appropriate amounts are received on the dates due, except that Broke, who acquired 500 shares on 1 January, defaults on the payment of the final call. On 1 June the shares are forfeited and reissued to Wealthy for £0.45 each.

(a) Enter the above transactions into the ledger accounts of Thatchers Ltd.
(b) Prepare an extract from the capital section of Thatchers Ltd balance sheet as at 1 June, after Broke's shares have been forfeited and reissued to Wealthy.

Required

(a)

Solution

Applications and Allotment Account

20X2		£	20X2		£
1 Jan	Capital	180,000	1 Jan	Bank	180,000

Call Account

20X2		£	20X2		£
31 Mar	Capital	119,900	31 Mar	Bank	119,900

Forfeited Shares Account

20X2		£	20X2		£
1 June	Capital[1]	250	1 June	Capital[2]	150
1 June	Share premium[3]	125	1 June	Bank[4]	225
		375			375

[1]500 shares @ nominal value £0.50 [2]500 shares @ £0.30 already accounted for
[3]500 shares × (£0.30 + £0.45 − £0.50) [4]500 shares reissued @ £0.45

Capital Account

20X2		£	20X2			£
1 June	Forfeited shares	150	1	Jan	Applic and allot	180,000
1 June	Balance c/d	300,000	31	Mar	Call	119,900
			1	June	Forfeited shares	
					Reissued	250
		300,150				300,150
			1	June Balance b/d		300,000

250 − 150 = # 500 shares @ £0.20 (being amount outstanding on reissued shares)

Share Premium Account

20X2	£	20X2		£
		1 June	Forfeited shares	
			Reissued	125

Bank Account

20X2		£	20X2		£
1	Jan Applic and allot	180,000			
31	Mar Call	119,900			
1	June Forfeited shares	225	1	June Balance c/d	300,125
		300,125			300,125
1	June Balance b/d	300,125			

(b)

Thatchers Ltd
Balance sheet (extract) as at
1 June 20X2

	£
Share capital:	
Authorized: 1,000,000 ordinary shares of £0.50 each	500,000
Issued: 600,000 ordinary shares of £0.50 fully paid	300,000
Share premium account	125

ACTIVITY

10.5

Required

Blaires Ltd has an authorized share capital of £1,000,000 divided into 4,000,000 ordinary shares with a nominal value of 25p each. On 1 July 20X1 3,000,000 shares were issued with the agreement that 20p was payable immediately and the balance outstanding payable on 30 September 20X1. The appropriate amounts are received on the due dates except that Mille Niam, who acquired 15,000 shares on 1 July, defaults on the payment of the final call. On 1 December 20X1 the shares are forfeited and reissued to Brusen for 15p per share.

(a)   Enter the above information into the ledger accounts of Blaires Ltd.
(b)   Prepare an extract from Blaires Ltd balance sheet as at 1 December 20X1.

THE RIGHTS ISSUE

A rights issue occurs where a company requires additional capital and the shares are offered to existing shareholders on a pro-rata basis according to their existing holdings. If the share issue described in Example 10.4 was a rights issue, it would mean that the existing shareholders of Griffin Ltd were offered one new share at £1.50 each for every two shares presently held. Public companies are legally required to raise additional share capital by way of a rights issue, unless this course of action is impractical, in which case an invitation to subscribe may be made to the general public. A particular attraction to the company of the rights issue is that it is an inexpensive method of raising funds as the formalities associated with the issue are kept to a minimum: for example, a full prospectus need not be issued. From the shareholders' point of view an advantage of this procedure is that control of the company remains in the same hands.

LOAN CAPITAL AND DEBENTURES

A company's memorandum usually authorizes the directors to raise finance by borrowing money as well as by issuing shares. Such loans may be secured or unsecured. A secured loan normally takes the form of a 'debenture', which may be defined as 'the written acknowledgement of a debt usually made under seal'. The security for the loan may take the form of either a fixed charge or a floating charge on the company's assets. A fixed charge exists where the asset on which the loan is secured is specified in the debenture deed. Ideally the asset should be one likely to appreciate rather than depreciate in value over time, such as land and buildings. As a further protection, the company is prevented from selling the charged asset without the debenture holder's express approval. A floating charge exists where the debenture is secured on particular categories of assets, for example, stocks and debtors, or the assets of the company generally. This form of debenture gives the company greater flexibility, since it is allowed to trade in the assets subject to the floating charge, and their composition may well change on a daily basis.

Debentures are usually issued for a specified period of time, after which they are redeemed. The debenture deed will, however, provide for early repayment in certain circumstances. For example, should the company default on an interest payment, a receiver may be appointed by the debenture holders to take control of the secured assets, sell them and repay the amount owed. The main differences between debentures, unsecured loans and share capital are summarized below.

1 Loans carry interest at a fixed rate payable regardless of profit levels. Dividends, even on preference shares, are payable only if profits are sufficient, and the directors decide to make a distribution approved by the shareholders attending the AGM.
2 Loan interest is an allowable expense in calculating taxable profit; dividends are not an allowable expense.
3 Loan interest is debited to the profit and loss account; dividends are debited to the appropriation account (see later in this chapter).
4 Unsecured loans and debentures are reported in the balance sheet as a non-current liability and deducted from the balance of total assets less current liabilities (see Figure 10.4). Each year, of course, loans and debentures come closer to their redemption date, and they must be reclassified as a current liability when repayable during the forthcoming accounting period. Share capital is reported as part of the shareholders' equity.
5 Debentures enjoy priority of repayment on liquidation. Unsecured loans rank alongside other unsecured creditors, such as trade creditors. Share capital is repaid, on liquidation, only if resources remain after all liabilities have been satisfied.
6 Loans are almost always redeemable; share capital is redeemable only if a number of conditions are satisfied. In particular, the redemption must be met either out of a fresh issue of shares or out of profits available for distribution. To the extent the redemption is met out of distributable profits, an equivalent amount must be transferred to a non-distributable 'capital redemption reserve' so as to maintain intact the company's permanent capital.
7 A company may at any time purchase its own debentures in the market; these then remain available for reissue until cancelled. A company may purchase its own shares only if the conditions applicable when there is a redemption of shares are satisfied. Where a company purchases its own shares, they must be cancelled immediately.

THE APPROPRIATION ACCOUNT

Profit is calculated in the trading and profit and loss account; the way in which profit is split between taxation, dividends, transfers to reserves and retention is dealt with in the appropriate account (see Figure 10.4). These allocations are now considered in detail.

Corporation tax

Sole traders and partnerships pay income tax on the profits arising from their business activities, whereas the profits of limited companies are subject to corporation tax. The rate of corporation tax depends on the level of profits, and is set out in the Budget and, later, incorporated in the annual Finance Act.

For example, in the financial year ending 2001 tax rates ranged from 10% on profits up to £10,000, to 30% on profits over £1,500,000. In the case of a profitable company, corporation tax may well represent the largest single cash outflow during an accounting period, and is therefore of considerable importance.

Corporation tax is levied on taxable profits, and readers must grasp that the figure for taxable profits is rarely the same as the profit figure reported in the company's accounts, which is called accounting profit. The reason for this is that the accountant and the government have different priorities when measuring profit. A good illustration concerns the treatment of capital expenditure. The aim of the accountant is to produce a profit figure that fairly represents the results of the firm for the year. For example, if it is estimated that an item of plant will last ten years, benefit the company equally each year and then be worthless, the accountant would consider it appropriate to make a *straight-line depreciation* charge of 10 per cent for each of those years. A major priority of the government is to ensure equity between taxpayers, and it is for this reason that they replace the depreciation charge, which may vary considerably from one company to another, with fixed rates of capital allowance, which are also laid down in the annual Finance Act. The current rate of capital allowance on plant and machinery is fixed at 25 per cent per annum on the *reducing balance* basis.

There are many other adjustments that produce less marked differences between accounting profit and taxable profit. For instance, the cost of business entertainment (e.g. taking clients out to dinner), other than for overseas customers, is disallowed for tax purposes but would be treated as a business cost when accounting profit is computed.

Corporation tax is payable nine months after the end of the accounting period to which it relates. The corporation tax charge is disclosed in the profit and loss appropriation account as a deduction from operating profit; in the balance sheet the amount payable appears as a current liability.

Swan Ltd was incorporated on 1 January 20X1, issued 150,000 ordinary shares of £1 each for cash and commenced business on the same day. Plant, purchased at a cost of £130,000, was expected to possess a four-year life and be worth £10,000 at the end of that time. The company reported a profit of £90,000 for 20X1, after charging depreciation of £30,000.

EXAMPLE
10.6

(a) A calculation of corporation tax payable for 20X1, so far as the information permits. For this purpose a capital allowance of 25 per cent and a corporation tax rate of 21 per cent are to be used.

(b) Enter the tax charge in the ledger accounts.

(c) Relevant extracts from the appropriation account of Swan Ltd for 20X1.

Required

Solution

		£
(a)	Accounting profit	90,000
	Add: Depreciation charge disallowed	30,000
		120,000
	Less: Capital allowance (£130,000 × 25%)*	(32,500)
	Taxable profit	87,500
	Corporation tax payable, £87,500 × 21% =	£18,375

Note *The remaining balance (£130,000 − £32,500 = £97,500) is carried forward and claimed against profits in future years.

(b)   Tax Charge Account

20X1		£	20X1		£
31 Dec	Corp tax liability	18,375	31 Dec	Transfer to P&L	18,375

Corporation Tax Liability Account

20X1		£	20X1		£
			31 Dec	Tax charge	18,375

(c) **Profit and Loss Appropriation Account for 20X1**

	£
Net profit before tax	90,000
Taxation	(18,375)
Profit after tax	71,625

ACTIVITY 10.6

Swallow Ltd made a profit for the year ending 31 March 20X0, after charging depreciation, of £180,000. The depreciation figure was based on fixed assets amounting to £400,000 which were being depreciated on a straight line basis over 8 years. The assets are 2 years old.

Required

(a) Calculate the corporation tax charge for 20X0 as far as the information permits. The corporation tax rate is 21% and the capital allowance is 25% reducing balance.

(b) Enter the tax charge in the ledger accounts.

(c) Prepare extracts from the appropriation account of Swallow Ltd for 20X0.

Value added tax (VAT)

Every business that trades in taxable items and has an annual turnover, including VAT, in excess of £50,000 must register for VAT purposes. For companies the accounting standard to be applied is SSAP 5. The consequence of registration is that VAT at the appropriate rate (at the time of writing 17.5 per cent) must be added to the selling price of goods and services and charged to the customer. Every three months the VAT collected, known as the output tax, is paid to the government after deducting any VAT the firm has itself paid on its purchases (the input tax). It is usually possible for a trader to reclaim VAT if the amount of input tax paid in any three-month period exceeds the amount of output tax collected. This may arise if, for example, a particularly expensive fixed asset is purchased, as VAT is charged by the supplier of such items and is immediately recoverable in full.

The accounting records of a registered trader have to be kept in such a way that all input tax and output tax is routinely identified so that the correct settlement can be made. This objective is achieved by identifying and recording separately the VAT element of transactions in a separate column in the books of prime entry. The total from the VAT analysis column of the sales day book is credited to a VAT account in the main ledger: the total from the VAT analysis column of the purchases day book is debited to the VAT account. Similar action must be taken in other books of prime entry, such as the cash book, goods returned day book or petty cash book, where transactions involving VAT are recorded. The VAT account is balanced every three months to find the amount due to HM Customs and Excise. The trading results of the enterprise are therefore reported net of VAT, and any balance on the VAT account at the balance sheet date is shown as a current asset or current liability. For example, if a company sells on credit an item for £235, of which £35 is VAT, the following entries are made in the books:

1   Debit the customer's account with £235. This is the full amount that has to be collected in respect of the sale.
2   Credit sales account £200. The company retains this amount after paying over the tax.
3   Credit VAT account with £35. This is the sum owed to the tax authorities as a result of the transaction and is a current liability until it is paid.

Note that the amount due from the customer is 117.5 per cent of the sales revenue which accrues to the company. Therefore, to find the VAT element of the gross price, it is multiplied by 17.5/117.5, and to find the sales value it is multiplied by 100/117.5. In the above example:

$$£235 \times 17.5/117.5 = £35$$
$$£235 \times 100/117.5 = £200$$

VAT is generally accounted for on the accruals basis but a cash basis can be used if agreed by Customs and Excise. The accounting period for VAT is most often on a monthly basis but both quarterly and annual schemes are operated in certain circumstances.

EXAMPLE
10.7

The following are summaries of the totals on the sales and purchases day books of Collector at the end of January:

Sales Day Book

Total	VAT	Sales
£	£	£
111,625	16,625	95,000

Purchases Day Book

Total	VAT	Materials	Cleaning	Advertisting
£	£	£	£	£
66,975	9,975	37,500	5,000	14,500

Petty Cash Book

Total	VAT	Stationery	Sundries	Motor expenses	Subscriptions
£	£	£	£	£	£
470	70	150	100	90	60

Required

Prepare the VAT account to record the above items, showing the balance due.

Solution

VAT Account

	£		£
Purchases day book	9,975	Sales day book	16,625
Petty cash book	70		
Balance due	6,580		
	16,625		16,625

Some items, such as food and childrens' clothing are subject to VAT but at a zero rate. A business that sells zero-rated items still has to maintain a VAT account so that input tax can be entered and reclaimed. Other items, such as the provision of health care, are exempt from VAT, which means that no tax is charged on their sale, but none of the related tax paid on inputs can be reclaimed; firms that trade only in exempt items do not need to register for VAT or keep a VAT account.

Dividends

Investors are willing to finance business activity because they expect that, at some future date, cash returns will exceed their initial investment by an amount sufficient to compensate them for risk and loss of liquidity. The investor in a limited company expects to receive cash returns in two forms, namely, dividends and the proceeds from the eventual sale of the shares. In the UK company law leaves directors to decide how much the firm can afford to pay as a dividend; the shareholders can only approve the amount proposed or choose to accept a lesser amount.

This rule is designed to prevent shareholders from insisting on a level of payout that might undermine the financial position of the concern and prejudice the claims of creditors.

Dividends are expressed in terms of pence per share and appear as a deduction in the appropriation account. Where the directors are fairly confident that results for the year will be satisfactory, it is common practice to pay an interim dividend during the financial year. The final dividend is usually paid some months after the end of the financial year, the amount payable being decided upon when the accounts have been prepared and profit for the year established.

The directors rarely pay out the entire profits in the form of dividends, and shareholders are usually willing to accept a decision to retain resources within the company because, although they forgo immediate income, the expectation is that reinvestment will produce greater future returns. Management usually aim for a reasonable balance between distributions and retentions.

Where the current year's profit is insufficient, dividends can be declared on the basis of undistributed profits brought forward. Where there are accumulated losses brought forward, these must be made good before a dividend is paid out of the current year's profit.

EXAMPLE 10.8

Hanbury Ltd has an authorized and issued share capital of £700,000 divided into 800,000 ordinary shares of 50p each and 300,000 8% preference shares of £1 each. The company made a net profit of £200,000 during 20X1 and, in July of that year, the company paid an interim ordinary dividend of 3p per share. At the year's end the directors declare the preference dividends and recommend a final ordinary dividend of 7p per share. The retained profit at 1 January 20X1 amounted to £94,000. A provision for corporation tax of £75,000 is to be made on the profit for the year.

Required

(a) Enter the above information in the ledger accounts for tax and dividends.
(b) Prepare the profit and loss appropriation account of Hanbury Ltd for 20X1.

Solution

(a)

Tax Charge Account

20X1	£	20X1	£
31 Dec Corp tax liability	75,000	31 Dec Transfer to P&L	75,000

Corporation Tax Liability Account

20X1	£	20X1	£
		31 Dec Tax charge	75,000

Ordinary Dividends Paid and Proposed Account

20X1	£	20X1	£
1 July Bank	24,000		
31 Dec Proposed dividends	56,000	31 Dec Transfer to P&L	80,000
	80,000		80,000

Preference Dividends Paid and Proposed Account

20X1		£	20X1		£
31 Dec	Proposed dividends	24,000	31 Dec	Transfer to P&L	24,000
		24,000			24,000

Proposed Dividends Account

20X1		£	20X1		£
			31 Dec	Ord dividends paid and proposed	56,000
			31 Dec	Pref dividends paid and proposed	24,000
31 Dec	Balance c/d	80,000			
		80,000			80,000
			31 Dec	Balance b/d	80,000

Bank Account

20X1		£	20X1		£
			1 July	Ord dividends paid and proposed	24,000

Note The directors can only pay an ordinary dividend if there are sufficient funds to cover the preference dividend first. Since an interim ordinary dividend was paid in July, it can be assumed that sufficient funds exist.

(b) **Profit and loss appropriation account of Hanbury Ltd for 20X1**

	£	£
Profit before tax		200,000
Taxation		(75,000)
Profit after tax		125,000
Less: Preference dividends:		
Proposed	24,000	
Ordinary dividends:		
Paid	24,000	
Proposed	56,000	(104,000)
Retained profit for the year		21,000
Retained profit at 1 January 20X1		94,000
Retained profit at 31 December 20X1		115,000

ACTIVITY
10.7

Required

Olympia Ltd was incorporated with an authorized share capital of 1,000,000 ordinary shares of £0.75 each and 600,000 6% preference shares of £1.00 each. The issued share capital (all issued at par) at 1 January 20X0 consisted of £600,000 ordinary shares and £550,000 preference shares. The company made a net profit before tax of £400,000 during 20X0 and, in July of that year, the directors paid an interim ordinary dividend of 5p per share. At the year end, 31 December 20X0, the directors declare the preference dividends and recommend a final ordinary dividend of 10p per share. The retained profit at 1 January 20X0 amounted to £194,000. A provision for corporation tax of £75,000 is to be made on the profit for the year.

(a) Enter the above information in the ledger accounts for tax and dividends.
(b) Prepare the profit and loss appropriation account of Olympia Ltd for the period ending 31 December 20X0.
(c) Prepare the capital section of the balance sheet of Olympia Ltd as at 31 December 20X0.

Provisions and reserves

A *provision* is legally defined as any amount written off or retained by way of providing for depreciation, renewals or diminution in the value of assets or retained by way of providing for any known liability of uncertain timing or amount. This definition covers three basic accounting adjustments.

1 The amount written off fixed assets by way of depreciation.
2 The amount written off current assets or investments to reflect the fact that book value exceeds the amount that is ultimately expected to be recoverable. Examples are a provision for bad debts or any provision necessary to reduce stock to net realizable value.
3 The amount set aside to meet a known liability, the amount of which can be reliably estimated. An example would be where a company sells goods with a warranty under which customers are covered for the cost of repairs of any manufacturing defects, say, within the first six months after purchase. An estimate could reliably be calculated based on past experience. A second example is a provision for taxation.

FRS 12, issued in September 1998, restricts the use of provisions, stating that:

A provision should only be recognized when:

(a) an entity has a present obligation as a result of a past event;
(b) it is probable that a transfer of economic benefits will be required to settle the obligation; and
(c) a reliable estimate can be made of the amount of the obligation.

A *reserve* is a transfer made out of profits at the directors' discretion. The reasons for transferring profits to reserves (and thereby keeping them from being distributed in the form of dividends) may be to help finance expansion, to enable dividends to be declared in a future year when profits are low or to earmark funds for the redemption of share capital or debentures (see later in this chapter).

The distinction between provisions and reserves is very important because it affects the measurement of profit and the way financial information is presented in the annual accounts. A provision is a cost associated with carrying on business activity, whereas a transfer to reserves is not. Provisions are therefore charged *above the line* (in the profit and loss account) and affect reported profits, whereas transfers to reserves are *made below the line* (in the appropriation account) and leave reported profit unaffected. Clearly it is important for management to identify accurately whether a particular item is in the nature of a provision or a reserve. Equally important, care must be taken when the amount of a provision is estimated, since any under- or overprovision will directly affect the accuracy of the reported profit figure.

For example, let us assume a company has a high proportion of debtors outstanding at the year end and past experience shows that a proportion of these will not pay. It would be unreasonable for the directors to ignore this fact as current assets would be overstated. Likewise it would be remiss of the directors to make a provision that was totally unrealistic. The amount of the provision should be made, as far as possible, on past experience and current knowledge.

In the balance sheet provisions are either deducted from the value of the asset to which they relate, e.g. depreciation of fixed assets and provision of bad debts; or included as a current liability, e.g. provision for taxation.

Reserves, on the other hand, remain part of the shareholders' interest and are listed after issued share capital and share premium on the face of the balance sheet (refer back to Figure 10.4).

Most of the matters discussed so far in this chapter are covered in Example 10.9.

EXAMPLE 10.9	Miskin Ltd commenced business on 1 January 20X2 and the following trial balance was extracted as at 31 December 20X2:		
		£	£
	Share capital		380,000
	8% debentures repayable 20X9		100,000
	10% unsecured loan repayable 30 June 20X3		20,000
	Tangible fixed assets at cost	480,000	
	Gross profit		152,000
	Trade debtors	61,500	
	Trade creditors		37,870
	Bank balance	7,400	
	Bad debts written off	320	
	Administration and selling expenses	63,200	
	Interest paid, 30 June 20X2	5,000	

Interim dividend paid	12,000	
Stock-in-trade at 31 December 20X2	60,450	
	689,870	689,870

The following additional information is provided:

1 The authorized share capital is £500,000, divided into ordinary shares of £1 each. The balance on the share capital account represents the proceeds from issuing 300,000 shares.
2 A provision for doubtful debts is to be made of 2 per cent on outstanding trade debtors.
3 Depreciation is to be charged on fixed assets at the rate of 4 per cent on cost.
4 The directors propose to recommend a final dividend of 5p per share.
5 Corporation tax of £180,000 is to be provided on the profits for 20X2.
6 A transfer of £10,000 is to be made to the general reserve.

(a) A profit and loss account and an appropriation account for 20X2. **Required**
(b) A balance sheet as at 31 December 20X2.

(a) **Solution**

Miskin Ltd
Profit and loss account and appropropriation account,
period ending 31 December 20X2

	£	£
Gross profit		152,000
Less: Administration and selling expenses	63,200	
Bad and doubtful debts (320 + (2% × 61,500))	1,550	
Interest (5,000 + 5,000 (1 July – 31 Dec 20X2))	10,000	
Provision for depreciation (4% × 480,000)	19,200	
		93,950
	£	£
Net profit before tax		58,050
Tax		−18,000
Profit after tax		40,050
Less: Dividends: Paid	12,000	
Proposed (5p × 300,000)	15,000	
Transfer to general reserve	10,000	
		−37,000
Retained profit for 20X2		3,050

(b)

Miskin Ltd
Balance sheet
as at 31 December 20X2

	£	£
Fixed assets		
Tangible fixed assets at cost		480,000
Less: Accumulated depreciation		−19,200
		460,800

Current assets		
Stocks	60,450	
Trade debtors (61,500 − 1,230)	60,270	
Bank	7,400	
	128,120	
Less: Creditors due within one year		
Unsecured loan repayable 30 June 20X3	20,000	
Trade creditors	37,870	
Corporation tax	18,000	
Dividend payable	15,000	
Accrual for interest	5,000	
	−95,870	
Working capital		32,250
Total assets less current liabilities		493,050
Less: Creditors due after more than one year		
8% debentures repayable 20X9		−100,000
		393,050
Financed by:		
Share capital		
Authorized: 500,000 ordinary shares of £1 each		500,000
Issued: 300,000 ordinary shares of £1 each		300,000
Share premium account (380,000 − 300,000)		80,000
General reserve		10,000
Retained profit		3,050
		393,050

ACTIVITY 10.8

The following information is provided in respect of the affairs of Newton Ltd, a trading company, for 20X0:

Draft profit and loss account, year to 31 December 20X0

	£000
Administration expenses	1,620
Selling costs	520
Distribution costs	140
Tax charge	63
Transfer to general reserve	200
Depreciation charge	250
Proposed dividend	100
Profit for the year	37
Retained profit brought forward from 19X9	290

Draft balance sheet, 31 December 20X0

Debit balances:	*£000*
Stock	724
Debtors	570
Plant and machinery at cost	1,840
Cash at bank	92
	3,226
Credit balances:	
Trade creditors	416
Provision for depreciation	520
General reserve	200
Dividend	100
Corporation tax	63
Share capital (£1 shares)	1,600
Profit and loss account	327
	3,226

Redraft the above accounts in order to make them more informative. The profit and loss account should show figures for gross profit, net profit and retained profit; the balance sheet should include appropriate classifications of assets and liabilities.

Required

REVALUATION RESERVE

Despite determined efforts on the part of successive governments to control inflation, prices have risen almost continuously since 1940. The process has had a significant effect on the usefulness of accounting statements based on the historical cost concept. The major balance sheet items, fixed assets and stocks, are reported at their original cost less, where appropriate, depreciation to comply with this concept. However, fixed assets may have been acquired many years ago when prices were much lower than today; therefore these assets are often reported in the balance sheet at figures far removed from their current value to the concern. This discrepancy has caused many individuals to question the usefulness of the balance sheet as a statement of a company's financial position, and uneasiness increased with the acceleration in the rate of inflation during the 1970s. The revaluation reserve was developed as a means of restoring an acceptable measure of reality to the corporate balance sheet. The adjustment is quite straightforward:

1. The book value of the fixed asset is increased from historical cost less depreciation to the revalued figure.
2. The surplus arising on revaluation is credited to a revaluation reserve, which is reported as part of the shareholders' equity in the balance sheet (see Figure 10.4).

The adjustment is entered in the books as follows:

Debit	Credit	With
Revaluation account	Fixed asset at cost account	Historical cost of fixed asset
Provision for depreciation account	Revaluation account	Accumulated depreciation
Fixed asset at revaluation account	Revaluation account	New valuation
Revaluation account	Revaluation reserve	Surplus arising on revaluation

The revaluation reserve is therefore an exception to the general rule that reserves are created as a result of transfers from reported profit.

EXAMPLE 10.10

The following information is extracted from the balance sheet of Messange plc at 31 December 20X4:

	£000
Freehold land and buildings at cost	2,100
Less: Accumulated depreciation	(1,300)
NBV	800

The land and buildings were revalued by a firm of chartered surveyors at £5,000,000 on 31 December 20X4. The directors have decided to incorporate the revaluation into the accounts.

Required

(a) Enter the above information in the ledger accounts.
(b) Prepare relevant extracts from the balance sheet of Messange plc as at 31 December 20X4.

Solution

(a) **Freehold Land and Buildings Account**

20X4		£000	20X4		£000
1	Jan Balance b/d	2,100	31 Dec Revaluation reserve		2,100
31	Dec Revaluation reserve	5,000	31 Dec Balance c/d		5,000
		7,100			7,100
20X5			20X5		
1	Jan Balance b/d	5,000			

Accumulated Depreciation (L&B) Account

20X4		£000	20X4		£000
31	Dec Revaluation reserve	1,300	1 Jan Balance b/d		1,300
		1,300			1,300

Revaluation Reserve Account

20X4	£000	20X4	£000
31 Dec Land and buildings	2,100	31 Dec Accum dep'n	1,300
31 Dec Balance c/d	4,200	31 Dec Land and buildings	5,000
	6,300		6,300
20X5		20X5	
		1 Jan Balance b/d	4,200

ACTIVITY
10.9

The following information is extracted from the balance sheet of Revaluation plc at 31 March 20X3:

	£000
Freehold land and buildings at cost	5,800
Less: Accumulated depreciation	(2,300)
NBV	3,500

The land and buildings were revalued by a firm of chartered surveyors at £7,000,000 on 31 March 20X3. The directors have decided to incorporate the revaluation into the accounts.

Required

(a)   Enter the above information in the ledger accounts.
(b)   Prepare relevant extracts from the balance sheet of Revaluation plc as at 31 March 20X3.

Today some large companies supplement their historical cost based accounting reports with financial statements fully adjusted to take account of the effect of changing price levels. This important development in corporate financial reporting procedures is the outcome of the inflation accounting debate that raged between 1970 and 1985. Inflation accounting techniques are examined at a more advanced stage of your financial accounting studies.

REDEMPTION OF DEBENTURES

It is essential that the directors plan a company's finances carefully and, in particular, ensure that a proper balance between short-term, medium-term and long-term funds is achieved. Both share capital and loan capital fall into the category of long-term finance, but share capital may be redeemable and loan capital will invariably be redeemable at some future date. It is management's job to ensure that the long-term capital base is not eroded as a result of the redemption. Indeed, in the case of share capital, the directors are under a strict legal obligation to ensure that this does not happen.

Company law imposes no conditions regarding the redemption of debentures. Debenture holders are treated in law as creditors rather than as providers of permanent capital. Consequently, there exists no requirement that the company should take steps to replace the resources paid out when redemption occurs. However, such obligations may either be imposed by the company's articles of association or be assumed voluntarily by the directors. Debentures may be repayable gradually over a period of years or, at the other extreme, the total amount borrowed may be repayable on a single future date. The effect on the company's finances will be less marked in the former situation, and it is often possible to make the necessary repayments out of cash generated from trading operations. In these circumstances the directors may transfer a sum, equal to the value of debentures redeemed, from profits to a debenture redemption reserve in order to acknowledge the fact that resources have been used in this way.

EXAMPLE 10.11

The debentures of Arches Ltd. are repayable by ten equal annual instalments of £10,000 commencing 31 December 20X1. The relevant balance sheet extracts, immediately before the first repayment, are as follows:

Balance sheet extracts at 31 December 20X1

	£
Creditors: amounts falling due with one year	
Debentures	10,000
Creditors: amounts falling due after more than one year	
Debentures	90,000
Issued ordinary share capital	200,000
Profit and loss account balance	50,000
	250,000

The company redeems one-tenth of the debentures on 31 December 20X1, at par, and transfers a similar amount from profit to the debenture redemption reserve.

Required

Revised extracts from the balance sheet of Arches after the first repayment of debentures has taken place.

Solution

Balance sheet extracts at 31 December 20X1

	£
Creditors: amounts falling due with one year	
Debentures	10,000
Creditors: amounts falling due after more than one year	
Debentures	80,000
Issued ordinary share capital	200,000
Debenture redemption reserve	10,000
Profit and loss account balance	40,000
	250,000

Note The company's cash balance will also have been reduced by the payment of £10,000.

ACTIVITY
10.10

Required

The debentures of Peaches Ltd on 1 January 20X0 amount to £500,000 and are repayable at par by equal annual instalments over eight years.

Extracts from the balance sheet of Peaches Ltd assuming that the repayment of debentures commences in (a) 20X0 and (b) 20X3.

Where the debentures are to be repaid on a single date, transfers to the debenture redemption reserve may be made over a number of years in anticipation of this event. Additional action must be taken, of course, to ensure that the necessary amount of cash is available to finance repayment when it falls due. One approach is to invest separately, each year, an amount of cash equal to the figure transferred to the debenture redemption reserve. These investments may be described, in the balance sheet, as 'debenture redemption investment fund', and the balance on this account appears as a separate item among the current assets of the company. The investments are sold, when the redemption date approaches, and the debentures redeemed out of the proceeds. The debenture redemption investment fund is seldom employed today.

The balance to the credit of the debenture redemption reserve remains legally available for distribution but, in reality, it forms part of the company's permanent capital. To acknowledge this fact, a further transfer may be made from the debenture redemption reserve to a non-distributable capital redemption reserve after the redemption has taken place; a second alternative is to capitalize the credit balance on the debenture redemption reserve by making a bonus issue of shares (see the next section).

BONUS (CAPITALIZATION, SCRIP) ISSUE OF SHARES

Figure 10.7 shows a typical balance sheet of a manufacturing company that has traded successfully for a number of years and financed a great deal of its expansion out of retained profits. Over the years Star plc has generated and retained profits amounting to £575,000 and the whole of this amount is legally available for distribution to the shareholders of the company. An examination of the information contained in the balance sheet in Figure 10.7 clearly shows that, in practice, the company would find it difficult to pay any dividend whatsoever. The company has a cash balance of just £2,000 to meet day-to-day cash outgoings and there is a bank overdraft of £136,000. Clearly the profits retained in the company, although initially in the form of cash, have since been reinvested in business assets. Consequently, although £575,000 remains legally available for distribution, in practice the company is unable to adopt this course of action. It is therefore argued that the equity section of the balance sheet does not fairly represent the financial position of Star plc.

	£	£
Fixed assets		
Plant and machinery at cost		850,000
Less: Accumulated depreciation		(360,000)
		490,000
Current assets		
Stock and work in progress	426,000	
Trade debtors and prepayments	250,000	
Cash-in-hand	2,000	
	678,000	
Less: Creditors falling due within one year		
Bank overdraft	136,000	
Trade creditors and accruals	207,000	
	343,000	
Net current assets		335,000
		825,000
Financed by		
Share capital (£1 ordinary shares)		250,000
Reserves (all distributable)		575,000
		825,000

FIGURE 10.7   Balance Sheet of Star plc as at 31 December 20X1

The directors are able to rectify the position by converting reserves into share capital. The procedure followed is to issue shareholders with additional shares in proportion to their existing holdings, and to make necessary adjustments to the relevant ledger accounts. The process is described as a capitalization of profits and the share issue to existing investors is called a bonus issue or a scrip issue. The adjustment is entered in the books as follows:

Debit	*Credit*	*With*
Retained profit	Share capital	The amount of the
(or reserves)		bonus issue

Assuming the directors of Star plc make a bonus issue of two shares for every one share presently held, the capital section of the balance sheet is revised as follows:

Balance sheet extract, Star plc, as at 31 December 20X1

Financed by:	£
Share capital (£1 shares)	750,000
Reserves	75,000
	825,000

The term 'bonus issue' is misleading. The implication is that the shareholder has received some additional financial benefit he or she did not previously enjoy. This is not the case. It is true that after the issue has taken place each shareholder holds three times as many shares, but the company receives nothing extra and its profit-earning potential remains unchanged. This can be demonstrated by examining the net asset value per share both before and after the bonus issue:

Net asset value per share

Before $\dfrac{£825,000}{£250,000} = £3.30$

After $\dfrac{£825,000}{£750,000} = £1.10$

A person who initially owned 100 shares had a total interest in the book value of the company's net assets of $100 \times £3.30 = £330$. After the bonus issue he or she owns 300 shares, but their underlying asset value has fallen to £1.10 each and the total book value of his or her interest remains unchanged at £330 ($300 \times £1.10$). The market price of the share falls by a similar proportion to reflect the larger number of shares in circulation.

It was noted earlier that the source of a bonus issue of shares is not limited to distributable profits; in particular, balances on the share premium account, revaluation reserve, debenture redemption reserve and capital redemption reserve may be applied in this way.

REPORTING FINANCIAL PERFORMANCE (FRS 3)

Earlier in the chapter the role of the Accounting Standards Boards in the development of accounting standards was discussed. One issue that they addressed in 1992 (among others) was the inadequacy of how profit was being reported and the ways in which comparability of performance was being compromised. Take, for example, a company that for many years operated under the same conditions but in its most recent year undertook a major reorganization of its operations with very high redundancy and reorganization costs being incurred. If a shareholder, or potential investor, were to analyse the performance of this company the latter year would be significantly out of line with previous years and hence the company would appear less profitable and therefore an unattractive investment. The poor performance, however, could be solely ascribed to the high reorganization costs which by their very nature are 'exceptional' in terms of size and incidence although they do fall within the ordinary activities of the business, i.e. they are costs that can be expected to occur in the normal running of a business.

FRS 3 was issued in October 1992 (amended in June 1993) and introduced:

- changes to the format of the profit and loss account;
- a note of historical cost profits and losses;
- a statement of total recognized gains and losses; and
- a reconciliation of movements in shareholders' funds.

The latter three points are outside the scope of an introductory text. The changes to the format of the profit and loss account can be seen in Figure 10.8. Turnover and operating profit are now split between continuing operations, acquisitions and discontinued operations. This helps the user of the accounts to distinguish between past and future performance.

	£000	£000
Turnover		
Continuing operations	650	
Acquisitions	150	
	800	
Discontinued operations	250	
		1,050
Cost of sales		(600)
Gross profit		450
Distribution costs	100	
Administrative expenses	80	
		(180)
Operating profit		
Continuing operations	240	
Acquisitions	100	
	340	
Discontinued operations (loss)	(70)	
		270
Loss on the disposal of discontinued operations*		(30)
Fundamental reorganization costs		(60)
Profit on disposal of fixed assets		70
Profit on ordinary activities before interest		250

Note
* A profit on disposal of discontinued operations would be added.
  A loss on disposal of fixed assets would be deducted.

FIGURE 10.8   Profit and Loss Account as per FRS 3

Certain exceptional items are now required to be shown on the face of the profit and loss account, namely:

(a)   profits or losses on the sale or termination of an operation;
(b)   costs of fundamental reorganizations or restructuring having a material affect on the nature and focus of the reporting entity's operations;
(c)   profits or losses on the sale of fixed assets.

Other exceptional items, such as the write-off of very large bad debts, should be charged to the profit and loss account in arriving at the profit or loss on ordinary activities.

GROUPS OF COMPANIES

There was a substantial increase in the average size of the business unit during the twentieth century which started with many industries still characterized by the 'one-man business'. Today the sole trader remains an important feature of business life but, in many industries, large-scale limited liability is dominant. This development has occurred as the result of both internal and external growth.

Internal expansion is brought about by the reinvestment of profits, whereas external growth involves combining together the activities of two or more separate entities in one of two ways: by purchasing either the assets of another business or its shares in order to obtain effective control of its operations. There are many reasons for business combinations which include the desire to safeguard essential sources of raw material or to guarantee wholesale and retail outlets for the products the company manufactures. The economic term used to describe the process whereby companies expand backwards or forwards along the chain of production and distribution is vertical integration. In contrast, horizontal integration occurs when companies at the same stage in the chain join together; this strategy may be adopted in order to reduce competition and perhaps also to reap some of the benefits commonly associated with large-scale production. Diversification occurs when companies expand into unrelated fields for such reasons as risk spreading or to utilize available funds when there is no room for further expansion in their present line of business.

The accounting problems associated with either of these types of business combination are not within the scope of an introductory textbook. However, students should have an appreciation of the nature and impact of business combination and so a few further comments are appropriate.

A combination based on the purchase of assets is dealt with in a straightforward manner. The assets acquired are revalued and incorporated into the purchasing company's books; any excess of price paid over the value attached to the assets purchased is attributed to goodwill (see the section on goodwill later in this chapter). Once this has been done, the assets are subsequently accounted for in the normal way.

A combination based on the purchase of shares arises where one company acquires sufficient shares in another to achieve effective control of its operations. For example, company A may acquire the entire share capital of company B. In these circumstances the arrangement is made between company A and the *shareholders* of company B; the transaction does not affect company B directly and it remains in existence as a separate legal entity. The reason for basing a combination on the acquisition of shares rather than assets are as follows:

- *Economy.* It is not necessary to purchase all the target company's shares, merely enough to ensure effective control of its operations.

- *Continuity.* Where the acquired company maintains a separate identity, its goodwill is more likely to survive unimpaired.

- *Decentralization.* Decentralization of both managerial and decision-making processes is facilitated where companies retain their own identity.

Combinations based on shares give rise to a group of companies within which the company that purchases the shares is called the 'parent company' and the company whose shares are acquired is called the 'subsidiary'. The relationship

FIGURE 10.9   Relationship between parent company and subsidiary company

between these is demonstrated in Figure 10.9. PC plc purchases the entire share capital of SC Ltd. The arrow in Figure 10.9 indicates that PC is the holding company and SC is the subsidiary, while the percentage superimposed on the arrow indicates the extent of the shareholding. Together PC and SC comprise a group of companies.

The shares in the subsidiary may be purchased for cash or in exchange for shares in the holding company, and the impact on the balance sheet of the holding company is indicated in Example 10.12.

EXAMPLE 10.12

A Limited purchases 50,000 shares with a par value of £1 each in B Limited. The agreed price is £70,000.

Required

State the effect of this transaction on the balance sheet of A Limited, assuming:

(a)   the transaction is paid for in cash; and
(b)   the purchase consideration is satisfied by the issue of 40,000 shares in A Limited each with a par value of £1.

Solution

(a)   The balance of cash in the balance sheet of A Limited is reduced by £70,000 and there appears instead an asset described as 'Investment in subsidiary £70,000'.
(b)   The investment in the subsidiary is again shown at £70,000. The corresponding credit entries are to increase the issued share capital of A Limited by £50,000 with the excess of £30,000 to the share premium account.

One company does not need to purchase the entire share capital of another for the latter to become its subsidiary – merely sufficient shares to obtain effective control of its operations. Acquisition of over 50 per cent of the voting share capital will normally be sufficient to achieve that objective.

The Companies Act imposes additional reporting requirements on parent companies. They must prepare both a profit and loss account and a balance sheet to cover the entire affairs of the group they control. In other words, the profit and loss account reports the combined turnover, costs and profits (or the share attributable to the holding company) of the parent company and its subsidiaries, while the group balance sheet combines together the assets and liabilities of the constituent companies. Where only a proportion of the shares is acquired, the amount of profit attributable to 'minority interests' must be shown in the profit and loss account and the proportion of assets attributable to them must be shown in the balance sheet (see Figure 1.2, which contains the relevant figures in relation to Marks and Spencer plc for the year ending 1999).

Almost all companies of significant size in the UK are parent companies. The largest have many subsidiaries. For example, the published accounts of Marks and Spencer plc list 25 subsidiaries in 1999.

GOODWILL AND INTANGIBLE FIXED ASSETS (FRS 10)

In 1997 the ASB returned to the issue of accounting for goodwill with the replacement of SSAP 22 by FRS 10. The standard has the following requirements:

1 Purchased goodwill and purchased intangible assets (e.g. patents and trade marks) should be capitalized as assets and shown in the balance sheet under the heading of intangible fixed assets.
2 Non-purchased (or inherent) goodwill should not be accounted for in a company's balance sheet.
3 Internally generated intangibles should only be included if there is a readily ascertainable market value.
4 The treatment of goodwill and intangible assets is either to write the assets off over their estimated useful life, or retain in the balance indefinitely (subject to annual review).

Goodwill is the excess of the price paid over the fair values (market values) of the net assets acquired.

RESEARCH AND DEVELOPMENT (SSAP 13)

For many large companies, such as those in the petroleum and pharmaceuticals industries, the involvement in research and development (R&D) is significant. The treatment of such expenditure depends on the nature of the research activity and the future expected outcome of the investment. SSAP 13 governs the treatment of R&D expenditure and specifies the following:

(a) Pure research is experimental or theoretical in nature with no specific aim or application, and as such there is no anticipated future benefit against which the expenditure can be charged. The expenditure should be written off against profit in the period incurred.
(b) Applied research has a specific practical aim or objective but the outcome is unknown. Again, there is no anticipated future benefit against which the expenditure can be charged. This expenditure should be written off against profit in the period incurred.

(c) Development expenditure involves the use of scientific or technical knowledge in order to produce new or substantially improved products or services prior to the commencement of commercial applications, or to improving substanially those already produced or installed. This expenditure can, if certain criteria are met, be capitalized and written off against future profit over its estimated useful economic life. Development expenditure that is capitalized appears as an intangible fixed asset on the balance sheet and is amortized from the date revenue is generated.

LIMITATIONS OF COMPANY ACCOUNTS

There is general agreement that shareholders and other external users find company accounts a useful basis for performance assessment and decision-making. At the same time it is accepted that they suffer from a number of important deficiencies. Some criticisms are as follows:

1   The accounts are usually well out of date. If they are prepared on a calendar-year basis, they are unlikely to be available until March or April of the following year. As such they will be of limited use to, say, a potential creditor as the financial position of a company may have changed dramatically since the accounts were prepared.
2   The information contained in the accounts is based on original cost rather than current value. For example, a freehold property purchased in 1950, for £100,000, might still be reported at this figure despite the fact that it is today worth £5 million. Most people would agree that this is absurd, but the use of £100,000 is fully in accordance with accepted accounting procedures.
3   The balance sheet reports some, but by no means all, of the assets belonging to an organization. In broad terms, an asset must possess a fairly readily identifiable cash value for it to be reported in the accounts. Certain assets, although extremely valuable, do not possess this characteristic and are not reported. For example, the favourable trading connections or goodwill of a company, built up over the years, will be omitted from the accounts.
4   Annual accounts are history, whereas the user wants to know what is likely to happen to a company in the future. Last year's accounts may show a good profit and a stable financial position, but trading conditions are subject to constant change, and a series of setbacks may result in heavy losses and a rapid deterioration in the company's financial structure.

Demands for the publication of information about future financial developments, such as cash forecasts and profit forecasts, have been resisted by management and accountants. The potential for inaccuracy, over-optimism on the part of management, the difficulty of auditing such information and the sensitivity of the information make its publication unacceptable. It is interesting to note, however, that management overcomes its opposition to the publication of forecasts when its company is under threat. For example, the directors often publish profit forecasts as a defensive measure to counter an unwelcome takeover bid. In general, however, information about future developments is restricted to the broad comments made by the chairperson in his or her report.

It must therefore be admitted that, although the improvement of financial reporting procedures continues to be the aim of most people in business and accountancy, much work remains to be done. The above limitations must therefore be borne in mind in assessing the usefulness of information reported in company accounts.

Readers should now attempt Questions 10.1 to 10.8.

10.1 The following trial balance was extracted from the accounts of Minto plc at 31 October 1986.

QUESTIONS

	£	£
Called-up share capital		200,000
Share premium		100,000
12% debentures		225,000
Fixed assets at cost:		
Freehold premises at cost	435,000	
Machinery and equipment	60,000	
Motor lorries	225,000	
Provisions for depreciation to		
1 November 1985:		
Freehold premises		30,000
Machinery and equipment		24,000
Motor lorries		62,000
Sales		791,600
Discounts allowed	14,200	
Discounts received		9,800
Purchases	458,200	
Debtors and creditors	54,100	31,400
Provision for doubtful debts at		
1 November 1985		3,700
Bad debts	2,900	
Wages and salaries	68,400	
Administrative expenses	32,800	
Research and development expenditure	9,600	
Debenture interest paid	13,500	
Directors' remuneration	40,000	
Retained profits at 1 November 1985		115,200
Stock at 1 November 1985	113,400	
Goodwill at cost	30,000	
Bank balance	35,600	
	1,592,700	1,592,700

Additional information relevant to the year ended 31 October 1986 is as follows:

(i)   Share capital is divided into 200,000 ordinary shares of £1 each and is all issued and fully paid.

(ii)   Stock held at 31 October 1986 is detailed as follows:

	Cost	Net realizable value
Category – small	£36,200	£26,700
Category – large	£47,800	£58,600
Category – magnum	£56,300	£46,800

(iii)   The provision for doubtful debts is to be increased to £4,500.

(iv)   Provision is to be made for depreciation as to:

machinery and equipment at 10 per cent per annum of cost;

motor lorries at 20 per cent per annum of cost; and

freehold premises – £6,000.

(v)   Corporation tax on the profits of the year is to be provided for at £33,000.

(vi)   Goodwill is to be amortized at 20 per cent of cost.

(vii)   A machinery replacement reserve is to be created of £15,000.

(viii)   An ordinary share dividend is proposed at the rate of 10p per share.

(ix)   Wages and motor expenses accruals amount to £1,500 and £900, respectively.

Required

(a)   Trading and profit and loss account for the year ended 31 October 1986.

(15 marks)

(b)   The balance sheet as on the above date in vertical format, and with appropriate subtotals. *(10 marks)*

(Total: 25 marks)

(ICSA, Introduction to Accounting, December, 1986)

10.2   You are presented with the following trial balance of Lincoln plc as at 31 December 1992.

	£000	£000
Share capital, 50p ordinary shares		1,000
Share premium		500
15% debentures		800
Profit and loss balance 1 January		200
Purchases and sales	2,400	5,000
Purchase returns and sales returns	100	150
Sales and purchase ledger control balances	1,000	400
Property: cost	800	
depreciation to 1.1.92		200
Land: at valuation on 1.1.83	900	
Machinery: cost	1,600	
depreciation to 1.1.92		500

Discounts for prompt payment	20	10
Operating expenses	1,300	
Interim dividends paid	100	
Debenture interest paid to 1.7.92	60	
Bank		30
Suspense account	210	
Stock at 1.1.92	300	
	8,790	8,790

The book-keeper has not recorded certain items, and seems to have only partially recorded others. Details are given below.

(a) Half of the debentures had been redeemed on 1 July 1992 at a cost of £380,000. Only one entry, in the bank account, had been made.

(b) During the year 1992 200,000 more ordinary shares, identical to those already in issue, had been issued at 110 pence per share. Again only one entry, in the bank account, had been made.

(c) The managing director has taken £10,000 of the purchases for his own use and no entries have been made for this.

(d) The land is to be revalued, as at 31 December 1992, at £1,500,000.

(e) Depreciation of 2% p.a. on cost needs to be provided on the property.

(f) One-tenth of the cost of machinery figure represents items which were fully depreciated down to their estimated scrap value of £10,000 prior to 1 January 1992. There have been no purchases or disposals of machinery during 1992. Depreciation of 10% p.a. on the reducing balance basis needs to be provided on the machinery, as appropriate.

(g) An amount of £50,000 had been paid during the year 1992 to a customer because of personal injury he had suffered as a result of a fault in the goods delivered to him. Only one entry, in the cash book, had been made.

(h) A final dividend of 5 pence per share, on all the shares in issue on 31 December 1992, is to be proposed.

(i) Closing stock at 31 December 1992 is £400,000. Half of this figure represents purchases still included in the purchase ledger control account balance at 31 December 1992.

(j) Any balance on the suspense account should be shown in the profit and loss account as a separate item.

Prepare the profit and loss account and balance sheet of Lincoln plc, in good order, as at 31 December 1992. Your layout and use of headings and subtotals should be designed to give the maximum of helpful information to the reader. All necessary workings should be clearly shown.

Required

(25 marks)

(ACCA Paper 1, The Accounting Framework, Practice Question)

10.3 (a) Within the field of periodic financial reporting, comment on and distinguish between 'accounting bases' and 'accounting policies' and relate them to the following fundamental accounting concepts:

    (i) the 'going concern' concept;

    (ii) the 'accruals' concept;

    (iii) the 'consistency' concept;

    (iv) the 'prudence' concept.

(13 marks)

(b) Explain how the directors of a company attempt to ensure that the annual published financial statements portray a 'true and fair view'.

(12 marks)

(Total: 25 marks)

(ICSA, Financial Accounting I, December, 1984)

10.4 The following trial balance was extracted from the books of Porchester Ltd on 31 March 20X6:

	£	£
Ordinary share capital (£1 shares)		500,000
Retained profit to 1 April 20X5		1,039,000
10% debentures repayable 20X9		300,000
Freehold land and buildings at cost	400,000	
Plant and machinery at cost	1,300,000	
Provision for depreciation on plant and machinery at 1 April 20X5		512,000
Debtors and prepayments (including trade debtors, £360,000)	370,080	
Stock and work in progress at 31 March 20X6	984,020	
Bank balance	268,000	
Provision for doubtful debts at 31 March 20X6		15,000
Creditors and accrued expenses		351,500
Gross profit for the year		1,020,800
Administration expenses	216,900	
Selling expenses	150,400	
Bad debts written off	8,700	
General repairs and maintenance	25,200	
Debenture interest to 30 September 20X5	15,000	
	3,738,300	3,738,300

Additional information is provided as follows:

1 The company's freehold property was revalued at £900,000 on 1 October 20X5. The directors have decided to use this figure for the purpose of the accounts.

2 The company made a bonus issue of two ordinary shares, fully paid, for each share held on 1 October 20X5. No entry has been made in the books in respect of the issue.

3 The directors propose to pay a dividend of 5 pence per share of the ordinary share capital at 31 March 20X6.

4 The company purchased additional plant costing £120,000 on 31 March 20X6. The plant was delivered to the company's premises on that date together with the purchase invoice to be paid within seven days, but no entry has been made in the books in respect of the transaction.

5 Depreciation is to be provided at 25 per cent, reducing balance, on all plant and machinery owned by the company at the year end, except the plant referred to under 4 above. Ignore depreciaton of freehold property.

6 Corporation tax of £150,000, due for payment on 1 January 20X7, is to be provided out of the trading profit for the year.

7 The company's authorized share capital is £2,000,000 divided into ordinary shares of £1 each.

The profit and loss account and profit and loss appropriation account of Porchester Ltd for the year ended 31 March 20X6, together with the balance sheet at that date. Particular attention should be given to layout, although the accounts need not necessarily be in a form appropriate for publication.

Required

10.5 What is the purpose of a bonus issue of shares? Using the information prepared in your answer to Question 10.4, consider whether the issue was reasonable in amount.

10.6 The trial balance of Southgate plc at 31 December 20X9 was as follows:

	£	£
Ordinary share capital (shares £1 each)		500,000
Freehold property at cost	500,000	
Furniture and equipment at cost	375,000	
Provision for depreciation of furniture and equipment, 1 January 20X9		59,500
Debtors and prepayments	105,000	
Stock and work in progress at 31 December 20X9	104,200	
Creditors and accruals		85,300
Balance at bank	72,000	
Gross profit on trading		416,500
Rent and rates	30,000	
Office salaries	142,600	
Advertising costs	21,000	
Transport costs	23,600	
Profit and loss account balance, 1 January 20X9		278,500

Taxation due but unpaid on 20X8 profits		103,600
Deposit on new equipment	10,000	
Temporary investment	60,000	
	1,443,400	1,443,400

You are given the following additional information:

1 The company has contracted to purchase new equipment at a cost of £50,000. A deposit of £10,000 was paid during December 20X9 and the remainder will be paid during January 20Y0 when delivery is expected.

2 Depreciation is to be provided on furniture and equipment, other than the new equipment referred to under 1, at the rate of 10 per cent on cost.

3 The figure for rent and rates in the above trial balance covers the 15 months to 31 March 20Y0.

4 During December 20X9 the company used part of the profit and loss account balance at 1 January 20X9 to make a bonus issue of one new share for every five shares already held. The issue was made at par but has not yet been written into the books.

5 During November 20X9 the company's freehold premises were valued at £650,000 by a firm of professional valuers. The company's directors have decided to write the revaluation into the 20X9 accounts and credit the surplus arising to revaluation reserve.

6 Taxation is to be provided at 50 per cent on the company's net profit from trading operations.

Required

(a) The profit and loss account of Southgate for 20X9 and balance sheet at 31 December 20X9. Each accounting statement should be presented in vertical format.

(b) Your comments on the suggestion, from one director, that the company should pay a dividend of 10p per share on the issued share capital in view of the large bank balance and the fact that no dividend was paid for 20X8.

Note   Ignore depreciation of freehold property.

10.7 The following balances existed in the accounting records of Koppa Ltd at 31 December 19X7.

		£000
Development costs capitalized, 1 January 19X7		180
Freehold land as revalued 31 December 19X7		2,200
Buildings	– cost	900
	– aggregate depreciation at 1 January 19X7	100
Office equipment	– cost	260
	– aggregate depreciation at 1 January 19X7	60
Motor vehicles	– cost	200
	– aggregate depreciation at 1 January 19X7	90

Trade debtors	1,360
Cash at bank	90
Trade creditors	820
12% debentures (issued 19X0 and redeemable 20Y7)	1,000
Called up share capital – shares of 50p each	1,000
Share premium account	500
Revaluation reserve	200
Profit and loss account 1 January 19X7	1,272
Sales	8,650
Purchases	5,010
Research and development expenditure for the year	162
Stock 1 January 19X7	990
Distribution costs	460
Administrative expenses	1,560
Debenture interest	120
Interim dividend paid	200

In preparing the company's profit and loss account and balance sheet at 31 December 19X7 the following further information is relevant.

(a) Stock at 31 December 19X7 was £880,000

(b) Depreciation is to be provided for as follows:

Land	Nil
Buildings	2% per annum on cost
Office equipment	20% per annum, reducing balance basis
Motor vehicles	25% per annum on cost

Depreciation on buildings and office equipment is all charged to administrative expenses. Depreciation on motor vehicles is to be split equally between distribution costs and administrative expenses.

(c) The £180,000 total for development costs as at 1 January 19X7 relates to two projects:

	£000
Project 836: completed project	82
(balance being amortized over the period expected to benefit from it;	
amount to be amortized in 1997: £20,000)	
Project 910: in progress	98
	180

(d) The research and development expenditure for the year is made up of:

	£000
Research expenditure	103
Development costs on Project 910 which continues to satisfy	
the requirements in SSAP 13 for capitalization	59
	162

(e)   The freehold land had originally cost £2,000,000 and was revalued on 31 December 19X7.

(f)   Prepayments and accruals at 31 December 19X7 were:

	Prepayments £000	Accruals £000
Administrative expenses	40	11
Sundry distribution costs	–	4

(g)   The share premium account balance arose as a result of the issue during 19X7 of 1,000,000 50p ordinary shares at £1.00 each. All shares qualify for the proposed final dividend to be provided for (see note below).

(h)   A final dividend of 20p per share is proposed.

Required

Prepare the company's profit and loss account for the year ended 31 December 19X7 and balance sheet as at that date, in a form suitable for publication as far as the information provided permits.

(24 marks)

(ACCA Paper 1, The Accounting Framework, June 1998 (modified))

10.8   (a)   FRS 32, *Reporting Financial Performance*, includes requirements governing the treatment of certain items in the published profit and loss account.

Required

Explain how FRS 3 requires discontinued operations and acquisitions to be dealt with in the profit and loss account. What are the advantages of these requirements to users of financial statements?   (7 marks)

(b)   The trial balance of Leonardo Ltd at 30 September 19X8 included the following items.

	Dr £000	Cr £000
Sales		6,840
Opening stock	1,200	
Purchases	3,670	
Distribution costs	880	
Administrative expenses	590	
Interest payable	300	
Costs of a fundamental reorganization of the company's operations	560	
Profit on sale of head office building (the company plans to move its central administration into a rented building)		1,200
Provision for doubtful debts 1 October 19X7		150

In preparing the company's profit and loss account the following further information is to be taken into account:

(i) Stock was taken on 27 September 19X8 (all valued at cost) and amounted to £950,000. Between that date and the close of business on 30 September 19X8, goods costing £68,000 were sold and there were no further receipts of goods. These sales are included in the sales total of £6,840,000.

(ii) During the year a debt of £400,000 proved to be irrecoverable and is to be written off. The provision for doubtful debts is to be increased to £200,000.

(iii) The tax charge on the profit from ordinary activities was £300,000.

Prepare the company's profit and loss account for the year ended 30 September 19X8 for publication.

Required

(10 marks)

(ACCA Paper 1, The Accounting Framework, December 1998 (modified))

SOLUTIONS TO ACTIVITIES

Solution to Activity 10.1

Share Capital Account

	£			£
		1 Jan	Balance b/d	2,500,000
		1 Jan	Bank	1,000,000

Bank Account

	£		£
1 Jan Balance b/f	2,500,000		
1 Jan Share capital	1,000,000		

Solution to Activity 10.2

Milliott Ltd
Balance sheet (extract) as at
1 January 20X1

	£
Share capital:	
Authorized: 8,000,000 ordinary shares of 50p each	4,000,000
Issued: 7,000,000 ordinary shares of 50p each fully paid	3,500,000

Solution to Activity 10.3

Applications and Allotment Account

		£			£
2	Share capital	300,000	1	Bank	300,000
4	Share capital	500,000	3	Bank	500,000
		800,000			800,000

First and Final Call Account

		£			£
5	Share capital	200,000	6	Bank	200,000

Capital Account

		£				£
					Balance b/f	2,500,000
				2	Applic and allotment	300,000
				4	Applic and allotment	500,000
	Balance c/d	3,500,000		5	First and final call	200,000
		3,500,000				3,500,000
					Balance b/d	3,500,000

Bank Account

			£			£
		Balance b/d	2,500,000			
1	Applic and Allotment		300,000			
3	Applic and Allotment		500,000			
6	First and final call		200,000		Balance c/d	3,500,000
			3,500,000			3,500,000
		Balance b/d	3,500,000			

Solution to Activity 10.4

(a)

Capital Account

		£				£
	Balance c/d	4,000,000	1 Jan X2	Balance b/d		3,500,000
			31 Dec X2	App and Allot		500,000
		4,000,000				4,000,000
				Balance b/d		4,000,000

Share Premium Account

		£			£
			31 Dec X2	Bank	500,000

Application and Allotment Account

		£			£
31 Dec X2	Share capital	500,000	31 Dec X2	Bank	1,000,000
31 Dec X2	Share premium	500,000			
		1,000,000			1,000,000

Bank Account

			£			£
1	Jan X2	Balance b/d	3,500,000			
31	Dec X2	App and Allot	1,000,000	31 Dec X2	Balance c/d	4,500,000
			4,500,000			4,500,000
1	Jan X3	Balance b/d	4,500,000			

(b)

Milliott Ltd
Balance sheet (extract) as at
31 December 20X2

Share capital:	£
Authorized and issued:	
8,000,000 ordinary shares of 50 p each	4,000,000
Share premium account	500,000

(a) *Solution to Activity 10.5*

Applications and Allotment Account

		£			£
I Jul	Capital	600,000	I Jul	Bank	600,000
		600,000			600,000

Call Account

		£			£
30 Sept	Capital	149,250	30 Sept	Bank	149,250
		149,250			149,250

Forfeited Shares Account

		£			£
I Dec	Capital[1]	3,750	30 Sept	Capital[2]	3,000
I Dec	Share premium[3]	1,500	I Dec	Bank[4]	2,250
		5,250			5,250

Notes [1] 15,000 shares @ nominal value £0.25   [2] 15,000 shares @ £0.20
[3] 15,000 shares × (£0.20 + £0.15 − £0.25)   [4] 15,000 shares reissued @ £0.15

Capital Account

		£			£
30 Sept	Forfeited shares	3,000	I Jul	Applic and Allot	600,000
			30 Sep	Call	149,250
I Dec	Balance c/d	750,000	I Dec	Forfeited shares	3,750
		753,000			753,000
			I Dec	Balance b/d	750,000

Share Premium Account

	£			£
		I Dec	Forfeited shares	1,500

Bank Account

		£		£
1 Jul	Applic and Allot	600,000		
30 Sept	Call	149,250		
1 Dec	Forfeited shares	2,250		

(b)

Blaires Ltd
Balance sheet (extract) as at
1 December 20X1

Share capital:		£
Authorized: 4,000,000 ordinary shares of £0.25 each		1,000,000
Issued: 3,000,000 ordinary shares of £0.25 fully paid		750,000
Share premium account		1,500

Solution to
Activity 10.6

		£
(a)	Accounting profit	180,000
	Add: Depreciation charge disallowed*	50,000
		230,000
	Less: Written-down allowance†	(75,000)
	Taxable profit	155,000
	Corporation tax payable, £155,000 × 20% =	£31,000

Notes   * £400,000/8

† £400,000 − (£400,000 × 25%) = 300,000 × 25% = 75,000

(b)

Tax Charge Account

20X0		£	*20X0*		£
31 Mar	Corp tax liability	31,000	31 Mar	Transfer to P&L	31,000

Corporation Tax Liability Account

20X0		£	*20X0*		£
			31 Mar	Tax charge	31,000

(c) **Profit and Loss Appropriation Account for 20X0**

	£
Net profit before tax	180,000
Taxation	(31,000)
Profit after tax	149,000

(a)

Solution to Activity 10.7

Tax Charge Account

20X0		£	20X0		£
31 Dec	Corp Tax Liability	75,000	31 Dec	Transfer to P&L	75,000

Corporation Tax Liability Account

20X0		£	20X0		£
			31 Dec	Tax charge	75,000

Ordinary Dividends Paid and Proposed Account

20X0		£	20X0		£
1 July	Bank*	40,000			
31 Dec	Proposed dividends[†]	80,000	31 Dec	Transfer to P&L	120,000
		120,000			120,000

Notes * £0.05 × 800,000 (800,000 = £600,000/75p)

[†] £0.10 × 800,000

Preference Dividends Proposed Account

20X0		£	20X0		£
31 Dec	Proposed dividends*	33,000	31 Dec	Transfer to P&L	33,000
		33,000			33,000

Note *6% × 550,000

Proposed Dividends Account

20X0		£	20X0		£
			31 Dec	Ord divis paid and prop	80,000
31 Dec	Balance c/d	113,000	31 Dec	Pref divis paid and prop	33,000
		113,000			113,000
			31 Dec	Balance b/d	113,000

Bank Account			
20X1	*£*	*20X1*	*£*
		2 July Ord dividends paid and proposed 40,000	

Note The directors can only pay an ordinary dividend if there are sufficient funds to cover the preference dividend first. Since an interim ordinary dividend was paid in July, it can be assumed that sufficient funds exist.

(b) **Profit and loss appropriation account of Olympia Ltd for 20X0**

	£	£
Profit before tax		400,000
Taxation		(75,000)
Profit after tax		325,000
Less: Preference dividends:		
Proposed	33,000	
Ordinary dividends:		
Paid	40,000	
Proposed	80,000	(153,000)
Retained profit for the year		172,000
Retained profit at 1 January 20X0		194,000
Retained profit at 31 December 20X0		366,000

(c)

Olympia Ltd
Balance sheet (extract) as at
31 December 20X0

	£
Share Capital:	
Authorized: 600,000 6% preference shares @ £1 each	600,000
1,000,000 ordinary shares @ £0.75 each	750,000
Issued: 550,000 preference shares @ £1 fully paid	550,000
800,000 ordinary shares @ £0.75 fully paid	600,000
P&L reserve	366,000

Solution to
Activity 10.8   In order to answer this question you have to work backwards, starting with balance of profit (i.e. profit after tax).

Newton Ltd

Profit and loss account and appropropriation account,
period ending 31 December 20X0

	£000	£000
Gross profit		3,030
Less: Distribution costs (520 + 140)	660	
Administrative expenses (1,620 + 250)	1,870	
		2,530
Net profit before tax		500
Tax		− 63
Profit after tax		437
Less: Proposed dividends	− 200	
Transfer to general reserve	− 200	
		− 400
Profit for 20X0		37
Retained profit brought forward		290
Retained profit carried forward		327

(b)

Newton Ltd

Balance sheet as at

31 December 20X0

	£000	£000
Fixed assets		
Plant and machinery (at cost)		1,840
Less: Accumulated depreciation		−520
		1,320
Current assets		
Stock	724	
Trade debtors	570	
Bank	92	
	1,386	
Less: Creditors due within one year		
Trade creditors	− 416	
Corporation tax	− 63	
Proposed dividend	− 100	
	− 579	
Working capital		807
Total assets less current liabilities		2,127
Financed by:		
Share capital		

Issued: 1,600,000 ordinary shares of £1 each		1,600
General reserve		200
Retained profit		327
		2,127

Solution to
Activity 10.9

(a)

Freehold Land and Buildings Account

20X3		£	20X3		£
1 April	Balance b/d	5,800	31 March	Revaluation reserve	5,800
31 March	Revaluation reserve	7,000	31 March	Balance c/d	7,000
		12,800			12,800
1 April	Balance b/d	7,000			

Accumulated Depreciation (L&B) Account

20X3		£	20X3		£
31 March	Revaluation reserve	2,300	1 April	Balance b/d	2,300
		2,300			2,300

Revaluation Reserve Account

20X3		£	20X3		£
31 March	Land and buildings	5,800	31 March	Accum dep'n	2,300
31 March	Balance c/d	3,500	31 March	Land and buildings	7,000
		9,300			9,300
			31 March	Balance b/d	3,500

(b)

Balance sheet extracts at 31 March 20X3

	£000
Fixed Assets:	
Freehold land and buildings	7,000
Financed by:	
Revaluation reserve	3,500

Solution to
Activity 10.10

(a)

Balance sheet extracts at 31 December 20X0

	£
Creditors: amounts falling due with one year	
Debentures	62,500
Creditors: amounts falling due after more than one year	
Debentures	437,500

(h)

Balance sheet extracts at 31 December 20X3

	£
Creditors: amounts falling due after more than one year	
Debentures	500,000

The objectives of this chapter are to:

- explain the uses of the cash flow statement as part of the annual accounts package;
- outline the required format of a cash flow statement so that it complies with FRS 1 (revised);
- show how the individual figures contained in a cash flow statement are derived;
- illustrate the construction of a complete cash flow statement; and
- demonstrate the interpretation of the information contained in cash flow statements.

INTRODUCTION

For many years limited companies have been legally obliged to publish each year a balance sheet and profit and loss account. During the 1960s, a number of companies voluntarily added to these two reports a third financial statement called 'the statement of source and application of funds', which was often abbreviated to 'statement of funds'. The production of the statement of funds was regulated in 1975 with the issue of SSAP 10, which required virtually all companies to include one as part of their annual accounts. SSAP 10 was replaced in 1993 by FRS 1, *Cash Flow Statements*, which changed the focus of the published statement from funds, generally defined as working capital, to cash. These developments reflect the recognition of an important gap in the information provided to external users of accounting reports. FRS 1 (revised in 1996) is applicable to all financial statements intended to give a true and fair view of the financial position and profit or loss, although there are some exceptions which include subsidiaries and small entities (as defined by company legislation; see Figure 10.2).

The balance sheet sets out the financial state of a business at a particular point in time, whereas the profit and loss account reports some, but not all, of the transactions undertaken during an accounting period; it includes only those transactions that directly give rise to revenues and expenditures. Other transactions, such as issues of shares and debentures and the purchase of fixed assets, are not reported in the profit and loss account since they are capital as opposed to revenue transactions. The inclusion of a cash flow statement as part of the annual accounts brings the following benefits:

- The concept of a cash flow is one which lay people can be expected to understand and so it helps to remove some of the misunderstanding which may arise when users of accounts do not understand the concepts and conventions that underlie such features as the depreciation charge.
- The survival of a company depends on its ability to meet its liabilities when they fall due, and this requires cash. The cash flow statement allows the user to judge an enterprise's ability to generate positive future cash flows and meet its financial obligations, such as the payment of dividends or repayment of loans.
- It enables the effect of investments, undertaken during the financial period, on the organization's financial position to be assessed.
- It explains the reasons for differences between profits and cash flows arising from trading activity.
- The value of a business reflects the amount of cash it is expected to generate in the future, and so the cash flow statement, although reporting historical events, provides a useful input to business valuation models based on estimates of likely future cash flows.

The next part of this chapter shows how the cash flow statement is presented, explains the calculation of the various figures it contains and describes the ways in which it can aid interpretation.

FORMAT

A cash flow statement can be defined as that statement sets out, in an orderly manner, the cash which has been raised and generated by a business during the year and the ways in which this cash has been spent. For publication purposes, FRS 1 (revised) requires that the cash flows are classified under the following standard headings:

- *Net cash flow from operating activities.* These are the cash flows which result from trading activities. Therefore this section contains the cash flows resulting from operations that are reported in the profit and loss account. All of the cash flows are to be reported net of value added tax, and the net amount, payable or recoverable in respect of VAT, is to be included as an item within this section.

- *Returns on investments and servicing of finance.* These are the receipts, such as interest received and dividends received, resulting from the ownership of investments and payments to non-equity providers of finance, for example loan interest and preference dividends.

- *Taxation.* This covers cash flows resulting from the taxation of revenue and capital profits, and for most companies that means corporation tax.

- *Capital expenditure and financial investment.* These cash flows arise from the purchase or sale of fixed assets, including long-term investments made in the shares or debentures of other companies and their eventual sale or repayment.

- *Acquisitions and disposals.* Receipts from the sale of, or payments to acquire associate, joint venture or subsidiary companies are included under this heading. (It is highly unlikely that you will come across this in your introductory studies.)

- *Equity dividends paid.* These cash outflows relate to dividends paid on ordinary shares.

- *Management of liquid resources.* This section includes cash flows relating to current asset investments that can be disposed of without disrupting business and that can be converted into cash or traded on the open market. Examples include short-term bank deposits and small investments in shares.

- *Financing.* These are cash flows that take place between the company and its external providers of finance. Cash receipts come from issuing shares, loans or debentures, and cash payments from their redemption.

The overall effect of the cash transactions is a net increase or decrease in the cash balance. In outline, the cash flow statement appears as shown in Figure 11.1.

	£000
Net cash flow from operating activities	X
Returns on investment and servicing of finance	X
Taxation	X
Capital expenditure and financial investment	X
Acquisitions and disposals	X
Equity dividends paid	X
Management of liquid resources	X
Financing	X
Net cash inflow/(outflow)	X

FIGURE 11.1   Outline of cash flow statement

The preparation of the cash flow statement for a company usually starts with the profit and loss account for a year, together with its opening and closing balance sheet. It is then necessary to convert the flows of resources, such as sales or dividends, into cash flows, using the techniques given in Chapter 4 where the reverse operation was carried out, namely converting cash flows into resource flows. The next section shows the practical application of these methods.

STATEMENT CONSTRUCTION

The profit and loss account and balance sheet from which a cash flow statement is to be prepared are given in Figure 11.2.

The information contained in Figure 11.2 will now be used to calculate the values to be included in a cash flow statement. Each of the elements identified in Figure 11.1 is dealt with separately and is then included in the complete statement. After the complete statement has been compiled, a number of related complications are considered.

Tide Ltd
Profit and Loss Account
period ending 31 December 20X4

	£000	£000
Turnover		3,620
Less: Opening stock	224	
Purchases	1,760	
Closing stock	−293	
Cost of goods sold		−1,691
Gross profit		1,929
Less: Depreciation	104	
Administration expenses	1,136	
Distribution costs	275	
Loss on sale of fixed asset	25	
		1,540
Operating profit		389
Interest received	26	
Interest paid	−10	
		16
Profit before tax		405
Tax		−90
Profit after tax		315
Dividends: Preference – Paid	−6	
Proposed	−6	
Ordinary – Paid	−39	
Proposed	−174	
		−225
Retained profit for the year		90
Retained profit brought forward		178
Retained profit carried forward		268

Tide Ltd
Balance Sheet
as at 31 December 20X4 and 20X3

	20X4 £000	20X3 £000
Fixed assets		
Plant at book value, 1 January	945	1,000
Additions	530	20
Disposals at book value	−40	–
Depreciation charge	−104	−75
	1,331	945
Current assets		
Stock	293	224
Trade debtors	586	549
Bank	–	53
	879	826
Less: Creditors due within one year		
Bank overdraft	−171	–
Trade creditors	−181	−156
Corporation tax	−90	−117
Proposed dividend: Preference	−6	−6
Ordinary	−174	−114
	−622	−393

Working capital	257	433
Total assets less current liabilities	1,588	1,378
Less: Creditors due after more than one year		
Debentures	–	– 200
	1,588	1,178
Financed by:		
Share capital		
6% Preference shares @ £1	200	200
Ordinary shares @ £1	1,000	800
Share premium	120	–
Retained profit	268	178
	1,588	1,178

FIGURE 11.2   Profit and loss account and balance sheet of Tide Ltd
for the year to 31 December 20X4

Net cash flow from operating activities

There are two alternative ways in which this may be calculated: the direct method
and the indirect method.

The *direct method* calculates the cash flow by comparing the cash received from
customers with the outflows for goods and services paid to suppliers and employees.
Items such as depreciation and the loss on sale of fixed assets are not included as
they do not involve the movement of cash. See below for a fuller explanation.

EXAMPLE 11.1

From the information given in Figure 11.2 calculate the net cash flow from operating activities using the direct method.

Solution

	£000
Cash from sales (W1)	3,583
Cash paid for:	
Purchases (W2)	(1,735)
Administrative expenses	(1,136)
Distribution costs	(275)
Net cash flow from operating activities	437

Workings:	W1	W2
	Sales	*Purchases*
	£000	*£000*
From profit and loss account	3,620	1,760
Add: Opening debtors/creditors	549	156
Less: Closing debtors/creditors	(586)	(181)
Cash flow	3,583	1,735

The opening debtors and creditors are added to the figures from the profit and loss account as they represent revenues and expenditures which took place in 20X3 (the previous year) which are converted into cash in 20X4 (the current year). The closing debtors and creditors are deducted because the sale or purchase took place in 20X4, but the related cash flow will not occur until 20X5 (the following year).

The *indirect method* produces exactly the same net cash flow as the direct method, but starts with the operating profit and makes adjustments for items in the profit and loss account which do not match their corresponding cash flow. This method is demonstrated in Example 11.2.

From the information given in Figure 11.2 calculate the net cash flow from operating activities using the indirect method.

EXAMPLE
11.2

	£000	
		Solution
Operating profit	389	
Adjustments for items not involving cash:		
Depreciation	104	
Loss on sale of fixed asset	25	
Further adjustments:		
Increase in stocks	(69)	
Increase in debtors	(37)	
Increase in trade creditors	25	
Net cash flow from operating activities	437	

Remember, the aim of a cash flow statement is to identify the amount of cash that has been generated in an accounting period and so any items that do not result in a cash movement should be ignored, and any items that result in a cash movement should be considered. Adjustments are necessary, therefore, to convert accounting profit into cash profit for the period concerned. Examples of, and reasons for, the adjustments are as follows:

- *Depreciation.* When an asset is purchased there is a cash outflow which is reported under the capital expenditure heading. The subsequent depreciation of the asset does not involve further cash outflows as depreciation is the method of charging the cost of the asset against profit over its useful life. Therefore, depreciation does not involve cash and should be added back to operating profit. (For a fuller explanation see the section on complexities below.)

- *Profit or loss on sale of a fixed asset.* The disposal of an asset will generate a cash inflow which is reported under the capital expenditure heading. The difference between what the business receives from the sale and the net book value of the asset, however, will give rise to a profit or loss. This profit or loss is included in the profit and loss account but does not represent any cash movement and so should be adjusted for when calculating cash profit. A profit on sale should be deducted from, and a loss added to, accounting profit. (For a fuller explanation see the section on complexities below.)

- *Credit sales and purchases.*   These are included in the profit and loss account even though the cash has not yet been received or paid. Conversely, a credit sale or purchase made in the previous year would be excluded from current profit even though the cash has been received or paid. The adjustments necessary for these are to add the opening debtors/creditors figures to, and deduct the closing debtors/creditors figures from, the operating profit figure. A quick way is to add or subtract the movement between the opening and closing balances (as demonstrated in Example 11.2 above).

- *Stock.*   Opening stock is added to purchases when calculating cost of sales even though the purchase of it took place in the previous year, and closing stock is deducted from cost of sales despite being purchased in the current period. The adjustments necessary for this are to add the opening stock figure to, and deduct the closing stock figure from, the operating profit figure. A quick way is to add or subtract the movement between the opening and closing balances (as demonstrated in Example 11.2 above).

FRS 1 requires companies to publish:

- a single figure for net cash flow from operating activities on the face of the cash flow statement; and
- a note which shows the reconciliation of the cash flow from operating activities with the profit from operating activities.

In addition, companies are free to publish additional information showing the results calculated on the direct method if they so wish.

The direct method of calculation has the advantage of being a clear statement of cash inflows and outflows and so is easily comprehended, while the indirect method highlights the reasons for differences between operating profit and operating cash flow.

Returns on investment and servicing of finance

This section contains the cash receipts of interest and dividends and payments of interest and non-equity dividends.

EXAMPLE 11.3

From the information given in Figure 11.2 calculate the returns on investments and servicing of finance.

	£000	Solution
Interest received	26	
Interest paid	(10)	
Dividends paid (W1)	(12)	
Net cash outflow	4	
W1		
Interim preference dividend for 20X4	6	
Final dividend paid for 20X3 from opening		
balance sheet	6	
	12	

Taxation

The tax paid in 20X4 is the amount included as a current liability in the opening balance sheet (i.e. balance sheet of 20X3), in this case £117,000. The charge for 20X4 is a liability in that year's balance sheet and will cause a cash outflow in 20X5.

Capital expenditure and financial investment

This covers the cost of acquiring fixed assets and investments and the cash inflow from the disposal of any of these items.

From the information given in Figure 11.2 calculate the amounts to be included under the heading of capital expenditure and financial investment.

EXAMPLE
11.4

	£000	Solution
Payments to buy fixed assets	(530)	
Receipts from the sale of fixed assets (W1)	15	
	(515)	
W1		

Disposal of Plant Account

	£000		£000
Plant	40	Proceeds from sale (bal fig)	15
		Loss on sale	25
	40		40

Equity dividends paid

The payment of dividends on ordinary shares is included under this heading.

EXAMPLE 11.5

From the information given in Figure 11.2 calculate the amount of equity dividends paid during the year.

Solution

	£000
Interim ordinary dividend	(39)
Proposed ordinary dividend of 20X3	(114)
	(153)

Financing

The issue of shares or debentures and their repayment are recorded under this heading, and so the figures are calculated by comparing the opening and closing balance sheets for these items to see whether there has been any increases or decreases.

EXAMPLE 11.6

From the information given in Figure 11.2 calculate the amounts to be included under the heading of financing.

Solution

	£000
Issue of shares (W1)	320
Repayment of debentures	(200)
	120
W1	
Increase in share capital	200
Increase in share premium	120
	320

It is now possible to combine all of the calculations done so far to produce a full cash flow statement for Tide Ltd, and this is shown in Figure 11.3.

SOME COMPLEXITIES OF THE CASH FLOW STATEMENT

This section examines some of the complexities associated with the cash flow statement:

- the depreciation charge as a source of cash;
- reconstructing the profit and loss account;
- movements in fixed assets.

Tide Ltd
Cash Flow Statement
for the year to 31 December 20X4

	£000	£000
Net cash flow from operating activities (note 1)		437
Returns on investment and servicing of finance:		
Interest received	26	
Interest paid	– 10	
Preference dividends paid	– 12	
		4
Taxation		– 117
Capital expenditure and financial investment:		
Acquisition of fixed assets	– 530	
Proceeds from the disposal of fixed assets	15	
		– 515
Equity dividends		– 153
Net cash outflow before financing		– 344
Financing:		
Issue of shares	320	
Redemption of debentures	– 200	
		120
Decrease in cash (note 2)		– 224

Note 1 Reconciliation of operating profit to net cash inflow from operating activities:

	£000
Operating profit	389
Adjustments for items not involving cash:	
Depreciation	104
Loss on sale of fixed asset	25
Further adjustments:	
Increase in stocks	(69)
Increase in debtors	(37)
Increase in trade creditors	25
	437

Note 2 Change in cash balance during the year:

	£000
Opening balance in hand	53
Closing overdraft	(171)
Decrease in cash	(224)

FIGURE 11.3   Cash flow statement of Tide Ltd for the year to
31 December 20X4

Depreciation and cash flow

The fact that the year's depreciation charge is added to operating profit as a source
of cash requires further consideration. During the course of trading activity, a

company generates revenue, principally in the form of sales receipts, and incurs expenditure comprising a wide range of different outlays, some of which result in an outflow of cash in the current accounting period and others which do not. Most outlays fall into the first category, for example, expenditure on purchases of materials, wages, salaries and rent. There are, however, a small number of items, the most important of which is depreciation, that are charged against profit but do not result in a current outflow of cash.

The purpose of the depreciation charge is to reflect the fact that sales revenue has benefited, during the period under review, from the use of fixed assets acquired in a previous accounting period. The effect of making the charge is to earmark an equivalent amount of cash for retention within the business, which may be used, in due course, to help finance replacement of the asset when it is worn out. Because depreciation is charged in the profit and loss account, but does not result in a current outflow of funds, it must be added back to reported profit in order to identify cash generated from operations, i.e.:

$$\text{Cash generated from operations} = \text{Profit} + \text{Depreciation}$$

Students often find it difficult to grasp the fact that the depreciation charge is represented by an equivalent inflow of cash. The link is demonstrated in Example 11.7.

EXAMPLE 11.7

The balance sheet of Pencil Ltd, which purchases and sells goods for cash, is as follows at 31 December 20X1:

Balance sheet as at 31 December 20X1

	£	£
Fixed assets at cost		1,800
Less: Depreciation		540
		1,260
Current assets		
Stock	400	
Cash	200	600
		1,860
10% Loan repayable 20X7		500
		1,360
Financed by:		
Share capital		1,000
Retained profit		360
		1,360

During 20X2 cash sales and cash purchases amounted respectively to £4,000 and £2,500. The stock level remained unchanged during the year and £600 was paid out for wages and other operating expenses. In addition, loan interest was paid on 31 December 20X2, and depreciation of £240 was charged on fixed assets.

Required

(a)   The cash account for 20X2.

(b)   The trading and profit and loss account for 20X2.

(c)   The balance sheet at 31 December 20X2.

(d)   A calculation of cash generated from operations during 20X2, i.e. profit + depreciation.

(a)   **Cash account for 20X2**   Solution

	£		£
Balance b/d	200	Purchases	2,500
Sales	4,000	Wages	600
		Interest	50
		Balance c/d	1,050
	4,200		4,200
Balance b/d	1,050		

(b)   **Trading and profit and loss account for 20X2**

	£	£
Sales		4,000
Opening stock	400	
Purchases	2,500	
	2,900	
Less: Closing stock	− 400	
Cost of goods sold		2,500
Gross profit		1,500
Wages	600	
Interest	50	
Depreciation	240	−890
Net profit		610

(c)   **Balance sheet at 31 December 20X2**

Fixed assets at cost		1,800
Less: Depreciation		780
		1,020
Current assets		
Stock	400	
Cash	1,050	1,450
		2,470
10% Loan repayable 20X7		− 500
		1,970
Financed by:		
Share capital		1,000
Retained profit (360 + 610)		970
		1,970

(c)   Cash generated from operations:

	£
Profit	610
Add: Depreciation	240
Cash from operations	850

A note of warning   A common misconception is that the depreciation charge produces an inflow of cash, and that the amount of cash available can be increased by raising the charge. This is wrong. Cash is generated from trading transactions and the depreciation charge is simply a 'book entry' that earmarks a proportion of funds generated from operations for retention within the business. If the depreciation charge in Example 11.7 is increased from £240 to £400, profit falls from £610 to £450 and cash generated from operations remains unchanged at £850 (depreciation £400 + profit £450). An effect of raising the charge is, however, to earmark a larger amount of cash for retention within the business in the current year; later in the asset's life, charges and retentions will be correspondingly lower because the balance that remains to be written off at 31 December 20X2 is reduced by £240.

ACTIVITY 11.1

Assume the same facts as appear in the solution to Example 11.7.

Required

Calculate the closing cash balance of Pencil, on 1 January 20X3, in each of the following circumstances:

(a)   The entire profit of £610 is paid out as dividends on 1 January 20X3.

(b)   The depreciation charge is amended to £400 and the entire profit of £450 is paid out as dividends on 1 January 20X3.

Note   No other transactions occurred on 1 January 20X3.

Reconstructing the profit and loss account

In some cases a profit and loss account may not be provided, and so the operating profit for the year has to be reconstructed from examining the changes between the opening and closing balance sheets. This technique is illustrated in Example 11.8.

The following are the summarized balance sheets of Ebbs Ltd at 31 December 20X2 and 20X1:

EXAMPLE
11.8

	20X2	20X1
	£000	£000
Fixed assets at book value	1,300	1,200
Current assets		
Stock	220	200
Debtors	300	250
Cash	15	10
	535	460
Current liabilities		
Trade creditors	160	140
Corporation tax	50	45
Dividend	55	35
	265	220
Working capital	270	240
	1,570	1,440
Financed by:		
Ordinary shares of £1 each	1,000	1,000
Profit and loss account	570	440
	1,570	1,440

The company paid an interim dividend of £15,000 during 20X2.

Calculate the profit from trading activities of Ebbs Ltd for 20X2.   **Required**

	£000	
		Solution
Retained profit 31 December	570	
Retained profit 1 January	440	
Increase	130	
Tax charge	50	
Interim dividend	15	
Final dividend	55	
Profit for the year	250	

Movement in fixed assets

Quite often a company purchases and sells fixed assets during the year. The balance sheet may only show the 'net' figure and so it is necessary to prepare a fixed asset schedule that shows all the movements during the year. The preparation of the schedule is based on the following known relationships:

$$Cost\ of\ fixed\ assets = \text{Opening balance} + \text{Additions} - \text{Cost of assets sold}$$
$$= \text{Closing balance}$$

$$Accumulated\ depreciation = \text{Opening balance} + \text{Charge for year} - \text{Accumulated depreciation on asset sold}$$
$$= \text{Closing balance}$$

This information would be represented in the T accounts as follows:

Fixed Asset Account

Balance b/d	XXX	Disposals at cost	XXX
Additions	XXX	Balance c/d	XXX
	XXX		XXX
Balance b/d	XXX		

Accumulated Depreciation Account

Accumulated depreciation on asset sold	XXX	Balance b/d	XXX
Balance c/d	XXX	Depreciation charge for year	XXX
	XXX		XXX
		Balance b/d	XXX

EXAMPLE 11.9

The following information is extracted from the balance sheet of Staple Ltd at 31 December:

	20X0	20X1
	£	£
Fixed assets	40,000	57,500
Less: Accumulated depreciation	– 22,700	– 31,600
	17,300	25,900

On 1 July 20X1, Staple sold a motor vehicle for £750. The machine had cost £6,000 some years ago, and accumulated depreciation at 31 December 20X0 was £4,900. The company's policy is to charge a full year's depreciation in the year of purchase and none in the year a vehicle is sold.

Required

(a) Calculations of additions during the year and depreciation charged.

(b) Calculate the profit or loss on disposal of vehicles.

(c) Show the information to be included in the cash flow statement relating to motor vehicles and indicate in which section of the statement each item would appear.

(a)

Solution

	Cost £	Dep'n £
Opening balance	40,000	22,700
Add: Purchases/depreciation charge for year	23,500*	13,800*
Less: Sales	6,000	− 4,900
Closing balance	57,500	31,600

Note *These are the balancing figures.

	£
(b) Book value (cost £6,000 − depreciation £4,900)	1,100
Less: Sales proceeds	(750)
Loss on sale	350

(c)

	£	Location
Depreciation charged	13,800 ⎫	Reconciliation of profit and
Loss on sale of vehicle	350* ⎬	cash flow from operating
		activities
Sale proceeds	750 ⎫	
Purchase of motor	⎬	Investing activities
vehicle	23,500 ⎭	

Note *The loss on disposal of £350 is debited to the profit and loss account to make up for the fact that insufficient depreciation has been charged. Like depreciation, the loss on sale is a non-cash expense and must be added back to the profit to produce the figure for cash generated from operations. Any profit on sale, credited to the profit and loss account, must likewise be deducted from profit, as the entire sale proceeds appear in the statement in the 'investing activities' section.

Use of ledger accounts to determine cash payments or receipts

As mentioned above, the balance sheet only shows the 'net' figure and does not highlight any movements in assets and liabilities. The process described above, i.e. the use of T accounts, for obtaining the cash flow associated with fixed assets can be applied to other assets and liabilities. The information available is entered in the ledger account and the balancing figure represents the cash movement. For example, the opening balance of accruals for electricity was £1,000 and the closing balance £1,500 and the electricity expense charged to the profit and loss account during the period was £4,000. What is the amount paid for electricity?

Electricity Account

Bank (bal. fig.)	3,500	Balance b/d	1,000
Balance c/d	1,500	Transfer to P&L A/c	4,000
	5,000		5,000
		Balance b/d	1,500

These latter complexities are now covered in Activity 11.2.

ACTIVITY
11.2

Small public company
Profit and loss account
period ending 30 September 1993

	£000	£000
Turnover		6,206
Net operating costs:		
Raw materials and consumables	2,932	
Staff costs	609	
Depreciation of plant	152	
*Other operating charges	1,150	
		− 4,843
Operating profit		1,363
Interest charges		− 180
Profit before taxation		1,183
Tax		− 285
Profit after taxation		898
Dividends: Preference	80	
Ordinary	190	− 270
Retained profit for the year		628
Retained profit brought forward		647
Retained profit carried forward		1,275

Note   *Other operating charges include the profit or loss on sale of plant and the write-off of goodwill.

Small public company
Balance sheets
as at 30 September 1992 and 1993

	1993 £000	1992 £000
Fixed assets		
Intangible: Goodwill	216	250
Tangible		
Acquired brands at cost	2,800	2,500
Land and buildings at valuation (1992 at cost)	2,500	1,765
Plant and machinery	2,160	1,100
	7,676	5,615
Current assets		
Stock	2,833	2,261
Debtors and prepayments	1,690	1,348
Cash and deposits	315	217
	4,838	3,826
Creditors: amount falling due within one year		
Trade creditors	− 351	− 307
Corporation tax	− 285	− 255
Proposed dividend: Preference	− 40	− 40
Ordinary	− 95	− 90
	− 771	− 692
Net current assets	4,067	3,134
Total assets less current liabilities	11,743	8,749
Creditors: amounts falling due after more than one year		
Debentures	− 1,500	− 1,602
	10,243	7,147
Financed by:		
Share capital		
8% Preference shares @ £1	1,000	1,000
Ordinary shares @ £1	6,400	5,500
Share premium	833	–
Revaluation reserve	735	–
Profit and loss account	1,275	647
	10,243	7,147

During the financial year 1992/93 the company sold plant with a book value of £102,000 for £131,000.

Required	(a)	A reconciliation of the operating profit with the cash inflow from operating activities.
	(b)	A cash flow statement for the company for the period ending 31 December 1993.
	(c)	A reconciliation of the movement in cash between 1992 and 1993.

(ICSA, Financial Accounting, December 1993, modified)

INTERPRETATION USING THE CASH FLOW STATEMENT

The preparation of a cash flow statement is not an end in itself. Its purpose is to provide some insights into the financial policy pursued by management during the year and to show the effects of that policy on the changes in the financial position of the company which have taken place. The interpretation of the information contained in the statement is now discussed.

Over-capitalization

A company sometimes finds itself with cash in excess of operating requirements. This may occur because initial financial requirements were overestimated and too much capital was raised at the outset. A second possible reason is a sharp contraction in the level of business operations, for example, the closure of a segment of a business or the sale of available freehold property. It is essential that excess funds should not be allowed to lie idle, and the usual solution is for management to make plans for the investment of these resources. Where this is not possible, cash should be returned to the shareholders in the form of a reduction of capital. Stringent legal formalities must be complied with when undertaking such a scheme, to ensure that the position of the creditors is not jeopardized.

Financing long-term investment

It is management's job to ensure that inflows and outflows of cash are properly matched, i.e. cash available for only a short period of time should only be used for a short-term application, while long-term investment must be paid for out of long-term finance. For example, the purchase of a fixed asset should be paid for by raising a long-term loan, or by issuing shares, or by retaining profits permanently within the business. The reason for this is that a company is likely to suffer acute financial embarrassment if it attempts to finance the purchase of factory premises, for example, using a short-term source of finance such as a bank overdraft. The new acquisition is expected to generate sufficient revenue to cover its cost and produce an adequate balance of profit, but this process will probably take a number of years and short-term finance will have to be repaid long before it is complete.

Over-trading

Over-trading is a condition that arises when a company attempts to do too much too quickly and, as a result, fails to maintain a satisfactory balance between profit maximization and financial stability. Over-trading usually occurs when a company rapidly expands its scale of business activities but fails, first, to make available sufficient long-term finance for this purpose. Where a company has over-traded some, or all, of the following features will be apparent from an examination of consecutive balance sheets:

* A sharp increase in expenditure on fixed assets.
* A decrease in the balance of cash, and perhaps the emergence of a bank overdraft.
* The structure of the current assets becomes less liquid, probably because the proportion of current assets 'tied up' in stock increases dramatically.
* A sharp increase in creditors caused by the company's inability to pay debts as they fall due.

The actual *causes* of over-trading are clearly demonstrated in the cash flow statement, which shows how much long-term finance has been made available during the year and how it has been used.

Madoc is confused and worried, and has come to you for advice. He tells you that, although he made a bigger profit in 20X7 than in 20X6, and has also made fewer drawings, he does not seem to be any better off and is finding it difficult to pay his creditors.

    The balance sheets of Madoc's business at the end of 20X6 and 20X7 are as follows:

EXAMPLE
11.10

Balance sheet at 31 December

	20X6	20X7
	£000	£000
Machines at cost	10,000	20,500
Less: Depreciation	− 3,000	− 5,500
	7,000	15,000
Stock	1,700	4,900
Debtors	1,800	3,700
Bank	3,500	400
	7,000	9,000
Creditors	− 3,000	− 10,000
Working capital	4,000	− 1,000
Net assets	11,000	14,000
Financed by:		
Opening capital	12,000	11,000

Add: Net profit	5,000	7,000
Less: Drawings	– 6,000	– 4,000
Closing capital	11,000	14,000

Required

Explain to Madoc what has happened, and support your explanation with an appropriate numerical statement. Briefly advise Madoc on future policy.

Solution

The causes of Madoc's problems can be identified from a cash flow statement:

	£
Cash flow from operating activities:	
Profit	7,000
Depreciation	2,500
Increase in stock	– 3,200
Increase in debtors	– 1,900
Increase in creditors	7,000
	11,400
Investing activities	
Purchase of fixed assets	– 10,500
Financing	
Drawings	– 4,000
Decrease in cash balance	– 3,100

The cause of Madoc's confusion is that he mistakenly believes that profit produces an equivalent increase in the bank balance. This may happen in certain circumstances, but only if no additional investment takes place. The above cash flow statement shows that Madoc has invested heavily in additional fixed assets and there have also been substantial increases in stocks and debtors. In total, these outlays significantly exceed cash generated from operations; the result is that the bank balance has fallen dramatically and the amount owed to creditors has more than trebled.

Madoc is in a very difficult financial position, as a result of *over-trading*, and it is important that he undertakes no further investment at this stage. He should also keep drawing to a minimum and use future profits to reduce his firm's reliance on short-term credit.

The situation shown in Example 11.10 is a relatively simple one. The principles of interpretation are now applied to the cash flow statement of Tide Ltd, as shown in Figure 11.3, to see what messages it contains:

- The company has a substantial net cash flow from operations, and note 1 explains the extent to which this differs from operating profit. Funds from operations (represented by operating profit, depreciation charge and loss on sale of fixed assets) are mainly responsible for cash generation, some of which has been used to finance the increase in stock and debtors, to the extent that this has not been covered by the increase in trade creditors.

- The 'Returns on investment and servicing of finance' and 'Equity dividends paid' show that the main outflow is dividends paid, which absorbs about one-half of net cash flow from operating activities.
- 'Taxation' discloses that paying corporation tax during the year has absorbed about 40 per cent of the net cash flow.
- 'Capital expenditure and financial investment' reveals that a substantial outlay has been made during the year. This is the largest single item in the cash flow statement and is mainly responsible for a net outflow of cash before financing of £344,000.
- The company has made a significant issue of shares, most of the cash from which has been used to repay the debentures. A net balance of £120,000 is shown in the 'Financing' section to help defray the net investment made during the accounting period.
- The overall outcome is a substantial decrease in cash of £224,000, with a cash balance of £53,000 at the start of the year turning into an overdraft of £171,000 at the end as a result of these developments.
- The concluding impression is of a company which has undertaken a significant expansion, with the result that its liquidity position has been put under strain.

Retrieving financial stability

The management of a company that has over-traded must take prompt steps to correct the financial imbalance, otherwise it is quite possible that the company will fail. There are a number of possible courses of action open to management. These include the following:

1 *Reduce the level of business investment.* Money is tied up in both fixed assets and current assets, and management should look carefully at the feasibility of releasing cash resources by reducing the amount invested in each of these areas. It is also possible that there is a building or a piece of land that can be sold without any unfavourable repercussions for the company's operating capability. Ratio analysis may be used to examine stock levels and debtor levels to discover whether these are unduly inflated. The company's stock ordering, processing and distribution policies will come under scrutiny, as will the effectiveness of the company's system of credit control. The possibility of reducing the investment in debtors, by offering discounts for prompt payment, may also be examined. It must, of course, be borne in mind that discounts, although helpful in improving cash flow, reduce sales proceeds and therefore profit. The employment of the services of a debt factor and the sale and lease-back of freehold property are other options that need to be investigated if there is a substantial liquidity problem that cannot be solved by more conventional means.

2   *Raise additional finance.*   The total finance to be raised depends on the period over which the cash shortage is expected to persist. Temporary cash difficulties may be overcome by arranging a bank overdraft facility or a short-term loan. Severe over-trading is likely to be corrected, however, only by raising long-term finance in the form of share capital or debentures. Access to either of these sources of long-term finance depends on the particular circumstances of the company under review. If loan finance is presently at a low level and the company has adequate security in the form of tangible assets, the issue of a debenture may well be appropriate. A share issue is, however, more likely to be the answer to the company's financial problems.

The fact that the company is in financial difficulties obviously places a question mark against the competence of the management team. They have not been successful in anticipating the present cash flow problems, and a potential lender might be doubtful whether management is able to do better in the future. It is the shareholders who will be at greatest financial risk if the company goes into liquidation. They are the last source of finance to be repaid and, in a forced sale, assets are likely to realize significantly less than their book values, often leaving little or nothing over for the providers of equity finance. On the other hand, if the company recovers, the shareholders have most to gain in the form of profits distributed to them in dividends or reinvested on their behalf. At a time of financial difficulty, it will therefore be necessary for the shareholders to confirm their confidence in the future of the company and subscribe to a rights issue.

3   *Cash generated from operations.*   The third possibility is for the company to recover on the basis of internally generated funds. The component elements of internal funds flow are usually net profit before tax plus depreciation. Tax must, of course, be paid out of this balance, but management is able to exercise a fair amount of discretion concerning the disposition of what remains. Usually, of course, a dividend is paid and investments are made in fixed assets, stocks and debtors. At a time of severe cash shortage, it is important that such outlays are kept to a minimum so that funds generated from operations may instead be used to improve the financial stability of the concern. Indeed, it may be necessary to abandon the payment of a dividend and, if possible, delay the replacement of old plant until the financial position improves. In the case of a profitable company, funds generated from operations and retained within the business can quickly restore an element of financial stability.

4   *A combination of remedies.*   A number of possible schemes have been considered to help the recovery of a company that has over-traded. It is unlikely that any individual course of action will completely solve the problem. Steps may be taken to economize on working capital and raise, say, a two-year loan to 'tide the company over' until sufficient finance has been generated internally to complete the recovery. Quite obviously, the appropriate remedy will depend entirely on the particular circumstances of the company in difficulty.

Problems of the kind discussed in this section are often avoidable. Financial imbalance is usually the result of management's failure to plan future financial developments. Forward planning and the use of forecast accounts to help management decide how to allocate resources are discussed in Chapter 14.

Readers should now attempt Questions 11.1–11.5

11.1 The balance sheets of Southall Ltd at 31 December 20X1 and 31 December 20X2 are as follows:

QUESTIONS

Balance sheets as at 31 December 20X1 and 20X2

	20X1		20X2	
	£000	£000	£000	£000
Fixed assets				
Plant at cost	52.0		70.0	
Less: Accum depreciation	− 16.5		− 22.7	
		35.5		47.3
Vehicles at cost	10.0		10.0	
Less: Accum depreciation	− 3.6		− 4.8	
		6.4		5.2
		41.9		52.5
Current assets				
Stock	10.2		12.6	
Trade debtors	8.3		13.7	
Bank	4.9		–	
	23.4		26.3	
Less: Creditors due within one year				
Bank overdraft			− 1.3	
Trade creditors	− 5.1		− 5.8	
	− 5.1		− 7.1	
Working capital		18.3		19.2
		60.2		71.7
Financed by:				
Share capital		50.0		54.0
Profit and loss account		10.2		17.7
		60.2		71.7

A cash flow statement for the year ending 31 December 20X2.

11.2   The following balances relate to the affairs of Tufton Ltd as at 31 March 20X0 and 20X1.

	20X0 £	20X1 £
Share capital	500,000	600,000
Retained profit	395,800	427,100
10% Debentures	200,000	300,000
Creditors	179,800	207,500
Proposed dividends	50,000	60,000
Bank overdraft	–	36,900
	1,325,600	1,631,500
Plant at cost	658,300	796,900
Less: Depreciation	263,500	371,600
	394,800	425,300
Freehold property at cost	300,000	350,000
Stock	327,100	608,300
Debtors	265,700	247,900
Cash at bank	38,000	–
	1,325,600	1,631,500

You are given the following information:

(i)   During the year to March 20X0, plant with a written-down value of £202,500 was sold for £169,500. This plant had originally cost £390,000.

(ii)   A bonus issue of one ordinary share for every five held was made out of retained profit on 1 June 20X0.

Required   A cash flow statement for the year to 31 March 20X1.

11.3   The following information is provided for Sharpener Ltd:

Balance sheets as at 31 December

	20X4 £	20X5 £
Fixed assets		
Cost	650,000	680,000
Less: Accumulated depreciation	– 176,500	– 203,700
	473,500	476,300
Current assets		
Stock	126,400	127,500
Trade debtors	97,700	95,000
Bank balance	23,600	–
	247,700	222,500

Less: Creditors due within one year		
Bank overdraft		– 37,900
Trade creditors	– 72,900	– 87,100
Proposed ordinary dividend	– 44,000	– 44,000
	– 116,900	– 169,000
Working capital	130,800	53,500
Total assets less current liabilities	604,300	529,800
Less: Creditors due after more than one year		
6% Debentures repayable 20X9	– 100,000	– 20,000
	504,300	509,800
Financed by:		
Share capital	400,000	400,000
Retained profit	104,300	109,800
	504,300	509,800

During 20X5 the directors offered to repay the debentures, and this invitation was accepted by the majority of the debenture holders.

(a) A cash flow statement for 20X5.   **Required**
(b) A brief explanation for the decline in the bank balance based on the information contained in the statement.

11.4 The summarized final accounts of Jordin plc are detailed below.

Profit and loss account for the year ended 31 May

	1996	1997
	£m	*£m*
Sales	500	550
Cost of goods sold	(240)	(260)
Overheads	(182)	(204)
Interest payable	(20)	(16)
Net profit	58	70
Corporation tax	(18)	(21)
Dividends	(22)	(24)
Retained profit	18	25

Balance sheet as at 31 May	1996	1997
	£m	*£m*
Fixed assets at cost	1,180	1,290
Cumulative depreciation	(624)	(666)
	556	624

Stock	60	57
Trade debtors	91	129
Cash at bank	56	–
Trade creditors	(44)	(53)
Corporation tax	(18)	(21)
Dividends`	(16)	(12)
Bank overdraft	–	(14)
Debentures	(200)	(160)
	485	550
Ordinary shares at £1	180	210
Share premium	120	130
Retained profits	185	210
	485	550

Note No fixed assets were disposed of during the year ended 31 May 1997.

Required

(a) Prepare a cash flow statement in accordance with FRS 1, in respect of Jordin plc for the year ended 31 May 1997. (12 marks)

(ICSA, Paper 6, Introduction to Accounting, June 1997 (modified))

11.5 The balance sheets of Rapier Ltd at 30 September 1996 and 30 September 1997 are given below.

Balance sheets as at 30 September

	1996		1997	
	£000	£000	£000	£000
Fixed assets (see note 1)				
Cost	600		730	
Aggregate depreciation	220		240	
		380		490
Current assets				
Stock	81		90	
Debtors	90		86	
Cash	4		7	
	175		183	
Creditors: amounts falling due within one year				
Trade creditors	48		50	
Bank overdraft	13		18	
Proposed dividends	18		22	
	79		90	
Net current assets		96		93
Total assets less current liabilities		476		583

Creditors: amounts falling due after more than one year			
10% debentures (see note 2)	(100)		(50)
	376		533
Capital			
Called up share capital			
Ordinary shares of £1 each	150		200
Share premium account	50		80
Revaluation reserve	–		50
Profit and loss account	176		203
	376		533

Notes 1 *Fixed assets*

During the year fixed assets which had cost £100,000, and which had a book value at 30 September 1996 of £20,000, were sold for £25,000.

2 *Debentures*

Interest is due half-yearly on 31 March and 30 September and was paid on the due dates. £50,000 of the 10% debentures were repaid on 30 September 1997.

3 *Share capital*

The increase in share capital took place on 1 January 1997.

4 An interim dividend of 5 pence per share was paid on 6 May 1997 to holders of all the shares in issue at that date.

5 Taxation has not been allowed for and is to be ignored in your answer.

(a) Prepare a cash flow statement for the year ended 30 September 1997 using the indirect method.   **Required**

Your answer should comply as far as possible with the requirements of FRS 1 as revised in October 1996 and should include the reconciliation of operating profit to net cash flow from operating activities.

The note reconciling net cash flow with movement in net debt is *not* required.

(16 marks)

(b) Give two examples of ways in which a cash flow statement can assist users in assessing a company's liquidity and financial adaptability.   (4 marks)

(20 marks)

(ACCA, Paper 1, The Accounting Framework, December 1997)

SOLUTIONS
TO
ACTIVITIES

Solution to
Activity 11.1

	(a)	(b)
	£	£
Cash balance at 31 December 20X2	1,050	1,050
Less: Dividends	(610)	(450)
Cash balance at 1 January 20X3	440	600

Note The increase in the depreciation charge, under (b), reduces the maximum dividend payable by £160 and, as a result, the remaining cash balance is £160 higher at £600.

Solution to
Activity 11.2

(a) Reconciliation of cash flow from operating activities:

	£000
Operating profit	1,363
Adjustments for items not involving cash:	
Depreciation	152
Profit on sale of plant (W1)	(29)
Goodwill written off (W2)	34
Further adjustments:	
Increase in stocks	(572)
Increase in debtors	(342)
Increase in trade creditors	44
Net cash inflow from operating activities	650

W1 **Disposal of Plant Account**

	£000		£000
Plant (NBV)	102	Proceeds from sale	131
Profit on sale	29		
	131		131

W2 **Goodwill Account**

	£000		£000
Balance b/d	250	**Written off (bal fig)**	34
		Balance c/d	216
	250		250
Balance b/d	216		

(b)

Small public company
cash flow statement
period ending 30 September 1993

	£000	£000
Net cash flow from operating activities (Part (a))		650
Returns on investment and servicing of finance:		
Interest paid	180	
Preference dividends paid (W1)	80	
		− 260
Taxation (W2)		− 255
Capital expenditure and financial investment:		
Acquisition of brands (W3)	− 300	
Acquisition of plant (W4)	− 1,314	
Proceeds from the disposal of plant	131	
		− 1,483
Equity dividends (W5)		− 185
Net cash outflow before financing		− 1,533
Financing:		
Issue of shares (W6)	1,733	
Redemption of debentures (W7)	− 102	
		1,631
Decrease in cash (Part (c))		98

W1 **Preference Dividend Account**

	£000		£000
Bank (bal fig)	80	Balance b/d	40
Balance c/d	40	Dividend for year	80
	120		120
		Balance b/d	40

W2   The tax paid is the liability for 1992.

W3	£000
Brands at 30 September 1992	2,500
Brands at 30 September 1993	2,800
Increase	300

W4 **Plant and Machinery Account**

	£000		£000
Balance b/d	1,100	Depreciation	152

Acquisition (bal fig)	*1,314*	Disposal (NBV)	102
		Balance c/d	2,160
	2,414		2,414
Balance b/d	2,160		

W5   Ordinary Dividend Account

	£000		£000
Bank (bal fig)	*185*	Balance b/d	90
Balance c/d	95	Dividend for year	190
	280		280
		Balance b/d	95

W6	£000
Ordinary shares at 30 September 1992	5,500
Ordinary shares at 30 September 1993	6,400
	900
Share premium	833
Increase	1,733

W7	£000
Debentures at 30 September 1992	1,602
Brands at 30 September 1993	1,500
Decrease	102
(c)	£000
Cash and deposits at 30 September 1992	217
Cash and deposits at 30 September 1993	315
Increase	98

12 Interpretation of accounts: ratio analysis

The objectives of this chapter are to:

- explain the need for profitability and financial stability in both the short and long term;
- introduce ratios as a tool to investigate corporate performance, together with their strengths and weaknesses;
- illustrate the calculation of significant accounting ratios and discuss the interpretation of the results;
- classify ratios and examine the relationships between them; and
- show how the cash flow statement and ratios can be used together to investigate the financial performance and position of a company.

THE NEED FOR PROFIT AND CASH

It is widely accepted that the maximization of profit is a major business objective, and it is part of management's job to devise an effective means of achieving this aim. Management must recognize, however, that there exists an effective constraint on the rate of expansion, and this limitation is the quantity of cash available at any point in time. If management pursues a policy of expansion without first taking steps to ensure that sufficient cash is available for this purpose, the consequence will be, at the very least, financial embarrassment and, at worst, bankruptcy or liquidation.

It is therefore important for management to plan carefully future business developments, and this planning process should concentrate attention on two separate, but related, areas: profitability and financial stability. Each area is of equal importance and any tendency to emphasize one aspect to the exclusion of the other is likely to produce unfavourable repercussions. For instance, preoccupation with financial stability is likely to discourage innovation. Constant changes in consumer demand are a fact of business life and the failure of management to anticipate, or at least respond to, these changes will result in a decline in the demand for the company's products to a level where the business is no longer viable. On the other hand, investment in a project that promises high profits in the near future, without first attempting to assess whether the company can afford the project, is equally ill advised. Recognition of the importance of financial stability should not cause management to ignore the need for profit, but it will cause management to follow a policy of *long-run* rather than *short-run* profit maximization.

A proper assessment of business performance must therefore focus attention on the adequacy of both profit and cash. The way in which ratio analysis is used to achieve such an assessment is examined in this chapter.

PRINCIPLES OF RATIO ANALYSIS

Accounting ratios are calculated by expressing one figure as a ratio or percentage of another with the objective of disclosing significant relationships and trends that are not immediately evident from the examination of individual balances appearing in the accounts. The ratio that results from a comparison of two figures only possesses real significance, however, if an identifiable economic relationship exists between the numerator and the denominator. For example, one would expect there to be a positive relationship between net profit and the level of sales. Assuming that each item sold produces a profit, one would expect a higher sales figure to produce more profit. So the knowledge that profit is £5 million is not particularly illuminating. What is of greater interest is net profit expressed as a percentage of sales (see later in this chapter).

The significance of an accounting ratio is enhanced by comparison with some yardstick of corporate performance. There are three options available, namely comparison with:

1 results achieved during a previous accounting period by the same company (trend analysis);
2 results achieved by other companies in the same business sector (interfirm comparisons); and
3 predetermined standards or budgets.

The advantage of making comparisons is that it enables users to classify a company's performance as good, average or poor in certain key areas. However, the user must realize that there are certain attractions and limitations attached to each of the three bases for comparison listed above.

1 Last year's results are readily available, in the case of limited companies, because there is a legal requirement for them to publish accounts giving corresponding figures for the previous accounting period. In the case of sole traders and partnerships, the ability to obtain access to the relevant data will depend on the particular circumstances of each case. For example, a banker can insist on the provision of relevant accounting information as a precondition for granting a loan. A limitation of trend analysis is that it provides little useful guidance about whether a business is doing as well as it should. For example, a comparison may show that there is an improvement in the net profit percentage, but last year's results may have been disastrous.
2 Problems with interfirm comparisons include the difficulty of finding a company engaged in a similar range of business activities, while differences in

accounting policies might detract from the significance of any findings. It is, however, important to discover how a company is performing in relation to its competitors since this throws a great deal of light on the efficiency of management and the long-term prospects of the concern.

3   A comparison of actual results with predetermined budgets or standards should, in theory, be the best test of whether the workforce has achieved a reasonable level of efficiency. However, establishing realistic standards is difficult and costly. Also, it is of little consolation to discover that work is being carried out efficiently if, due to the existence of a declining market, profits are falling. In practice, management rarely publishes budgeted future results, or standards, and so external users of accounting reports usually have to confine their attention to trend analysis and interfirm comparisons.

CLASSIFICATION OF ACCOUNTING RATIOS

A meaningful accounting ratio is calculated by comparing two financial balances between which there exists some identifiable economic relationship, such as profit and sales. The most important accounting ratio is the return on capital employed examined next in this chapter, while ratios designed to analyse profit margins, solvency, asset utilization and gearing are dealt with later. Finally, the relationship between the various financial ratios is examined.

Accounting ratios are used to build up a corporate profile of the company under investigation. The ratios rarely point unanimously in the same direction; profits, for example, may have declined during the same accounting period that solvency has improved. This emphasizes the importance of not attaching too much attention to individual accounting ratios, and a balanced assessment of the company's progress requires a careful examination to be made of the relative significance of the ratios that are calculated.

RETURN ON CAPITAL EMPLOYED

The amount of profit earned by a business is important but, to assess the relative performance of a number of businesses, or even the performance of the same business over a number of years, it is necessary to examine the figure for profit in relation to the amount of money invested (capital employed) in the business. The return on capital employed (ROCE) is calculated as follows:

$$\text{ROCE} = \frac{\text{Net profit}}{\text{Capital employed}} \times 100$$

It is generally acceptable to use either net profit before or net profit after tax for the purpose of this calculation. Whichever approach is adopted, it should be consistently applied. When tax complications are introduced later in this chapter, the pre-tax version is used.

EXAMPLE
12.1

The following information is provided for 20X1:

	Company A	Company B
	£	£
Net profit	100,000	150,000
Capital employed	500,000	1,500,000

Required

Calculate the ROCE for each company.

Solution

Company A: $\dfrac{£100,000}{£500,000} \times 100 = 20\%$

Company B: $\dfrac{£150,000}{£1,500,000} \times 100 = 10\%$

Company A has reported a net profit of £100,000 whereas company B has reported a net profit of £150,000, i.e. company B has generated 50 per cent more profit than company A, but, to achieve this, three times as much has been invested. When profit is related to the amount invested we find that company A has earned a return of 20 per cent compared with 10 per cent by company B. It is therefore clear that, contrary to the initial impression conveyed by the figures provided in the question, company A is by far the better business proposition for, say, the prospective investor.

ACTIVITY
12.1

The following information is provided for 20X5:

	ABC Ltd	XYZ Ltd
	£	£
Net profit	250,000	75,000
Capital employed	750,000	200,000

Required

Calculate the ROCE for each company.

Calculation of capital employed

Capital employed is the amount of money invested in the business. The two most common methods of calculating capital employed are as follows:

1   *Owners' (proprietors') capital employed.*   This is the amount invested by the owner or owners. It is the balance on the sole trader's capital account; the aggregate of the balances on the partners' capital and current accounts or, in the case of a limited company, the ordinary shareholders' capital plus share premium account, retained profits and any balances on reserve accounts. Using the asset-based approach, owners' capital employed is calculated by taking total assets and deducting non-ownership liabilities.

2   *Total capital employed.*   This is found by adding together all sources of finance, i.e. capital, long-term liabilities and current liabilities. Using the asset-based approach, total capital employed is calculated by combining the balances for each category of asset belonging to the business.

The following balances were extracted from the books of Compass Ltd at 31 December 20X2:

EXAMPLE

12.2

	£
Fixed assets	130,000
Ordinary share capital	100,000
Share premium account	20,000
10% loan repayable 20X8	50,000
Trade creditors	25,000
Current assets	105,000
Revaluation reserve	12,000
Proposed dividend	10,000
Retained profit	18,000

(a)   The balance sheet of Compass Ltd at 31 December 20X2.

(b)   The figures for:

Required

    (i)   owners' capital employed; and

    (ii)   total capital employed

(a)

Solution

Compass Ltd

Balance sheet as at 31 December 20X2

	£	£
Fixed assets		130,000
Current assets	105,000	
Creditors: amounts falling due within one year		
Trade creditors	(25,000)	
Proposed dividends	(10,000)	
	(35,000)	
Working capital		70,000
		200,000
Creditors: amounts falling due after more than one year		
10% loan repayable 20X8		(50,000)
		150,000
Financed by:		
Ordinary share capital		100,000
Share premium account		20,000
Revaluation reserve		12,000
Retained profit		18,000
		150,000

(b) (i)   Owners' capital employed, £150,000.

(ii)   Total capital employed, £235,000 (£130,000 fixed assets + £105,000 current assets).

ACTIVITY 12.2

The following balances were taken from the accounts of Moon plc at the end of 20X2.

Debits	£
Plant and machinery (cost)	850,000
Trade debtors and prepayments	250,000
Stock and work in progress	426,000
Cash in hand	2,000
Credits	
8% debentures repayable 20X9	150,000
Plant and machinery accumulated depreciation	360,000
Trade creditors and accruals	157,000
Revaluation reserve	90,000
Bank overdraft	136,000
Share capital (£1 ordinary shares)	250,000
Share premium account	100,000
Reserves (all distributable)	235,000
Corporation tax	50,000

Required

(a)   The balance sheet of Moon plc at 31 December 20X2.

(b)   The figures for:

(i)   owners' capital employed; and

(ii)   total capital employed

Matching profit with capital employed

The profit figure used for the purpose of calculating ROCE will differ depending on the version of capital employed under consideration:

- *Owners' capital employed.*   Use net profit before tax reported in the accounts.

- *Total capital employed.*   Use net profit before tax and before deducting interest charges, including interest on any bank overdraft.

The different purposes of these calculations are as follows: the former measures the return earned for ordinary shareholders; the latter directs attention to the efficiency with which management utilizes the total resources at its disposal.

Assume the same facts as for Example 12.2. In addition, the summarized profit and loss account of Compass Ltd for 20X2 is as follows:

EXAMPLE
12.3

	£	£
Gross profit		100,000
Distribution costs	17,000	
Administrative expenses	54,000	− 71,000
Operating profit		29,000
Interest paid		− 5,000
Profit before tax		24,000
Taxation		− 8,000
Profit after tax		16,000
Less: Dividends paid		− 10,000
Retained profit for the year		6,000
Retained profit brought forward		12,000
Retained profit carried forward		18,000

Calculations of the return on:

(a) owners' capital employed; and

(b) total capital employed.

Required

(a) Owners' capital employed:

$$\text{Return} = \frac{24,000}{150,000} \times 100 = 16\%$$

Solution

(b) Total capital employed:

$$\text{Return} = \frac{29,000^*}{235,000} \times 100 = 12.3\%$$

Note * £24,000 (net profit) + £5,000 (all interest charges).

The directors of Compass have managed to achieve a return of 12.3 per cent on the total resources at their disposal. The return earned on the owners' capital employed is significantly higher, at 16 per cent. There are two reasons for this:

1 Compass benefits from 'free' finance amounting to £35,000, consisting of the dividend not yet due (£10,000) and trade credit (£25,000). It is for this reason that business people usually take the maximum amount of finance offered in the form of credit by suppliers.

2 The directors have raised a long-term loan at a favourable rate of interest, i.e. the £850,000 loan repayable in 20X8 attracts interest at the rate of 10 per cent per annum and, because the return earned on total capital employed is higher (12.3 per cent), the

surplus accrues to the ordinary shareholders who are, as a result, better off. The division of total capital between shares and loans – technically referred to as gearing – is discussed further later in this chapter.

The rates of return, calculated in this section, are based on capital employed at the year end. Profit arises throughout the 12-month period, however, and a more precise calculation is made by using average capital employed during the year. Because the information needed to calculate average capital employed is rarely provided, and because absolute accuracy is not a priority, it is perfectly acceptable to use the year-end figure, which usually produces a close approximation.

ACTIVITY 12.3

Assume the same facts as for Activity 12.2. In addition, the summarized profit and loss account of Moon plc for 20X2 is as follows:

Profit and loss account of Moon plc for 20X2

	£	£
Gross profit		892,000
Distribution costs	220,000	
Administrative expenses	450,000	– 670,000
Operating profit		222,000
Interest paid		– 12,000
Profit before tax		210,000
Taxation		– 50,000
Profit after tax		160,000
Less: Dividends paid		– 30,000
Retained profit for the year		130,000
Retained profit brought forward		105,000
Retained profit carried forward		235,000

Required

Calculate the return on:

(a) owners' capital employed; and
(b) total capital employed.

PROFIT RATIOS

The purposes of profit ratios are to help assess the adequacy of profits earned, to discover whether margins are increasing or declining and to help choose between alternative courses of action. A proper appreciation of the significance of the gross profit margin and the net profit percentage is dependent upon a thorough understanding of the different ways in which business costs, both fixed and variable, respond to changes in the levels of production and sales (see Chapter 13).

Gross profit margin (percentage)

The gross profit margin is calculated, as a percentage, using the formula:

$$\text{Gross profit margin} = \frac{\text{Gross profit}}{\text{Sales}} \times 100$$

In the case of a trader, where cost of goods sold is a variable cost, the ratio is expected to remain *constant* when the level of sales rises or falls.

The sales, cost of goods sold and gross profit of Printer Ltd for 20X4 and 20X5 were: **EXAMPLE 12.4**

	20X4	20X5
	£	£
Sales	162,000	196,000
Cost of goods sold	(121,500)	(147,000)
Gross profit	40,500	49,000

Calculate the gross profit margin for each year.   **Required**

Gross profit margin: **Solution**

20X4 $\dfrac{40,500}{162,000} \times 100 = 25\%$

20X5 $\dfrac{49,000}{196,000} \times 100 = 25\%$

The sales, cost of goods sold and gross profit of Painter Ltd for 20X1 and 20X2 were: **ACTIVITY 12.4**

	20X1	20X2
	£	£
Sales	900,000	1,200,000
Cost of goods sold	(693,000)	(924,000)
Gross profit	207,000	276,000

Calculate the gross profit margin for each year.   **Required**

The constant gross profit margin results from the fact that for each additional unit sold, an extra unit is purchased, and prices, both for buying and selling, are unchanged. In practice, the margin does not always remain stable for reasons that include the following:

1   *A reduction in the unit cost of goods sold.*   Increased purchases, for example, may enable bulk purchase discounts to be obtained.
2   *Under- or overvaluation of stocks.*   If stocks are undervalued, for example, cost of goods sold is inflated and profit understated. An incorrect valuation may be the result of an error during stocktake or it may be due to fraud, for example, a businesswoman might intentionally undervalue her stocks so as to reduce the amount of tax payable. The closing stock of one period is the opening stock of the next, of course, and so the effect of errors cancels out unless repeated.
3   *Price variations.*   The directors may decide to cut the selling price in an attempt to increase sales. This reduces the gross profit margin but, provided sufficient extra units are sold, gross profit may still increase.

The gross profit margin of manufacturing businesses varies with changes in the level of activity even where prices are stable and stocks correctly valued. This is because manufacturing expenses include some fixed costs and, as production increases, the fixed costs are spread over a greater number of units, with the result that the total cost per unit falls.

EXAMPLE 12.5

Yale Ltd incurs annual fixed manufacturing costs of £75,000 and a variable manufacturing cost per unit of £5. Each unit sells for £10. In 20X1, 20,000 units were produced and sold; in 20X2, the figure was 25,000. There were no opening or closing stocks in either year.

Required

(a)   Calculate the average fixed manufacturing cost per unit.
(b)   Calculate the company's total gross profit and gross profit margin for each year.
(c)   Comment briefly on the results prepared in answer to parts (a) and (b).

Solution

(a)

	20X1	20X2
Average fixed manufacturing cost per unit	$\dfrac{£75,000}{20,000} = £3.75$	$\dfrac{£75,000}{25,000} = £3.00$

(b)

	20X1		*20X2*	
	£	£	£	£
Sales		200,000		250,000
Less: Variable costs	100,000		125,000	
Fixed costs	75,000		75,000	
		− 175,000		− 200,000
Gross profit		25,000		50,000
Gross profit margin:				

	20X1		*20X2*	
$\dfrac{\text{Gross profit}}{\text{Sales}}$	$\dfrac{£25,000}{£200,000} = 12.5\%$		$\dfrac{£50,000}{£250,000} = 20\%$	

(c)   An increase in sales of 25 per cent has resulted in an increase in gross profit of 100 per cent and in the gross profit margin of 60 per cent. This is because the average fixed cost per unit has fallen from £3.75 to £3.00.

ACTIVITY
12.5

The following information was taken from the records of Lock, Stock and Barrel Ltd for the periods ending 31 March 20X3 and 20X4:

Fixed manufacturing costs		£280,000
Unit variable manufacturing cost		£15
Unit selling price		£25
Units purchased and sold:	20X3	50,000
	20X4	70,000

There was no opening stock or closing stock in either year.

Required

(a)   Calculate the average fixed manufacturing cost per unit.
(b)   Calculate the company's total gross profit and gross profit margin for each year.

Net profit percentage

The net profit percentage expresses net profit as a percentage of sales. It is calculated as follows:

$$\text{Net profit percentage} = \frac{\text{Net profit}}{\text{Sales}} \times 100$$

The expenses debited to the profit and loss account are both fixed and variable with respect to sales. For example, interest paid on debentures is a fixed expense, provided that no further loans are taken out, while delivery costs are likely to respond to changes in the level of sales. The net profit percentage of traders and manufacturers can be expected to increase or decrease in line with the level of sales.

EXAMPLE
12.6

Crackle is a trader who buys and sells goods. His trading results for 20X6 and 20X7 were:

Summarized trading results:

	20X6	20X7
	£	£
Sales	80,000	100,000
Cost of goods sold	− 60,000	− 75,000
Gross profit	20,000	25,000
Expenses	− 10,000	− 12,000
Net profit	10,000	13,000

There were no opening or closing stocks, in either year. The cost of goods Crackle sells rose by 10 per cent on 1 January 20X7.

Required

(a) Calculate Crackle's gross profit and net profit margins for 20X6 and 20X7.

(b) Comment on the changes in the percentages calculated in part (a).

Solution

(a)

	20X6	20X7
Gross profit margin	$\dfrac{20,000}{80,000} \times 100 = 25\%$	$\dfrac{25,000}{100,000} \times 100 = 25\%$
Net profit percentage	$\dfrac{10,000}{80,000} \times 100 = 12.5\%$	$\dfrac{13,000}{100,000} \times 100 = 13\%$

(b) The gross profit margin has remained constant at 25 per cent, and so we can conclude that Crackle has been able to pass on the 10 per cent increase in costs to his customers. The growth in the value of sales is due not only to the price rise but also to an increase in the volume of sales. If sales had simply risen in line with the price rise, they would have amounted to only £80,000 + (£80,000 × 10%) = £88,000.

The value of sales has increased by 25 per cent, while expenses have increased by only 20 per cent (some of them must be fixed costs). As a result, the net profit percentage has increased from 12.5 to 13 per cent.

ACTIVITY 12.6

Snap is a trader who buys and sells goods. His trading results for 20X5 and 20X6 were:

Summarized trading results:

	20X5 £	20X6 £
Sales	400,000	500,000
Cost of goods sold	− 190,000	− 190,000
Gross profit	210,000	310,000
Expenses	− 63,000	− 100,000
Net profit	147,000	210,000

There were no opening or closing stock, in either year.

Required

Calculate Snap's gross profit and net profit margins for 20X5 and 20X6.

To examine the relative impact of changes in level of activity on the cost structure, it is useful to express all costs as a percentage of sales. This is demonstrated in Example 12.7, which also shows that changes in the gross profit margin have a 'knock-on' effect on the net profit percentage.

Stamp Ltd, a trading company, did not increase its selling prices between 20X6 and 20X7, but the cost of the goods it sells rose 1.25 per cent on 1 January 20X7. Its trading and profit and loss accounts for 20X6 and 20X7 were:

EXAMPLE
12.7

Summarized trading results:

	20X6	20X7
	£	£
Sales	50,000	60,000
Cost of goods sold	− 40,000	− 48,600
Gross profit	10,000	11,400
Rent	− 1,200	− 1,200
Other expenses	− 2,000	− 2,400
Net Profit	6,800	7,800

(a) Prepare statements for 20X6 and 20X7 in which each of the cost categories, the net profit and the gross profit are expressed as percentages of sales.

(b) Comment on the results shown in the statement prepared in part (a).

	20X6	20X7
	%	%
Sales	100.0	100.0
Cost of goods sold	80.0	81.0
Gross profit	20.0	19.0
Rent	2.4	2.0
Other expenses	4.0	4.0
Net profit	13.6	13.0

(b) The gross profit has risen, but the gross profit margin has fallen by 1 per cent as a result of the rise in the cost of the goods Stamp Ltd sells (1.25 per cent of cost is equivalent to 1 per cent of sales price where the gross margin is 20 per cent).

Turning to the profit and loss account, rent is a fixed cost, and its impact has fallen from 2.4 to 2 per cent. Other expenses continue to account for 4 per cent of sales. The net result is a fall in total profit and loss account costs from 6.4 to 6 per cent.

The overall impact is a fall in the net profit percentage by 0.6 per cent, although the amount of net profit has risen. If the gross profit margin could have been maintained by passing on the price rise to customers, the net profit percentage would also have risen.

Taking the information from Activity 12.6, prepare statements for 20X5 and 20X6 that express as a percentage of sales the expenses and cost of goods sold figures.

Readers should now attempt Question 12.1 at the end of this chapter.

Earnings per share and the price/earnings ratio

FRS 14 requires quoted companies to state their earnings per share (EPS) in the accounts, and shareholders use this figure as one basis for assessing the performance of their investment. The EPS is expressed in pence and is calculated as follows:

$$EPS = \frac{Earnings}{Equity\ shares}$$

where

1   earnings are defined as profit, after deducting taxation and any preference dividends (this is the amount available for the equity shareholders); and
2   equity shares are the number of ordinary shares in issue and ranking for dividend.

EXAMPLE 12.8

Walnut has an issued share capital of £1 million, divided into ordinary shares of 25p each, and 500,000 £1 preference shares carrying a dividend of 7 per cent. The following information is provided in respect of 20X0 and 20XI:

Profit and loss account extracts

	20X0	20XI
	£	£
Profit before taxation	700,000	900,000
Tax	− 165,000	− 200,000
Profit after taxation	535,000	700,000
Dividends: Preference	− 35,000	− 35,000
Ordinary	− 100,000	− 150,000
Retained profit for the year	400,000	515,000

Required

A calculation of the earnings per share for 20X0 and 20X1.

Solution

$$20X0:\ EPS = \frac{535,000 - 35,000^\dagger}{4,000,000^*} = 12.5p$$

$$20X1:\ EPS = \frac{700,000 - 35,000}{4,000,000^*} = 16.6p$$

Note   † Deduct preference dividend not attributable to equity shareholders.
* 4,000,000 shares = £1,000,000 / 0.25.

The following information is taken from the accounts of Johannah Ltd for the years ending 31 December 20X0 and 20X1.

	20X1	20X0
	£000	£000
Profit before tax	3,183	2,964
Tax	− 1,285	− 1,255
Profit after tax	1,898	1,709
Dividends: Preference	− 80	− 80
Ordinary	− 180	− 190
Retained profit for the year	1,638	1,439

The issued share capital for both years consisted of £5,500,000 50p ordinary shares and £1,000,000 £1 preference shares.

Calculate the earnings per share figure for 20X0 and 20X1.   Required

The EPS is also used as the basis for calculating the price/earnings (P/E) ratio, which is widely used by financial analysts as a means of assessing the performance of an individual company and comparing it with the performance and prospects of other companies in the same industry. The P/E ratio is calculated as follows:

$$\text{P/E ratio} = \frac{\text{Market price of share}}{\text{Most recent EPS}}$$

We can, therefore, see that the ratio is calculated by expressing the current market price of the share as a multiple of past earnings per share. The figure for market price is taken from the daily list issued by the London Stock Exchange and the earnings per share can be obtained from the company's most recent accounts. A number of daily newspapers give an up-to-date calculation of the P/E ratio of quoted companies. A high P/E ratio indicates that the market believes the company has good prospects, whereas a low P/E ratio suggests that the experts think that the next results published for the company are likely to show a deterioration. It follows from this that companies favoured by the stock market will have higher P/E ratios.

SOLVENCY RATIOS

Working capital ratio

A business must be able to meet its debts as they fall due if it is to maintain its creditworthiness and continue as a going concern. For this desirable state of affairs to exist, a business must have an adequate balance of working capital (i.e. current assets − current liabilities). A secure financial position is illustrated in Example 12.9.

EXAMPLE   The following balances were extracted from the books of Campion Ltd as at 31 December
12.9   20X1:

	£
Share capital	100,000
Reserves	75,000
Taxation due at 30 September 20X2	10,000
Trade creditors	15,000
Balance of cash at bank	5,000
Fixed assets at cost less depreciation	150,000
Stock	22,000
Trade debtors	23,000

Required   A calculation of Campion's working capital at 31 December 20X1.

Solution

	£	£
Current assets:		
Stock		22,000
Trade debtors		23,000
Bank balance		5,000
		50,000
Current liabilities:		
Trade creditors	15,000	
Taxation payable	10,000	
		− 25,000
Working capital		25,000

ACTIVITY   The following balances were extracted from the books of Potter Ltd as at 31 March 20X3:
12.9

	£000
Share capital	2,000
Reserves	1,500
Corporation tax liability	400
Trade creditors	600
Bank overdraft	100
Fixed assets at net book value	3,100
Stock	500
Trade debtors	1,000

Required   A calculation of Potter Ltd's working capital at 31 March 20X3.

The above calculation shows that Campion is able to pay its current liabilities
out of resources made available by the conversion of current assets into cash and,

in addition, it shows that £25,000 will remain after the necessary payments have been made. The fact that business activity is continuous means that additional purchases will be made during January 20X2 and more sales will also occur. Consequently, the £25,000 surplus will never actually arise in a single lump sum. Nevertheless, the working capital calculation provides a useful indication of the company's ability to meet its short-term debts as they fall due for payment, i.e. it focuses attention on the solvency position of the firm.

The significance that can be attached to the balance for working capital, taken in isolation, is limited. A figure of £25,000 suggests financial stability in the case of a small business, such as Campion, but probably not in a much larger enterprise. In another company, the deduction of current liabilities amounting to, say, £975,000 from current assets of £1,000,000 would also show a working capital balance of £25,000 but, in view of the much larger scale of short-term commitments, it would probably be regarded as a totally inadequate financial 'cushion'. It is for this reason that users of accounting statements pay more attention to the working capital (or current) ratio, which examines the proportional relationship between current assets and current liabilities. It is calculated as follows:

$$\text{Working capital ratio} = \frac{\text{Current assets}}{\text{Current liabilities}}$$

The working capital ratio of Campion is:

$$\text{Working capital ratio} = \frac{£50,000}{£25,000}$$

$$= 2 : 1$$

The purpose of the working capital ratio is to help assess the solvency position of a business, and a question naturally asked by students and business people is, 'What is an acceptable ratio?' Unfortunately it is not possible to give a definite answer because much depends on the nature of the trade in which the company is engaged. It may be assumed, for the purpose of illustration, that Campion is a trading company that purchases and sells goods on credit, and also that the company receives from suppliers the same period of credit as it allows to customers. Thirty days is the normal credit period, although the exact duration is unimportant because, provided a company allows customers, on average, the same period of credit as is granted by its suppliers, the amount of money due from customers will be received in time for the creditors to be paid as their debts fall due. Because Campion sells goods on credit none of the money presently tied up in stock will be converted into cash in time to pay the existing current liabilities as they mature. It is true that some stock will be sold in the next few days, but it will be a further 30 days, at least, before the cash is collected from the customer. It will be even longer before the remaining stock is converted into cash. The conclusion that arises from this analysis is that the working capital ratio must be sufficiently high to accommodate the inclusion of stock among the current assets. If stock comprises no more than 50 per cent of total current assets, as is the case at Campion, an adequate ratio of current assets to current liabilities is in the region of 2 : 1.

In practice a ratio of 2 : 1 is conventionally regarded as the acceptable norm. It cannot be emphasized too strongly, however, that this is a broad generalization that should be treated with great caution. For example, companies in certain sectors of the economy turn stock into cash very quickly and, for them, a ratio well below 2 : 1 is quite acceptable (the working capital ratio of Marks and Spencer plc at 31 March 1999 was 1.65 : 1). This state of affairs usually exists in the retail trade where sales are made mainly for cash. In circumstances where resources are tied up in stock for a much longer time period, as happens in the construction industry, a working capital ratio of perhaps 4 : 1 may be regarded as essential.

Readers should now attempt Question 12.2 at the end of the chapter.

Liquidity ratio

The purpose of the liquidity ratio is similar to that of the working capital ratio, in that it is designed to assess the ability of a business to meet its debts as they fall due. The calculation is as follows:

$$\text{Liquidity ratio} = \frac{\text{Liquid assets}}{\text{Current liabilities}}$$

It is a more rigorous test of solvency than the working capital ratio because it omits current assets that are unlikely to be converted into cash in time to meet liabilities falling due in the near future. The ratio is for this reason sometimes described as the 'acid test' of solvency. Non-liquid current assets that must be left out of the calculation include stock (unless sales are made on the cash basis, as in the case of a food supermarket, in which case stock is a liquid asset) and any trade debts not receivable in the near future because customers have been allowed an extended period of credit.

The liquidity ratio of Campion (Example 12.9) is as follows:

$$\text{Liquidity ratio} = \frac{£23,000 + £5,000}{£25,000}$$
$$= 1.12 : 1$$

This calculation shows that Campion Ltd has sufficient liquid assets to cover its current liabilities. A ratio of 1 : 1 is generally considered desirable in practice and, on the whole, this is a fair test. However, readers should be aware of the fact that the conventional method of calculation can understate the short-term financial position of the firm because, although current assets are carefully examined and less liquid items excluded, the same distinction is not made in the case of current liabilities. Normally all current liabilities are included despite the fact that some of the amounts outstanding, particularly taxation, may not be payable for a number of months. In Campion's case, for example, current liabilities include taxation that is not due for payment until 30 September 20X2, nine months after the balance sheet date. Readers should therefore be aware of the fact that the conventional method of calculating the liquidity ratio, which includes all current liabilities, is consistent with the accounting concept of 'prudence' but may, in certain circumstances, be a little over-cautious.

Readers should now work through Question 12.3 at the end of the chapter.

ASSET TURNOVER RATIOS

The ratios calculated in this section are designed to answer the following question: 'Is management making full enough use of the resources placed at its disposal by shareholders and creditors?'

Rate of stock turnover

This ratio measures the speed with which a company turns over its stock. The calculation is made as follows:

$$\text{Rate of stock turnover} = \frac{\text{Cost of goods sold}}{\text{Average stock level}}$$

where average stock is the opening plus closing stocks divided by 2.

The accounts of Treadmill Ltd show figures for cost of goods sold and average stock levels of £150,000 and £25,000, respectively.

EXAMPLE 12.10

Calculate the rate of stock turnover of Treadmill.

Required

$$\text{Rate of stock turnover} = \frac{150,000}{25,000} = 6 \text{ times a year}$$

Solution

Extracts of the trading account of Jogging Ltd for the years ending 30 June 20X0 and 20X1 were as follows:

ACTIVITY 12.10

Extract of Trading Account

	20X0		20X1	
	£000	£000	£000	£000
Sales		4,000		6,000
Opening stock	400		600	
Purchases	2,500		3,800	
	2,900		4,400	
Less: Closing stock	− 600		− 750	
Cost of goods sold		− 2,300		− 3,650
Gross profit		1,700		2,350

Calculate the rate of stock turnover of Jogging Ltd for 20X0 and 20X1.

Required

Two queries often raised by students concerning the calculation of the above formula are as follows: 'Why use cost of sales rather than sales?' and 'Why use average stock levels rather than closing stock?' The reason, in both cases, is to ensure that both the numerator and denominator are computed on a comparable basis.

Stocks, which make up the denominator, are valued at cost for accounting purposes, and the numerator must be computed on a similar basis. The sales figure can be used to produce a ratio that enables users to make helpful inter-period comparisons, when cost of sales figures are not available, but there is a risk that wrong conclusions will be drawn when there are changes in the gross profit margin from one accounting period to another.

Turning to the reason for using average stock levels, the numerator measures the cost of goods dispatched to customers during an accounting period, and the denominator should therefore represent the average investment in stock during the same period. The average is usually based on opening and closing stock figures but, because stock levels fluctuate a great deal, a more precise calculation would make use of stock levels at various dates during the year, perhaps at the end of each month.

The term 'ratio' is used loosely, in accountancy, to cover all the calculations that measure the relationship between two financial totals. We have already seen, for example, that net profit is conventionally expressed as a percentage of sales rather than as an actual ratio. In the case of the stock turnover ratio, many analysts prefer to present it in terms of the number of days (or weeks or months) that elapse between the dates on which goods are delivered by suppliers and dispatched to customers, i.e. the stockholding period. This can be done by dividing the result of the calculation presented in Example 12.10 into 365 (or 52 or 12), or by modifying the formula so as to achieve the desired result in a single step.

$$\text{Rate of stock turnover, in days} = \frac{\text{Average stock}}{\text{Cost of goods sold}} \times 365$$
$$= \frac{25,000}{150,000} \times 365$$
$$- 61 \text{ days}$$

Companies strive to keep the stockholding period as low as possible in order to minimize associated business costs. If Treadmill held its stock for an average of four months, rather than 61 days, its investment in stocks would double to approximately £50,000. Extra finance would then have to be raised, handling costs would increase and the potential loss from stock damage and obsolescence would be much greater. Although management's aim is to keep stocks to a minimum, it must nevertheless ensure that there are sufficient raw materials available to meet production requirements (in the case of a manufacturer) and enough finished goods available to meet consumer demand. It is, therefore, management's job to maintain a balance between these conflicting priorities.

The following information is provided in respect of the affairs of Hutchinson, which makes up its accounts on the calendar year basis:

EXAMPLE
12.11

	20X5	20X6
	£	£
Credit sales	500,000	600,000
Credit purchases	350,000	400,000
Cost of goods sold	330,000	360,000
Stock at 31 December	60,000	100,000
Debtors at 31 December	102,000	98,000
Creditors at 31 December	25,000	40,000
Average total assets at 31 December	185,000	300,000

Stock and debtors at 1 January 20X5 amounted to £70,000 and £98,000 respectively.

(a)   Calculations of the rate of stock turnover expressed (i) as a rate and (ii) in days, for each of the years 20X5 and 20X6.

(b)   Comment briefly on your results.

Required

(a)

Solution

(i)   Number of times

	20X5	20X6

Rate of stock turnover

$$\frac{\text{Cost of goods sold}}{\text{Average stock}}$$ $\dfrac{330}{65*} = 5 \text{ times}$ $\dfrac{360}{80^\dagger} = 4.5 \text{ times}$

Notes   *Average stock = (70,000 + 60,000) ÷ 2.

†Average stock = (60,000 + 100,000) ÷ 2.

(ii)   Number of days

	20X5	20X6

Rate of stock turnover in days

$$\frac{\text{Average stock}}{\text{Cost of goods sold}} \times 365$$ $\dfrac{65}{330} \times 365 = 72 \text{ days}$ $\dfrac{80}{360} \times 365 = 81 \text{ days}$

(b)   In 20X6 Hutchinson achieved a 20 per cent increase in sales from £500,000 to £600,000. In these circumstances, a proportionate increase in the volume of stock held might be expected. However, a disproportionate increase in stock levels, from £60,000 to £100,000, has occurred. This has been caused by a growth in the average stockholding period from 72 days to 81 days, i.e. it has taken the company, on average, 9 days longer to turn over stock in 20X6 than in the previous year.

ACTIVITY 12.11

The following information was extracted from the books of Muggles Ltd for the period ending 31 March 20X0, 20X1 and 20X2:

	20X0 £000	20X1 £000	20X2 £000
Stock at 31 March	133	459	729
Total sales	1,300	3,000	4,500
Total purchases	780	1,800	2,700
Trade debtors	200	690	1,200
Trade creditors	172	465	880
Total assets (i.e. total capital employed)	730	1,500	2,900
Net profit	219	405	725

Note   Cash sales amount to 20% of total sales in each of the three years. Credit purchases represent three-quarters of total purchases in each of the three years.

Required

Calculate the rate of stock turnover as the number of times per year and in days for 20X1 and 20X2.

Rate of collection of debtors

The period of credit allowed to customers is an important business decision. Too little credit makes it difficult to achieve a satisfactory level of sales, whereas too much credit deprives a company of essential liquid resources. The 'normal' credit period varies between industries but, in practice, it is quite usual for customers to take from six to eight weeks to pay their bills. The rate of collection of debtors is calculated, in days, as follows:

$$\text{Rate of collection of debtors} = \frac{\text{Average trade debtors}}{\text{Credit sales}} \times 365$$

Note that the denominator is confined to credit sales, since only these give rise to debts outstanding. Where the split between cash and credit sales is not given, the total sales figure may be used to calculate a ratio that gives useful comparative information provided there is no significant change in the proportion of total sales made for cash.

The debt collection ratio measures the effectiveness of a company's system of credit control. When an order is received, the credit controller (usually the owner in the case of a small business but a specialist function in the case of a large corporation) must assess the creditworthiness of the potential customer. This may involve taking up references, from say a bank, speaking to colleagues in the trade and perhaps examining a recent copy of the company's accounts. If it is decided to supply the goods requested, it is important that they should be invoiced immediately following dispatch. Any time lag inevitably increases the credit period and the volume of resources tied up in debts outstanding.

At the end of the credit period, often 30 days, a check should be made to ensure that cash has been received. Indeed, a list of debtor balances, classified by the length of time outstanding, should be prepared as a matter of systematic routine. If the credit period is exceeded, the customer's attention should be drawn to this fact by sending either a statement or a letter requesting immediate payment. The debt should subsequently be kept under continuous scrutiny and no further goods supplied until payment is made. Failure to respond to the second request for payment should result in determined attempts to recover the balance outstanding by such devices as persistent telephone calls or a solicitor's letter threatening legal action. Whether legal action will in fact be taken depends on the amount outstanding, the likelihood of recovery (has the customer the money?) and the costs involved.

Using the information given in Example 12.11, calculate the rate of collection of debtors, in days, for each of the years 20X5 and 20X6 and comment briefly on the results.

EXAMPLE 12.12

Solution

	20X5	20X6
Rate of collection of debtors in days		
$\dfrac{\text{Average debtors}}{\text{Credit sales}} \times 365$	$\dfrac{100^*}{500} \times 365 = 73$ days	$\dfrac{^*100}{600} \times 365 = 61$ days

Note * Average debtors = opening debtors plus closing debtors divided by 2.

The company has reduced the average period taken to collect debts from 73 days to 61 days. As a result, the average debtor balance outstanding has remained at £100,000, despite a significant increase in sales. Possible explanations are a strong demand for the company's product, enabling credit periods to be cut, or improved efficiency in the credit control department.

ACTIVITY 12.12

Using the information given in Activity 12.11, calculate the rate of collection of debtors, in days, for each of the years 20X1 and 20X2.

Rate of payment of creditors

This ratio measures the average period of time taken by companies to pay their bills. As a general rule, companies extract the maximum credit period from suppliers since, in the absence of discounts for prompt payment, it represents a free source of finance. At the same time, undue delays should be avoided as these will have a harmful long-run effect on the company's credit standing. The result of the calculation must be interpreted with particular care since not all suppliers grant similar credit terms but, provided there are no significant changes in the 'mix' of trade creditors, the average payments period should remain stable. The rate of payment of creditors is calculated, in days, as follows:

$$\text{Rate of payment of suppliers} = \frac{\text{Average trade creditors}}{\text{Credit purchases}} \times 365$$

A change in the rate of payment of suppliers' invoices may well reflect an improvement or decline in a company's liquidity. For instance, if a company is short of cash it is likely that creditors will be made to wait longer for the payment of amounts due to them. This may be an acceptable short-term strategy, particularly where suppliers are familiar with their customer's 'temporary' predicament and are willing to accept an extension of credit terms. Management should, however, take prompt steps to arrange for additional finance; otherwise supplies of goods will eventually be curtailed.

EXAMPLE 12.13

Using the information given in Example 12.11, calculate the rate of payment of creditors, in days, for each of the years 20X5 and 20X6 and comment briefly on your results.

Solution

	20X5	20X6
Rate of payment of creditors in days		
$\dfrac{\text{Closing creditors}}{\text{Credit purchases}} \times 365$	$\dfrac{25}{350} \times 365 = 26$ days	$\dfrac{40}{400} \times 365 = 36.5$ days

Hutchinson's figure for trade creditors at 1 January 20X5 is not provided. It is, therefore, impossible to calculate the ratio by using the average creditors figure for that year. We could make the calculation, based on averages, for 20X6 but, without a comparative figure for 20X5, this would be of little interpretative value. The best course is to do calculations, for each year, using the closing figures, instead of average figures, for trade creditors. This measures the approximate number of days' purchases represented by the closing balances of trade creditors. The result of the calculation is open to criticism since purchases are unlikely to have occurred at a uniform rate throughout the year. It must be remembered, however, that too much weight ought not to be attached to an individual ratio that should be used only to help build up an overall business profile.

Trade creditors have increased disproportionately between the end of 20X5 and 20X6; at the latter date the value of creditors outstanding represents 10½ days' additional purchases. One possible explanation is that the company is now making full use of credit periods allowed by suppliers. Alternatively, the company may simply be short of cash especially bearing in mind the length of time it is taking them to collect their debts from debtors.

As usual, ratios merely measure change and investigation is needed to discover what actions have caused these changes to occur.

Using the information given in Activity 12.11, calculate the rate of payment of creditors, in days, for each of the years 20X1 and 20X2.

ACTIVITY 12.13

The cash operating cycle

The period of time that elapses between the payment for goods supplied and the receipt of cash from customers in respect of their sale is called 'the cash operating cycle'. During this time period the goods acquired must be financed by the company. The shorter the length of time between the initial outlay of funds and the ultimate collection of cash, the smaller the value of working capital to be financed. The cash cycle is represented by:

$$\text{Stockholding period} + \text{Debt collection period}$$
$$- \text{Creditor payment period}$$

This is demonstrated in Example 12.14.

Using the figures calculated from the information given in Example 12.11 above, calculate the cash operating cycle of Hutchinson.

EXAMPLE 12.14

Solution

	20X5 Days	20X6 Days
Stockholding period	72.0	81.0
Debt collection period	73.0	61.0
	145.0	142.0
Credit payment period	− 26.0	− 36.5
Cash operating cycle	119.0	105.5

ACTIVITY
12.14

Using the figures calculated from the information given in Activity 12.11 above, calculate the cash operating cycle of Muggles Ltd.

Total asset turnover

It is management's job to make the fullest use of available resources; only if this objective is achieved are profits likely to be maximized. The stock turnover and debt collection ratios are designed to measure management's ability to control the level of investment in certain selected areas, whereas the 'total asset turnover' has the broader aim of assessing the extent to which management utilizes all available resources. It is computed as follows:

$$\text{Total asset turnover} = \frac{\text{Sales}}{\text{Average total assets}}$$

A high ratio indicates that management is using the assets effectively to generate sales; most probably the company is working at, or near, full capacity. Possible reasons for a decline in the ratio include the following:

1 A fall in either the stock turnover or debt collection ratios which have a 'knock-on' effect on the total asset turnover ratio.
2 Temporary inconveniences such as a strike or a fire which destroys essential equipment.
3 The collapse in demand for a product line, unless steps are promptly taken to dispose of the equipment or transfer it to an alternative use.
4 The acquisition of fixed assets. A new company needs to make arrangements for accommodation and for the installation of any necessary plant and equipment. These facilities are unlikely to be used to their full capacity immediately but, as business builds up, the level of utilization increases. The point is eventually reached where existing fixed assets are used to their full capacity, and further expansion of business activity involves the acquisition of additional plant. It normally takes some time before demand increases sufficiently to absorb the extra capacity and, meanwhile, fixed asset turnover declines.

EXAMPLE
12.15

Using the information given in Example 12.11, calculate the total asset turnover for each of the years 20X5 and 20X6 and comment briefly on your results.

Solution

	20X5	20X6
Total asset turnover		
$\dfrac{\text{Sales}}{\text{Average total assets}}$	$\dfrac{500}{185} = 2.7 : 1$	$\dfrac{600}{300} = 2 : 1$

The ratio may be expressed either in the above form or as an amount of sales per £1 invested in assets, i.e. sales were £2.70 per £1 invested in 20X5 and £2 per £1 invested in 20X6. It is apparent that a significant reduction in asset utilization has occurred.

Using the information given in Activity 12.11, calculate the total asset turnover for each of the years 20X1 and 20X2.

ACTIVITY
12.5

A limitation of the asset turnover ratio is that it gives a high result for companies using older assets. This is partly the effect of inflation, but also because company accounts show fixed assets at net book value, which declines each year.

RELATIONSHIP BETWEEN ACCOUNTING RATIOS

Analyses of corporate performance carried out by students, and even by trained accountants, are often unsatisfactory; a common weakness is the failure to explore the relationship between the various ratios that have been calculated. The essence of the relationship is contained in the following formula:

Primary ratio		Secondary ratios	
		Margin ×	*Utilization*
Return on total capital employed	=	Net profit percentage	× Total asset turnover

A principal managerial objective is to maximize the return on total capital employed, sometimes referred to as the 'primary ratio'. This objective can be accomplished in the following ways: by increasing the net profit percentage and/or by achieving a higher rate of asset utilization. It may well be that greater asset utilization, for instance more sales, can only be achieved by lowering prices, and management has to judge whether the larger volume of activity will be sufficient to justify the lower gross and net margins that result from implementing a policy of price reductions.

Double and Quick are suppliers of computer software. Quick rents premises and advertises his products in popular magazines. He supplies goods by mail order and insists on the receipt of cash before the software is dispatched. Double owns a shop in the centre of town and advertises heavily on local radio and television, as well as in trade journals. Goods are supplied over the counter for cash or on a credit basis. The following information is provided in respect of 20X4 for each of these businesses:

EXAMPLE
12.16

	Double	Quick
	£	*£*
Net profit	120,000	200,000
Sales	600,000	800,000
Average total capital employed	400,000	1,000,000

Required

Calculate the primary and secondary ratios for Double and Quick and comment on the results.

Solution

Applying the formula:

Return on capital employed = Net profit percentage × Total asset turnover

$$\text{Double:} \quad \frac{120,000}{400,000} \times 100 \quad = \quad \left(\frac{120,000}{600,000} \times 100 \right) \times \left(\frac{600,000}{400,000} \right)$$

$$30\% \quad = \quad 20\% \quad \times \quad 1.5$$

$$\text{Quick:} \quad \frac{200,000}{1,000,000} \times 100 \quad = \quad \left(\frac{200,000}{800,000} \times 100 \right) \times \left(\frac{800,000}{1,000,000} \right)$$

$$20\% \quad = \quad 25\% \quad \times \quad 0.8$$

The above calculations show that Double achieves the greater asset utilization (£1.50 of sales per £1 invested as compared with the £0.80 achieved by Quick) but his net profit percentage is lower (20 per cent compared with Quick's 25 per cent). Overall, Double's policy of maintaining a retail outlet in the centre of town seems to be more successful, i.e. the greater asset utilization more than compensates for the lower margins, and he achieves a rate of return on gross assets of 30 per cent.

ACTIVITY 12.16

Using the information given in Activity 12.11, calculate the primary and secondary ratios for Muggles Ltd for 20X1 and 20X2.

The above analysis may be extended by producing a 'pyramid' of accounting ratios in the form demonstrated in Figure 12.1. The pyramid can be used to tackle questions in a structured manner. It is not, of course, necessary to reproduce the ratios in pyramid format, though readers may decide that such a presentation is helpful. The first step is to calculate the primary ratio, i.e. the return on gross assets. Ideally, it will be possible to calculate comparative figures for a previous accounting period or another company in the same industry. The secondary ratios can then be calculated to discover profit margins and the extent of asset utilization. The discovery that the net profit percentage is stable would suggest that further investigation of profit margins is probably unnecessary. A significant

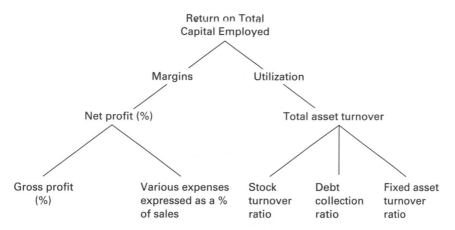

FIGURE 12.1   Pyramid of accounting ratios

variation in asset utilization, however, points to the need to calculate ratios further down the pyramid to discover the reasons for observed changes.

Readers should now attempt Questions 12.4 and 12.5 at the end of this chapter.

GEARING (OR LEVERAGE)

The return earned for shareholders is dependent on management's achievements in three key areas:

1 Profit margins.
2 Utilization of assets.
3 Gearing.

The previous section demonstrated the fact that the rate of return on gross assets is a function of profit margins and asset utilization, but it takes no account of the company's capital structure. The effect of gearing on the return earned for the equity shareholders is now examined.

Capital is derived from two sources: shares and loans. Quite often only shares are issued when a company is formed, but loans are usually raised at some later date. There are numerous reasons for issuing loan capital. For instance, the owners might want to increase their investment but minimize the risk involved, and this can be done by making a secured loan. Alternatively, management might require additional finance that the shareholders are unwilling to supply, and so a loan is raised instead. In either case, the effect is to introduce an element of gearing or leverage into the capital structure of the company. There are numerous ways of measuring gearing, but the debt/equity ratio is perhaps most commonly used. It is calculated as follows:

$$\text{Debt/equity ratio} = \frac{\text{Total financial debt}}{\text{Shareholders' equity}}$$

where total financial debt includes preference shares, loans from directors and bank overdrafts.

The use of debt capital is likely to affect the amount of profit accruing to the ordinary shareholders, and expansion is often financed in this manner with the objective of increasing, or 'gearing up', the rate of return on shareholders' capital employed. This objective can be achieved, however, only if the rate of return earned on the additional funds raised exceeds that payable to the providers of the loan.

EXAMPLE 12.17

The directors of Beulah Ltd are planning to undertake a new project that involves an investment of £10 million in fixed assets and working capital. The directors plan to finance the whole investment with a long-term loan bearing interest at 15 per cent per annum. The company's accountant forecasts an annual profit, before finance charges, of £2 million from the new project (ignore taxation).

Required

Calculate the financial benefit accruing to the equity shareholders from undertaking the project. Comment on the implications of your calculation.

Solution

	£m
Additional profit contributed by new project	2.0
Less: Interest charge, 15% of £10 million	(1.5)
Surplus	0.5

The existing shareholders are expected to be better off to the tune of £0.5 million each year as a result of undertaking the new project. This is because the new venture yields a return of 20 per cent whereas the loan creditors have contracted for interest at the lower rate of 15 per cent. Profit may, of course, not come up to expectations, and if it is less than £1.5 million the introduction of gearing will be detrimental to the ordinary shareholders. For example, if the new project generates profits before interest charges of £0.8 million, interest of £1.5 million must still be paid and the shortfall of £0.7 million (£1.5 million − £0.8 million) must be borne by the ordinary shareholders.

ACTIVITY 12.17

The following information has been reproduced from the solution to Example 10.9.

Miskin Ltd
Balance Sheet
As at 31 December 20X2

	£	£
Fixed assets		
Tangible fixed assets at cost		480,000

Less: Accumulated depreciation		19,200
		460,800
Current assets		
Stock	60,450	
Trade debtors (62,500 − 1,230)	60,270	
Bank	7,400	
	128,120	
Less: Creditors due within one year		
Unsecured loan repayable 30 June 20X3	20,000	
Trade creditors	37,870	
Corporation tax	18,000	
Dividend payable	15,000	
Accrual for interest	5,000	
	− 95,870	
Working capital		32,250
Total assets less current liabilities		493,050
Less: Creditors due after more than one year		
8% debentures repayable 20X9		− 100,000
		393,050
Financed by:		
Share capital		
Authorized: 500,000 ordinary shares of £1 each		500,000
Issued: 300,000 ordinary shares of £1 each		300,000
Share premium account (380,000 − 300,000)		80,000
General reserve		10,000
Retained profit		3,050
		393,050

Calculate the debt/equity ratio for Miskin Ltd.   **Required**

The shareholders of a highly geared company reap enormous benefits when there are increases in earnings before interest and tax. The interest payable on loan finance remains unchanged and a growing surplus accrues to a relatively small group of equity shareholders. The converse is also true, and a highly geared company is likely to find itself in severe financial difficulties if it suffers a succession of trading losses. It is not possible to specify an optimal level of gearing for companies but, as a general rule, gearing should be low in those industries where demand is volatile and profits are subject to fluctuation.

Readers should now attempt Question 12.6 at the end of this chapter.

CASH FLOW STATEMENT RATIOS

The cash flow statement, the preparation of which was explained in Chapter 11, shows the sources from which the company has derived cash during the year, how it has spent the cash and the resulting net impact on its cash position. Percentages can be used to show the relative balance between the inflows and outflows of cash, with the choice of which figure to use as a base (i.e. which one equals 100 per cent) depending on the purpose of the analysis. This is shown in Example 12.18.

EXAMPLE 12.18

The cash flow statement of Tide Ltd, as given previously in Figure 11.3, for the year to 31 December 20X4 is as follows:

Tide Ltd

Cash Flow Statement

for the year to 31 December 20X4

	£000	£000
Net cash flow from operating activities		437
Returns on investment and servicing of finance:		
Interest received	26	
Interest paid	− 10	
Preference dividends paid	− 12	
		4
Taxation		− 117
Capital expenditure and financial investment:		
Acquisition of fixed assets	− 530	
Proceeds from the disposal of fixed assets	15	
		− 515
Equity dividends		− 153
Net cash outflow before financing		− 344
Financing:		
Issue of shares	320	
Redemption of debentures	− 200	
		120
Decrease in cash		− 224

Required

(a) Explain how the cash flow generated from operations has been used.

(b) Discuss the manner in which the new fixed assets have been financed.

Solution

(a) Of the cash flow from operations, 34 per cent has been used to finance returns on investments and equity dividends, and 27 per cent was absorbed in paying taxation. The remaining 39 per cent contributed to the acquisition of fixed assets.

(b) The acquisition of fixed assets caused a cash outflow of £530,000. This was financed as follows:

- 3 per cent by selling other fixed assets;
- 32 per cent by cash generated from operations after taxation and servicing of finance;
- 23 per cent from issuing shares after repaying debentures;
- the balance of 42 per cent by running down the cash balance.

LIMITATIONS OF ACCOUNTING RATIOS

The various calculations illustrated in this chapter suffer from a number of limitations that should be borne in mind by anyone attempting to interpret their significance. The main limitations are as follows:

1 Accounting ratios can be used to assess whether performance is satisfactory, by means of interfirm comparison, and also whether results have improved, worsened or remained stable, by comparing this year's results with those achieved last year. The ratios do not, however, provide explanations for observed changes, and further inquiry is needed for this purpose. The external user's ability to obtain further information is usually extremely limited, for example, the shareholder may ask questions at the annual general meeting. It is only management that has direct access to the information needed to provide the right answer.

2 A deterioration in an accounting ratio cannot necessarily be interpreted as poor management. For example, a decline in the rate of stock turnover might appear undesirable, but further investigation might reveal the accumulation of scarce raw materials that enable the plant to continue working when competitors are forced to suspend production.

3 Too much significance should not be attached to individual ratios, for example, a 30 per cent rate of return on total capital employed might indicate that all is well, but this conclusion would be unjustified if further analysis revealed a liquidity ratio of 0.4 : 1.

4 Company financial statements are usually based on historical cost and, therefore, accounting ratios based on these figures would be expected to improve, irrespective of efficiency, during a period of rising prices; for example, total asset turnover of £3 per £1 invested might be computed from historical cost accounts, whereas a figure of £1.80 per £1 invested might be obtained if assets were restated at their current worth.

5 Differences in accounting policies may detract from the value of interfirm comparisons; for example, the valuation of stock on the AVCO basis rather than the FIFO basis would probably produce a much lower working capital ratio.

6 Financial statements and accounting ratios can be distorted as the result of 'one-off' large transactions such as cash raised from issuing a debenture and awaiting investment, or a profit on the sale of a fixed asset. Analysts should similarly be on their guard for evidence of 'window-dressing', perhaps designed to conceal a deteriorating financial position.

7 Particular care must be taken when interpreting accounting ratios calculated for seasonal businesses. Where sales are high at a particular time during the year, for example, at Christmas, stock might be expected to increase and cash to decline in the months leading up to the busy period. In these circumstances deteriorations in both the liquidity ratio and the rate of stock turnover are not necessarily causes for concern.

8 Consideration must be given to variations in commercial trading patterns when assessing the significance of accounting ratios computed for particular

companies. For example, a retail chain of supermarkets would be expected to have a much lower liquidity ratio and a much higher rate of stock turnover than a construction engineering firm. In this context, accepted 'norms' such as a working capital ratio of 2 : 1 must be used with care.

LINKING TOGETHER CASH FLOW ANALYSIS AND RATIO ANALYSIS

Accounting ratios can be used to assess the performance of a company during an accounting period. Comparisons with earlier years and the performance of other businesses provide useful yardsticks for assessing whether or not an improvement has occurred and for gauging whether or not results are as good as they could be. The cash flow statement complements these calculations by helping to explain how improvements in a company's financial position have been brought about or why a deterioration has occurred. Example 12.19 demonstrates how the two forms of financial analysis may be employed, alongside one another, to gain an understanding of the financial performance and position of a business enterprise. In addition, it shows how the annual accounts, although relating to a *past* time period, may be used as a basis for estimating likely future prospects.

EXAMPLE 12.19	Expansion Ltd is a private company that has carried on copper-mining activities for a number of years. At the beginning of 20X2 the company purchased a small established tin mine at a cost of £350,000; production commenced at once. Tin extracted from the new mine in 20X2 amounted to 600 tonnes. This is expected to increase to 900 tonnes by 20X8 and then decline gradually. Finance for the new mine was partly provided by an overdraft to be repaid by the end of 20X3.			

The summarized balance sheets for 31 December 20X1 and 20X2 are as follows:

	20X1		20X2	
	£	£	£	£
Fixed assets				
Mines at cost	465,000		815,000	
Less: Depreciation	−150,000		−190,000	
		315,000		625,000
Plant and equipment at cost	213,250		263,250	
Less: Depreciation	−56,200		−75,200	
		157,050		188,050
		472,050		813,050
Current assets				
Stocks of tin and copper	143,100		169,000	
Debtors	86,250		118,250	
Cash at bank	44,100		–	
	273,450		287,250	

Current liabilities

Overdraft	–		– 148,200	
Trade creditors and accrued				
expenses	– 63,000		– 138,100	
	– 63,000		– 286,300	
Working capital		210,450		950
		682,500		814,000
Financed by:				
Share capital (ordinary shares)		500,000		500,000
Profit and loss account		182,500		314,000
		682,500		814,000

The net profit earned during 20X2 was £181,500 (20X1 £103,000) of which £50,000 (20X1 £25,000) was paid out in dividends. Turnover increased from £1,060,000 in 20X1 to £1,500,000 in 20X2.

Examine the financial policies pursued by the directors of Expansion Ltd during 20X2 and comment on proposals to develop further by acquiring an additional site in the early months of 20X3. You should use a cash flow statement and relevant accounting ratios to support your analysis.

Required

Expansion Ltd
Cash Flow Statement
for the year to 31 December 20X2

Solution

	£
Net cash flow from operating activities (Note 1)	257,700
Capital expenditure and financial investment:	
Acquisition of fixed assets	– 400,000
Equity dividends	–50,000
Net cash outflow	– 192,300

Note 1: Cash flow from operations

	£
Profit	181,500
Depreciation	59,000
Increase in stock	– 25,900
Increase in debtors	– 32,000
Increase in creditors	75,100
	257,700

Ratios	20X1	20X2
Working capital ratio	4.3 : 1	1.0 : 1
Liquidity ratio	2.1 : 1	0.4 : 1

The company had surplus funds at the end of 20X1 and so decided to expand. It financed the remainder of the expansion with a two-year overdraft to be repaid out of funds generated from operations. The financial position at the end of 20X2 is weak due to the failure to raise sufficient long-term finance to meet the cost of the investment programme.

Examination of *Profitability*	*Ratios*	*20X1*	*20X2*
	Net profit percentage	9.7%	12.1%
	Return on total capital employed	13.8%	16.5%
	Return on owners' equity	15.1%	22.3%

A significant improvement in profitability has occurred, which might be expected to continue with further increases in output from the new mine. The company has paid a good dividend.

Conclusion and Prospects

Expansion has been funded out of short-term finance and the financial position at the end of 20X2 is weak. This is risky and an element of over-trading has undoubtedly occurred. The project is profitable, however, and it seems that the company will recover on the basis of funds generated from operations that, in 20X2, amounted to £240,500. Further expansion appears undesirable at present; there should be a delay of a year to 18 months. If this is not possible, the company should raise medium- or long-term finance to cover the cost of the additional site.

Readers should now attempt Questions 12.7–12.10 at the end of this chapter.

QUESTIONS

12.1   The summarized trading and profit and loss account of Rubber Ltd for 20X1 and its summarized balance sheet at 31 December 20X1 are as follows:

Trading and profit and loss account for 20X1

	£
Sales	180,000
Cost of sales	−126,000
Gross profit	54,000
Expenses (fixed)	−39,000
Net profit	15,000

Note   A dividend of £10,000 is proposed for 20X1.

Balance sheet as at 31 December 20X1

	£	£
Fixed assets		113,000
Current assets	70,000	
Less: Creditors due within one year		
General	− 23,000	
Dividend	− 10,000	
	− 33,000	

Working capital		37,000
		150,000
Financed by:		
Share capital		100,000
Retained profit		50,000
		150,000

The company could expand production to a sales level of £255,000 with no increase in fixed expenses and the cost of sales would remain the same percentage of sales as for 20X1.

Required

(a) Calculate the gross profit percentage, net profit as a percentage of sales and the return on capital employed for 20X1.

(b) A calculation of the level of sales that would have been necessary to increase the return on capital employed by 2 per cent.

Note For the purpose of the answer, capital employed is to be interpreted as issued capital plus retained profit on 31 December.

12.2 The balance sheets of Galston Ltd as at 31 December 20X5 and 20X6 are as follows:

Galston Ltd
Balance sheet
as at 31 December

	20X5			*20X6*
	£	£	£	£
Fixed assets at cost		303,000		367,500
Less: Accumulated depreciation		− 124,500		− 157,500
		178,500		210,000
Current assets				
Stocks	37,500		75,000	
Debtors	34,500		43,500	
Bank	18,000		1,500	
	90,000		120,000	
Less: Creditors due within one year				
	− 45,000		− 55,500	
Working capital		45,000		64,500
		223,500		274,500
Financed by:				
Share capital		150,000		150,000
Retained profit at 31 Dec 20X5		73,500		73,500
Profit for 20X5		–		51,000
		223,500		274,500

The figure of current liabilities as at 31 December 20X5 includes a proposed dividend of £7,500 for the year to that date. No decision has been taken yet about the dividend to be paid for 20X6, and nothing is included in the 20X6 balance sheet for such a dividend.

The directors are considering the dividend that should be paid for 20X6 in the light of the excellent results for that year.

Required

(a) Calculations of Galston's working capital and working capital ratio as at 31 December 20X5 and 31 December 20X6.

(b) A calculation of the maximum dividend that should be declared for 20X6 if the working capital ratio at 31 December 20X6 is to be the same as at 31 December 20X5.

(c) A brief discussion of the financial policy pursued by the directors of Galston Ltd in 20X6.

12.3 The following information has been extracted from the accounts of Lock Ltd, a wholesale trading company:

Balances at 31 December

	20X1	20X2
	£	£
Fixed assets	500,000	550,000
Trade debtors	125,000	150,000
Cash at bank	25,000	–
Proposed dividend	20,000	60,000
Overdraft	–	20,000
Trade creditors	80,000	100,000
Stock	150,000	200,000

Results for the year to 31 December

	20X1	20X2
	£	£
Sales	2,000,000	3,000,000
Cost of sales	1,000,000	1,450,000
Overhead costs	800,000	1,300,000

Required

(a) A statement showing the return on capital employed, the working capital ratio and the liquidity ratio. Your answer should be presented in the following form:

	20X1	20X2
Return on capital employed	_____	_____
Working capital	_____	_____
Working capital ratio	_____	_____
Liquidity ratio	_____	_____

(b) A brief discussion of the implications of the information calculated above.

Note For the purpose of your calculations, capital employed is defined as shareholders' equity.

12.4   Beta Ltd is reviewing the financial statements of two companies, Zeta Ltd and Omega Ltd. The companies trade as wholesalers, selling electrical goods to retailers on credit. Their most recent financial statements appear below.

Profit and loss accounts for the year ended 31 March 19X8

	Zeta Limited		Omega Limited	
	£ 000	£ 000	£ 000	£ 000
Sales		4,000		6,000
Cost of sales				
Opening stock	200		800	
Purchases	3,200		4,800	
	3,400		5,600	
Less: closing stock	400		800	
		3,000		4,800
Gross profit		1,000		1,200
Expenses				
Distribution costs	200		150	
Administrative expenses	290		250	
Interest paid	10		400	
		500		800
Profit before tax		500		400
Taxation		120		90
Net profit for the period		380		310

Balance Sheets as at 31 March 19X8

	Zeta Limited		Omega Limited	
	£ 000	£ 000	£ 000	£ 000
Fixed assets				
Tangible assets				
Warehouse and office buildings	1,200		5,000	
Equipment and vehicles	600		1,000	
		1,800		6,000
Current assets				
Stock	400		800	
Debtors – trade	800		900	
– sundry	150		80	
Cash at bank	–		100	
	1,350		1,880	

Current liabilities			
Creditors – trade	(800)		(800)
– sundry	(80)		(100)
Overdraft	(200)		–
Taxation	(120)		(90)
		150	890
		1,950	6,890
Long-term loan (interest 10% p.a.)		–	(4,000)
		1,950	2,890
Share capital		1,000	1,600
Revaluation reserve		–	500
Profit and loss account		950	790
		1,950	2,890

Required

(a) Calculate for each company a total of *eight* ratios which will assist in measuring the three aspects of profitability, liquidity and management of the elements of working capital. Show all workings. (8 marks)

(b) Based on the ratios you have calculated in (a), compare the two companies as regards their profitability, liquidity and working capital management. (8 marks)

(c) Omega Ltd is much more highly geared than Zeta Ltd. What are the implications of this for the two companies? (4 marks)

(20 marks)

(ACCA, Paper 1, The Accounting Framework, December 1998)

12.5 The following information is obtained in connection with the affairs of two companies, manufacturing specialized metal products, in respect of the year ended 31 December 20X5:

	Metalmax Ltd £000	Precision Products Ltd £000
Sales	800	950
Administration expenses	30	30
Selling expenses (including promotional costs)	45	60
Plant and machinery at cost	360	360
Depreciation to 31 December 20X4	110	110
Current assets	240	400
Trade creditors	120	320
Share capital (£1 ordinary shares)	200	200

It is also established that both companies incur variable costs of sales, excluding depreciation, of 80 per cent on sales. Depreciation should be charged at 15 per cent on the cost of machinery. Reserves may be treated as the balancing figure in the balance sheets.

(a) Summary trading and profit and loss accounts for the year ended 31 December 20X5 and balance sheets at that date for each company to facilitate comparison.

(b) A comparison of the profitability of the two companies during 20X5 and of their respective financial positions at the end of the year. Relevant accounting ratios should be used to support the discussion.

Notes 1 Within the current asset totals are included balances in respect of stocks and work in progress as follows:

Metaimax Ltd	£120,000
Precision Products Ltd	£200,000

2 Ignore taxation.

12.6 The following information is provided relating to the affairs of two companies engaged in similar trading activities:

	Hot Ltd	Cold Ltd
	£	£
Ordinary share capital	800,000	500,000
15% debentures	200,000	500,000

Each company earned a trading profit before finance charges of £110,000 in year 1 and £190,000 in year 2. Corporation tax is charged at 50 per cent on the trading profits after finance charges have been deducted. The company pays out as dividends its entire post-tax profits, i.e. there are no reserves.

(a) Summary profit and loss accounts, dealing with the results of each of the two companies' activities during years 1 and 2, so far as the information given above permits.

(b) Calculations of profits before tax expressed as percentages of ordinary share capital for each company in respect of both years 1 and 2.
(c) A discussion of the returns earned for shareholders over the two-year period.

12.7 The following information relates to the affairs of General Engineering plc:

Balance sheets at 31 December

	£000	20X7 £000	£000	20X8 £000
Fixed assets				
Plant at cost less depreciation		2,600		2,760
Property at cost less depreciation		800		700
Investment at cost		300		250
		3,700		3,710

Current assets			
Stocks and work in progress	900	2,120	
Debtors	660	700	
Deposits at bank	290	620	
	1,850	3,440	
Less: Creditors due within one year			
Creditors	− 520	− 720	
Proposed final dividend	− 400	− 400	
	− 920	− 1,120	
Working capital	930	2,320	
	4,630	6,030	
Less: Creditors due after more than one year			
Long term loan (12%)	–	−300	
	4,630	5,730	
Financed by:			
Issued share capital	2,000	2,500	
Share premium account	–	200	
Retained profit	2,630	3,030	
	4,630	5,730	

Extracts from the profit and loss account for 20X8

	£000
Trading profit for the year after charging all costs, including depreciation of plant, £250,000, and depreciation of property, £100,000	700
Interest and dividends received, less interest paid	20
Net profit from ordinary activities	720
Add: Profit from the sale of an investment	80
	800
Less: Proposed dividend	− 400
Retained profit for the year	400
Retained profit at 1 January 20X8	2,630
Retained profit carried forward	3,030

During 20X8 investments that had cost £50,000 some years earlier were sold for £130,000.

Required

(a)   A cash flow statement for the year to 31 December 20X8.

(b)   A discussion of the change in the financial position of General Engineering between the end of 20X7 and the end of 20X8. You are not required to examine the profitability of the firm, but should use the working capital and liquidity ratios to help assess financial developments.

Note Ignore taxation.

12.8 Emerald Ltd and Garnet Ltd are two companies engaged in manufacturing electrical appliances. Both operate from rented premises. Their financial statements at 31 March 1997 were as follows.

Profit and loss accounts
for the year ended 31 March 1997

	Emerald		Garnet	
	£000	£000	£000	£000
Sales		1,075		756
Less: Costs of sales				
Materials	(360)		(280)	
Manufacturing wages	(130)		(140)	
Depreciation of plant	(125)		(74)	
Other manufacturing costs	(100)	(715)	(80)	(574)
Gross profit		360		182
Saundry expenses		(125)		(95)
Operating profit		235		87
Interest on debentures		(10)		(30)
Net profit before tax		225		57
Taxation		(50)		(15)
Net profit after tax		175		42
Proposed dividend		(100)		(40)
Retained profit		75		2

Balance sheets as at 31 March 1997

	Emerald		Garnet	
	£000	£000	£000	£000
Fixed assets				
Plant and machinery				
Cost	1,250		1,480	
Aggregate depreciation	(450)	800	(1,160)	320
Office equipment				
Cost	65		180	
Aggregate depreciation	(20)	45	(82)	98
Motor vehicles				
Cost	60		50	
Aggregate depreciation	(20)	40	(20)	30
		885		448

Current assets		
Stock	210	170
Debtors: trade	400	300
sundry	50	40
Cash at bank	20	
	680	510

Creditors: amounts falling due within one year		
Trade creditors	(100)	(140)
Sundry (including taxation)	(80)	(60)
Bank overdraft	(100)	(280)
Proposed dividend	(100)	(40)
	(380)	(520)

Net current assets		300	(10)
Total assets less current liabilities		1,185	438

Creditors: amounts falling due
in more than one year

10% debentures		(100)	(300)
		1,085	138

Capital			
Called up share capital		600	100
Profit and loss account		485	38
		1,085	138

Required

(a) Calculate the following ratios for both companies:

    (i)   current ratio;

    (ii)   quick ratio/acid test;

    (iii) debtors' collection period in days;

    (iv) return on capital employed (ROCE);

    (v)   return on owners' equity (before taxation);

    (vi) gearing ratio;

    (vii) interest cover;

    (viii) dividend cover (ignore tax relating to dividends);

    (ix) gross profit percentage on sales;

    (x)   operating profit percentage on sales.   (10 marks)

(b) Comment briefly on the relative profitability, liquidity and risk of the two companies.

    (10 marks)

    (20 marks)

(ACCA, Paper 1, The Accounting Framework, June 1997)

12.9   Pereniv Ltd

You work in the accounts department of Pereniv Ltd, a company which manufactures materials which it supplies to electrical goods manufacturers. Normal credit terms in the industry, for both suppliers and customers, require payment within 30 days from the end of the month in which the goods were invoiced.

Latlest Ltd and Nelumbo Ltd are both new customers of Pereniv Ltd, so neither has a sales ledger account with Pereniv Ltd. Latlest Ltd, has recently ordered materials worth £100,000 from Pereniv Ltd. Nelumbo Ltd wishes to purchase materials worth £300,000 from Pereniv Ltd.

You have obtained summaries of the final accounts of Latlest Ltd and Nelumbo Ltd for the year ended 31 March 1999. These are set out below.

Profit and loss accounts

	Latlest Ltd	Nelumbo Ltd
	£000	£000
Sales	35,505	57,330
Cost of sales Materials	6,250	13,150
Labour and production overheads	14,320	24,565
Gross profit	14,935	19,615
Non-production overheads	11,738	15,432
Trading profit	3,197	4,183
Debenture interest	1,120	800
Profit before taxation	2,077	3,383
Tax on profit	765	834
Profit after taxation	1,312	2,549
Dividends	392	567
Retained profit for the year	920	1,982
Retained earnings at 1 April 1998	1,783	2,498
Retained earnings at 31 March 1999	2,703	4,480

Balance sheets at 31 March 1999

Fixed assets	24,903	32,413
Materials stock	1,047	645
Finished goods stock	1,732	5,269
Trade debtors	6,136	15,432
Other debtors	1,799	1,007
Bank and cash	68	97
	35,685	54,863
Materials creditors	743	2,836
Other creditors	331	707
Bank overdraft	3,003	14,738
8% debentures	14,000	10,000
£0.50 ordinary shares, fully paid	5,600	6,300
Reserves	12,008	20,282
	35,685	54,863

Required

(a) Calculate the following liquidity ratios for Latlest Ltd and for Nelumbo Ltd:

    (i)   current ratio;

    (ii) quick ratio (or acid test ratio);

    (iii) days materials in stock;

    (iv) days of finished goods in stock;

    (v) debtors collection period;

    (vi) creditors payment period;

    (vii) operating or cash cycle.

    Present your results in the form of a table.   (14 marks)

(b) Comment on the liquidity of each company. Advise Pereniv Ltd whether it should extend credit to Latlest Ltd or to Nelumbo Ltd.   (6 marks)

      (20 marks)

    (ICSA, Paper 6, Introduction to Accounting, June 1999)

12.10 The following trial balance has been extracted from the ledgers of JK Ltd at 31 March 1993:

	£	£
Sales (all on credit)		647,400
Stock (1 April 1992)	15,400	
Trade debtors and creditors	82,851	41,936
Purchases (all on credit)	321,874	
Carriage in	13,256	
Carriage out	32,460	
Electricity	6,994	
Business rates	8,940	
Wages and salaries	138,292	
Postage and stationery	6,984	
Rent	14,600	
VAT control		16,382
PAYE control		4,736
Motor vehicles: at cost	49,400	
depreciation		21,240
Bank deposit account	90,000	
Bank current account	77,240	
Ordinary shares of £1 each		50,000
Profit and loss – unappropriated profit		76,597
	858,291	858,291

The following notes are also relevant:

(i) Stock at 31 March 1993, valued at cost, was £19,473.

(ii) Prepaid rent amounted to £2,800.

(iii) Accruals are estimated as follows:

	£
Electricity	946
Wages and salaries	2,464

(iv) Depreciation on motor vehicles is to be provided at 25 per cent per annum using the reducing balance method.

(v) Accrued interest on the bank deposit account amounts to £7,200.

(vi) A provision for corporation tax of £30,000 is to be made on the profits of the year.

(vii) No interim dividend was paid but the directors propose a final dividend of £0.05 per share.

(a) Prepare JK Ltd's trading, profit and loss and appropriation account for the year ended   **Required**
31 March 1993, in vertical format.   (10 marks)

(b) Prepare JK Ltd's balance sheet at 31 March 1993, in vertical format.   (7 marks)

(c) Calculate and comment briefly on the debtors' and creditors' payment periods and the stockholding period of JK Ltd.   (10 marks)

(Total: 27 marks)

(CIMA, Accounting, May 1993)

SOLUTIONS
TO
ACTIVITIES

ABC Ltd: $\dfrac{£250,000}{£750,000} \times 100 = 33.3\%$ *Solution to*
Activity 12.1

XYZ Ltd: $\dfrac{£75,000}{£200,000} \times 100 = 37.5\%$

(a)   **Moon plc**   *Solution to*
Balance sheet as at 31 December 20X2   *Activity 12.2*

	£	£
Fixed assets		
Plant and machinery at cost		850,000
Less: Accumulated depreciation		(360,000)
		490,000
Current assets		
Stock and work in progress	426,000	
Trade debtors and prepayments	250,000	
Cash in hand	2,000	
	678,000	

Less: Creditors amounts falling due within one year		
Bank overdraft	136,000	
Trade creditors	157,000	
Corporation tax	50,000	
	343,000	
Working capital		335,000
		825,000
Less: Creditors amounts falling due after more than one year		
8% debentures repayable 20X9		(150,000)
		675,000
Financed by:		
Share capital (£1 ordinary shares)		250,000
Share premium account		100,000
Revaluation reserve		90,000
Reserves (all distributable)		235,000
		675,000

(b) (i) Owners' capital employed, £675,000.

(ii) Total capital employed, £1,168,000 (£490,000 + £678,000)

Solution to Activity 12.3

(a) Owners' capital employed:

$$\text{Return} = \frac{210,000}{675,000} \times 100 = 31.1\%$$

(b) Total capital employed:

$$\text{Return} = \frac{222,000}{1,168,000} \times 100 = 19.0\%$$

Solution to Activity 12.4

Gross profit margin: 20X1 $\frac{207,000}{900,000} \times 100 = 23\%$

20X2 $\frac{276,000}{1,200,000} \times 100 = 23\%$

Solution to Activity 12.5

(a) Average fixed manufacturing cost per unit 20X3   20X4

$$\frac{£280,000}{50,000} = £5.60 \qquad \frac{£280,000}{70,000} = £4.00$$

(b)

	20X3		20X4	
	£000	£000	£000	£000
Sales		1,250		1,750
Less: Variable costs	750		1,050	
Fixed costs	280		280	
		− 1,030		− 1,330
Gross profit		220		420

Gross profit margin:

	20X3	20X4
Gross profit	$\dfrac{£220,000}{£1,250,000} = 17.6\%$	$\dfrac{£420,000}{£1,750,000} = 24\%$
Sales		

Solution to
Activity 12.6

	20X5	20X6
Gross profit margin	$\dfrac{£210,000}{£400,000} = 52.5\%$	$\dfrac{£310,000}{£500,000} = 62\%$

Net profit margin	$\dfrac{£147,000}{£400,000} = 36.75\%$	$\dfrac{£210,000}{£500,000} = 42\%$

Solution to
Activity 12.7

	20X5	20X6
	%	%
Sales	100.0	100.0
Cost of goods sold	47.5	38.0
Expenses	16.0	20.0

Solution to
Activity 12.8

$$20X1: \text{EPS} = \frac{1,898,000 - 80,000}{11,000,000} = 16.53\text{p}$$

$$20X0: \text{EPS} = \frac{1,709,000 - 80,000}{11,000,000} = 14.81\text{p}$$

Solution to
Activity 12.9

	£000	£000
Current assets:		
Stock		500
Trade debtors		1,000
		1,500
Current liabilities:		
Bank overdraft	100	
Trade creditors	600	
Corporation tax liability	400	
		−1,100
Working capital		400

Solution to		*20X0*	*20X1*
Activity 12.10	Rate of stock turnover		

$$\frac{\text{Cost of goods sold}}{\text{Average stock}} \qquad \frac{2,300}{500^*} = 4.6 \text{ times} \qquad \frac{3,650}{675^\dagger} = 5.4 \text{ times}$$

Notes *Average stock = (400 + 600) ÷ 2.
† Average stock = (600 + 750) ÷2.

Solution to
Activity 12.11

Number of times

	20X1	*20X2*
$\dfrac{\text{Cost of goods sold}}{\text{Average stock}}$	$\dfrac{1,474^*}{296^\dagger} = 4.98 \text{ times}$	$\dfrac{2,430^{**}}{594^\ddagger} = 4.09 \text{ times}$

Notes   *Cost of goods sold:

	Opening stock	133,000
	Purchases	1,800,000
	Less: Closing stock	(459,000)
		1,474,000

**Cost of goods sold:

	Opening stock	459,000
	Purchases	2,700,000
	Less: Closing stock	(729,000)
		2,430,000

† Average stock: (133,000 + 459,000) ÷ 2.
‡ Average stock: (459,000 + 729,000) ÷ 2.

Number of days:

	20X1	*20X2*
$\dfrac{\text{Average stock}}{\text{Cost of goods sold}} \times 365$	$\dfrac{296}{1,474} \times 365 = 73 \text{ days}$	$\dfrac{594}{2,430} \times 365 = 89 \text{ days}$

Solution to
Activity 12.12

Rate of collection of debtors in days

	20X1	*20X2*
$\dfrac{\text{Average debtors}}{\text{Credit sales}} \times 365$	$\dfrac{445^*}{2,400^\dagger} \times 365 = 68 \text{ days}$	$\dfrac{945^{**}}{3,600^\ddagger} \times 365 = 96 \text{ days}$

Notes   * Average debtors: $(200 + 690) \div 2$.

**Average debtors: $(690 + 1,200) \div 2$.

†Credit sales: $3,000 \times 80\%$.

‡Credit sales: $4,500 \times 80\%$.

Rate of payment of creditors in days

Solution to
Activity 12.13

	20X1	*20X2*

$$\frac{\text{Average creditors}}{\text{Credit purchases}} \times 365 \qquad \frac{318.5*}{1,350^\dagger} \times 365 = 86 \text{ days} \qquad \frac{672.5**}{2,025^\ddagger} \times 365 = 121 \text{ days}$$

* Average creditors: $(172,000 + 465,000) \div 2$.
** Average creditors: $(465,000 + 880,000) \div 2$.
† Credit purchases: $1,800 \times 75\%$.
‡ Credit purchases: $2,700 \times 75\%$.

Solution to
Activity 12.14

	20X1	*20X2*
	Days	*Days*
Stockholding period	73	89
Debt collection period	67	96
	140	185
Credit payment period	−86	−121
Cash operating cycle	54	64

Solution to
Activity 12.15

	20X1	*20X2*
Total asset turnover		

$$\frac{\text{Sales}}{\text{Average total assets}} \qquad \frac{3,000}{1,115*} = £2.69 \qquad \frac{4,500}{2,200^\dagger} = £2.05$$

Notes   * Average total assets: $(730,000 + 1,500,000) \div 2$.

† Average total assets: $(1,500,000 + 2,900,000) \div 2$.

Solution to
Activity 12.16

$$20X1: \frac{405,000}{1,115,000*} \times 100 = \left(\frac{405,000}{3,000,000} \times 100\right) \times \left(\frac{3,000,000}{1,115,000}\right)$$

$$36.3\% \qquad = \qquad 13.5\% \qquad \times \quad 2.69$$

20X2: $\dfrac{725,000}{2,200,000^{\dagger}} \times 100$ $=$ $\left(\dfrac{725,000 \times 100}{4,500,000}\right)$ $\times$ $\left(\dfrac{4,500,000}{2,200,000}\right)$

32.9% $=$ 16.1% $\times$ 2.045

Notes   * Average total assests employed: (730 + 1,500)/2.
         $\dagger$ Average total assets employed: (1,500 + 2,900)/2.

Solution to
Activity 12.17   Debt/equity ratio $= \dfrac{100,000 + 20,000}{393,050} = 30.5\%$

13 Decision-making

The objectives of this chapter are to:

- introduce the use of accounting information as part of the decision-making process;
- show how costs behave in response to changes in the level of activity;
- define and distinguish between fixed costs and variable costs and between direct costs and indirect costs;
- define and distinguish between cost centres and cost units;
- differentiate between production cost centres and service cost centres;
- show how to trace direct costs (materials and labour) to cost centres and cost units;
- demonstrate how to apportion overhead costs to cost centres;
- explain the calculation of overhead recovery rates;
- assess the relative merits of different methods of overhead recovery and introduce activity-based costing;
- explain and illustrate the use of break-even analysis;
- show how to carry out investment appraisal using payback, return on capital employed and net present value techniques;
- compare and contrast the different methods of investment appraisal; and
- show how to prepare forecasts of cash flow, the profit and loss account, the balance sheet and the cash flow statement.

INTRODUCTION

The accounting process has many aspects and, so far, this book's emphasis has been on recording, reporting and analysing the financial consequences of past economic activity. The essence of this approach is that it is an after-the-fact exercise and concentrates on events that have already taken place. An important application of accounting techniques is to provide a basis on which management decisions of the following type can be taken:

1 Whether existing activity should be expanded or reduced.
2 Whether a new product should be introduced.
3 How existing production techniques could be improved.
4 Whether new products should be manufactured or purchased ready-made.
5 The manufacturing techniques to be used for new products.

All possible business decisions must be examined in the light of their expected impact on profit, and management must be satisfied, before resources are committed, that any proposed activity, or change in existing activity, will add to overall profit. Financial forecasts are therefore needed so that the likely outcomes of alternative courses of action can be analysed and the most profitable ones adopted.

This chapter introduces the study and interpretation of cost behaviour that must be understood as the basis for preparing forecasts. It reviews some of the analytical techniques available to assist management when it makes investment decisions, and it examines the impact of anticipated activity on cash flow, funds flow, profit and the balance sheet.

COST BEHAVIOUR

The manner in which production or trading activity is organized sets the capacity of the undertaking and influences its costs. For example, the acquisition of a particular machine sets the maximum output that can be achieved before an additional machine must be bought. Similarly, the size of premises used by a shop determines their cost and the maximum number of product lines that can be displayed and stored; above a certain level, further space is needed. The capacity of the business sets the upper level of activity and the output of a firm is the extent to which the available capacity is utilized – the lowest level is zero, and the greatest is the largest amount permitted by available capacity. Management must decide what the likely output will be and arrange capacity accordingly, bearing in mind the costs of servicing the capacity and that growth may take place. In the long run it may prove cheaper to acquire at the start of a project the additional capacity likely to be needed so as to take advantage of the economies of scale that can result from the use of capital-intensive techniques.

It is necessary for management to understand how costs behave, or are likely to behave, so that they can be controlled, and the most appropriate mix of inputs, with their related costs, selected. This section examines a number of ways in which costs can be analysed to enable management to gain this understanding.

Fixed and variable costs

Business costs may be classified according to how they behave in response to changes in output:

- *Fixed costs.* These remain constant over a range of output and include such items as rent and depreciation. For example, the rent for premises or a straight-line depreciation charge related to a machine are constant irrespective of whether these assets are being used at full capacity or well below. However, if an output in excess of the existing full capacity is contemplated, then an additional set of fixed costs must be incurred to provide additional capacity.

- *Variable costs.* These vary in direct proportion to output, and include the costs of raw materials and manufacturing wages. For example, if no production takes place, then no raw materials have to be purchased while, at full capacity, the total cost of materials is the number of units produced times the material cost per unit.

Forecast output is unlikely to be achieved exactly in practice, and calculations of the profit expected at different levels of output are helpful in making a decision about whether a new project should be undertaken. This is shown in Example 13.1.

EXAMPLE
13.1

The management of Glass Ltd is considering the possibility of manufacturing a new product that will sell at £15 per unit. Existing capacity is fully utilized, and so a new factory would have to be rented and plant, with a life of ten years, purchased. The expected costs are:

	£
Annual factory rent	10,000.00
Purchase price of plant	75,000.00
Raw material cost per unit	2.10
Labour cost per unit	1.50
Other variable costs	1.00
Fixed costs (excluding rent and depreciation)	6,500.00

Note The company depreciates plant on the straight-line basis assuming a zero residual value.

Required

Forecast the profit that will be made from sales of the new product at the alternative annual rate of:

(a) 2,500 units;
(b) 5,000 units.

Solution

	(a)	2,500 units		(b)	5,000 units	
	£	£	£	£	£	£
Sales			37,500			75,000
Fixed costs						
Rent	10,000			10,000		
Depreciation	7,500			7,500		
Other	6,500			6,500		
		24,000			24,000	

Variable costs						
Raw materials	5,250			10,500		
Labour	3,750			7,500		
Other	2,500			5,000		
		11,500			23,000	
Total costs			35,500			47,000
Profit			2,000			28,000

Output has doubled, but profit has increased 14 times. This result is examined later in the chapter.

Another use of forecasts, of the type prepared in Example 13.1, is to help decide the method of production; the choice often lies between 'capital-intensive' and 'labour-intensive' techniques. Capital-intensive production uses automatic machines, such as the 'robots' seen on car production-lines, and requires a large investment in plant with a consequent high level of fixed costs. Variable costs are lower as each additional unit produced requires only a small labour input. Additional potential benefits from capital-intensive methods are that raw materials are used more efficiently, and therefore cost less per unit, and there is a lower rejection rate at the stage of inspecting the finished product. Labour-intensive methods use relatively little plant and have low fixed costs, but high variable costs per unit as each additional item produced requires a large input of labour.

EXAMPLE 13.2

The directors of Hasard Ltd are sure that 10,000 units a year of a newly developed product can be sold at £90 each. They are undecided about how to produce it. The alternatives are

	Method 1	Method 2
	£	£
Investment in plant with a ten-year life	125,000	750,000
Fixed costs (excluding depreciation)	185,000	200,000
Variable cost per unit		
Raw materials	35	30
Labour	20	5
Other	6	2

Note   The company calculates depreciation on the straight-line basis assuming a zero scrap value.

Required

Prepare financial statement to show the likely profit from each of the two methods at the expected level of sales.

Forecast trading results

Solution

		Method 1			Method 2	
	£	£	£	£	£	£
Sales			900,000			900,000
Fixed costs						
Depreciation	12,500			75,000		
Other	185,000			200,000		
		197,500			275,000	
Variable costs						
Raw materials	350,000			300,000		
Labour	200,000			50,000		
Other	60,000			20,000		
		610,000			370,000	
Total costs			– 807,500			– 645,000
Profit			92,500			255,000

Readers should now try Question 13.1 at the end of the chapter.

Some costs are neither completely fixed nor fully variable – they are termed 'semi-variable'. Although semi-variable costs respond to volume changes, they do not change in direct proportion to them. It is possible for semi-variable costs to remain constant over a relatively small range of activity, and each successive set of costs may differ in price from its predecessor. For example, an increase in manufacturing output creates additional work in the accounts department. The initial load may be carried by an accountant who performs alone all the necessary activities. When his or her capacity is exceeded, a book-keeper may be added to the staff, and then a clerk. Each additional employee, hired to increase the capacity of the accounts department in response to an increase in manufacturing output, adds relatively less to costs as an accountant is paid more than a book-keeper, who in turn earns more than a clerk. This type of response to changes in output occurs in the case of general expenses in Question 13.2 at the end of this chapter, which should now be attempted.

Direct and indirect costs

Direct costs are those that can be traced in full to an individual costing unit. Indirect costs are those that relate only partially to a particular costing unit and must be apportioned to it. Care has to be taken when interpreting results based on apportioned (joint) costs as they have to be met in full irrespective of whether activity in a particular department continues or is discontinued. An initial examination of results may produce the conclusion that a department or branch is making a loss and so should be closed, but it must be remembered that its share of apportioned costs will then have to be met by the remaining cost centres.

EXAMPLE 13.3

The business of Bits & Co. is divided into three departments of equal size: A, B and C. The departmental results for 20X7 were:

Departmental trading results

	Department			Total
	A	B	C	
	£000	£000	£000	£000
Sales	50	120	180	350
Cost of goods sold	− 25	− 60	− 90	− 175
Gross profit	25	60	90	175
Departmental wages	− 10	− 20	− 30	− 60
	15	40	60	115
Rent (shared equally)	− 20	− 20	− 20	− 60
Profit (loss)	(5)	20	40	55

Mr Bits is considering closing department A because it is making a loss. He says it is better to leave the floor space empty than to use it to lose money.

Required

Prepare a statement to show Mr Bits the effect on total profit if department A is closed.

Solution

Revised departmental trading results

	Department		Total
	B	C	
	£000	£000	£000
Sales	120	180	300
Cost of goods sold	− 60	− 90	− 150
Gross profit	60	90	150
Departmental wages	− 20	− 30	− 50
	40	60	100
Rent (shared equally)*	− 30	− 30	− 60
Profit (loss)	10	30	40

Note *Rent shared equally between the remaining departments.

Department A should be kept open as it meets 75 per cent of its share of apportioned costs. Total profit is reduced by £15,000 if it is closed. The revised departmental trading results show that the plan of Mr Bits to close department A is based on his failure to appreciate the difference between direct and indirect costs.

It is sometimes argued that, because the account information that results can lead to wrong decisions, the apportionment of indirect costs should not be made. If indirect costs are not apportioned, the departmental trading results of Bits & Co would be presented as follows:

	Department			Total
	A	B	C	
	£000	£000	£000	£000
Sales	50	120	180	350
Cost of goods sold	− 25	− 60	− 90	− 175
Gross profit	25	60	90	175
Departmental wages	− 10	− 20	− 30	− 60
Departmental surplus	15	40	60	115
Rent				− 60
Profit				55

The above presentation highlights the fact that all departments are making a positive *contribution* to general overhead costs that are not controllable at the departmental level. In the short run, therefore, the question is whether the continued operation of a particular department or the acceptance of a sales order will make a contribution towards fixed costs (which are broadly equivalent to overheads or indirect costs). We will also see that the theory of contribution costing underpins break-even analysis as a means of planning business activity and making investment decisions.

The nature of a cost, i.e. whether it is direct or indirect, has to be decided in accordance with the costing unit under examination. For example, if the costing unit is a manufacturing department, then the depreciation of machines located in it and the salary of the departmental supervisor are direct costs. However, if the costing unit is a single item of output, then the depreciation and supervisor's salary are indirect costs as they also relate to the rest of the output. Raw materials and manufacturing wages are examples of direct costs where the costing unit is a single item of output.

TOTAL COSTING AND OVERHEAD RECOVERY RATES

Earlier in this chapter we saw that direct costs (usually these are the variable costs) are of most relevance for the purpose of decision-making. For example, a company will keep a department open provided revenues cover variable costs that, in the short run, may well consist mainly of direct materials and direct labour costs. In the longer run, more costs become avoidable – the next annual rental becomes payable and fixed assets must be replaced – with the result that at this stage avoidable costs (which now include fixed as well as variable costs) may not be covered and the department closed.

For a company to survive and prosper in the long run it must cover not only its direct costs but also its indirect costs. A company therefore needs to be aware of the total costs involved in supplying a particular product despite the fact that, in certain circumstances, it may be willing to accept a price below that figure. It is normal practice for companies to operate a system of total or absorption costing, despite some doubts concerning its validity, as the basis for many business decisions.

The operation of a system of total costing requires the collection of costs at cost centres which may be defined as: *a department or section of a department or any other convenient basis on which it is helpful to collect costs for decision-making purposes.* If we were to consider a printing company, for example, then costs could be collected in the following cost centres: typesetting department; printing department; cutting and binding department; and service departments (which could include despatch, canteen, administration).

The first problem is to devise a satisfactory system for allocating and apportioning costs to cost centres. This is examined in the next subsection.

The following stage is to recharge the costs collected at the cost centres to the cost units, which are usually the products manufactured. This is examined in the subsection below entitled 'Total unit cost'.

Accounting for materials, labour and overheads

Materials   The usual approach is to raise a materials requisition note to authorize the issue of goods from the stores to production. The requisition note identifies the cost centre to which the materials have been allocated and is used as the originating document for the purpose of recharging material issued from the stores to the cost centre. The method of pricing the issue may be FIFO, LIFO, AVCO or some other acceptable basis.

Labour   Job cards are kept for each employee to show where each individual is spending his or her time. The weekly or monthly payroll is then analysed in conjunction with the job cards to determine the charge to various cost centres. Not all labour costs can be charged directly to cost centres and the remainder are treated as part of the indirect costs or overheads.

We can therefore see that, provided a suitable system of record-keeping is developed, it is a fairly straightforward matter to trace direct material costs and direct labour costs to cost centres. The costs are incurred at the cost centre and it is merely necessary to ensure that the records are capable of identifying that fact.

Overheads   In this case it is not possible to identify the cost directly with a cost centre and so the approach adopted is to apportion overheads between cost centres on some logical basis. Some examples are as follows:

Expense	Basis of apportionment
Rent and rates	Square metre of floor space occupied
Wages of time-keeper	Number of employees in department
Canteen costs	Number of employees in department
Insurance costs	The insurable value of items in the department
Lighting	The number of power points
Heating	The number of radiators

We can see that the aim is to establish a logical relationship between the cost incurred and the method of apportionment. For example, the rent and rates payable in respect of a building are related to the size of the building, and it would therefore seem sensible to apportion the total cost between departments located within the building based on their relative size.

There is one further problem. Cost centres are made up of two types: production cost centres, where goods are manufactured; and service cost centres, which assist the production cost centres but do not themselves produce goods. The costs of the service cost centres, once established, must therefore be recharged to the production cost centres on a logical basis.

Hannah Ltd has two production departments and a service department. Each department produces a single product. The budgeted costs for 20X0 are as follows:

EXAMPLE
13.4

Direct costs	£
Materials	
Production department A	100,000
Production department B	250,000
Service department	150,000
Labour:	
Production department A	55,000
Production department B	250,000
Service department	100,000
Indirect costs	
Depreciation	100,000
Stores	20,000
Rent	36,000
Power	120,000

The following further information is provided:

Department	Value of plant (£)	Stores requisitions (number)	Floor space m²	Machine horse power	Labour hours	Machine hours
A	200,000	300	10,000	200	70,000	20,000
B	160,000	600	8,000	120	30,000	80,000
Service	140,000	100	2,000	80	–	–

It is agreed that the service department serves the two production departments equally.

Required

A statement (overhead analysis sheet) showing the apportionment of the overhead (indirect) costs to the three departments (primary apportionment) and the overhead costs of the service department recharged to the operating departments (secondary apportionment).

Solution

Overhead Analysis Sheet

Type of expense	Basis of apportionment	Total £000	Production department A £000	Production department B £000	Service department £000
Depreciation	Book value of plant	100.0	40.0	32.0	28.0
Stores	Materials requisitions	20.0	6.0	12.0	2.0
Rent	Floor space	36.0	18.0	14.4	3.6
Power	Machine horse power	120.0	60.0	36.0	24.0
		276.0	124.0	94.4	57.6
Materials and labour		250.0			250.0
		526.0	124.0	94.4	307.6
Recharged equally			153.8	153.8	−307.6
		526.0	277.8	248.2	–

Based on the information provided, the most appropriate basis for allocating the total depreciation charge of £100,000 would seem to be the book value of plant. For similar reasons, stores costs are allocated on the basis of material requisitions, rent on the basis of floor space and power on the basis of machine horse power. The result of this process is to apportion £57,600 to the service department. These costs, together with the material and labour costs of the services department, amounting to £250,000, are then reallocated to the two production departments on an equal basis.

Total unit cost

It may be helpful to summarize, at this stage, the process involved in the recovery of total manufacturing costs. The three steps are as follows:

1   Apportion overhead costs to cost centres (usually departments) in the manner described above.
2   Recharge the costs of service cost centres to production cost centres on some logical basis, as demonstrated above.
3   Recharge the total overheads apportioned to a cost centre to cost units (usually products) based on the selected overhead recovery rate (see below).

The process may be shown diagrammatically as in Figure 13.1.

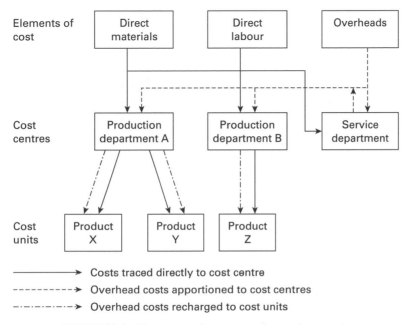

FIGURE 13.1   Tracing costs to cost centres and cost units

The elements of cost are direct materials, direct labour and overheads. The continuous arrow shows that the material and labour costs can be traced directly to each of the two production departments and the service department. In due course, these costs can be allocated to the products produced (where there are a large number of homogeneous products – for example, car tyres – an average cost is used for this purpose). The dashed arrows represent the apportionment of overheads to each of the three departments, and the one rising upwards from the service department indicates its total costs are recharged to production departments. The final stage (dot–dashed arrows) is the use of overhead recovery rates to recharge overheads to products. In the case of production department A, it can be seen that its overhead costs are split between two products (X and Y) whereas production department B's overheads must be recovered as part of the cost of the product Z.

The calculations involved in the final stage are now considered.

Overhead recovery rates   The overheads allocated to each production centre must now be recharged to the cost units – products X, Y and Z. The method of recovering these overheads is to attach them to a variable with which there can be established some kind of causal relationship. Traditionally, five methods have been employed in British industry:

- percentage on direct materials;
- percentage on direct labour;
- percentage on total direct (prime) costs;
- machine hour rate;
- direct labour hour rate.

The justification for adding a 'percentage' based on direct material, or direct labour, or total direct cost is that the level of overheads attaching to a particular product is a consequence of one or other of these variables. It is unlikely that the causal relationship would be strong but, where direct materials or direct labour are the dominant element of total cost and the level of overheads fairly modest, any distortion of the total cost figure resulting from its adoption is unlikely to be great.

Because overheads are usually a function of time, an hourly rate is therefore more appropriate. In circumstances where production is labour-intensive, a labour hour rate might be seen as most appropriate; where production is capital-intensive a machine hour rate should be preferred. It is a criticism of British industry that the percentage on direct labour method remains in widespread use; it has the merit of simplicity but, in circumstances where the ratio of overhead costs to direct labour is substantial, its adoption may well mean the provision of highly misleading figures for total cost and wrong decisions being reached.

The calculation of overhead recovery rates will be illustrated in Example 13.5.

EXAMPLE 13.5

Using the information contained in Example 13.4, calculate the overhead recovery rates using direct materials, direct labour, labour hour rate and machine hour rate.

Solution

Percentage on direct materials

$$\frac{\text{Allocated overheads}}{\text{Budgeted direct material costs}} \times 100$$

Department A: $\dfrac{277,800}{100,000} \times 100 = 277.8\%$

Department B: $\dfrac{248,200}{250,000} \times 100 = 99.3\%$

Percentage on direct labour

$$\frac{\text{Allocated overheads}}{\text{Budgeted direct labour costs}} \times 100$$

Department A: $\dfrac{277,800}{55,000} \times 100 = 505.1\%$

Department B: $\dfrac{248,200}{250,000} \times 100 = 99.3\%$

Direct labour hour rate

$$\frac{\text{Allocated overheads}}{\text{Budgeted labour hours}} \times 100$$

$$\text{Department A} = \frac{277,800}{70,000} \times 100 = \text{£3.97 per hour}$$

$$\text{Department B} = \frac{248,200}{30,000} \times 100 = \text{£8.27 per hour}$$

Machine hour rate

$$\frac{\text{Allocated overheads}}{\text{Budgeted machine hours}} \times 100$$

$$\text{Department A} = \frac{277,800}{20,000} \times 100 = \text{£13.90 per hour}$$

$$\text{Department B} = \frac{248,200}{80,000} \times 100 = \text{£ 3.10 per hour}$$

We can therefore see significant differences in total costings, depending upon the method used to recover overheads. For example, product X is costed at £3,223 using the percentage on direct labour and £2,340 using the machine hour rate. Clearly both figures for total cost cannot be correct (of course they may both be incorrect), and the use of an inappropriate method leads to misguided pricing decisions and assessments of profitability.

We do not know which method is correct without further investigation of the circumstances prevailing within the factory. However, it does seem that production of products X and Y is relatively labour-intensive (note the larger number of labour hours worked compared with machine hours and the high level of direct labour cost), suggesting that the labour hour method may be most appropriate. Product Z, on the other hand, is relatively capital-intensive (note the large number of machine hours and low labour costs) and the machine hour rate may be more appropriate in this case.

Activity-based costing

The traditional models for recovering overheads have come under increasing criticism in recent years. The main objection is that a single (global) method is used to recover the entire overheads allocated to a cost centre. It is argued that this is misguided on the grounds that there is likely to be a range of different factors that affect individual types of overhead cost, and this fact is ignored by the traditional methods. Different factors are of course recognized for the purpose of allocating overheads to cost centres, but this procedure is not carried through in the identification of overhead costs with cost units.

Advocates of activity-based costing (ABC) argue that, as the result of improvements in information technology, links between individual overheads and cost units, which may have been impossible in earlier times when the traditional methods were developed, can now be forged. ABC involves the following:

- The identification of 'cost drivers', i.e. the activity which causes the overhead to be incurred. For example, the cost of running the buying department may be a function of the number of orders placed and so the cost of the buying department should be allocated to individual product lines based on the number of orders placed during the accounting period.
- The accumulation of overhead costs, by cost unit (product), in accordance with the cost drivers.
- The apportionment of batches of overheads to product lines in accordance with the extent to which they utilize the cost driver.

The outcome is that the product bears a fairer share of overheads and more relevant data are generated for the purposes of pricing and monitoring business performance. Readers should now try Question 13.3 at the end of this chapter.

Marginal (contribution) costing

A useful technique to apply when examining the way in which fixed and variable costs respond to changes in the level of activity is to calculate the 'contribution' each unit sold makes towards fixed costs. Analysis based on this approach assumes that the revenue from each unit is applied first to meet its related variable costs, and any surplus, the contribution, is then set against total fixed costs. Once the fixed costs have been completely recovered, the contribution of each additional unit sold adds to profit. The contribution of each unit is calculated by the formula:

$$\text{Selling price per unit} - \text{Variable cost per unit} = \text{Contribution}$$

EXAMPLE 13.6

Product Z incurs the following variable costs per unit:

	£
Materials	5.00
Wages	4.50
Expenses	1.25

Required

Calculate the contribution of product Z if its selling price per unit is:
(a) £12;
(b) £15.

Solution

The total variable cost is

	£
Materials	5.00
Wages	4.50
Expenses	1.25
	10.75

(a)   Contribution = £12 − £10.75 = £1.25.
(b)   Contribution = £15 − £10.75 = £4.25.

The technique of contribution costing is used in break-even analysis and margin of safety and target profit calculations, which are dealt with later in this chapter.

Break-even analysis

A forecast of sales should be prepared as part of the appraisal of whether a particular project should be undertaken. The volume of anticipated sales sets the capacity that has to be provided and also determines the total value of variable costs. Forecasts cannot be wholly accurate, and so it is usual to examine results based on a number of alternative outcomes. A particularly useful piece of information is the volume of sales needed to achieve break-even point, which occurs where total costs equal total revenues and neither a profit nor loss is made. Looked at another way, a company breaks even when the contribution from sales is exactly equal to fixed costs. The break-even point is calculated with the formula:

$$\frac{\text{Fixed costs}}{\text{Contribution per unit}} = \text{Break-even point, measured in units sold}$$

The break-even point in terms of the value of sales can be calculated by multiplying the number of units by the selling price per unit.

The importance of the break-even point is that below it a loss is suffered, and above it a profit is earned. It is, therefore, very important that management selects projects that are likely to achieve at least enough sales to break even. The following example will help explain the concept of contribution and the break-even point.

A company manufactures a product that sells for £20 per unit. The variable cost of manufacture is £14 per unit and the total fixed costs amount to £60.

The contribution per unit is £6 per unit (£20 − £14) and the break even point is 10 units (£60 / £6). Contribution means a contribution towards covering fixed costs, and so if we assume that fixed costs represent a hole we need 10 lots of £6 to fill it. In other words, we need to sell 10 items to cover our fixed costs. If any more items are sold then profit is earned. See diagram below:

EXAMPLE
13.7

**EXAMPLE
13.8**

The directors of Cumberland Ltd are considering an investment project that has a maximum output of 50,000 units and is expected to involve the following costs and revenues:

	£
Annual fixed costs	100,000.00
Selling price per unit	10.00
Variable cost per unit	6.00

Required

(a)   Calculate the sales in terms of both units and value that have to be made for the project to break even.

(b)   Calculate the profit or loss that would occur if sales are:

   (i)   1,000 units less than those needed to break even; and

  (ii)   1,000 units more than those needed to break even.

Solution

(a)   Contribution $= £10 - £6 = £4$

Break-even point

(in units) $= \dfrac{£100,000}{£4} = 25,000 \text{ units}$

Break-even point

(in value) $= 25,000 \text{ (units)} \times £10 \text{ (selling price per unit)}$
$= £250,000.$

(b)

	(i) 1,000 less	(ii) 1,000 more
Sales in units	24,000	26,000
	£	£
Contribution (unit sales × £4)	96,000	104,000
Fixed costs	100,000	100,000
Profit (loss)	(4,000)	4,000

Note   An alternative way to calculate the effect of changes in the level of sales on profit is to calculate the increase, or decrease, in the contribution. In this case, the starting point is zero, and the contribution from sales of 1,000 units is $1,000 \times £4 = £4,000$. Therefore, an increase in sales of 1,000 units gives a profit of £4,000 and a decrease in sales of 1,000 units gives a loss of £4,000.

The certainty with which sales can be forecast may influence the choice of production method and also affect decisions about which products to trade in. Where there is great uncertainty, production methods and products with low break-even points may be chosen to minimize the risk of losses. However, the choice of a method or product with a low break-even point may restrict the total profits that can be earned if high sales are achieved.

The directors of Trestle Ltd are considering the following alternative methods of manufacturing a new product:

EXAMPLE
13.9

	Method 1	Method 2
	£	£
Plant with a life of ten years	50,000.00	150,000.00
Other annual fixed costs	3,000.00	3,000.00
Variable cost per unit	7.00	6.50
Selling price per unit	8.00	8.00

The plant is expected to have a zero scrap value at the end of its life, and the company uses the straight-line method of depreciation.

Method 2 has a lower variable cost because it uses less labour and has lower wastage rates for raw materials.

(a) Calculate the break-even point for each method of production.

(b) Calculate the profit or loss for each method that results from sales levels of 10,000 units, 20,000 units and 30,000 units.
(c) What is the greatest loss that might be suffered under each method?
(d) Advise management on which method should be adopted.

(a)

	Method 1		Method 2	
	£		£	
Fixed costs				
Depreciation	5,000		15,000	
Other	3,000		3,000	
	8,000		18,000	
Contribution	£8 – £7	= £1	£8 – £6.50	= £1.50
Break-even point	8,000	= 8,000	18,000	= 12,000
	1	units	1.50	units

(b)

	Method 1	Method 2
	£	£
10,000 units		
Contribution	10,000	15,000
Fixed costs	– 8,000	– 18,000
Profit (loss)	2,000	– 3,000
20,000 units		
Contribution	20,000	30,000
Fixed costs	– 8,000	– 18,000
Profit	12,000	12,000

30,000 units		
Contribution	30,000	45,000
Fixed costs	− 8,000	− 18,000
Profit	22,000	27,000

(c)   The greatest loss occurs when there is no contribution (i.e. zero output), and is equal to the fixed costs. Therefore, the maximum loss of method 1 is £8,000 and of method 2 is £18,000.

(d)   Once method 2 breaks even, £1.50 is added to profit by every additional unit sold, while method 1 adds only £1. However, method 1 breaks even at a lower level of sales. Both methods make the same profit at sales of 20,000 units.

The decision about which method to select therefore rests on expected sales. If 20,000 is the maximum level of expected sales, then method 1 is better; if sales are expected to exceed easily that level, then method 2 is better.

Readers should now work through Question 13.4 at the end of this chapter.

It is sometimes useful, for example when preparing a report for consideration at a meeting, to present the result of break-even analysis in the form of a graph. Figure 13.2 shows how this is done.

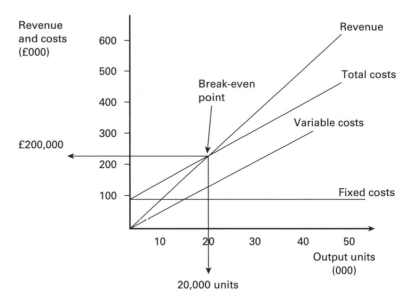

FIGURE 13.2   A break-even graph

All of the relationships expressed in the graph are represented by straight lines, and so each of them can be plotted by calculating two points. This is done by considering the costs and revenues that arise at levels of output of zero and full capacity which, in Example 13.8 was 50,000 units.

	Zero output	*Full capacity*
Revenue	$0 \times £10 = £0$	$50,000 \times £10 = £500,000$
Fixed cost	£100,000	£100,000
Variable cost*	$0 \times £6 = £0$	$50,000 \times £6 = £300,000$
Total cost	£0 + £100,000	£300,000 + £100,000
(Variable plus		
fixed costs)	= £100,000	= £400,000

Note   *It is possible to omit this line without reducing the usefulness of the chart, especially to save excessive contents when the results of two alternatives are being plotted on the same graph.

The break-even point can be found in terms of either units or value and is where the total cost line crosses the revenue line. At levels of sales below this point a loss is made, and above it a profit. The extent of the divergence between the revenue and total cost lines above the break-even point indicates the rate of growth in profit as sales increase.

The graph should not be extended beyond the stated full capacity as, after this point, an additional set of fixed costs has to be incurred, and no information is given on the resulting cost structure, or how demand in this region would be met.

Question 13.5 at the end of this chapter should now be worked.

Profit–volume graph

The relationship between the volume of activity and profit can also be expressed in a profit–volume graph which shows the profit (or loss) arising at various levels of output. When output is zero, a loss equal to the fixed costs is suffered; each additional unit sold reduces the loss by an amount equal to its contribution until the break-even point is reached. Thereafter, each extra unit's contribution adds to profit until maximum output is achieved. Figure 13.3 shows the profit-volume graph using the information given in Example 13.8.

The relationship between profit and volume is a straight line, and so can be plotted using figures for profit or loss at zero and maximum levels of activity. In the case of Figure 13.3 these two figures are:

1 at zero output a loss of £100,000, the fixed costs, results; and
2 at full capacity the profit is (50,000(output) × £4 (contribution per unit)) − £100,000 (fixed costs) = £100,000.

The break-even point is found where the profit–volume line crosses zero, indicating that neither a profit nor loss is made at that point.

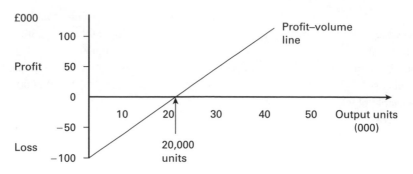

FIGURE 13.3   A profit–volume graph

The margin of safety

The margin of safety gives an indication of how vulnerable a company is to changes in the volume of sales. It shows, as a percentage, how far sales can fall from their expected level before the break-even point is reached – a fall to below this point results in a loss. The margin of safety is calculated, using data on either value or units, by the formula:

$$\frac{\text{Expected sales} - \text{Sales at break-even point}}{\text{Expected sales}}$$

EXAMPLE 13.10

Using the information in Example 13.8, calculate, using both values and quantities, the margin of safety of the project under consideration by Cumberland if the expected annual sales are 40,000 units.

Solution

Quantity:

$$\frac{40,000 \text{ (Expected sales)} - 25,000 \text{ (Break-even point)}}{40,000 \text{ (Expected sales)}} = 37.5\%$$

Value:

$$\frac{400,000 \text{ (Expected sales)} - 250,000 \text{ (Break-even point)}}{400,000 \text{ (Expected sales)}} = 37.5\%$$

Note   The same result is obtained using either values or quantities.

The margin of safety can also be calculated using actual results, in which case the formula is:

$$\frac{\text{Actual sales} - \text{Actual break-even point}}{\text{Actual sales}}$$

Target profit calculation

Once the contribution is known, it is also possible to calculate the level of sales needed, in terms of either value or quantity, to earn a given amount of profit. First, sales have to be sufficient to earn a total contribution equal to fixed costs, and then sufficient additional sales must be made to give the required profit. The formula to calculate the sales, in units, for a particular profit is:

$$\frac{\text{Fixed costs} + \text{Required profit}}{\text{Contribution}} = \text{Sales in units}$$

The value of sales can then be calculated by multiplying the number of units by the selling price per unit.

The directors of Carp Ltd are considering the manufacture of a new product that sells at £16 per unit. Its manufacture would involve annual fixed costs of £147,500 and a variable cost per unit of £9.50. The directors are willing to undertake the project if a profit of £80,000 can be made.

EXAMPLE
13.11

Calculate the sales required, in terms of both quantity and value, to produce the desired profit.

Required

Solution

	£
Selling price per unit	16.00
Variable cost per unit	9.50
Contribution	6.50

$$\text{Required sales} = \frac{£147,500 + £80,000}{£6.50}$$

$$= 35,000 \text{ units}$$

or

$$35,000 \times £16 = £560,000$$

Readers should now work through Question 13.6 at the end of this chapter.

INVESTMENT APPRAISAL

Management must decide how to invest the resources at its disposal, and usually the funds available are not sufficient to carry out all the possible projects that have been put forward, even if they all appear profitable. Some decisions still remain even after an initial decision of which projects to pursue has been taken; for example, once it has been decided to acquire a piece of machinery, the options remain of whether to buy it or lease it. Therefore, a selection process has to be carried out to choose those projects to be undertaken, and to decide how the plans are to be put into operation. A number of techniques have been developed to help management make such decisions, and some of the more common ones are now described.

Payback

The payback method of investment appraisal is based on the time taken by a project to generate the amount of cash that has been invested in it. The decision of which projects to undertake depends on the speed with which the available projects recover their initial investment:

1 If there is no limit on the funds available, all projects that recover their invest-ment within a set period of time are chosen.
2 If funds are limited, those projects that recover their investment the quickest are selected.

EXAMPLE 13.12

The management of Applause Ltd is considering the following proposed investment projects. All of the fixed assets are expected to have a life of five years, at the end of which their value will be zero:

	Project		
	A	B	C
	£	£	£
Initial investment in fixed assets	25,000	50,000	60,000
Cash inflows:			
Year 1	10,000	30,000	10,000
Year 2	10,000	20,000	20,000
Year 3	10,000	15,000	20,000
Year 4	10,000	5,000	40,000
Year 5	10,000	5,000	60,000

Assume that the cash flows arise evenly throughout the year.

Required

(a) Calculate the payback period of each project.
(b) State which projects would be chosen if all projects that pay back in three or less years are selected.
(c) State which projects would be chosen if only £70,000 is available for investment, i.e. only one of the projects can be undertaken.

Solution

(a) Project A pays back the initial investment of £25,000 in 2.5 years, i.e. £10,000 + £10,000 + (£10,000 × 0.5). Project B pays back £50,000 in 2 years, i.e. £30,000 + £20,000. Project C pays back £60,000 in 3.25 years, i.e. £10,000 + £20,000 + £20,000 + (£40,000 × 0.25).
(b) Projects A and B would be chosen as they both pay back in three or less years. Project C is rejected as it takes more than three years to earn a sum equal to its initial investment.
(c) Only one of the projects can be chosen as the combination of any two of them involves an outlay in excess of the £70,000 available. Project B recovers the sum invested most quickly, and so it would be selected.

The selection of investment projects on the basis of their payback periods has been criticized because it ignores cash received after the payback period and so it may exclude a very profitable project if the bulk of its returns are not expected until near the end of its life – for example, project C in Example 13.12. A counter to this argument is that companies do not like to take risks and are exposed to less risk if projects are chosen that recover their cash outlay most quickly. A further advantage of payback is that it focuses on earlier rather than later forecasts, which become less reliable the further they are projected into the future.

Return on capital employed

The calculation of the ROCE was explained in Chapter 12 and can be used to choose between alternative investment projects:

1   If there is no limit on the funds available, all projects that have a ROCE in excess of a stated minimum are chosen.
2   If funds are limited, those projects that have the higher ROCE are selected.

It is usual to base the calculation of the forecast ROCE on the average investment as, over the life of the project, the value of the fixed assets decreases from their cost price at the start of the project to their scrap value at the end. The average investment is found by the formula:

$$(\text{Cost of fixed assets} - \text{scrap value}) \div 2$$

The management of Applause Ltd in Example 13.12 decide to use the expected ROCE of the projects under consideration as the basis on which to make their investment decision.

EXAMPLE 13.13

(a)   Calculate the ROCE of each project.

Required

(b)   State which projects would be selected if all those with a ROCE of 25 per cent or more are to be undertaken.
(c)   State which project would be carried out if only one can be selected.

(a)

Solution

	Project		
	A	*B*	*C*
Annual profit (loss)*	£	£	£
Year 1	5,000	20,000	(2,000)
Year 2	5,000	10,000	8,000
Year 3	5,000	5,000	8,000
Year 4	5,000	(5,000)	28,000
Year 5	5,000	(5,000)	48,000
	25,000	25,000	90,000

Average annual profit	5,000		5,000		18,000	
Average capital invested	12,500		25,000		30,000	
Expected ROCE	$\dfrac{5,000}{12,500}$	= 40%	$\dfrac{5,000}{25,000}$	= 20%	$\dfrac{18,000}{30,000}$	= 60%

Note   *Calculated by deducting a straight-line depreciation charge from the forecast cash flows of each project. The depreciation charges are: project A, £5,000 (£25,000/5); project B, £10,000 (£50,000/5); and project C, £12,000 (£60,000/5).

(b)   Projects A and C are selected as they give a return on capital employed of 25 per cent or more.

(c)   Project C is chosen as it has the highest ROCE.

Example 13.13 produces a different selection of projects compared with payback. Because all the returns over the life of the project are included, project C becomes the most desirable whereas project B is excluded. However, it can be argued that the returns in the more distant future should not be given the same weight as the more imminent ones, as they carry greater uncertainty and, even if they transpire as predicted, they are less valuable as it has been necessary to wait longer for them.

Net present value

The NPV method of investment appraisal brings into consideration all the cash flows over the life of a project, but gives decreasing weight to them the further into the future they are expected to arise. The weights applied are based on the time value of money, a concept that holds that sums of money received in the future are worth less than the same sum received today. The link between the present and future values is determined by the rate of interest, also known as the discount rate, faced by the entity making the calculation. For example, if a firm's discount rate is 10 per cent per annum, then £100 receivable in two year's time is worth only £82.65 today as £82.65 invested at a compound annual interest rate of 10 per cent will accumulate as follows:

	£
Invested today	82.65
Year 1 interest (86.65 × 10%)	8.26
Value at end of year 1	90.91
Year 2 interest (90.91 × 10%)	9.09
Value at the end of year 2	100.00

Based on this calculation, it can be stated that the present value of £100 in two years' time at a 10 per cent discount rate is £82.65. Note the operation of compound interest whereby the interest earned is added to the sum invested at the end of each year, and so itself earns interest from then on.

To avoid the need to make complicated calculations, tables of discount factors are available that show, for different discount rates, the present value of £1 received at various times in the future. Such a table of discount factors is shown in Table 13.1. This table is used to find the present value of future sums of money by multiplying the sums by the appropriate discount factor. For example: the present value of £10,000 receivable in 4 years' time by a firm with a cost of capital of 15 per cent is £10,000 × 0.572 = £5,720; and the present value of £15,000 receivable in 3 years' time by a firm with a cost of capital of 10 per cent is £15,000 × 0.751 = £11,265.

Table 13.1 Discount table showing the present value of £1

	Discount factor		
Discount rate	10%	15%	20%
Year			
0	1.000	1.000	1.000
1	0.909	0.870	0.833
2	0.826	0.756	0.694
3	0.751	0.658	0.579
4	0.683	0.572	0.482
5	0.621	0.497	0.402
6	0.564	0.432	0.335
7	0.513	0.376	0.279

The steps to carry out an investment appraisal using NPV are as follows:

1 Calculate the cash flows of the project. The cash outflow of the initial investment takes place immediately and is given a weight of 1. The other cash flows are assumed to take place at the end of the year in which they occur.
2 Determine the discount rate. This is the rate of interest paid to borrow funds to carry out the project – it is also known as the firm's cost of capital.
3 Use a discount factor table to find the factors appropriate to the timing of the cash flows (from step 1) and the discount rate (from step 2).
4 Calculate the present values of the cash flows from step 1 by applying the factors found in step 3.
5 The present values, positive and negative, from step 4 are summed to find the NPV.
6 If there is no limit on the funds available, all projects with a positive NPV are chosen. If funds are limited and the initial investments are the same, the project with highest positive NPV is selected. Where the initial investments are

not equal, the project with the highest profitability index in excess of 1 is selected. The profitability index is calculated by the formula:

$$\frac{\text{Present value of cash inflows}}{\text{Initial investment}} = \text{Profitability index}$$

EXAMPLE 13.14

Required

The directors of Applause Ltd determine that the company's cost of capital is 15 per cent.

Using the information on cash flows in Example 13.12, but assuming that the annual cash inflow from project A is £5,000:

(a) calculate the NPV of each project;
(b) calculate the profitability index of each project;
(c) state which projects would be accepted if unlimited funds were available; and
(d) state which project would be accepted if limited funds were available and only one could be undertaken.

Solution

(a)

	Discount factor	Project A cash flow	Project A present value	Project B cash flow	Project B present value	Project C cash flow	Project C present value
Investment	1.000	− 25,000	− 25,000	− 50,000	− 50,000	− 60,000	− 60,000
Year 1	0.870	5,000	4,350	30,000	26,100	10,000	8,700
2	0.756	5,000	3,780	20,000	15,120	20,000	15,120
3	0.658	5,000	3,290	15,000	9,870	20,000	13,160
4	0.572	5,000	2,860	5,000	2,860	40,000	22,880
5	0.497	5,000	2,485	5,000	2,485	60,000	29,820
NPV			− 8,235		6,435		29,680

(b) **Profitability index**

Project A	Project B	Project C
16,765/25,000	56,435/50,000	89,680/60,000
− 0.67	= 1.13	− 1.49

(c) If funds are unlimited, projects B and C would be chosen as they both have positive NPVs.
(d) If only one project could be undertaken, project C would be chosen as it has the highest profitability index, i.e. it gives the greatest NPV per £ invested.

As is the case with all techniques of investment appraisal, it must be remembered that NPV analysis is only a guide for management and relies on forecasts of the future that must be subject to uncertainty. Management also has to contend with the fact that different techniques can give different advice, and so judgement must be exercised when making a final selection.

Readers should now try Questions 13.7 and 13.8 at the end of this chapter.

FORECAST RESULTS

Management is often faced with a number of alternative courses of action, especially when it is considering the long-term development of the company. It is of great assistance to management to prepare forecasts that predict the likely outcome of alternatives so that choices are based on the best possible information available.

Forecasts cannot be completely accurate, as many of the factors that influence actual results, such as the cost of raw materials and the actual demand for the product, are outside the control of management. However, this does not invalidate the exercise of preparing forecasts since the alternative is to make decisions without evaluating the outcome of management's expectations. To prepare forecasts, management must answer such vital questions as, 'How many units do you expect to sell?', 'What will be the selling price per unit?' and 'How much labour, at what cost, will it take to produce each unit?' Forecasts bring together the answers to all these questions in accounting statements, and show the expected impact of alternatives on key financial magnitudes such as cash, profit and working capital. Cash forecasts are considered in the next subsection of this chapter, the forecast trading and profit and loss account and balance sheet are then dealt with, and finally how to prepare a forecast cash flow statement of funds.

The availability of spreadsheets for use on computers has greatly assisted the preparation of forecasts. Any reader familiar with these programs will see clearly how they could be used and appreciate their benefits when studying this section. However, the fact that a forecast has been prepared on a computer does not mean that the underlying techniques are correct, and so it is important that the correct approaches, as described in this section, are understood and used. One of the main benefits of using a spreadsheet to prepare a forecast is the ability, with careful design, to compute revised solutions in response to changes in key variables. This facility is so useful that readers are advised to acquire the ability to use spreadsheets if they have to prepare forecasts on a routine basis.

Cash forecasts

Management must ensure that the company can afford any new project that is under consideration, i.e. that the company will not run out of cash if a particular plan is followed. Additional external finance, such as a bank overdraft, can be sought if the company's own cash resources are insufficient, but lenders will only be willing to provide funds that are likely to be repaid. The impact of plans on the cash resources of a company can be predicted using a cash forecast, and this is also of great interest to any person or organization, such as a bank, which is approached for funds. If cash forecasts are not prepared, a company may suddenly find itself short of cash or holding unproductive surplus funds in its bank account. A cash forecast enables a company to foresee a deficit, for which appropriate funding can be sought, or a surplus for which uses can be prepared in advance.

The preparation of a monthly cash forecast involves the identification of the cash flows expected to take place in each month and the calculation of the forecast cash position at the end of each month. The following techniques are used to predict cash transactions:

1 *Sales.* Cash sales are entered in the forecast as receipts for the month in which they take place. The time lag has to be taken into account for credit sales – for example, cash from March sales may not be received until April.
2 *Purchases.* Cash purchases are entered in the month in which they take place. The time lag has to be taken into account for credit purchases – for example, cash for October purchases may not be paid until November.
3 *Regular items.* Regular payments are entered in the appropriate month, possibly with adjustments for a lag between the date when the expense is incurred and when it is paid.
4 *Irregular items.* Irregular items, such as the purchase of fixed assets or the payment of tax, are also entered according to their incidence.

EXAMPLE 13.15

Hamel runs a shop that makes all of its sales for cash. Forecasts for the first half of 20X6 are:

Sales	January to March – £25,000 per month
	April to June – £30,000 per month
Purchases	A gross margin of 20 per cent on selling prices is made.
	Every item sold is immediately replaced.
	Suppliers are paid in the month following delivery.
Payments	Wages and other expenses, £4,000 per month.
	Drawings, £1,000 per month.
	Delivery van cost £7,000; received on 1 January and paid for in February.
Opening balances	Owed to suppliers £16,000.
	Cash £1,000.

Ignore interest on any overdraft that may arise.

Required

(a) Calculate the value of monthly purchases.
(b) Prepare a cash forecast for Hamel for the first six months of 20X6 that shows the cash balance at the end of each month.
(c) Comment on the position shown by the forecast.

Solution

(a)

	Sales	Purchases (Sales − 20%)
	£000	£000
January	25	20
February	25	20
March	25	20

			30		24
April			30		24
May			30		24
June			30		24

(b)

	Jan	Feb	March	April	May	June	Total
	£000	£000	£000	£000	£000	£000	£000
Cash in Sales	25	25	25	30	30	30	165
Cash out							
Purchases	16	20	20	20	24	24	124
Wages and other expenses	4	4	4	4	4	4	24
Drawings	1	1	1	1	1	1	6
Delivery van		7					7
	21	32	25	25	29	29	161
Opening balance	1	5	(2)	(2)	3	4	1
+ Cash in	25	25	25	30	30	30	165
Cash out	(21)	(32)	(25)	(25)	(29)	(29)	(161)
Closing balance	5	(2)	(2)	3	4	5	5

(c) The purchase of the van creates a cash deficit in February and March, but this is made good from trading cash inflows by April. The bank should be approached for a temporary loan – an overdraft would be best. By the end of June the business is accumulating a cash surplus that will continue to increase if trade stays at the same level. Thought should be given to how any permanently spare cash is to be used.

Note the columnar layout of the solution to part (b) of the example. The use of this presentation is recommended because:

1 it saves time as the descriptions of cash flows do not have to be repeated for each month;
2 errors are less likely to occur as any inconsistent entries are more easily identified; and
3 it aids comparison throughout the period covered by the forecast of the individual elements of cash flow.

Forecast trading and profit and loss account and balance sheet

The preparation of a trading and profit and loss account and balance sheet from the cash account, and opening and closing values for assets and liabilities, was explained in Chapter 3 in the context of past results. Once the cash forecast has been prepared, the same techniques may be applied to prepare a forecast trading and profit and loss account and balance sheet.

EXAMPLE
13.16

The balance sheet of Hamel at 31 December 20X5 was:

	£	£
Fixed assets		
Premises		10,000
Current assets		
Stock	18,500	
Cash	1,000	
	19,500	
Current liabilities		
Trade creditors	16,000	
		3,500
		13,500
Capital		13,500

Hamel expects to undertake the transactions given in Example 13.15 during the first six months of 20X6. You may assume that the monthly cash forecast has been prepared, which gives a summary of cash transactions in the 'total' column.

The van is expected to have a life of five years and a zero scrap value at the end of that time. Hamel uses the straight-line method to calculate depreciation.

Required

Prepare Hamel's forecast trading and profit and loss account for the six months to 30 June 20X6 and a balance sheet at that date.

Solution

Forecast trading and profit and loss account

	£	£
Sales		165,000
Less: Cost of goods sold (W1)		132,000
Gross profit		33,000
Wages	24,000	
Depreciation (0.5 × 7,000 / 5)	700	
		24,700
Net profit		8,300

Balance sheet

	£	£
Fixed assets		
Premises		10,000
Van	7,000	
Less: Depreciation	700	6,300
		16,300
Current assets		
Stock	18,500	
Cash	5,000	
	23,500	

Current liabilities
Trade creditors   24,000

	500
	15,800
Capital	13,500
Add: Profit	8,300
	21,800
Less: Drawings	(6,000)
	15,800

W1

Purchases = Payments − Opening creditors + Closing creditors

Purchases = 124,000 − 16,000 + 24,000 (June purchases) = 132,000.

The level of stock has remained unchanged and so purchases and cost of goods sold have the same value.

Forecast cash flow statement

The preparation of the cash flow statement from historical data was dealt with in Chapter 11. The same principles can be applied to prepare a cash flow statement from forecast data such as those in Example 13.16 (question and solution).

EXAMPLE
13.17
Required

Prepare the forecast cash flow statement of Hamel for the six months to 30 June 20X6 using the information given in Example 13.16 (question and solution).

Solution

Cash flow statement for the six months to 30 June 20X6

	£
Net cash flow from operating activity (Note 1)	17,000
Returns on investment and servicing of finance	
Drawings	(6,000)
Investing activities	
Payments to buy fixed assets	(7,000)
Increase in cash	4,000
Note 1: Net cash flow from operating activities	
Profit	8,300
Depreciation	700
Increase in creditors	8,000
	17,000

13.1 Glen Eagles is the proprietor of a small but long-established manufacturing business that has consistently made an annual profit of £20,000. The financial results of the business have shown little change in recent years, and the financial position has been very stable, supported by the fact that annual drawings have generally been lower than the profit. The expectation is that there will be little change over the next few years and that the level of profit will be maintained.

Eagles has recently been invited by Troon Ltd to increase his production to meet an export demand in a market where the prospects of development and increased sales are very substantial. Additional plant with a life of ten years, and a zero residual value at the end of that period, will be needed for such an expansion. Machines that will produce 46,000 items per annum are available at a cost of £36,000 each.

The selling price per item is £1, and the variable costs of manufacture for the export market will be 55p per item. Additional general expenses will amount to £10,000 for the first £46,000 increase in sales, but will fall to £4,000 for each £46,000 block of additional sales above the first £46,000.

Eagles has no private resources. The existing liquid resources of the business would cover any additional working capital required, and also provide £10,000 towards the capital cost of the new project. A bank is willing to lend up to £100,000 to Eagles at an interest rate of 15 per cent per annum.

An alternative proposal is made to Eagles. Troon Ltd offers him £120,000 in cash for his entire business and is prepared to retain his services as a manager on a ten-year contract at a salary of £14,000 per annum plus an additional £3,000 per annum for each £46,000 increase in turnover.

Eagles can expect to invest the proceeds of the sale of his business to earn interest of 10 per cent per annum.

(a) Statements reporting on the profit likely to be received from overseas sales at the rate of £46,000, £92,000 and £138,000 per annum, respectively.

(b) Prepare a report to Eagles that shows the results of the alternative course of action open to him.

13.2 Tassell Ltd is a manufacturing company specializing in the production of two machines, XX and YY. The manufacturing process for the two machines is different and this necessitates a separate production department for each. The managing director of the company is considering a revised selling price for each machine.

The estimated costs for the next 12 months are as follows:

	Admin. & Support Services	Dept. of Manufacturing XX	YY	Stores Dept
	£	£	£	£
Direct wages	–	891,880	144,900	–
Direct materials	–	2,043,216	5,924,800	–
Rent and rates	81,000			

Power	23,200			
Heat and light	11,740			
Salaries and indirect wages	196,300	128,640	64,185	144,415
Insurance of:				
Buildings	8,910			
Machinery	5,750			
Office equipment	1,000			
Depreciation of:				
Buildings	5,940			
Machinery	23,000			
Office equipment	4,000			
Miscellaneous expenses	2,190	12,210	6,875	5,775

Other than salaries and indirect wages and miscellaneous expenses, the overheads have not yet been spread on to individual cost centres.

Additional information for the forthcoming year is as follows:

| | | Dept. of Manufacturing | | |
	Admin. & Support Services	XX	YY	Stores Dept
No. of employees	14	71	17	12
Stores requisitions	20	600	840	–
Value of:				
Buildings (whole site)	£540,000			
Machinery	–	£110,000	£420,000	£45,000
Office equipment	£60,000	–	–	–
Floor area (sq. metres)	220	800	600	1,080
Cubic capacity (metres)	–	3,200	2,300	5,540
Direct labour hours	–	121,620	22,560	–
Machine operating hours	–	12,000	46,000	–
Units produced	–	162,160	322,000	–

(a) Prepare an overhead analysis sheet for Tassell Ltd in respect of the year. Clearly show the basis of apportionment where appropriate.   **Required**
(15 marks)

(b) Calculate an appropriate overhead recovery rate for each productive cost centre.
(2 marks)

(c) The managing director of Tassell Ltd has decided to add £1.80 to each unit of XX and YY to cover other costs and profit element. Establish a selling price for each product which covers the company's direct costs; overheads; other costs; and profit element.
(5 marks)

(Total 22 marks)

(ICSA, Introduction to Accounting)

13.3 During 20X4 Feather Ltd, which has a maximum possible output of 100,000 units, sold 60,000 units of a product and made a net profit of £20,000. The contribution per unit was £2, and the selling price was £5 per unit.

A competitor entered the market in November 20X4, and is selling a very similar product to Feather's at £4.60 per unit. The management of Feather decides that it must introduce automation to meet this challenge and decides upon the following plan for 20X5:

(a) Reduce the selling price per unit to £4.50. This should increase sales to 90,000.
(b) Introduce new machinery with the result that annual fixed costs increase by £80,000.
(c) The new machinery will decrease variable costs by £1 per unit.

Required

(a) Prepare the summary profit and loss account for 20X4, showing sales, variable costs, fixed costs and profit.
(b) Calculate the break-even level of sales for 20X4 in terms of units and £s.
(c) Prepare the forecast profit and loss account for 20X5, showing sales, variable costs, fixed costs and profit.
(d) Calculate the break-even level of sales for 20X5 in terms of both units and £s.

13.4 Use the information in Question 13.3 to prepare a break-even chart that shows the results of both 20X4 and 20X5.

13.5 The summarized profit and loss account of Latchmere Ltd for 20X6 is as follows:

	£	£
Sales (100,000 units @ £2 each)		200,000
Raw materials	50,000	
Wages	100,000	
Depreciation	10,000	
		160,000
Gross profit		40,000
General expenses		20,000
Net profit		20,000

The company's plant has now reached its maximum level of production and the directors are considering proposals for expansion. Two plans have been suggested:

1 The purchase of additional plant of the same type and capacity as that in use at present, and which will operate at exactly the same raw materials and wages costs per unit as the existing plant, in the expectation of doubling the level of sales. It is thought that a market exists at the current selling price of £2 per unit. The plant will cost £100,000.
2 The purchase of additional plant, at a cost of £200,000, capable of manufacturing a similar product with the same raw material content as the current product, but for which the wages cost will be reduced to 15 per cent of the expected selling price of £2 per unit.

Under both plans, additional general expenses amounting to £5,000 will be incurred for any increase in turnover up to £100,000 (total sales £300,000) and a further £10,000 will be incurred for any increase in turnover above £100,000 and up to £200,000 (total sales £400,000). The cost of production and the selling price per unit of the first £200,000 of sales will be the same as for 20X6, and the profit on those sales will be unchanged.

For both plans, the life of the new plant will be ten years, at the end of which it will have a zero scrap value. The purchase will be financed by a fixed-term ten-year loan at 10 per cent per annum.

(a) Prepare a trading and profit and loss account of Latchmere Ltd for 20X7 assuming that plan 1 is implemented and that the expected sales increase of £200,000 is achieved. **Required**

(b) Calculate the minimum increase in sales needed under plan 2 to ensure that the net profit after charging interest is equal to the profit it is calculated will be produced under plan 1.

(c) Calculate the sales necessary in 20X7 under plan 2 that give the company as a whole the same net profit, after interest, as was earned in 20X6, that is, £20,000.

13.6 The directors of Axmede Ltd have decided that the company has £100,000 available for investment in fixed assets and are considering the following two alternative projects, both of which are expected to have a life of four years, at the end of which the plant will have a zero scrap value:

	Project Zero	Project Nemo
	£000	£000
Initial investment in fixed assets	80	90
Cash inflows:		
Year 1	50	30
2	40	30
3	30	40
4	20	60
	140	160

The company's cost of capital is 20 per cent.

(a) Calculate the payback period of each project. **Required**
(b) Calculate the return on capital employed of each project.
(c) Calculate the net present value of each project.
(d) Calculate the profitability index of each project.
(e) Advise management as to which project it should undertake.

13.7 The balance sheet of Harris Ltd as at 30 November 1993 is shown below:

	£000		£000
Fixed assets	775	Share capital	800
Stock	240	Reserves	318

Trade debtors	384	Trade creditors	297
Cash at bank	27	Accruals	11
	1,426		1,426

You are informed that:

(i) The firm's anticipated sales and purchases for the next six months are:

	£000	£000
December	410	205
January	290	224
February	364	236
March	392	249
April	440	273
May	484	293

(ii) Customers are allowed one month's credit and Harris Ltd takes a similar period of credit from suppliers. (You may assume that these terms and conditions are strictly adhered to.)

(iii) Expense creditors will be paid during December.

(iv) Overheads for the next six months are estimated at £71,000 per month. This figure includes £14,000 depreciation and £43,000 in respect of wages and salaries. Payments will be made during the month in which the expense is incurred.

(v) The firm experts to purchase some new capital equipment during late May. The cost of the equipment will be £360,000 and be paid for during the months of purchase.

(vi) The accountant of Harris Ltd had negotiated a loan of £350,000 from the firm's bank to be paid during late May to cover the cost of new capital equipment.

(vii) The firm expects to sell its stock at a mark-up of 100 per cent.

Required

(a) Prepare a cash budget for Harris Ltd in respect of the six months ending 31 May 1994. (8 marks)

(b) Advise the firm's accountant whether there is a need for a loan to cover the purchase of the new capital equipment. (3 marks)

(c) Calculate Harris Ltd's net profit or net loss for the six months ending 31 May 1994. (7 marks)

(ICSA, December 1993)

13.8 Hilary Pringle plans to set up in business on 1 January 19X6 with a capital of £5,000 with which she will open a bank account for her business. Early in January she will buy fixtures and fittings for her shop estimated to cost £2,000, which she will pay in cash. Hilary expects to have to replace her fixtures and fittings in four years' time and will at that time donate her old ones to charity. She has already made arrangements for renting a shop from 1 January when she will be required to pay £1,500 rent for the six months to 30 June. Hilary estimates that her monthly expenses (wages, telephone, insurance, etc.) will average £400 per month and will be paid as incurred, and she realizes she will have to draw £300 per month for living expenses.

Hilary will sell some goods for cash, expected receipts £1,000 per month, but most of her sales will be on credit and are expected to be £2,000 in January rising by £1,000 per month thereafter. Credit customers will be expected to settle their accounts in the month following delivery – for example, sales in January will be paid for in February.

Hilary has arranged credit accounts with various suppliers who require her to pay two months after delivery. Purchases planned are £4,000 per month for the first three months. The customary gross profit/sales ratio in Hilary's type of business is 25 per cent.

1   Produce a statement showing the forecast receipts, payments and balance of cash for each of the months January to March 19X6.

2   Produce a forecast profit and loss statement for that period and a balance sheet at 31 March 19X6.

Required

(AAT, Numeracy and Accounting)

Standard costing and budgetary control

The objectives of this chapter are to:

- identify the types of comparisons made in order to monitor the achievement of business objectives;
- identify, distinguish between and appreciate the main features of a system of budgetary control, i.e. planning, forecasting, coordination and control;
- explain the advantages of a system of budgetary control;
- distinguish between budgets and forecasts;
- demonstrate the preparation of budgets for sales, purchases and cash;
- show how the results of individual budgets are summarized in a budgeted profit and loss account and budgeted balance sheet;
- outline the nature and purpose of a system of standard costing;
- explain the advantages of a system of standard costing;
- calculate the main variances for sales, materials and overheads;
- identify reasons for favourable and unfavourable variances and demonstrate possible interrelationships between them; and
- familiarize students with the nature of the main overhead variances.

INTRODUCTION

A principal aim of business organizations is the maximization of profit within the constraints imposed by the need to ensure long-run financial stability. In other words, the aim is long-run rather than short-run profit maximization. It was noted in Chapter 12 that three types of comparisons might be made in order to monitor the achievement of these objectives – time series analysis; interfirm comparisons; and standards and budgets – and the use of the first two types of comparison has already been considered.

In this chapter we consider, for the first time, the use of standards and budgets to help ensure the most efficient use of available resources. For this purpose, systems of standard costing and budgetary control are installed by management and, unlike the other methods of performance appraisal, their utilization is confined to the internal user group. The *purpose* of the two systems is identical; their aim is to estimate what future achievements should be and thereby provide an objective yardstick against which actual performance can be measured. The difference is that budgetary control is concerned with aggregate costs and revenues at departmental or company level, whereas standard costing is concerned with the costs and revenues relating to individual goods and services.

BUDGETARY CONTROL

The main features of a system of budgetary control are as follows:

- *Planning and forecasting* levels of business activity.
- *Coordinating* different aspects of business activity so they work in harmony with one another.
- *Controlling* performance and costs.

The key words are therefore *planning, forecasting, coordinating* and *control,* and their combined purpose is to achieve maximum profitability consistent with long-run financial stability.

The advantages of a system of budgetary control may be summarized as follows:

- The company's business objectives are established, e.g. maximization of profit; maximization of market share; the provision of employment opportunities; survival; financial stability; and the supply of quality products. Some of these objectives are clearly complementary, but they may contain an element of conflict, e.g. preoccupation with survival may conflict with profit maximization – which must be resolved. The outcome of this difficult process is that the firm 'knows where it is going'.

- Targets for sales, production, etc., are identified, which are achievable assuming a reasonable level of efficiency. For example, it is no use assuming a level of sales that cannot be met in order to show a budgeted profit, which is, in reality, unlikely to be achieved.

- The activities of each department and individual are coordinated in order to ensure, for example, that there are sufficient skilled personnel to enable production targets to be met. The result is that the budgets are not simply a set of vague and unrelated hopes and wishes. They must cover the whole of the organization to ensure that all activity is geared towards achieving the budget objective. Coordination ensures that, provided each individual in charge of a budget centre (typically a department) fulfils his or her responsibilities, the organization as a whole moves in the right direction.

- The responsibilities of individuals are stated so that each employee knows what is expected of him or her. In particular, the budgetary process facilitates delegation of responsibilities to individuals in charge of specified areas of activity, called budget centres.

- Actual results are recorded and compared with budgets, enabling the identification of deviations, both favourable and unfavourable. Management is then able to concentrate on areas that require corrective action to be taken. This is called 'management by exception'.

The main differences between budgets, considered here, and the forecasts, considered in the previous chapter, are as follows:

- A forecast is what is expected to happen assuming existing business conditions remain constant, e.g. advertising policy or geographical areas of operation remain unchanged.
- A budget sets out what is achievable following the introduction of changes designed to improve operating efficiency.

PREPARATION OF BUDGETS

A budget is a financial plan based on targeted future activity and is used to control that activity. It is possible to make a number of estimates of the financial outcome under different assumptions, and the one that best meets the firm's objectives and is within its capabilities is chosen.

The sales budget

This is the logical first stage in the planning process as the predicted volume of sales determines most of the other features of the organization, such as the amount of office accommodation required and the number of employees to be engaged. The sales manager must analyse the market in which the firm intends to operate and consider such questions as: the products to be sold; the geographical areas in which the product is to be sold; the potential size of the market; when the sales will take place; the price to be charged; and the number of units to be sold.

The sales budget (similarly all other budgets), once prepared, must be compared with the firm's resources to see it if can be achieved and whether it contributes towards the realization of an adequate level of profit. If not, consideration must be given to the effect of charging a higher price and possibly reducing sales, or the effect of charging a lower price and increasing the level of activity. The impact on sales of increasing the level of advertising might also be considered.

EXAMPLE 14.1

Paxton Ltd is a new company incorporated on 1 December 20X0. It is located in Bristol with sales agencies in the South West and in Wales. Forecasts have been made of sales levels under different assumptions and the following budgetary information has been agreed:

- Sales in the South West amount to 200 units in March 20X1 and increase by 20 per cent in each of the next two months. The target level of sales for the month of May to then be repeated in each subsequent month.
- Sales in Wales to commence at 250 units in the month of February, remaining at that level each month until October. Sales in November and December and in January 20X2 to amount to twice the level previously achieved.
- The budgeted selling price is £50 per unit.

The sales budget for Paxton Ltd for each of the months of 20XI. **Required**

Sales Budget for each of the months of 20XI **Solution**

Month	South West	Wales	Total	Price per unit £	Value £
January					
February		250	250	50	12,500
March	200	250	450	50	22,500
April	240	250	490	50	24,500
May	288	250	538	50	26,900
June	288	250	538	50	26,900
July	288	250	538	50	26,900
August	288	250	538	50	26,900
September	288	250	538	50	26,900
October	288	250	538	50	26,900
November	288	500	788	50	39,400
December	288	500	788	50	39,400
					299,700

The sales budget, therefore, sets out the monthly targets for managers responsible for each geographical location and gives the total sales value for inclusion in the trading account for the year. Of course, trading accounts could be prepared more regularly for management if required, for example, on a monthly or quarterly basis.

The purchases (production) budget

All companies operating a system of budgetary control require a purchases budget; in the case of a manufacturing company, a production budget is also required. We concentrate on the preparation of a purchases budget for a trading organization, though similar principles would be applied for the purpose of preparing a production budget.

The essential requirement, when preparing the purchases budget, is to make sure that purchases are sufficient so that goods are available for delivery to customers as and when required. The contents of the purchases budget therefore depend on

- the budgeted sales for the budget period; and
- planned increases or decreases in stock.

EXAMPLE 14.2

Paxton Ltd (see Example 14.1) is to purchase and take delivery of 500 units of stock in December 20X0. The company's buyer will subsequently make purchases sufficient to meet budgeted sales for the forthcoming month. The budgeted purchase price is £30 per unit.

Required

The purchases budget for Paxton Ltd for each of the 13 months to December 20X1.

Solution

Purchases Budget for the 13 months to December 20X1.

Month	Units purchased	Price per unit £	Value £
20X0			
December	500	30	15,000
20X1			
January	250	30	7,500
February	450	30	13,500
March	490	30	14,700
April	538	30	16,140
May	538	30	16,140
June	538	30	16,140
July	538	30	16,140
August	538	30	16,140
September	538	30	16,140
October	788	30	23,640
November	788	30	23,640
December	788	30	23,640
			218,460

Units Purchased = Units Sold

Other expense budgets

There are separate budgets for costs incurred in respect of administration, selling and distributing a company's products. A specific manager should be given responsibility for each budget and the costs should be measured, monitored and controlled as carefully as purchases and production costs.

The cash budget   This shows the cash implications of each of the above budgets. However, it also reflects the impact of capital transactions, such as the purchase of fixed assets and the issue of shares and loans. The basic principles involved in the preparation of the cash budget are similar to those explained in Chapter 12 relating to cash forecasts. In particular, the impact of 'time lags' between sales and the receipt of cash and between purchases and the payment of cash must be given effect.

The policy of Paxton Ltd (see Examples 14.1 and 14.2) is to allow two months' credit to customers and it has agreed one month's credit with its suppliers. The company will issue 100,000 shares of 50p each for cash, at par value, on 1 December 20X0. An annual rental of £5,000 will be paid, in advance, on 1 December, and fixed assets costing £30,000 paid for on 31 December 20X0. Operating expenses (including wages) will amount to £4,000 per month, commencing December 20X0, and these costs will be paid for in the month they are incurred.

EXAMPLE 14.3

A cash budget for the 13 months to December 20X1 showing the surplus or deficit at the end of each month. Ignore interest payable.

Required

Cash budget for the 13 months to 31 December 20X1

Solution

Month	Opening balance £	Share issue £	Sales £	Purchases £	Fixed assets £	Rent £	Other Expenses £	Closing Balance £
20X0								
December		50,000			− 30,000	− 5,000	− 4,000	11,000
20X1								
January	11,000			− 15,000			− 4,000	− 8,000
February	− 8,000			− 7,500			− 4,000	− 19,500
March	− 19,500			− 13,500			− 4,000	− 37,000
April	− 37,000		12,500	− 14,700			− 4,000	− 43,200
May	− 43,200		22,500	− 16,140			− 4,000	− 40,840
June	− 40,840		24,500	− 16,140			− 4,000	− 36,480
July	− 36,480		26,900	− 16,140			− 4,000	− 29,720
August	− 29,720		26,900	− 16,140			− 4,000	− 22,960
September	− 22,960		26,900	− 16,140			− 4,000	− 16,200
October	− 16,200		26,900	− 16,140			− 4,000	− 9,440
November	− 9,440		26,900	− 23,640			− 4,000	− 10,180
December	− 10,180		26,900	− 23,640		− 5,000	− 4,000	− 15,920

The following can be noticed:

- The two months' credit allowed to customers means that the sales made in November and December, amounting to £39,400 each month, will not be received until after the end of the present budget period, giving rise to closing debtors of £78,800.
- Similarly, purchases in the month of December amounting to £23,640 are not paid until January 20X1, and these will appear in the budgeted balance sheet at 31 December 20X1 as trade creditors.
- Cash inflows are budgeted to exceed outflows in the month of December 20X0, but the cash balance of £11,000 is soon converted into an overdraft due to the fact that there are no sales proceeds until the month of April. The budgeted maximum cash deficiency is £43,200 at the end of April and this then falls quite quickly up to the end of December. The budgeted overdraft then increases marginally due to the need to purchase additional stock to meet the budgeted increase in sales in Wales during the months of November and December 20X1 and January 20X2.

The master budget When each budget has been finalized, their overall results can be brought together in a master budget for the organization as a whole. The master budget consists of a budgeted profit and loss account and budgeted balance sheet. It is the responsibility of management to review the contents of the master budget in order to assess whether the results appear satisfactory, particularly in terms of profitability and financial stability. If the results are unsatisfactory in any respect, action must be taken to achieve an improvement. This is the advantage of the budgeting exercise: problems can be identified in time for corrective action to be taken.

EXAMPLE 14.4	The fixed assets of Paxton Ltd (see Examples 14.1–14.3) which were purchased on 31 December 20X0 are expected to have a useful life of six years and a residual value of £3,000 at the end of that period.
Required	(a) The budgeted profit and loss account for Paxton Ltd for the period to 31 December 20X1 and the budgeted balance sheet of that date. (b) Brief comments on the budgeted profitability and cash position.
Solution	(a) **Budgeted trading and profit and loss account for the period to 31 December 20X1**

	£	£
Sales (see Example 14.1)		299,700
Purchases (see Example 14.2)	218,460	
Less: Closing stock	38,640 W1	
Cost of goods sold		179,820
Gross profit		119,880
Rent	5,417 W2	
Depreciation	4,500 W3	
Other expenses	52,000	61,917
Net profit		57,963

Budgeted balance sheet at 31 December 20X1

	£	£
Fixed assets at cost		30,000
Less: Accumulated depreciation		4,500
		25,500
Current assets		
Stock	38,640	
Trade debtors (see Example 14.3)	78,800	
Prepaid rent	4,583 W4	
	122,023	
Current liabilities		
Trade creditors (see Example 14.3)	23,640	
Cash deficit (see Example 14.3)	15,920	
	39,560	

Net current assets	82,463
Total assets less current liabilities	107,963
Share capital	50,000
Net profit	57,963
	107,963

W1 £15,000 (base stock) + £23,640 (purchases to meet budgeted sales in January 20X2).

W2 £5,000 (payment December 20X0) + £5,000 × 1/12 (payment December 19X1).

W3 £30,000 (cost) − £3,000 (estimated residual value)/6.

W4 £5,000 × 11/12.

(b) The budgeted results are very encouraging and might well be even better in 20X2 due to the following: there will be no need to pay rent and expenses for a month in which no production takes place, as was the case in December 20X0; and sales are budgeted to continue in January 20X2 at a much higher level than in January 20X1.

There is a cash deficiency of £15,920 at the end of the year. The cash budget will have drawn to management's attention the need to arrange additional finance of approximately £45,000 on a short-term basis to meet the budgeted deficiency in the early months of 20X1. A bank overdraft would seem to be a suitable form of finance in the circumstances.

Summary

We now present the budget process in the form of a diagram (Figure 14.1). This reminds us that the organizational objectives are first decided upon by management and, on that basis, results are forecast for a future accounting period using a range of different assumptions. The outcomes are examined by management, which must take steps to review the expected results in the light of organizational objectives: these include the need to ensure that actions are fully coordinated and that the plans indicate an adequate level of profitability and financial stability. The plans are then formalized, as budgets, and managers responsible for activity at budget-centre level are informed of their responsibilities. These managers will have played a full part in the budgeting process and should, therefore, have confidence in the budget process and in the budgets being achievable. Actual results are then recorded in accordance with the budgetary framework in order to facilitate comparison. Differences between budget and actual are identified and reported to management at the appropriate level, so that corrective action can be taken. The information obtained also feeds into the future budgeting process and business objectives will be reviewed.

Readers should now attempt Question 14.1 at the end of this chapter.

STANDARD COSTING

A system of standard costing makes use of predetermined standard costs relating to each element of cost (labour, material and overhead) for each type of product

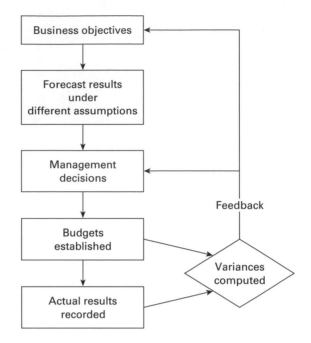

FIGURE 14.1   Management planning, decision-making and control

manufactured or service supplied. The actual costs incurred are then compared with standard costs as work proceeds. The difference between actual and standard is termed the variance, and this is analysed to help identify the reason for it so that inefficiencies may immediately be brought to the attention of the responsible managers and corrective action taken.

We can therefore see that there are broad similarities between standard costing and budgetary control; the essential difference is that we are concerned here with controlling costs at the level of the individual or product rather than at the level of the department.

The first stage in the operation of a system of standard costing is to establish the standards. It may be necessary to employ work-study engineers to measure time taken on particular jobs and the materials used. It is possible to distinguish between ideal (or theoretical) standards that assume 100 per cent efficiency and expected (or attainable) standards given the conditions prevailing in a particular business organization. Ideal standards are almost certain not to be achievable and are likely to have a demotivating effect on personnel. For this reason, systems of standard costing are usually based on a reasonably ambitious but achievable level of efficiency. The advantages of a system of standard costing may be summarized as follows:

- The installation of a system of standard costing requires the company to review existing practices and this often results in substantial improvements being made.
- Standard costs are a more meaningful yardstick than the alternatives, which are to compare results with those of a previous year or a different company. For example, this year's results may be better than last year's but last year's results may have been abysmal, so the observed improvement, although welcome, does not indicate whether the firm has achieved its potential.
- Variances are quickly identified, enabling corrective action to be taken before further losses are unnecessarily incurred.
- There is a saving in management time in that attention is focused on problem areas.
- The system identifies areas of achievement as well as difficulty, and draws management's attention to areas of success, which the company may be able to exploit more fully.
- The system promotes cost consciousness; individuals know that standards have been set and that the financial results of their work are under scrutiny.

CALCULATION OF VARIANCES

The broad operation of a system of variance analysis is illustrated in Figure 14.2. The overall variance is the difference between the actual profit and the budgeted profit for a particular product line. The simple explanation for the overall variance is that revenue has been lower than expected and/or costs have been higher. These magnitudes are reflected, respectively, in the 'total sales variance' and the 'total cost variance'. These two variances may then be the subject of further analysis, and the appropriate calculations are now considered.

Variances arise for two basic reasons.

- The actual volume of activity differs from the standard volume of activity, giving rise to a volume variance.
- The actual price may differ from the standard price, giving rise to a price variance.

The variances may be either favourable (F) or unfavourable (U), giving rise to three possible combinations:

- Both variances favourable.
- Both variances unfavourable.
- One variance favourable and one unfavourable.

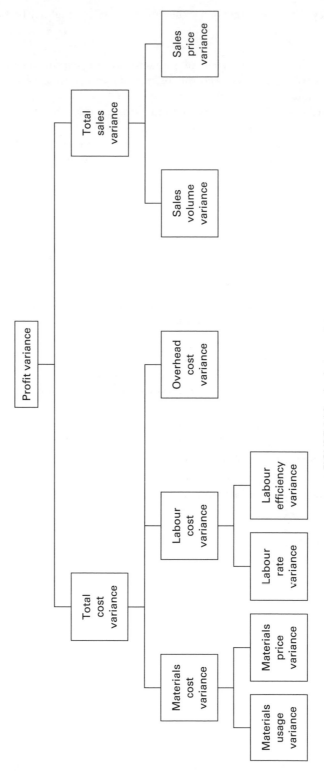

FIGURE 14.2 Analysing variance

Sales variances

The total sales variance may be analysed into the sales volume variance and the sales price variance, as indicated in Figure 14.2. The calculations of the three variances are as follows. We calculate total sales variance as:

Total sales variance = Actual sales proceeds − Standard sales proceeds

A positive sales variance indicates a favourable situation (actual revenue exceeds standard) and a negative figure an unfavourable variance. The sales volume variance is given by:

$$Sales\ volume\ variance = (\text{Actual quantity} \times \text{Standard price})$$
$$- (\text{Standard quantity} \times \text{Standard price})$$

The calculation may be shown algebraically as

$$(AQ - SQ)\ SP$$

where AQ is actual quantity, SQ standard quantity and SP standard price.

The effect of this calculation is to value any variation in actual quantity from standard quantity at standard price. Finally, sales price variance is:

$$Sales\ price\ variance = (\text{Actual price} \times \text{Actual quantity})$$
$$- (\text{Standard price} \times \text{Actual quantity})$$
$$= (AP - SP)\ AQ$$

where AP is actual price, SP standard price and AQ actual quantity.

The effect of this calculation is to identify, for the actual quantity of sales, the effect of any variation between actual price and standard price.

There are three main reasons for the sales volume variance:

- Competition being weaker/stronger than expected.
- Success/failure of advertising campaign.
- A rise or fall in prices causing the volume of sales to be higher or lower than expected.

Factors giving rise to sales price variance include:

- The need to reduce prices to respond to unforeseen competition.
- An unanticipated change in fashion.
- Unanticipated rise/fall in demand for product.

EXAMPLE   The budgeted sales for the month of January are 500 units at a price of £250 per unit.
14.5   Actual sales amounted to 480 items at £225 per unit.
Required   Calculations for the month of January:

(a)   the total sales variance;
(b)   the sales volume variance;
(c)   the sales price variance.

Solution   (a)   Total sales variance = (480 × £225) – (500 × £250) = £17,000 (U).
(b)   Sales volume variance = (480 – 500) £250 = £5,000 (U).
(c)   Sales price variance = (£225 – £250) 480 = £12,000 (U).

There has been an unfavourable total sales variance of £17,000 which has come about
because

- the volume of sales has fallen 20 units below standard, producing an unfavourable
  volume variance of £5,000; and
- the units have been sold at £25 below standard price producing an unfavourable price
  variance of £12,000.

The nature of, and relationship between, the variances can be shown diagrammatically as in Figure 14.3. In this instance, the outer rectangle on the graph
represents the standard sales proceeds ($SQ \times SP$) whereas the inner rectangle
represents actual sales proceeds ($AQ \times AP$). The shaded area, in total, represents
the total sales variance. It comprises two parts:

- The sales price variance (area A) representing the actual level of sales made at
  a price of £25 below standard.
- The sales volume variance (area B) represents the shortfall in sales, 20 units,
  valued at the standard price of £250 per unit.

It should be noted that, in practice, the above analysis of the total sales variance
into volume and price is unlikely to exhaust the possibilities available. In particular, it is possible to calculate a sales mixture variance where a company deals in a
range of products and the standards are based on an assumed ratio concerning the
sales of particular items. If the ratio alters then this causes a total sales variance
despite the fact that the sales price of each item and the overall sales volume may
not have altered. For example, a company may plan to sell 10,000 units of A at £50
and 5,000 units of B at £10. If the sales prices remain unchanged but the quantities of sales achieved are reversed, this has an enormous impact on the total sales
figure which can be pinpointed by calculating the sales mixture variance. This is
beyond the scope of an introductory text, however, and is not considered further.

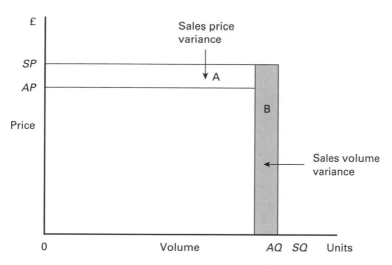

FIGURE 14.3 The nature of and relationship between variances

Total cost variance

$$Total\ cost\ variance = \text{Actual cost} - \text{Standard cost}$$
$$\text{(for actual level of production)}$$

A positive cost variance indicates an unfavourable situation (actual cost exceeds standard) and a negative figure a favourable one.

Materials variances

The materials cost variance arises because actual materials costs differ from standard; it may be calculated as follows:

$$Materials\ cost\ variance = \text{Actual materials cost} - \text{Standard materials cost}$$
$$\text{(for actual level of production)}$$

This may then be analysed into usage and price variances as follows:

$$Materials\ usage\ variance = (\text{Actual quantity} \times \text{Standard price})$$
$$- (\text{Standard quantity} \times \text{Standard price})$$
$$= (AQ - SQ)\ SP$$

$$Materials\ price\ variance = (\text{Actual price} \times \text{Actual quantity})$$
$$- (\text{Standard price} \times \text{Actual quantity})$$
$$= (AP - SP)\ AQ$$

Reasons for the materials usage variance include the following:

- Careful/careless use of materials.
- The use of materials of a better or worse quality than expected.
- The use of defective materials.
- Pilfering.
- The use of the wrong type of material.
- The work being done by employees more skilled or less skilled than anticipated.

And factors giving rise to materials price variance include:

- The failure to obtain anticipated trade discounts.
- The level of inflation being higher/lower than expected.
- Change in the rate of import duties.

EXAMPLE 14.6

The standards for component No. 124–8 are as follows:

Price of raw material input – £5 per kilo.
Quantity of raw material input – 4 kilos per unit.

Actual production data for the month of February:

1,000 units of component No. 124–8 produced.
Price of material input – £6 per kilo.
Quantity of material used – 4,500 kilos.

Required

Calculations for the month of February:

(a) the materials cost variance;
(b) the materials usage variance;
(c) the materials price variance.

Solution

(a) Materials cost variance = $(4,500 \times £6) - (4,000 \times £5) = £7,000$ (U).
(b) Materials usage variance = $(4,500 - 4,000)\ £5 = £2,500$ (U).
(c) Materials price variance = $(£6 - £5)\ 4,500 = £4,500$ (U).

We can therefore see that all three variances are unfavourable. These are clearly matters that require management's attention. At this stage, however, the causes of the unfavourable variances are unknown. It is therefore necessary to conduct investigations with the relevant managers or supervisors, perhaps at shop floor level, in order to obtain satisfactory explanations for these losses in order to enable corrective actions to be taken.

Labour variances

The labour cost variance arises because actual labour costs differ from standard; it may be calculated as follows:

$$\textit{Labour cost variance} = \text{Actual labour cost} - \text{Standard labour cost}$$
$$\text{(for actual level of production)}$$

The total variance may, again, be analysed into the quantity and price elements using, in this case, the terms 'efficiency' as a measure of the time taken to do the job, and 'rate' representing the amount paid for doing the job:

$$\textit{Labour efficiency variance} = (\text{Actual hours} \times \text{Standard rate})$$
$$- (\text{Standard hours} \times \text{Standard rate})$$
$$= (AH - SH)\, SR$$

where AH is actual hours, SH standard hours and SR standard rate; and,

$$\textit{Labour rate variance} = (\text{Actual rate} \times \text{Actual hours})$$
$$- (\text{Standard rate} \times \text{Actual hours})$$
$$= (AR - SR)\, AH$$

where AR is actual rate, SR standard rate and AH actual hours.

Reasons for the labour efficiency variance include the following:

- Inadequate or improved training of employees.
- Dissatisfaction among the workforce or unexpected rise in morale.
- Poor working conditions, for example, inadequate ventilation.
- Machinery breakdowns.

Reasons for labour rate variance include the following:

- Employing the wrong grade of labour.
- An excessive amount of overtime worked.
- Wage increases higher/lower than anticipated due to effective/ineffective trade union action.

The labour standards for component No. 124–8 are as follows:

EXAMPLE
14.7

Labour rate £20 per hour.
Hours of work – 2 hours per component.

Actual production data for the month of February:

1,000 units of component No. 124–8.
Labour rate paid – £21 per hour.
Hours worked – 1,950.

Required

Calculations for the month of February:

(a)   the labour cost variance;
(b)   the labour efficiency variance;
(c)   the labour rate variance.

Solution

(a)   Labour cost variance = (1,950 × £21) − (2,000 × £20) = £950 (U).
(b)   Labour efficiency variance = (1,950 − 2,000) £20 = £1,000 (F).
(c)   Labour rate variance = (£21 − £20) 1,950 = £1,950 (U).

It can therefore be seen that an unfavourable labour rate variance results from the fact that employees were paid £1 per hour more than expected. This unfavourable variance has been partially offset by the fact that the output was produced in 50 hours less than had been expected. One might speculate that the company has employed a higher grade of labour than anticipated to do the work, resulting in it being performed more efficiently than had been expected. These suspicions must, of course, be the subject of investigation.

Overhead variance

The overhead cost variance is the difference between the total standard and total actual overhead cost. It may be further analysed into the overhead expenditure (budget) variance and volume variance, and even further to take account of efficiency and changes in the length of a calendar month between one budget period and another. For the purpose of this introductory text we do not need to examine overhead variances in detail but simply note some of the reasons why they arise:

Expenditure (budget) variance. Particular items of overhead, e.g. rent, cost more than expected.
Volume variance. This covers factors, such as machine breakdowns, which cause the factory to be idle and the level of output to be less than anticipated.
Efficiency variance. This arises because of factors similar to those that account for the labour efficiency variance, e.g. machinery breakdowns.
Calendar variance. Differences in the length of budget periods, e.g. a 30-day month compared with a 31-day month.

The relationship between variances

We have considered each variance separately, but readers should be aware of the fact that business activity involves interaction between a range of different resource inputs and that factors which may have favourable effects in one direction may produce negative outcomes elsewhere.

It is therefore important for management to ensure that activities are fully coordinated and that actions are not taken that, although improving apparent performance in one area, may have unfavourable repercussions for the performance of a company as a whole. For example, the decision might be taken to engage a lower grade of labour than anticipated when setting the budget in order to reduce personnel costs and produce a favourable labour rate variance. The low-cost employees may, however, take much longer to do the job, producing an unfavourable labour efficiency variance, and may fail to process materials with sufficient care, resulting in an unfavourable materials usage variance. In a similar vein, the purchase of cheap materials (to produce a favourable materials price variance) may result in more materials being used (unfavourable materials usage variance) and more time being taken due to a high rejection rate (unfavourable labour efficiency variance).

Readers should now attempt Questions 14.1–14.4.

14.1   The following information is available from the books of Abbington Ltd for the financial year ended 31 October 1993:   **QUESTIONS**

Trading and profit and loss account for the year ended 31 October 1993

	£000	£000
Sales		1,300
Cost of goods sold		910
Gross profit		390
Administration costs	70	
Selling and distribution costs	40	
Financial charges	10	
Depreciation of fixed assets	30	
		150
Net profit		240

Balance sheet as at 31 October 1993

	£000	£000	£000
Fixed assets at cost			1,100
Less: Aggregate depreciation			230
NBV			870
Current assets			
Stock		120	
Trade debtors	100		
Less: Provision for doubtful debts	10		
		90	
Balance at bank		390	
		600	

Current liabilities		
Trade creditors	100	
Accrued expenses	20	120
		480
		1,350
Share capital and reserves		
Issued capital (50p ordinary shares)		400
11% £1 preference shares		50
Share premium		200
Retained profit		700
		1,350

The newly appointed managing director decided that in order to increase profits it is absolutely necessary to control costs. Thus he decided to introduce budgetary control.

The following forecast information is available for the year ending 31 October 1994:

1 The sales are forecast to increase to £1.6 million for the year.

2 A more efficient buying programme is expected to increase the gross profit/sales ratio to 32 per cent.

3 In order to finance further expansion as the recession recedes, a rights issue of one new ordinary share for every two shares currently held is to be made on 1 August 1994. It is expected that the issue will be fully subscribed and it will also be underwritten. The issue price is 65p per share, fully paid.

4 Despite inflationary pressures the managing director is determined to reduce costs. The forecast level of costs as a proportion of sales is: administration costs 5 per cent; selling and distribution costs 3½ per cent. There will be no change in financial charges as compared to 1992–3.

5 Owing to the recession bad debts are expected to rise substantially and thus the provision for doubtful debts is to be increased to 15 per cent of trade debtors. Forecast trade debts as at 31 October 1994 are £150,000.

6 A general reserve will be created on 31 December 1994 of £300,000.

7 Land and buildings which cost £350,000 (nil depreciation as at 31 October 1993) are to be written down to £200,000 due to the falling prices in the property market.

8 Dividends during 1993–4 will be restricted to paying

   (i) the preference dividend for the year; and

   (ii) a final ordinary dividend of 3p per share, but only on the shares issued before 1 August 1994.

   The dividends would be paid on 1 January 1995.

9 All fixed assets other than land and buildings will be depreciated at 10 per cent per annum based on the cost of assets held at the end of the financial year. There are to be no additions or disposals of fixed assets during 1993–4.

10 Other forecast balances as at 31 October 1994:

	£000
Expense creditors	17.00
Trade creditors	97.00
Stock	290.00
Balance at bank	760.50

(a) A budgeted trading, profit and loss and appropriation account for the year ending 31 October 1994.

Required

(18 marks)

(b) A budgeted balance sheet as at 31 October 1994.

(16 marks)

(c) Identify ways in which profits could be increased by making better use of forecast current assets.

(16 marks)

(AEB, Accounting, November 1993)

14.2 Bragg Ltd manufactures a household product. The standard cost of this article is:

Direct material   3 kilogrammes at £1.25 per kilogram
Direct labour   3 hours at £5.10 per hour

The company manufactures this product in batches of 50,000 units per month and all production is completed by the end of the period.

In June 1992 the actual results were:

Direct materials   158,000 kilograms costing £189,600
Direct labour   156,000 hours costing £819,000

Prior to the compilation of the actual results some of the senior management were asked to comment on the possible outcome of the comparison exercise that would take place.

The purchasing manager stated that he had obtained very good terms from his suppliers and there should be a favourable price variance. The personnel manager reported that no increase in wage rates had been agreed so there should be no variance emerging in the wage rate calculation. Finally, the production manager was of the opinion that the labour force was efficient and the usage of materials would be improved.

(a) Calculate the following variances:

Required

(i)   total direct cost variance.
(ii)   direct material price and usage variances;
(iii) direct labour rate and efficiency variances.

(12 marks)

(b) In light of the variances calculated in (a), comment on the managers' views.

(8 marks)

(c)   A report to the senior management team in respect of the advantages and disadvantages of standard costing.

(5 marks)

(AEB, Accounting, November 1992)

14.3   Nester Ltd manufactures towing equipment and operates a standard costing system. A standard cost sheet for model A94 is as follows:

Raw materials   3 kilos at £2 per kilo
Direct labour per model   I hour at £4 per hour

The actual production of this model for the period I January to 31 March 1993 resulted in the following details:

Number of items produced   2,000
Quantity of material used   6,400 kilos
Purchase price of material   £2.20 per kilo
Labour hours worked   1,800 hours
Actual labour rate   £4.10 per hour

There was no defective output and all production was complete.

Required

(a)   Calculate the material and labour variances for the production period from I January 1993 to 31 March 1993.

(12 marks)

(b)   Comment on the labour rate and efficiency variances calculated above.

(6 marks)

(c)   Define standard costing.

(6 marks)

(d)   Describe how standard costing may be useful to management.

(6 marks)

(AEB, Accounting, November 1992)

14.4   Phelan Forests Ltd produces timber for the paper industry. The company's output is measured in cubic metres of timber. All its output is delivered to one customer, a paper mill. Phelan Forests Ltd has no stocks of felled timber as deliveries to the paper mill are made each day. Phelan Forests Ltd pays extraction fees of £20 per cubic metre of timber felled to the owners of the forest.

Phelan Forests Ltd has a budgetary control system which is based upon fixed budgets, i.e. no adjustment is made for changes in the volume of output. You have recently taken over the administration of Phelan Forests Ltd. You note that actual monthly output is frequently very different from the budgeted output. You are concerned to find that Phelan Forests Ltd's management pays littlle attention to the variances contained in the monthly budget report.

The budgetary control report for May 1999 is set out below. You have identified that those items which are marked with a V are variable and change directly with output.

Phelan Forests Ltd – Budget Report for month of May 1999

Item	Fixed Budget		Actual	Variances ( ) = adverse
Quantity produced (cubic metres)	1,000		1,150	150
	£		£	£
Revenue	100,000	V	120,750	20,750
Costs				
Extraction fees	20,000	V	23,000	(3,000)
Wages and salaries				
Production labour	20,000	V	24,150	(4,150)
Maintenance	2,000		1,950	50
Supervision	3,000		2,800	200
Management and administration	4,500		4,650	(150)
	29,500		33,550	(4,050)
Fuel, oil and spares				
Saws	1,000	V	1,035	(35)
Tractors and winches	500	V	460	40
Vans and trucks	250		275	(25)
	1,750		1,770	(20)
Expenses				
Production	1,250	V	1,495	(245)
Maintenance	1,500		1,550	(50)
Management and administration	2,300		2,890	(590)
Buildings	850		720	130
	5,900		6,655	(755)
Depreciation				
Saws	400	V	460	(60)
Tractors and winches	1,500	V	1,725	(225)
Vans and trucks	2,500		2,500	0
Maintenance equipment	1,300		1,300	0
Office equipment and furniture	950		950	0
	6,650		6,935	(285)
Total costs	63,800		71,910	(8,110)
Profit (loss)	36,200		48,840	12,640

Required

(a) Redraft the May 1999 budget report in a marginal costing format and at the same time replace the original fixed budget with a flexible budget. You do not need to include an 'original budget' column in your revised report.

(b) Write a memorandum to G.V. Singh, Phelan Forest Ltd's general manager, which:

(i)   sets out the problems with the original budget report format;

(ii) explains how the introduction of marginal costing, combined with flexible budgeting, could improve the monthly budget report.

(ICSA, Paper 6, Introduction to Accounting, June 1999 (modified))

Appendix: solutions to questions

Odd-numbered solutions appear here, as well as 6.2, 6.4 and 6.6. All other even-numbered solutions appear in the Solutions Manual.

Business transactions: 2, 3, 4. Personal transaction: 1. Part business/part personal **QUESTION 2.1** transaction: 5.

(a) **Balance sheet of Roger's business, 1 September 20X0**   QUESTION 2.3

	£		£
Cash at bank	1,200	Capital	1,200

(b) **Balance sheet of Roger's business, 2 September 20X0**

	£		£
Machine	750	Capital	1,200
Bank (£1,200 + £1,000)	2,200	Endridge Local Authority	1,000
		Creditors	750
	2,950		2,950

(c) **Balance sheet of Roger's business, 3 September 20X0**

	£		£
Machines (£750 + £1,820)	2,570	Capital	1,200
Stock	420	Endridge Local Authority	1,000
		Creditors	750
		Bank overdraft	
		(£2,200–£1,820–£420)	40
	2,990		2,990

(d) **Balance sheet of Roger's business, 4 September 20X0**

	£		£
Machines	2,570	Capital	1,200
Stock (£420 + £215)	635	Endridge Local Authority	1,000
		Creditors (£750 + £215)	965
		Bank overdraft	40
	3,205		3,205

QUESTION 2.5   (a)   **Balance sheet of Daley at 31 December 20X1**

	£		£
Business premises	9,000	Capital	
Stock	5,250	(balancing figure)	13,450
Trade debtors	3,340	Loan from Weakly	3,000
Cash	1,750	Trade creditors	2,890
	19,340		19,340

(b)   **Balance sheet of Daley at:**

	1 Jan	2 Jan	3 Jan	4 Jan	5 Jan	6 Jan	7 Jan
Sources of finance	£	£	£	£	£	£	£
Capital	13,450	13,450	13,450	13,450	13,450	13,450	13,450
Add: Profit					180	180	180
Less: Drawings							(100)
					13,630	13,630	13,530
Loan from							
Weakly	3,000	3,000	3,000	3,000	3,000	2,000	2,000
Trade creditors	3,390	3,390	2,720	2,980	2,980	2,980	2,980
	19,840	19,840	19,170	19,430	19,610	18,610	18,510
Assets							
Business premises	9,000	9,000	9,000	9,000	9,000	9,000	9,000
Typewriter	500	500	500	500	500	500	500
Stock	5,250	5,250	5,250	5,510	5,160	5,160	5,060
Trade debtors	3,340	3,150	3,150	3,150	3,150	3,150	3,150
Cash	1,750	1,940	1,270	1,270	1,800	800	800
	19,840	19,840	19,170	19,430	19,610	18,610	18,510

QUESTION 2.7

1   *Accountancy.*   This is a system for recording and reporting business transactions, in financial terms, to interested parties who use this information as the basis for decision-making and performance assessment.

2   *Entity concept.*   It is assumed, for accounting purposes, that the business entity has an existence separate and distinct from owners, managers and other individuals with whom it comes into contact during the course of its trading activities.

      The assumption requires business transactions to be separated from personal transactions and accounting statements to concentrate on the financial position of the firm and its relationship with outsiders.

3   *Balance sheet.*   This is a financial statement that shows, on the one hand, the sources from which a business has raised finance and, on the other, the ways in which those monetary resources are employed. The balance sheet sets out the financial position at a particular moment in time and has been colourfully described as an instantaneous financial photograph of a business.

4   *Realization concept.*   This assumes that profit is earned or realized when the sale takes place. The justification for this treatment is that a sale results in the replacement of stock by either cash or a legally enforceable debt due from the customer.

5   *Trade credit.*   This is the period of time that elapses between the dates goods are supplied and paid for.

6   *Trading cycle, credit transactions.*   This is a series of transactions that begins with the delivery of stock from suppliers. The stock is then sold and delivered to customers, resulting in a profit being realized or a loss incurred. Next, cash is collected from customers and the cycle is completed by paying suppliers the amount due.

7   $A = C + L$.   This formula expresses the balance sheet relationship between sources of finance and assets where

- C = Capital invested by the owners, including retained profits
- L = Liabilities
- A = Assets

The balance sheet must always balance because all assets appearing on the righthand side of the balance sheet must be financed, and the various sources employed appear on the left.

8   *Owner's capital.*   This is the amount of the initial investment in the concern, to which are added any further injections of capital plus profit earned, and from which are deducted drawings made by the owner for personal use.

9   *Money measurement concept.*   Assets are reported in the balance sheet only if the benefit they provide can be measured or quantified, in money terms, with a reasonable degree of precision.

10   *Fixed assets.*   These are purchased and retained to help carry on the business. Fixed assets are not sold in the normal course of business and their disposal will usually occur only when they are worn out, e.g. machinery.

11   *Current assets.*   These are assets that are held for resale or conversion into cash, e.g. stock-in-trade and trade debtors.

12   *Current liabilities.*   These are debts payable within 12 months of the balance sheet date, e.g. trade creditors and a bank overdraft.

13   *Gross assets.*   These are the total assets belonging to a business entity and therefore include both fixed assets and current assets.

14   *Historic cost.*   The cost of an item at the date of purchase.

Balance sheet of C. Forest at 31 December 20X2					QUESTION 2.9
	£	£		£	£
Fixed assets			Opening capital		52,380
Leasehold premises		25,000	Add: Profit		12,600

Plant and machinery		26,500	Less: Drawings	(10,950)
		51,500		54,030
			Loan repayable 20X9	9,000
Current assets			Current liabilities	
Stock-in-trade	14,200		Loan repayable 20X3	2,500
Trade debtors	14,100		Trade creditors	10,600
Cash-in-hand	270	28,570	Bank overdraft	3,940	17,040
		80,070		80,070

QUESTION 3.1 (a) Gross assets, £6,700. Net assets, £6,500 (gross assets £6,700 – liabilities £200). Working capital, £4,500 (current assets £4,700 – current liabilities £200).

(b)

Trans.	Profit	Net assets	Gross assets	Working capital
1	NIL	NIL	NIL	NIL
2	NIL	Increase, £500	Increase, £500	Increase, £500
3	Decrease, £100	Decrease, £100	Decrease, £100	Decrease, £100
4	NIL	Decrease, £50	Decrease, £50	Decrease, £50
5	NIL	NIL	Increase, £150	NIL
6	NIL	NIL	NIL	Decrease, £700

QUESTION 3.3 A Trade debtors have paid £5,000 and this has reduced the bank overdraft from £10,000 to £5,000.

B Stocks costing £11,000 have been purchased on credit.

C Stocks costing £14,000 have been sold for £20,000, causing a bank overdraft of £5,000 to be converted into a bank balance of £15,000 and creating a profit of £6,000 which has been added to capital.

D A loan of £25,000 has been raised to purchase equipment.

E Stocks costing £10,000 have been withdrawn by the owner, resulting in capital being reduced by that amount.

F Accrued expenses amounting to £1,000 have been paid, and a further £1,000 has been withdrawn by the owner.

G The owner has injected £50,000 worth of cash, which has been used to acquire buildings.

H Bad debts of £3,000 have been written off and this has reduced the balance of debtors and capital by that amount.

I The sum of £5,000 has been paid to creditors in satisfaction of £6,000 owing. This has given rise to a discount received of £1,000 which has been credited to capital.

J Prepaid expenses amounting to £2,000 have been reimbursed.

(a) **Balance sheet at 31 December 20X4**

	£	£
Fixed assets		
Furniture and fittings at cost		
less accumulated depreciation		400
Current assets		
Stock	2,040	
Debtors	1,900	
Bank	480	
	4,420	
Less current liabilities		
Trade creditors	(1,630)	
Working Capital		2,790
		3,190
Capital (equal to assets − liabilities)		3,190

(b) **Trading and profit and loss account of Stoll for 20X5**

	£	£
Sales		32,004 W2
Less: Purchases	25,100 W1	
Add: Opening stock	2,040	
Less: Closing stock	(1,848)	
Cost of goods sold		25,292
Gross profit		6,712
Less: General expenses	2,524	
Rent	300	
Depreciation	40	2,864
Net profit		3,848

Workings

Convert cash flows to flows of goods.

	£
W1 Purchases: Payments to suppliers	24,800
Less: Opening creditors	(1,630)
Add: Closing creditors	1,930
	25,100

	£
W2 Sales: Received from debtors	31,560
Less: Opening debtors	(1,900)
Add: Closing debtors	2,344
	32,004

Balance sheet of Stoll at 31 December 20X5

	£	£
Fixed assets		
Furniture at cost less depreciation		360
Current assets		
Stock	1,848	
Debtors	2,344	
Bank	816	
	5,008	
Less: Current liabilities		
Trade creditors	1,930	
Working capital		3,078
		3,438
Financed by:		
Opening capital		3,190
Add: Net profit		3,848
Less: Drawings		(3,600)
		3,438

QUESTION 4.3 (a) **Stondon**
Balance sheet as at 31 December 20X3

	£	£
Fixed assets		800
Furniture and fittings		2,500
Motor van at cost less depreciation		3,300
Current assets:		
Stock	6,891	
Trade debtors	4,124	
	11,015	
Current liabilities:		
Bank overdraft	782	
Trade creditors	3,586	
	(4,368)	
		6,647
		9,947
Capital = (A – L)		9,947

(b)

	£
Capital at 31 December 20X3	9,947
Less: Capital at 31 December 20X2	7,940

Increase in capital		2,007	
Add: Drawings		12,840	
		14,847	
Less: Capital introduced		4,200	
Net profit for 20X3		10,647	

(c) **Trading and profit and loss account for 20X3**

	£		£	
Sales (25,067 × 4)			100,268	(4)
Less: Purchases (by difference)	76,708	(8)		
Add: Opening stock	5,384	(7)		
Less: Closing stock	(6,891)	(6)		
Cost of goods sold			75,201	(5)
Gross profit			25,067	(3)
Less: Running expenses			14,420	(2)
Net profit			10,647	(1)

Note The numbers in brackets indicate the order in which the trading and profit and loss account is reconstructed.

(a) **Bar trading account for 20X8**   QUESTION 4.5

	£	£	
Sales		107,600	
Opening stock	8,200		
Add: Purchases	81,248 W2		
Less: Closing stock	(11,936)		
Costs of goods sold		77,512	
Gross profit		30,088	

(b) **Income and expenditure account for 20X8**

	£		£
Rent	2,800	Bar profit	30,088
Rates	2,000	Subscriptions	12,400
General expenses	5,448 W3	Interest	4,160
Depreciation	3,040 W4		
Salaries	16,840		
Surplus	16,520		
	46,648		46,648

(c) **Balance sheet at 31 December 20X8**

	£	£
Fixed assets		
Furniture	30,400	

Less: Depreciation	3,040	27,360
Current assets:		
Investments	75,200	
Stocks	11,936	
Bank	3,680	
	90,816	
Current liabilities:		
Creditors – Supplies	4,568	
Expenses	248	
	(4,816)	
		86,000
		113,360
Accumulated fund		96,840
Add: Surplus		16,520
		113,360

W1   **Balance sheet at 1 January 20X8**

	£		£
Furniture	30,400	Accumulated fund (A–L)	96,840
Investments	49,200	Creditors: Supplies	4,080
Stocks	8,200	Expenses	160
Bank	13,280		
	101,080		101,080

W2	*Purchases*	£
	Payments for purchases	80,760
	Less: Opening creditors	(4,080)
	Add: Closing creditors	4,568
		81,248

W3	*General expenses*	£
	Payments for general expenses	5,360
	Less: Opening creditors	(160)
	Add: Closing creditors	248
		5,448

W4   *Depreciation*
£30,400 × 10% = £3,040.

QUESTION 4.7   **AB Sports and Social Club**
Income and expenditure account for period ending 31 December 1995

	£	£
Income:		
Subscriptions (note 1)		10,690
Bar and cafe profit (note 2)		9,200
Sale of sportswear (note 3)		1,400

	£	£	£
Hire of sportswear (note 4)			1,700
Deposit account interest			800
			23,790
Expenditure:			
Rent of clubhouse		6,000	
Grounds person		10,000	
Heating oil (note 5)		4,500	
Depreciation (5,000 × 10%)		500	
			(21,000)
Surplus of income over expenditure for the period			2,790

AB Sports and Social Club
Balance sheet as at 31 December 1995

	£	£	£
Fixed assets:			
Equipment (5,000 − 4,000)			1,000
Current assets:			
Heating oil		700	
Bar and café stocks		5,000	
Sports equipment for sale (4,000 − 2,000)		2,000	
Sports equipment for hire (1,000 + 500)		1,500	
Subscriptions in arrears		90	
Bank deposit account (10,000 + 6,000)		16,000	
Bank current account		1,300	
		26,590	
Current liabilities:			
Creditors for bar and café purchases	800		
Creditors for sportswear	450		
Creditors for heating oil	200		
Subscriptions in advance	200		
		(1,650)	
			24,940
			25,940
Accumulated fund b/f			23,150
Surplus for year			2,790
Accumulated fund c/f			25,940

Note 1 Subscriptions:	£
Advance b/f 01.01.95	40
Cash received	11,000
Outstanding 31.12.95	90
	11,130
Less: Arrears w/o (10 + 230)	(240)

Advance c/f 31.12.95		(200)
		10,690

Note 2 Bar and café profit:		£
Sales		20,000
Opening stock	7,000	
Purchases (9,000 + 800 − 1,000)	8,800	
	15,800	
Less: Closing stock	(5,000)	
Cost of goods sold		(10,800)
Profit		9,200

Note 3 Sale of sportswear:		£
Sales		5,000
Opening stock	3,000	
Purchases	3,100	
	6,100	
Less: Closing stock	(4,000)	
Cost of goods sold		(2,100)
Gross profit		2,900
Sportswear written down		(1,500)
Net profit		1,400

Note 4 Hire of sportswear:		£
Receipts		3,000
Opening stock	750	
Purchases	1,550	
	2,300	
Less: Closing stock	(1,000)	
Cost of goods sold		(1,300)
Profit		1,700

Note 5 Heating oil		£
Opening stock		1,000
Purchases (4,000 + 200)		4,200
		5,200
Less: Closing stock		(700)
Expense for year		4,500

Bank Account QUESTION 5.1

January		£	January			£
1	Capital introduced	5,000	2	Van		4,000
1–31	Cash sales	2,250	3	Rent		100
1–31	Debtors	450	1–31	Creditors		2,500
			15	Drawings		110
			30	Insurance		120
			31	Balance c/d		870
		7,700				7,700
February						
1	Balance b/d	870				

Double column cash book QUESTION 5.3

	Cash £	Bank £		Cash £	Bank £
Capital		10,000	Premises		8,000
Loan	5,000		Equipment		2,750
Cash		750	Van	4,000	
Sales	5,500		Bank	750	
Cash		4,250	Purchases	1,000	3,000
			Wages	100	
			Drawings	150	
			Rates		250
			Bank	4,250	
			Balance c/d	250	1,000
	10,500	15,000		10,500	15,000
Balance b/d	250	1,000			

(a) Revised Cash Book QUESTION 5.5

	£		£
31 Dec Balance c/d	10,734.75	Overdraft originally entered as a debit (need to double the amount)	14,000.24
		Discounts should not be entered	500.02
Dec payment overstated	63.00	Bank charges	80.00
Dec receipts understated	2.00	Standing order	50.00
Standing order	117.98		
Balance c/d	3,712.53		
	14,630.26		14,630.26

Bank reconciliation statement

	£	£
Balance as per bank statement		(3,472.34)
Less: Outstanding payments		
Cheque no. 7657	123.45	
Cheque no. 7660	19.84	
		(143.29)
		3,615.63
Balance as per cash book		3,712.53
Remaining difference		96.90

(b)   The remaining difference relates to a period prior to the current bank statement being issued. Possible causes include:

- unpresented cheques from November or earlier;
- receipts or payments omitted from the cash book;
- transposition errors prior to November;
- recording transactions more than once;
- not recording dishonoured (bounced) cheques;
- recording non-cash items in the cash book such as discounts allowed or received.

QUESTION 5.7   (a)   **Cash Book**

March 1993	£	March 1993	£
		Balance b/d	6,076
Understated	600	Bank charges	48
Correction (154–145)	9	Dividend cheque	340
		Standing order	110
Balance c/d	6,150	Dishonoured cheque	185
	6,759		6,759

Bank Reconciliation

	£
Overdraft on statement	(2,129)
Outstanding lodgement	1,550
Outstanding cheques	(4,920)
Standing order (120 × 3)	(360)
Credit transfer	(291)
Balance in cash book	(6,150)

(b)   It is necessary to prepare a bank reconciliation to identify:

- Items in the cash book that are not on the bank statement, which should comprise only outstanding lodgements and cheques. The lodgements should be traced to the following bank statement, and any undue delay investigated; outstanding cheques should be monitored and followed up as the date when they expire approaches.

- Items on the bank statement that are not in the cash book. Where such items are found to be correct, they should be entered in the cash book. Any that do not relate to the company should be reported to the bank as errors to be corrected.

By enabling these checks to be carried out, the bank reconciliation provides proof that the company's record of its bank transactions is correct and also identifies any errors made by the bank. It aids the internal control of the company as the day-to-day running of the cash book can be delegated and then checked by management by using the reconciliation statement.

QUESTION 6.1

	Debit £	Credit £
Capital		8,500
Trade creditors		4,600
Plant and machinery	4,500	
Stock	2,700	
Debtors	5,200	
Cash	700	
	13,100	13,100

QUESTION 6.2

Sales day book (SDB)

Customer	£
Vision	7,000
Sister	4,000
Batty	2,700
Flat	200
Broke	300
	14,200

Purchases day book (PDB)

Supplier	Total £	Goods for resale £	Motor expenses £	Office expenses £
Tele	3,000	3,000		
Trany	2,000	2,000		
Valve	2,400	2,400		
Garage	100		100	
Paper	50			50
	7,550	7,400	100	50

Returns inwards day book (RIDB)

Customer	£
Vision	300
Batty	200
	500

Returns outwards day book (RODB)

Supplier	£
Trany	100
Valve	150
	250

Cash book (CB) receipts (debit)

Detail	Discount £	Cash £	Debtors £	Sundry £
Balance b/d		700		
Vision	50	6,350	6,350	
Sister	40	3,500	3,500	
Batty	25	2,600	2,600	
Scrap		100		100
	115	13,250	12,450	100

Cash book (CB) payments (credit)

Detail	Discount £	Cash £	Creditors £	Wages £	Motor expenses £	Sundry £
Tele	55	2,950	2,950			
Trany	35	1,950	1,950			
Valve	20	2,200	2,200			
Plantmax		1,000				1,000
Wages		1,500		1,500		
Accom.		600				600
Supplies		250				250
Garage		300			300	
	110	10,750	7,100	1,500	300	1,850
Balance c/d		2,500				
		13,250				

Capital

	£			£
			Journal	8,500

Purchase Ledger Control Account

		£			£
January	RODB	250	January	Journal	4,600
	CB Discounts	110		PDB	7,550
	CB Cash	7,100			
	Balance c/d	4,690			
		12,150			12,150

Plant and Machinery

		£			£
January	Journal	4,500	January	Balance c/d	5,500
	CB	1,000			
		5,500			5,500

Stock

		£		£
January	Journal	2,700		

Sales Ledger Control Account

		£			£
January	Journal	5,200	January	RIDB	500
	SDB	14,200		CB Discounts	115
				CB Cash	12,450
				Balance c/d	6,335
		19,400			19,400

Sales

		£			£
January	RIDB	500	January	SDB	14,200
	Balance c/d	13,700			
		14,200			14,200

Purchases

		£			£
January	PDB	7,400	January	RODB	250
				Balance c/d	7,150
		7,400			7,400

Motor Expenses

		£			£
January	PDB	100	January	Balance c/d	400
	CB	300			
		400			400

Office Expenses

		£			£
January	PDB	50	January	Balance c/d	300
	CB	250			
		300			300

Discounts Allowed

		£		£
January	CB	115		

Discount Received

	£			£
		January	CB	110

Sale of Fixed Assets

		£		£
January	CB	100		

Wages

		£		£
January	CB	1,500		

Rent

		£		£
January	CB	600		

QUESTION 6.4   **Sales Ledger**

Vision

		£			£
January	Balance b/d	2,500	January	RIDB	300
	SDB	7,000		CB Discounts	50
				CB Cash	6,350
				Balance c/d	2,800
		9,500			9,500

Sister

		£			£
January	Balance b/d	1,500	January	CB Discounts	40
	SDB	4,000		CB Cash	3,500
				Balance c/d	1,960
		5,500			5,500

Batty

		£			£
January	Balance b/d	1,200	January	RIDB	200
	SDB	2,700		CB Discounts	25
				CB Cash	2,600

		£			£
			Balance c/d		1,075
		3,900			3,900

Flat

		£			£
January	SDB	200			

Broke

		£			£
January	SDB	300			

Purchases ledger

Tele

		£			£
January	CB Discounts	55	January	Balance b/d	2,300
	CB Cash	2,950		PDB	3,000
	Balance c/d	2,295			
		5,300			5,300

Trany

		£			£
January	RODB	100	January	Balance b/d	1,000
	CB Discount	35		PDB	2,000
	CB Cash	1,950			
	Balance c/d	915			
		3,000			3,000

Valve

		£			£
January	RODB	150	January	Balance c/d	1,300
	CB Discount	20		PDB	2,400
	CB Cash	2,200			
	Balance c/d	1,330			
		3,700			3,700

Garage

		£			£
			January	PDB	100

Paper

		£			£
			January	PDB	50

Sales Ledger   QUESTION 6.5

	£
Vision	2,800
Sister	1,960
Batty	1,075

Flat	200
Broke	300
As per control account	6,335

Purchase ledger

	£
Tele	2,295
Trany	915
Valve	1,330
Garage	100
Paper	50
As per control account	4,690

QUESTION 6.6

	Debit	Credit
	£	£
Cash	2,500	
Capital		8,500
Creditors		4,690
Plant and machinery	5,500	
Stock	2,700	
Debtors	6,335	
Sales		13,700
Purchases	7,150	
Motor expenses	400	
Office expenses	300	
Discounts allowed	115	
Discounts received		110
Wages	1,500	
Rent	600	
Sale of fixed asset		100
	27,100	27,100

QUESTION 6.7 (a) (i) Real accounts represent assets, or items of property other than claims against external persons. Balances on real accounts are, in normal circumstances, assets, for example, when motor vehicles, furniture or plant and machinery are purchased, real accounts under those headings are debited.

         (ii) Personal accounts are those which show the relationship of the business with other persons or firms. A debit balance on a personal account is an asset and represents the right to receive money in the future. A credit balance is a liability.

        (iii) Nominal accounts are used to record items of income and expense. Debit balances are expenses and credit balances are income.

(b) (i) Fixed asset at cost £10,000 – real account.

(ii) Wages £700 – nominal account.

(iii) Discounts received £1,400 – nominal account.

(iv) Balance due from Double Ltd £1,500 – personal account.

Sales Ledger Control Account   QUESTION 6.9

20X1		£	20X1		£
1 October	Balance b/d	102,300	1 October	Balance b/d	340
	Sales	630,800		Cash	498,660
				Returns	2,700
				Discounts	
				purchase ledger	11,790
				Contras	5,200
				Bad Debts	3,950
20X2			20X2		
30 September	Balance c/d	510	30 September	Balance c/d	210,970
		733,610			733,610

Note Items 4, 6 and 8 do not belong in the sales ledger control account.

(a) **Creditors Ledger Control Account**   QUESTION
                                                                                     6.11

	£		£
Discounts r/d	3,608	Balance: 1 December 1989	45,870
Cash and cheques paid	231,570	Purchases	249,560
Sales ledger set-offs	818		
Returns outwards	4,564		
Balance: 30 November 1990	54,870		
	295,430		295,430

(b)

(i) **Corrected Creditors Ledger Control Account**

Item		£
	Balance: 30 November 1990	54,870
2	Invoice omitted	1,850
3	Credit note	(870)
4	Petty cash payments	(625)
		55,225

(ii) Corrected total on the individual creditors accounts

Item		£
	Given total	51,120
1	Invoice omitted	1,125
2	Invoice omitted	1,850
3	Credit note	(870)
5	Undercast	2,000
		55,225

	Transaction	Original document	Book of original entry	Double entry
QUESTION 6.13	Purchase of goods on credit	Purchase invoice Goods received note	Purchases day book	As part of total: Debit purchases Credit creditors
	Goods returned by credit customer	Credit note	Returns inwards day book	As part of total: Debit sale Credit debtors
	Petty cash payment	Petty cash voucher supported by receipts	Petty cash book	The entry in the petty cash book is the credit; the debit is to the entertainment account
	Credit card sales	Card voucher and invoice for card charges	Cash book	Debit cash book; credit sales On subsequent receipt of invoice for card charges to support direct debit: Debit charges Credit cash book
	Recovery of bad debt	Cheque received	Cash book journal	Reinstate the debt: Debit debtors Credit bad debts Record receipt: Debit cash Credit debtors

Trading and profit and loss account for the year to 30 June 20X7

	£	£
Sales		108,920
Opening stock	9,470	
Purchases	72,190	
Closing stock	(9,960)	
Cost of goods sold		71,700
		37,220
Gross profit		
Depreciation	3,000	
Rent	1,000	
Wages	14,330	
Other costs	4,590	
		22,920
Net profit		14,300

Balance sheet at 30 June 20X7

	£	£
Fixed assets		
At cost		35,000
Less: Accumulated depreciation		
(12,500 + 3,000)		15,500
		19,500
Current assets		
Stock	9,960	
Debtors	7,350	
Cash	1,710	
	19,020	
Current liabilities		
Creditors	6,220	
		12,800
		32,300
Capital		
At 1 July 19X6		30,350
Profit		14,300
		44,650
Drawings		(12,350)
		32,300

QUESTION 7.3   **Insurance Account**

20X8		£	20X8		£
1 January	Balance b/d	450	31 December	Balance c/d	510
June	Cash	1,020		Profit and loss	
				account	960
		1,470			1,470

Rates Account

20X8		£	20X8		£
1 January	Balance b/d	290	31 December	Balance c/d	390
March	Cash	780		Profit and loss	
September	Cash	780		account	1,460
		1,850			1,850

Gas Account

20X8		£	20X8		£
March	Cash	850	1 January	Balance b/d	600
June	Cash	840	31 December	Profit and loss	
September	Cash	610		account	3,340
December	Cash	960			
31 December	Balance c/d	680			
		3,940			3,940

Electricity Account

20X8		£	20X8		£
February	Cash	900	1 January	Balance b/d	300
May	Cash	820	31 December	Profit and loss	
August	Cash	690		account	3,050
November	Cash	550			
31 December	Balance c/d	390			
		3,350			3,350

QUESTION 7.5   (a)   **Sales ledger control account**

	£		£
Balance b/d	156,937	B. Clyde – bad debt	560
		M. Poppins – bad debt	227
		Balance c/d	156,150
	156,937		156,937

Bad debts account

	£		£
Balance b/d	750	Profit and loss account	1,537
Sales ledger control			
account	560		

| Sales ledger control account | 227 | | |
| | 1,537 | | 1,537 |

Doubtful debts account

	£		£
provision for doubtful debts account	1,648	Profit and loss account	1,648

Provision for doubtful debts account

	£		£
Balance c/d	4,248	Balance b/d	2,600
		Doubtful debts account*	
		S. Wars	340
		M. Express	78
		M. Ash	80
		Increase in provision	1,150
	4,248		4,248

Note   *Total value £1,648.

(b)   **Balance sheet – extract**

	£
Debtors	156,150
Less: Provision for doubtful debts	4,248
	151,902

(a)   **S. Top – Journal**

		Debit	Credit
		£	£
1.	Plant and machinery	2,750	
	Repairs to machinery		2,750
	Transfer of purchase of lathe wrongly recorded		
2.	Repairs	350	
	Manufacturing wages		350
	Transfer of repair costs wrongly recorded		
3.	Bad debts	1,290	
	Debtors		1,290
	Irrecoverable debts due from J. Jones written off		

4.	Drawings	200	
	Rates		200
	Transfer of rates on S. Top's private house		
5.	Purchases	1,500	
	Creditors		1,500
	Goods received but not recorded at year end		
6.	Provision for depreciation	1,000	
	Machinery		1,000
	Fully depreciated machine scrapped during year		
7.	Drawings	150	
	Purchases		150
	Goods taken for S. Top's personal use		
8.	Delivery	125	
	Purchases		125
	Transfer of delivery cost wrongly recorded		

(b) **Statement of effect of adjustments on profit**

		Decrease profit £	Increase profit £
1.	Expense capitalized		2,750
3.	Increase in bad debts	1,290	
4.	Expense charged to owner		200
5.	Increase in purchases	1,500	
7.	Purchases charged to owner		150
		2,790	3,100
			2,790
	Net increase in profit		310

QUESTION 8.1 (a) There are two main tests:

(i) Expenditure that enhances the ability of the firm to earn profits is capital, whereas expenditure designed merely to maintain the existing level of operations is revenue.

(ii) Capital expenditure is incurred on the purchase of assets that are expected to possess a useful life that extends over a number of accounting periods; moreover, it is not intended to sell these assets in the normal course of business. Revenue expenditure is incurred in acquiring goods and services that are consumed in a short space of time. A correct allocation is important, because otherwise profit and asset values are wrongly reported. For example, the misallocation of capital to revenue causes both profit and gross assets to be understated.

(b) (i) *Revenue* This is a normal repair to make good wear and tear.

(ii) *Capital* Hourly capacity is increased.

(iii) *Capital* This is part of the cost of acquiring the new asset.

(iv) *Capital* This increases the firm's productive capacity.

(v) *Capital* This expenditure is needed to make the plant ready for use.

(a) **QUESTION 8.3**

	(i) Straight-line	(ii) Diminishing balance	(iii) Units of output
	£	£	£
Year 1	7,000	15,400	5,600
Year 2	7,000	6,930	7,000
Year 3	7,000	3,119	7,700
Year 4	7,000	1,403	7,700
	28,000	26,852	28,000

Workings

Straight line = 28,000/4 = £7,000 per annum (full year).

Diminishing balance = 55% charge applied to net book value at the beginning of the year.

Units of output = £28,000/200,000 = 14p per hour

(b) **Minilab Account**

	£			£
1.1.X1 Cost	28,000	30.6.X3	Asset disposals account	28,000

Provision for depreciation

	£			£
30.6.X3 Asset disposals account	17,500	1.1.X3	Opening balance	14,000
		30.6.X3	Depreciation account	3,500
	17,500			17,500

Asset Disposals Account

	£			£
30.6.X3 Minilab account	28,000	30.6.X3	Provision for depreciation	17,500
		30.6.X3	Cash	10,000
		30.6.X3	Loss on sale	500
	28,000			28,000

QUESTION 8.5 The fundamental rule is that stock should be valued at the *lower* of cost and net realizable value, taking each item or groups of similar items separately.

Valuation of stock calculated as follows:

Product	Cost	NRV	Lower of cost and NRV
A	2,400	2,760	2,400
B	1,290	740	740
C	3,680	750	750
D	2,950	4,760	2,950
E	6,280	9,730	6,280
Value of stock			13,120

QUESTION 8.7 *Perpetual inventory.* Stock records are written up on a regular basis to record receipts and issues of stock and the quantity on hand after each transaction. Sometimes the records are also maintained in terms of values and, where this is done, values for total issues (cost of goods sold) and closing stock are readily available under this system. Where values are not recorded, the cost of goods sold is obtained as the balancing item (see below).

Periodic stocktake. Stocks are physically counted and valued at the end of each accounting period. The figure for cost of goods sold is the balancing item obtained by applying the formula:

Opening stock + Purchases − Closing stock = Cost of goods sold

QUESTION 8.9 (a)   AVCO basis − stock card

		Receipts			Issues			Balance	
	Units	Price	Total	Units	Price	Total	Units	Price	Total
		£	£		£		£	£	£
1 Jan.	50	165	8,250				50	165.00	8,250
10 Jan.	200	143	28,600				250	147.40	36,850
31 Jan.				180	147.40	26,532	70	147.40	10,318
1 Feb.	120	170	20,400				190	161.67	30,718
28 Feb.				120	161.67	19,401	70	161.67	11,317
2 March	220	210	46,200				290	198.33	57,517
31 March				250	198.33	49,583	40	198.33	7,934
	590		103,450	550		95,516	40		7,934

FIFO basis

Receipts, 590

Issues, 550

Balance: 40 units

Balance of stock valued at most recent prices

Stocks: £210 × 40 = £8,400

(b) **Trading Account, January–March 1993**

		FIFO	LIFO
		£	£
Sales:	£175 × 180	31,500	
	£215 × 120	25,800	
	£230 × 250	57,500	
		114,800	114,800
Purchases		103,450	103,450
Closing stock		8,400	7,934
Cost of goods sold		95,050	95,516
Gross profit		19,750	19,284

(c) The basic rule is that stock should be valued at the lower of cost and net realizable value. This rule is designed to ensure compliance with the prudence concept which requires that:

- profits should not be recognized until they are realized; and
- provision should be made for all foreseeable losses.

For the purpose of applying the rule, the comparison between cost and net realizable value should be made in respect of individual items of stock or groups of similar items. This is to ensure that full provision is made for foreseeable losses.

Stock must be valued for the purpose of the published accounts on the total cost basis, including any overhead costs incurred in bringing the stock into its present condition and location. This complies with the accruals concept by ensuring that the full cost of an item of stock is matched with the related revenue when the sales take place. Companies may use FIFO, AVCO or certain other acceptable methods to match stock purchases with stock sales. Whichever method is selected should be applied consistently to ensure comparability of results from one accounting period to the next. It can be seen from the above example that, in circumstances where prices are rising, the use of FIFO will result in a higher stock valuation and a higher figure for gross profit.

Examples are as follows:

QUESTION 8.11

(a) Insurance premiums received before the period covered by the insurance; rents received before the rental period.
(b) Cash sales of goods; sale of goods on credit where the cash is collected in the same accounting period.
(c) Collection of customers' accounts in the period following the sale; receipt of interest after the period to which it relates.

(d) Prepayment of insurance premiums or subscription fees.

(e) Payments for office salaries and telephone charges in the period in which they are used (debit entry is to an expense account).

(f) Payment of suppliers' accounts outstanding at the year end; payment for rent accrued at the year end.

QUESTION 8.13

(a) (i) *Dual aspect.* This means the financial effect of each transaction undertaken by a business must be entered in the books twice: a debit entry to record items such as the acquisition of an asset, an expense incurred, a revenue reduced or a loan repaid; and a credit entry to record a liability incurred, a revenue received, an expense reduced or an asset reduced.

(ii) *Consistency.* The consistency concept requires businesses to use the same valuation methods each year when preparing accounting statements. The need for the consistency concept arises because there is available a variety of different ways of valuing particular assets and liabilities.

(iii) *Prudence.* The prudence concept (sometimes also called the concept of conservatism) requires the accountant to make full provision for all expected losses and not to anticipate revenues until they are realized. The justification for the accruals concept is that the risks inherent in overstatement (for example, overstating profit) are much greater than result from an understatement.

(iv) *Matching/accruals.* The accountant measures profit for a period of time, such as a year, by comparing or 'matching' revenue and expenditure identified with that time period. For this purpose, revenue is assumed to be realized when a sale takes place, while costs are matched against revenue when the benefit of the expenditure is received rather than when the cash payment is made.

(v) *Going concern.* This assumes that the business is a permanent venture and will not be wound up in the foreseeable future. This means that the accountant can assume that the business will remain in existence long enough to enable the recovery of the initial investment, and that liquidation values can be ignored.

(b) (i) *Dual aspect.* An example would be the sale of goods on credit for £2,000. The debit entry would be to 'trade debtors' and shown as a current asset in the balance sheet; the credit entry would be to 'sales' and included in the profit and loss account.

(ii) *Consistency.* In the case of stock, alternative methods include first in first out (FIFO), last in first out (LIFO), and the weighted average cost method (AVCO). Once the method of stock valuation has been selected, it should be adopted in subsequent years.

(iii) *Prudence.* A company may have made a sale on credit which is recognized in the manner indicated under (i). If it becomes apparent that the debtor is unlikely to repay the amount owing, provision has to be made for this foreseeable loss. The amount involved is written off in the profit and loss account, and the balance of trade debtors is reduced by a corresponding amount.

(iv) *Matching/accruals.* A company may have purchased a fixed asset for £30,000 which it expects to last for four years and then have residual value of £2,000. In these circumstances the total amount to be written off is £28,000 and, applying the straight-line method, £7,000 must be matched against revenue arising over each of the four years.

(v) *Going concern.* The resale value of the fixed asset referred to under (iv) may fall to, say, £15,000 immediately following acquisition. This change in market price is considered to be irrelevant as there is no intention to resell the asset. Provided the company remains in existence for four years, it is perfectly legitimate to ignore the decline in the resale value of the fixed asset and, instead, depreciate the asset at the rate of £7,000 per annum.

(a) **Realization Account**

	£		£
Freehold land and property	80,000	Mars capital account:	
Equipment	9,000	Property	120,000
Motor car	3,000	Equipment	11,000
Stock	24,000	Stock	26,000
Debtors	6,500	Debtors	6,100
Cash – expenses	1,500	Total assets acquired	163,100
Profit on realization		Saturn capital account:	
Jupiter	21,000	Car	2,900
Mars	10,500		
Saturn	10,500		
	166,000		166,000

(b) **Bank Account**

	£		£
Mars capital account	90,000	Balance b/d	6,400
		Realization expenses	1,500
		Creditors	4,100
		Capital accounts:	
		Saturn	32,600
		Mars	45,400
	90,000		90,000

(c)   **Capital Account**

	Jupiter	Mars	Saturn		Jupiter	Mars	Saturn
	£	£	£		£	£	£
Realization				Balance b/d	55,000	32,000	25,000
account		163,100	2,900	Realization			
				account	21,000	10,500	10,500
Mars	30,600			Jupiter		30,600	
Cash	45,400		32,600	Cash		90,000	
	76,000	163,100	35,500		76,000	163,100	35,500

(d)   **Balance sheet at 1 July 1984**

	£	£
Fixed assets		
Freehold land and premises		120,000
Equipment		11,000
		131,000
Current assets		
Stock	26,000	
Debtors	6,100	
		32,100
		163,100
Less:		
Loan from Jupiter	30,600	
Bank loan	90,000	
		120,600
		42,500
Financed by:		
Capital account – Mars		42,500

The above balance sheet shows that the balance on the capital account of Mars represents his personal investment in the business; a substantial part of the firm's assets are financed by funds from outside sources.

QUESTION 9.3   **Trading and profit and loss account for the year to 31 March 20X3**

	£	£
Sales		150,000
Opening stock	30,000	
Purchases	110,000	
Goods lost	(700)	
Stock drawings	(340)	
Closing stock	(40,000)	
Cost of goods sold		98,960
Gross profit		51,040

Depreciation	1,500	
Wages (14,500 + 500)	15,000	
Rent (5,000 − 1,000)	4,000	
Expenses	3,000	
Heat and light	1,200	
Delivery	5,300	
		30,000
Net trading profit		21,040
	£	£

Appropriation:

Interest on drawings:		
Bean		200
Stalk		300
		21,540
Salaries:		
Bean	2,000	
Stalk	4,000	
		6,000
		15,540
Interest:		
Bean	1,500	
Stalk	500	
		2,000
		13,540
Residue:		
Bean	6,770	
Stalk	6,770	
		13,540

Balance sheet at 31 March 20X3

	£	£	£
Fixed assets			6,000
Less: Depreciation			1,500
			4,500
Current assets:			
Stock		40,000	
Debtors		14,000	
Debtor for goods lost		700	
Prepaid rent		1,000	
Cash		4,500	
		60,200	

Current liabilities:			
Creditors	11,500		
Accrued wages	500		
		12,000	
Working capital			48,200
			52,700

	£	£	£
	Bean	*Stalk*	
Capital	30,000	10,000	40,000
Current accounts:			
Balance 1 April 20X2	3,000	5,000	
Interest on drawings	(200)	(300)	
Drawings: Cash	(7,000)	(9,000)	
Stock	(340)	–	
Interest on capital	1,500	500	
Salaries	2,000	4,000	
Share of residue	6,770	6,770	12,700
	5,730	6,970	52,700

QUESTION 9.5 (a)   **Realization Account**

	£		£
Freehold land and buildings	300,000	Loan	40,000
Plant and machinery	115,900	Creditors	118,400
Motor vehicle	58,600	Proceeds:	
Stocks	110,600	Land and buildings	380,000
Debtors	89,400	Plant and machinery	88,000
Creditors settled	115,000	Motor vehicles	38,000
Loan (including interest)	41,000	Gamma – debtors	20,000
Dissolution expenses	2,400	Gamma – stock	120,000
Balance to partners:		Gamma – car	14,000
Alpha (5/10)	31,450	Beta – car	9,000
Beta (3/10)	18,870	Proceeds–debtors	68,400
Gamma (2/10)	12,580		
	895,800		895,800

(b)

Capital Accounts

	Alpha £	Beta £	Gamma £		Alpha £	Beta £	Gamma £
Realization a/c				Balance b/d	233,600	188,900	106,200
				Balance on the			
MV	–	9,000	14,000	realization a/c	31,450	18,870	12,580
Stock	–	–	120,000				
Debtors	–	–	20,000				
Balance c/d	265,050	198,770	–	Balance c/d			35,220
	265,050	207,770	154,000		265,050	207,770	154,000

(c)

Cash Account

	£		£
Balance	12,600	Creditors	115,000
Proceeds:		Loan	41,000
Land and buildings	380,000	Dissolution expenses	2,400
Plant and machinery	88,000	Due to Alpha	265,050
Motor vehicles	38,000	Due to Beta	198,770
Debtors	68,400		
Due from Gamma	35,220		
	622,220		622,220

Loan interest = £40,000 × 10% × 3/12 = £1,000.

(a) **Trading and profit and loss account year to 31 October 1986**

QUESTION 10.1

	£	£
Sales		791,600
Less: Opening stock	113,400	
Purchases	458,200	
Closing stock	(121,300) W1	
Cost of goods sold		450,300
Gross profit		341,300
Less: Discounts allowed less received	4,400 W2	
Bad and doubtful debts	3,700 W3	
Wages and salaries	69,900 W4	
Administrative expenses	33,700 W5	
Research and development expenditure	9,600	
Directors' remuneration	40,000	
Depreciation	57,000 W6	
Goodwill amortized	6,000	

Debenture interest		27,000	251,300
Net profit			90,000
Less: Corporation tax			33,000
			57,000
Retained profit at 1 November 1985			115,200
			172,200
Less: Ordinary dividends		20,000	
Transfer to machinery replacement reserve		15,000	35,000
Retained profit at 31 October 1986			137,200

(b) **Balance sheet at 31 October 1986**

Fixed assets	£	£	£
Tangible	Cost	Depreciation	
Freehold premises	435,000	36,000	399,000
Machinery and equipment	60,000	30,000	30,000
Motor lorries	225,000	107,000	118,000
			547,000
Intangible: Goodwill			24,000
Current assets			
Stock		121,300	
Debtors		49,600 W7	
Bank		35,600	
		206,500	
Less: Creditors due within one year			
Creditors		31,400	
Corporation tax		33,000	
Dividends		20,000	
Accruals		15,900 W8	
		100,300	
Net current assets			106,200
Total assets less current liabilities			677,200
Less: Creditors due in more than one year			
12% debentures			225,000
			452,200
Financed by			
Called-up share capital			200,000
Share premium account			100,000
Machinery replacement reserve			15,000
Retained profit			137,200
			452,200

W1 26,700 (NRV) + 47,800 (Cost) + 46,800 (NRV) = 121,300.

W2 14,200 − 9,800 = 4,400.

W3 2,900 (Bad debts) + 800 (Increase in doubtful debt provision) = 3,700.

W4   68,400 + 1,500 (Accruals) = 69,900.

W5   32,800 + 900 (Accruals) = 33,700.

W6   6,000 (Machinery and equipment) + 45,000 (Lorries) + 6,000 (Premises)
      = 57,000.

W7   54,100 – 4,500 (Provision for doubtful debts) = 49,600.

W8   1,500 + 900 + 13,500 = 15,900.

(a) Accounting bases is the term used, in SSAP 2, to describe the various methods that
     have been developed for valuing assets and liabilities. For example, the alternative bases
     available to account for the decline in value of fixed assets include reducing balance
     basis, straight-line and the units of service method.

     Accounting policies is the term used to describe the particular accounting bases
     adopted by a company for the purpose of valuing assets and liabilities when preparing
     the accounts. The policies adopted must be described by the company in its report. The
     accounting policies used by a company must be consistent with the following four
     fundamental accounting concepts:

     (i)   *The going concern concept*, which assumes that the company will continue in
           business for the foreseeable future. The main significance of this assumption is that
           the liquidation values of fixed assets can be ignored and it is instead assumed that
           the company will remain in business long enough to enable the resources tied up
           in fixed assets to be fully recovered.
     (ii) *The accruals concept*, which requires revenues and expenses to be reported in
           the periodic profit and loss account as they are earned and incurred rather than
           when the amounts of cash are received and paid.
     (iii) *The consistency concept*, which requires the company to employ the same
           accounting policy for valuing a particular asset in each consecutive accounting
           period. The purpose of this is to enable comparisons to be made.
     (iv) *The concept of prudence*, which stipulates that a company should not take credit
           for profits before they are earned but should make provision for all foreseeable
           losses.

     An accounting policy such as the reducing balance basis conforms to each of the four
     fundamental concepts. It spreads the cost of the fixed asset, over a number of accounting
     periods, on the assumption that the company will continue indefinitely as a going concern.
     It allocates the cost of the fixed asset less residual value between accounting procedures
     based on benefits received. This achieves compliance with both the accruals concept
     and the consistency concept. Compliance with the prudence concept is also assured
     because, by the time the asset is written off, all foreseeable losses are provided for.

(b) Compliance with the requirements of SSAP 2 goes a long way towards ensuring that
     the published accounts show a true and fair view. There are, however, other matters that
     require attention in the case of a limited company. It is necessary for the directors to

take steps to ensure that there is compliance with the Companies Act 1985 and the many other SSAPs and FRSs issued by the accounting profession. In the case of quoted companies, there are further stock exchange rules that have to be satisfied, for example, the obligation to publish interim accounting statements. These regulations are useful because they ensure an adequate level of disclosure, comparability between accounting periods and comparability between one company and another.

It is, of course, important for the directors to ensure that their company's accounts portray a true and fair view, because a reputation for openness and frankness is likely to make it easier to raise the finance needed to carry on business operations. At the same time, it is necessary to guard against the possibility of the directors manipulating the accounts in order to make the company appear a more attractive proposition than is justified by the underlying commercial performance. It is for this reason that the Companies Act makes provision for appointment of independent auditors to report whether the accounts prepared and presented to the shareholders and filed with the Registrar of Companies portray a true and fair view.

QUESTION 10.5

The purpose of the bonus issue is to give formal acknowledgement to the fact that profits, retained by the directors in previous years, have been permanently invested in business assets and no longer remain available for distribution. At 31 March 20X6 the company has cash available of £268,000, of which £75,000 is required to finance the proposed dividend, and £120,000 is needed to pay for the plant recently purchased. This leaves a modest balance to meet operating expenses. It is therefore clear that the company has no surplus cash resources, and it was therefore perfectly reasonable to capitalize the bulk of the retained profits. It is possible to argue that a smaller bonus issue might have been made some years earlier, but certain formalities are involved and it is not a process management will wish to undertake on a regular basis.

QUESTION 10.7

Koppa Limited
Profit and loss account, period ending 31 December 19X7

	£000	£000
Turnover		8,650
Opening stock	990	
Purchases	5,010	
	6,000	
Less: Closing stock	(880)	
Cost of goods sold		(5,120)
Gross profit		3,530
Distribution costs (460 + 25 + 4)		(489)

Administrative expenses
$\quad$ (1,560 + 162 + 20 − 59 + 83 − 40 + 11)   (1,737)

Operating profit	1,304
Debenture interest	(120)
Profit for the year	1,184
Dividends	(600)
Retained profit for the year	584
Retained profit brought forward	1,272
Retained profit carried forward	1,856

Koppa Limited
Balance sheet as at 31 December 19X7

	£000	£000	£000
Fixed assets			
Intangible fixed assets:			
$\quad$ Development costs (180 + 59 − 20)			219
Tangible fixed assets:			
$\quad$ Freehold land and buildings			
$\quad\quad$ (2,200 + 900 − 100 − 18)			2,982
$\quad$ Office equipment (260 − 60 − 40)			160
$\quad$ Motor vehicles (200 − 90 − 50)			60
			3,421
Current assets:			
Stock		880	
Debtors		1,360	
Prepayments		40	
Bank		90	
		2,370	
Creditors: amounts falling due within one year			
Creditors	820		
Proposed dividends	400		
Accruals	15	(1,235)	
Net current assets (working capital)			1,135
Total assets less current liabilities			4,556
Creditors: amounts falling due after more			
$\quad$ than one year			
12% Debentures			(1,000)
			3,556
Share capital and reserves:			
Share capital: shares of 50p each			1,000
Share premium			500
Revaluation reserve			200
Profit and loss account (1,272 + 584)			1,856
			3,556

QUESTION 11.1

A useful starting-point when answering this type of question is to prepare a worksheet which shows the differences between the closing and opening balance sheet and lists them according to whether they represent an inflow or outflow of cash. For this question, the worksheet appears as follows:

Worksheet

	20X1 £	20X1 £	20X2 £	20X2 £	Differences Inflow £	Differences Outflow £
Fixed assets						
Plant at cost	52,000		70,000			18,000
Less: Depreciation	16,500	35,500	22,700	47,300	6,200	
Transport at cost	10,000		10,000			
Less: Depreciation	3,600	6,400	4,800	5,200	1,200	
		41,900		52,500		
Current assets:						
Stocks	10,200		12,600			2,400
Debtors	8,300		13,700			5,400
Bank	4,900		–		4,900	
	23,400		26,300			
Less: Current liabilities						
Trade creditors	5,100		5,800		700	
Bank overdraft	–		1,300		1,300	
	5,100		7,100			
Working capital		18,300		19,200		
		60,200		71,700		
Fianaced by:						
Share capital		50,000		54,000	4,000	
Profit and loss account		10,200		17,700	7,500	
		60,200		71,700	25,800	25,800

Cash flow statement for 20X2

	£
Net cash flow from operating activities*	7,800
Returns on investment and servicing of finance	–
Taxation	–
Investing activities	(18,000)
Financing	4,000
Increase (decrease) in cash	(6,200)

Note *Net cash flow from operating activities

Profit	7,500
Depreciation	7,400
Increase in stock	(2,400)
Increase in debtors	(5,400)
Increase in creditors	700
	7,800

Sharpener Ltd
Cash flow statement for 20X5

QUESTION
11.3

	£	£
Net cash flow from operating activities (note 1)		98,500
Returns on investment and servicing of finance:		
Debenture interest paid		(6,000)
Taxation		–
Capital expenditure and financial investment:		
Purchase of fixed asset		(30,000)
Equity dividends paid		(44,000)
Financing:		
Repayment of debentures		(80,000)
Decrease in cash (note 2)		(61,500)

Note 1: Net cash flow from operating activities	£
Retained profit for the year (109,800 – 104,300)	5,500
Add: Dividends	44,000
Debenture interest (6% × 100,000)*	6,000
Profit before interest	55,500
Adjustments:	
Depreciation (203,700 – 176,500)	27,200
Increase in stock	(1,100)
Decrease in debtors	2,700
Increase in creditors	14,200
	98,500

*Assumed that debenture interest paid before redemption took place.

Note 2: Reconciliation of movement in cash	£
Bank balance at end of 20X4	23,600
Decrease in bank during year (bal. fig)	(61,500)
Bank balance at end of 20X5	(37,900)

(b)   The company plans to pay out nearly all of its profits in the form of dividends, while the funds retained in the business by way of the depreciation charge have been used to purchase fixed assets. There are no other long-term sources of finance and the debentures have been repaid by increasing the amount of credit taken from suppliers and running down the bank balance. The result is a large bank overdraft and, probably, severe liquidity problems.

QUESTION
11.5

(a)   **Rapier Ltd**
Cash flow statement for 1997

	£000	£000
Net cash flow from operating activities (note 1)		161
Returns on investment and servicing of finance:		
Debenture interest paid		(10)
Taxation		–
Capital expenditure and financial Investment:		
Purchase of fixed asset (note 2)	(180)	
Sale of fixed asset	25	(155)
Equity dividends paid (note 3)		(28)
Financing:		
Issue of shares (note 4)	80	
Repayment of debentures	(50)	30
Decrease in cash (note 5)		(2)

Note 1: Net cash flow from operating activities	£000
Retained profit for the year (203 – 176)	27
Add: Dividends paid (0.05 × 200) + 22	32
Debenture interest (10% × 100)	10
Profit before interest	69
Adjustments:	
Depreciation*	100
Profit on sale (25 – 20)	(5)
Increase in stock	(9)
Decrease in debtors	4
Increase in creditors	2
	161

*Depreciation for the year:	
Opening balance	220
Less: Depreciation on disposed asset	
(100 – 20)	(80)
Add: Depreciation for year (bal. fig.)	100
Closing balance	240

Note 2: Purchase of fixed asset   £

    NBV Balance b/d forward from 1996   380

    Add: Revaluation   50

    Less: Disposal at NBV   (20)

    Depreciation for year   (100)

    Purchase of plant (bal. fig.)   180

    NBV Balance at end of 1997   490

Note 3: Equity dividends paid   £

    Balance b/d forward from 1996   18

    Dividends: Interim   10

        Proposed   22

                         50

    Less: Balance at end of 1997   (22)

    Dividends paid in year   28

Note 4: Cash flow from issue of shares   £

    Increase in share capital   50

    Increase in share premium   30

                         80

Note 5: Reconciliation of movement in cash   £

    Bank balance at end of 1996 (4 − 13)   (9)

    Decrease in bank during year (bal. fig)   (2)

    Bank balance at end of 1997 (7 − 18)   (11)

(b) A cash flow statement shows the movement in cash during the accounting period and identifies the reasons for the movement. The amount of cash generated from operations is highlighted together with other sources of income such as the issue of shares or the sale of fixed assets. The more cash that is raised from operations the better the company's financial position.

(a) Gross profit margin $\dfrac{54{,}000}{180{,}000} \times 100 = 30\%$

QUESTION 12.1

    Net profit as a % of sales $\dfrac{15{,}000}{180{,}000} \times 100 = 8.3\%$

    Return on capital employed $\dfrac{15{,}000}{150{,}000} \times 100 = 10\%$

(b)   An increase in the ROCE to 12.5 per cent would require additional profit of £150,000 × 2.5% = £3,750. The gross profit margin is 30 per cent and an additional turnover of £3,750 × (100 ÷ 30) = £12,500 would produce the required increase in net profit.

QUESTION 12.3   (a)

	20X1		20X2	
Return on capital employed	$\frac{200}{700} \times 100$	28.6%	$\frac{250}{720} \times 100$	34.7%
Working capital		200		170
Working capital ratio	$\frac{300}{100}$: 1	3 : 1	$\frac{350}{180}$: 1	1.9 : 1
Liquidity ratio	$\frac{125 + 25}{100}$: 1	1.5 : 1	$\frac{150}{180}$: 1	0.8 : 1

Workings

Balance sheet, 31 December

	20X1		20X2	
	£000	£000	£000	£000
Fixed assets		500		550
Current assets: Stock	150		200	
Trade debtors	125		150	
Cash at bank	25		–	
	300		350	
Less: Current liabilities: Trade creditors	80		100	
Proposed dividend	20		60	
Overdraft	–		20	
	100		180	
Working capital		200		170
Shareholders' equity (capital employed)		700		720

Profit and loss account

	20X1		20X2	
Sales		2,000		3,000
Less: Cost of sales	1,000		1,450	
Overhead costs	800	1,800	1,300	2,750
Net Profit		200		250

(b)   Lock Ltd earned a high rate of return on the shareholders' investment during 20X1, which has been improved on during 20X2. The balance sheet, at 31 December 20X1, shows a strong financial position, with the working capital and liquidity ratios each at a high level for a wholesale trading company. There has been a significant decline in the solvency position during the year. The ratios suggest that the company will find it difficult to meet its debts as they fall due for payment. The proposal to pay a final dividend three times last year's level may need to be reconsidered.

(a) **Trading and profit and loss accounts for 20X5**

	Metalmax		Precision Products	
	£000	£000	£000	£000
Sales		800		950
Less: Variable cost of sales	640		760	
Depreciation	54		54	
Cost of sales		694		814
Gross profit		106		136
Less: Administration expenses	30		30	
Selling expenses	45	75	60	90
Net profit		31		46

Balance sheets at 31 December 20X5

	Metalmax		Precision Products	
	£000	£000	£000	£000
Plant and machinery at cost		360		360
Less: Depreciation		164		164
		196		196
Current assets				
Stock and work in progress	120		200	
Other current assets	120		200	
	240		400	
Less: Current liabilities	120		320	
Working capital		120		80
		316		276
Share capital		200		200
Reserves		116		76
		316		276

(b)

Accounting ratios	Metalmax	Precision Products
Gross profit margin	13.3%	14.3%
Net profit percentage	3.9%	4.8%
Return on total capital employed	7.1%	7.7%
Return on owners' equity	9.8%	16.7%
Working capital ratio	2 : 1	1.25 : 1
Liquidity ratio	1 : 1	0.6 : 1

Metalmax is the more solvent, whereas Precision Products is the more profitable.

Variable cost of sales is 80 per cent in the case of both companies. Precision Products produces the higher gross profit margin because, on the basis of an identical investment in fixed assets, it produces a significantly higher level of sales. The selling expenses of Precision

Products are much higher, perhaps due to the fact that they advertise their products more heavily and distribute them more widely. However, the company retains its advantage and achieves the higher net profit margin. The rates of return on both versions of capital employed are higher at Precision Products. The difference is substantial in the case of return on owners' equity. This is because a large proportion of Precision Products' current assets are funded out of the 'free' finance provided by trade creditors. The consequence of this, however, is that Precision Products' solvency position, at the end of 19X5, is extremely weak. Metalmax, with a working capital ratio and liquidity ratio in line with conventional 'norms', is in a sound financial condition.

QUESTION 12.7

(a) **Cash flow statement for 20X8**

	£000	£000
Net cash flow from operating activities (Note 1)		(10)
Returns on investment and servicing of finance		
Interest received	20	
Dividends paid	(400)	
Net cash flow		(380)
Investing activities		
Payments to buy fixed assets	(410)	
Receipts from sale of fixed assets	130	
		(280)
Net cash outflow before financing		(670)
Financing		
Issuing of shares (500 + 200)	700	
Long-term loan	300	
		1,000
Increase in deposits at bank		330

Note 1

Reconciliation of operating profit to net cash inflow from operating activities:

	£000
Operating profit	700
Depreciation charge	350
Increase in stocks	(1,220)
Increase in debtors	(40)
Increase in trade creditors	200
	(10)

(b)

Accounting ratios	20X7	20X8
Working capital	2 : 1	3.1 : 1
Liquidity	1 : 1	1.2 : 1

The financial position at the end of 20X7 appears satisfactory when judged on the basis of relevant accounting ratios. The liquidity ratio is 1:1 and the working capital ratio is 2:1, both of which are about right for an engineering firm. At the end of 20X8, the working capital appears to be too high and the company is verging on excess liquidity.

The statement of funds shows that the company both raised and generated long-term funds significantly in excess of present business requirements. Funds generated from operations more than cover the dividend and plant acquisition, yet the company has issued shares, raised a loan and benefited from the sale of investments. A great deal of the surplus finance is tied up in stocks; a non-income-producing asset. The company's system of stock control should be examined to check whether it is being operated efficiently.

The effect of financial developments during 20X8 is a very strong financial position at the end of the year, but there is some doubt whether available resources are being effectively employed. Perhaps additional resources have been raised to finance *future* expansion, but there is no indication that this is the case.

QUESTION
12.9

(a)

	LATLEST	NELUMBO
(i) Current ratio		
$\dfrac{\text{Current assets}}{\text{Current liabilities}}$	$\dfrac{10{,}782}{4{,}077} = 2.64:1$	$\dfrac{22{,}450}{18{,}281} = 1.23:1$
(ii) Quick ratio		
$\dfrac{\text{Current assets} - \text{stock}}{\text{Current liabilities}}$	$\dfrac{8{,}003}{4{,}077} = 1.96:1$	$\dfrac{16{,}536}{18{,}281} = 0.9:1$
(iii) Days material stock		
$\dfrac{\text{Material stock}}{\text{Material cost of sales}} \times 365$	$\dfrac{1{,}047}{6{,}250} \times 365 = 61.1\,\text{days}$	$\dfrac{645}{13{,}150} \times 365 = 17.9\,\text{days}$
(iv) Days finished goods stock		
$\dfrac{\text{Finished goods stock}}{\text{Cost of sales}} \times 365$	$\dfrac{1{,}732}{20{,}570} \times 365 = 30.7\,\text{days}$	$\dfrac{5{,}269}{37{,}715} \times 365 = 51\,\text{days}$
(v) Debtors days		
$\dfrac{\text{Trade debtors}}{\text{Sales}} \times 365\,\text{days}$	$\dfrac{6{,}136}{35{,}505} \times 365 = 63.1\,\text{days}$	$\dfrac{15{,}432}{57{,}330} \times 365 = 98.3\,\text{days}$
(vi) Creditor days		
$\dfrac{\text{Material creditors}}{\text{Material cost of sales}} \times 365$	$\dfrac{743}{6{,}250} \times 365 = 43.4\,\text{days}$	$\dfrac{2{,}836}{13{,}150} \times 365 = 78.7\,\text{days}$
(vii) Operating or cash cycle		
(iii) + (iv) + (v) − (vi)	$61.1 + 30.7 + 63.1$ $- 43.4 = 111.5$	$17.9 + 51 + 98.3$ $- 78.7 = 88.5$

(b)   *Latlest Ltd.* Current assets are over two and a half times as great as current liabilities which is satisfactory. The liquidity position is also good, with adequate debtor and cash balances.

The stock turnover efficiency is not very good as it takes two months to convert materials to finished goods.

Creditors are paid on average in 43 days, which is reasonable.

The cash cycle of 16 weeks (115.5/7) is on the long side, mainly due to the slow material turnover.

Extension of credit terms to Latlest seems reasonable as there is nothing to suggest in the ratios that the company is a credit risk.

Nelumbo Ltd, The current ratio shows that current assets exceed current liabilities but the liquidity ratio is not so good. There are more current liabilities than cash and debtors.

Material stock turnover appears efficient in that it takes just over two weeks. This could be due to efficient material management or could be indicative of supply problems.

The number of days taken to turnover finished goods equates to around seven weeks, which is very high. This could indicate a problem with sales.

It is taking the company over 3 months to collect its debts from debtors and as a consequence is taking a long time to pay its creditors. The company is at risk of losing its credit-worthiness.

Extension of credit terms of Nelumbo is not advisable, given the poor performance of the business to date.

QUESTION 13.1

(a)

	£	£	£	£	£	£
Sales		46,000		92,000		138,000
Variable cost	25,300		50,600		75,900	
Depreciation	3,600		7,200		10,800	
General expenses	10,000		14,000		18,000	
Interest*	3,900		9,300		14,700	
		42,800		81,100		119,400
Profit		3,200		10,900		18,600
^Calculation:						
Cost of plant		36,000		72,000		108,000
Available for investment		10,000		10,000		10,000
Balance to be borrowed		26,000		62,000		98,000
Borrowings at 15%		3,900		9,300		14,700

(b)   Eagles can either retain ownership of the business or sell it to Troon Ltd and remain as manager. Under either of these options his income varies according to the level of sales, and is calculated as follows:

	£	£	£	£
Sales	*Existing*	*+ 46,000*	*+ 92,000*	*+ 138,000*
RETAIN OWNERSHIP				
Existing profit	20,000	20,000	20,000	20,000
Profit from exports	–	3,200	10,900	18,600
Total income	20,000	23,200	30,900	38,600
SELL TO TROON LTD				
Invest proceeds of sale to				
earn annual interest	12,000	12,000	12,000	12,000
Salary as manager	14,000	14,000	14,000	14,000
Bonus for additional sales	–	3,000	6,000	9,000
Total	26,000	29,000	32,000	35,000

It can be seen that Eagles is better off selling the business and working as manager unless the largest increase in sales under consideration can be achieved. He must consider whether this is likely. Also, the relief of no longer having the responsibility of both owning and managing the business may be attractive, together with the possession of personal capital in the form of cash. These considerations may induce him to sell the business even if he considers the higher income from retention can probably be achieved.

(a) **Summary profit and loss account 20X4**

	£
Sales (60,000 × £5)	300
Variable costs (60,000 × £3*)	180
Total contribution	120
Fixed costs†	100
Net profit	20

Notes *£5 (selling price) - £2 (contribution) = £3 (variable cost).
     †Balancing figure.

(b) $\dfrac{\text{Fixed costs}}{\text{Contribution}} = \dfrac{£100,000}{£2} = 50{,}000 \text{ units}$

       50,000 x £5 = £250,000

(c) **Summary profit and loss account 20X5**

	£000
Sales (90,000 × £4.50)	405
Variable costs (90,000 × £2)	180
Total contribution	225
Fixed costs (£100,000 + £80,000)	180
Net profit	45

(d) $\dfrac{\text{Fixed costs}}{\text{Contribution}} = \dfrac{£180,000}{(£4.50 - £2)} = 72,000$ units

$$72,000 \times £4.50 = £324,000$$

QUESTION 13.5	(a)		£	£
		Sales		400,000
		Raw materials	100,000	
		Wages	200,000	
		Depreciation	20,000	
				320,000
		Gross profit		80,000
		General expenses (20,000 + 15,000*)	35,000	
		Interest	10,000	
				45,000
		Net profit		35,000
	(b)		£	£
		Selling price per unit		2.00
		Variable costs:		
		Raw materials	.50	
		Wages	.30	
				.80
		Contribution		1.20
		Fixed costs:		£
		Depreciation		20,000
		Interest		20,000
		Expenses*		15,000
				55,000
		Additional profit:		
		Profit under plan 1		35,000
		Existing profit		20,000
				15,000

Sales $= \dfrac{55,000 + 15,000}{1.20} = 58,333$ units or $58,333 \times £2 = £116,667.$

Note   *The increase in sales is greater than £100,000 and so the full additional general expenses are incurred.

(c) The condition necessary for the company as a whole to make the same profit as in 20X6 is that the extra sales break even. This point is calculated as follows:

$$£$$

Fixed costs of plan 2:

	£
Depreciation	20,000
Interest	20,000
Expenses[†]	5,000
	45,000

$$\text{Break-even sales} = \frac{45,000}{1.2} = 37,500 \text{ units or } 37,500 \times 2 = £75,000.$$

Note   [†]As the increase in sales is less than £100,000, the additional expenses are limited to £5,000.

(a) **Cash flow forecast for the six months to 31 May 1994**

QUESTION 13.7

	Dec. £000	Jan. £000	Feb. £000	March £000	April £000	May £000
Cash in						
Sales	384	410	290	364	392	440
Loan						350
	384	410	290	364	392	790
Cash out						
Creditors	297	205	224	236	249	273
Accruals	11					
Wages and salaries	43	43	43	43	43	43
Overheads	14	14	14	14	14	14
Equipment						360
	365	262	281	293	306	690
Summary						
Opening balance	27	46	194	203	274	360
Cash in	384	410	290	364	392	790
Less: Cash out	(365)	(262)	(281)	(293)	(306)	(690)
Closing balance	46	194	203	274	360	460

(b) The company's bank balance, if the loan is not raised, will be £460,000 - £350,000 = £110,000. This is a very healthy balance and so, unless the company has other anticipated commitments, the loan is not required.

(c)   **Profit and loss account for the six months to 31 May 1994**

	£000
Sales	2,380
Less: Cost of sales (2,380/2)	1,190
Gross profit	1,190
Overheads (71 × 6)	426
Net profit	764

QUESTION   (a)   **Budgeted trading profit and loss account and appropriation account, year to**
14.1   **31 October 1994**

	£000	£000
Sales		1,600
Cost of goods sold (68%)		1,088
Gross profit (32%)		512
Administration costs (5%)		80
Selling and distribution costs (3.5%)		56
Bad debts (£150,000 × 15%) − £10,000		12.5
Depreciation (£150,000 + (£750,000 × 10%))		225
Financial charges		10
		383.5
Net profit		128.5
Dividends: Ordinary 3p × 800,000	24	
Preference	5.5	29.5
Retained profit for year		99
Retained profit brought forward		700
		799
Transfer to general reserve		300
Retained profit carried forward		499

(b)   **Budgeted balance sheet as at 31 October 1994**

	£000	£000
Land and buildings at valuation		200
Other fixed assets at cost	750	
Less: Aggregate depreciation	305	445
		645
Current assets		
Stock		290
Trade debtors	150	
Less: Provision	22.5	127.5
Balance at bank		760.5
		1,178

Current liabilities

Trade creditors	97	
Expense creditors	17	114
Net current assets		1,064
		1,709
Ordinary share capital		600
11% preference shares		50
Share premium £200,000 + (15p × 400,000)		260
General reserve		300
Retained profit		499
		1,709

(c) The most noticeable feature of the forecast current assets is the massive balance of cash at bank, which amounts to £760,500. This seems substantially in excess of operating requirements and could be utilized to improve profitability in the following ways:

- Repay the 11 per cent preference shares and avoid the preference dividend of £5,500 per annum.
- Explore remunerative ways of investing surplus cash available. Possibilities include the acquisition of income-producing securities or shares in another company.

There has also been a significant increase in stock and debtors, and steps should be taken to see whether these can be reduced, generating further cash available for investment.

(a)

QUESTION 14.3

Material cost variance =		
(£2.20 × 6,400) − (£2 × 6,000*) = 2,080	(U)	
Material usage variance =		
(6,400 − 6,000*) £2	800	(U)
Material price variance =		
(£2.20 − £2) 6,400	1,280	(U)
Labour cost variance =		
(4.10 × 1,800) − (£4 × 2,000)	620	(F)
Labour efficiency variance =		
(1,800 − 2,000) £4	800	(F)
Labour rate variance =		
(£4.10 − £4) 1,800	180	(U)

Note *3 kilos × 2,000

(b)   The labour rate variance is favourable, and possible reasons include:

  - employing the wrong (lower) grade of labour; and
  - wage increases lower than anticipated due to ineffective trade union action.

The labour efficiency variance is unfavourable and possible reasons include:

  - inadequate training of employees;
  - dissatisfaction among the workforce; and
  - poor working conditions, for example inadequate ventilation.

(c)   A system of standard costing makes use of predetermined standard costs relating to each element of cost (labour, material and overhead) for each type of product manufactured or service supplied. The actual costs incurred are then compared with standard costs as work proceeds. The difference between actual and standard is termed the *variance*; variances are analysed to help identify their causes so that inefficiencies may immediately be brought to the attention of the responsible managers and corrective action taken.

(d)   A system of standard costing is useful to management for the following reasons:

  - The installation of a system of standard costing requires the company to review existing practices, and this often results in substantial improvements being made.
  - Standard costs are a more meaningful yardstick than the alternatives, which are to compare results with those of a previous year or a different company.
  - Variances are quickly identified, enabling corrective action to be taken before further losses are unnecessarily incurred.
  - There is a saving in management time in that attention is focused on problem areas.
  - The system identifies areas of achievement as well as difficulty, and draws management's attention to areas of success which the company may be able to exploit more fully.
  - The system promotes cost consciousness, individuals know that standards have been set and that the financial results of their work are under scrutiny.

Index